SEP 25 1990

FEB
DATE DUE

OCT

MAY
DATE DUE
01 97

MAR
DATE DUE

APR
DATE
11 94

15 97

JUN
DATE DUE
03 97

Sports Illustrated

PRO FOOTBALL
'89-90

Sports Illustrated PRO FOOTBALL '89-90

By Peter King

Oxmoor House

Published by Oxmoor House, Inc.
1271 Avenue of the Americas
New York, New York   10020

ISBN: 0-8487-1023-1
ISSN: 1049-3670

Manufactured in the United States of America
First Printing 1990

Pro Football '89-90
Senior Editor: *Morin Bishop*
  Editorial Assistants: *Stacey Harmis, Roxana Lonergan*
  Copyreader: *Pamela Roberts*
  Reporter: *Stefanie Krasnow*
Director of Photography & Research: *Geraldine Howard*
  Photo Researchers: *Lorna Bieber, Janine Jones,
  Molly Winkleman*
Production Manager: *Jerry Higdon*
  Associate Production Manager: *Rick Litton*
  Production Assistant: *Terry Beste*
Designer: *Bob Cato*

Original work by the following SPORTS ILLUSTRATED
senior writers provided the basis for portions of
Pro Football '89-90:
  Curry Kirkpatrick: feature on Deion Sanders.
  Franz Lidz: feature on Jerry Glanville.
  Jill Lieber: features on Dan Hampton and Art Shell.
  Rick Reilly: stories on the Houston-Pittsburgh
wild-card game, the Denver-Pittsburgh divisional playoff game
and the Denver-Cleveland conference championship game.
  Rick Telander: story on the Buffalo-Cleveland
divisional playoff game.
  Ralph Wiley: features on Anthony Carter and Randall
Cunningham.
  Paul Zimmerman: feature on Reggie White and stories
on the Rams-Giants wild-card game, the Vikings-49ers
divisional playoff game, the Rams-49ers conference
championship game and the Super Bowl between Denver and
San Franciso.

Special thanks to *Joe Marshall,* Director of Special Projects,
SPORTS ILLUSTRATED, and to *Robert Mitchell,* Photo Editor,
SPORTS ILLUSTRATED.

To order SPORTS ILLUSTRATED magazine, write to:
SPORTS ILLUSTRATED, Subscription Service Department,
P.O. Box 60001, Tampa, Florida 33660-0001

Contents

Introduction
The More Things Change... Y

You'll be on your couch in 10 years or so, watching TV in the middle of the night because you can't sleep, and the *NFL Films* show reviewing the 1989 season will come on, and you'll watch.

You'll be struck by the number of changes wrought by this one solitary year. You'll see 229 players change teams, as the first step toward a modern-age free-agency system is instituted, with Cincinnati going down and Kansas City up, in large part because of it. You'll see the film clips of a quivering Pete Rozelle resigning as commissioner and of a very corporate-looking Paul Tagliabue taking over. You'll see a Chicago cult hero, Jim McMahon, traded. You'll see a black head coach, Art Shell, hired by the Raiders. You'll see the sport's first $3 million man, quarterback Randall Cunningham of the Eagles. You'll see highlights from the season the Cowboys got awful and the Bears got bad, the Packers got good and the Chiefs got much better. You'll see the Broncos with a defense. You'll see the Steelers transformed.

You'll see new offensive stars—Barry Sanders of the Lions, Christian Okoye of the Chiefs, Don Majkowski and Sterling Sharpe of the Packers, Dalton Hilliard of the Saints and Mark Carrier of the Bucs.

In the midst of all this newness, you'll see two maddening constants:

1. Close games.
2. The 49ers.

Parity first. In the first week of the season, Cleveland traveled to Pittsburgh and came away with an easy 51-0 win. In Week 6, Pittsburgh visited Cleveland. Same matchup, same outcome, right? Wrong. Pittsburgh won 17-7. This was the fourth straight year in which more than 45% of all games were decided by a touchdown or less. While the merits of

the closeness could be argued, the fans loved it, turning out in record numbers all across the league. TV ratings were up too, presaging the big dollars the NFL would get in its next television contract.

"I don't know how much healthier the game could be on the field," general manager George Young of the Giants said near season's end. "We've got good, close, competitive games, which is what the fans have always wanted, and we've got great individual performances. Any team can win any week. I don't know anyone who would want it any different, do you?"

San Francisco, like a sullen dinner guest, refused to get in the parity mood. How impressive it was that the team of the decade was also the champion of 1989 and remained the team to beat as the league entered the '90s. Virtually all the great teams since 1960 have been good for a while, fallen a bit, then rebuilt toward greatness again. The 49ers had no such slip, maintaining a decade-long level of excellence almost unmatched in NFL history.

Good coaching and shrewd drafting were certainly the main reasons for this sustained greatness. But both factors were greatly enhanced by generous infusions of cash from owner Eddie DeBartolo Jr.—one NFL club source says the 49ers lost $9 million in their Super Bowl-winning 1988 season—and by the 49ers' unsentimental approach to personnel changes. "That might be what hurt some other great teams," DeBartolo says. "In this business, if you hang on to a guy too long, it can kill you."

Almost everyone in the NFL has an Eddie D. money story. In New York several years ago, DeBartolo rented a Manhattan night spot called Stringfellow's for a private party. It was a favorite place of comedian Eddie Murphy, who came to the door that night trying to get in. Management asked DeBartolo if Murphy could come and sit at a corner table, away from the party. Sure, said DeBartolo. If he pays a $250,000 cover charge. Murphy declined. Another DeBartolo story: In New Jersey for a Giants-49er game, DeBartolo hired a 10-limo convoy to take him and his guests to the game. He let the drivers stand in the rear of the party's seating area at Giants Stadium so they would be able to watch the game. Nine of the drivers watched impassively. The 10th rooted openly for the Giants. At the end of the night, nine of the drivers got $100 tips. The 10th got $50. Another DeBartolo story: After the strike of 1987, he gave all of his players $10,000 bonuses to help make up for the money they had lost. The NFL fined him $50,000 for it, and the players took up a collection to pay the fine. That's the kind of regard they have for him.

DeBartolo's theory of team management is simple: Give your team every possible edge, regardless of cost. Give the front office the scouting staff it needs. Give the coaching staff the chance to look at every waiver-wire castoff. Give the players everything, within reason, that money can buy. The 49ers were the sport's highest-paid team in 1989, with an average salary of $376,300. When they traveled longer than an hour, DeBartolo hired wide-body jets so that each player could have at least one open seat next to him. Each player was served the equivalent of two first-class airplane meals per flight, prepared expressly for the team by United Airline's two West Coast head chefs. About two-thirds of the players got single rooms on the road; most NFL players have to double up.

In the '80s, the club responded. Beginning in 1981, with Bill Walsh at the helm, the club ran off records of 13-3, 3-6 (in the strike year of 1982), 10-6, 15-1, 10-6, 10-5-1, 13-2 and 10-6. In spite of parity, the DeBartolo largess was paying off.

One's appreciation of the 49ers is only heightened by a look at the rest of the league. In football, nothing seems to last. Take the Bears and the Giants, Super Bowl powerhouses expected to dominate for years to come. Neither team could maintain its superior level of play. The 49ers had some constants—Walsh, Joe Montana and Ronnie Lott—but were still retooled several times as the decade wore on. In many ways, what the 49ers accomplished in winning four Super Bowls in nine years is even more impressive than the Steelers' four championships in six years during the 1970s. Pittsburgh performed its miracles with a largely stable unit, brilliantly coached by Chuck Noll and carefully assembled by the Rooneys. The 49ers, in contrast, changed on the fly, with Montana using Earl Cooper, Ricky Patton and Dwight Clark in '81; Wendell Tyler, Roger Craig and Russ Francis in '84; and Craig, Jerry Rice and John Taylor in '88 and '89. They also operated with a defense that squeezed the most out of a shifting cast of veterans and middle-round youngsters, turning them over quickly when they were no longer productive.

Compare the Steelers at the end of the '70s with the 49ers at the end of the '80s, and you see why the 49ers might be poised for the most prolonged period of dominance in NFL history. The Steelers had Mark Malone behind Terry Bradshaw. The 49ers have Steve Young behind Joe Montana. The Steelers had no relief behind L.C. Greenwood, Dwight White and Joe Greene, all of whom ended the decade over 30. The 49ers enter the '90s with a frisky pass rush of Dan Stubbs, Pierce Holt, Larry Roberts, Charles Haley and Kevin Fagan, none of whom are past their fifth NFL season. The Steelers had, by necessity, the fiscally conservative ownership of the Rooneys, whose football team was the family's main business and

Deep pockets, deep heart: DeBartolo gave Matt Millen one of his trademark hugs after the 49ers routed Minnesota 41-13 in the playoffs.

who were not going to pay $7.5 million for a free-agent outside linebacker. The 49ers have DeBartolo, and, well, you get the feeling he would pay that much for a water boy if the Gatorade he carried had some mystical power in it.

The 49ers also have a new coach, George Seifert, who is white-haired like Walsh but does not possess his predecessor's ego. Before the 49er game against the Eagles in Week 3, Seifert talked with emotion and humility about being in charge of this talented team. "A minitradition has been established," Seifert said then. "We have to follow. It's what's expected of us."

The next day, the 49ers twice trailed the Eagles by 11 points in the fourth quarter before charging back to win behind Montana's four fourth quarter touchdown passes. A teary DeBartolo, once perfectly tailored, got all mussed up as the final seconds ticked off, because he simply had to embrace every 49er he could find. "I love you, Ronnie!" he said to Lott, locking him in a bear hug.

The 49ers finished the regular season at 14-2, then swept away their three playoff opponents with almost disdainful ease, outscoring them 126-26. In a decade of rampant materialism, it was only right that the team with the best financial resources—as well as the best natural ones—should finish the '80s as king.

Measuring Greatness	Overall W L T	PCT.	Home W L T	PCT.	Away W L T	PCT.	Playoffs W L
Lest there remains some unenlightened corner of the world that does not accept the 49ers as the team of the decade, here are the numbers on the 10 most successful teams in the '80s. Can anyone dispute the greatness of a team that wins 73% of its games on the road?							
San Francisco	104-47-1	.688	40-27	.645	55-20-1	.730	13-4
Washington	97-55	.638	52-23	.693	45-32	.584	11-3
Miami	94-57-1	.622	53-21-1	.713	41-36	.532	
Denver	93-58-1	.615	58-19	.753	35-39-1	.473	6-5
Chicago	92-60	.605	54-22	.711	38-38	.500	
L.A. Raiders	90-63	.588	49-27	.645	40-36	.526	
L.A. Rams	86-66	.566	46-30	.605	40-36	.526	
Cleveland	83-68-1	.549	46-29-1	.620	37-40	.481	
N.Y. Giants	81-70-1	.536	46-31	.597	35-39-1	.473	6-
Cincinnati	81-71	.533	47-29	.618	34-42	.447	

FIRST QUARTER

Preseason & Weeks 1-6

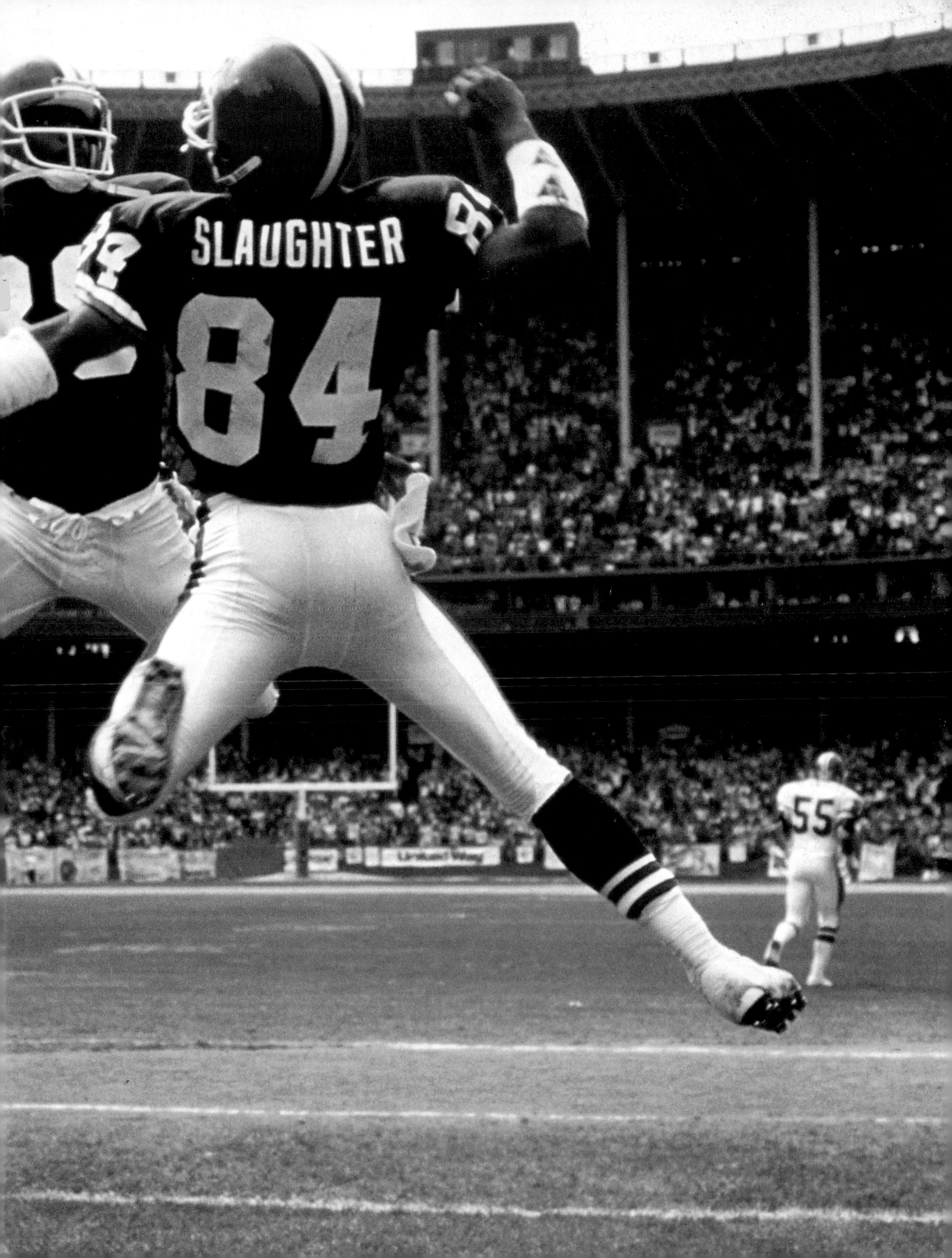
SLAUGHTER
84
55

Ch-ch-ch-changes

As the 1989 season began, there was a strange, new look to the NFL landscape. On the field and off, the league was in a state of flux, shaken by what rock superstar David Bowie once expressed in a simple phrase: ch-ch-ch-changes.

The NFL, in its quest to avoid unlimited free agency, for the first time established a limited free-agency system—so-called Plan B—whereby each club was allowed to protect only 37 players on its roster. That left an average of 20 people per team free to peddle their services elsewhere. When the two-month signing period was over on April 1, a total of 229 Plan B free agents had changed clubs.

In March, Pete Rozelle resigned after 29 years as league commissioner, because he wanted to enjoy the rest of his life away from the litigious world of the NFL. "I didn't want to die in office," he said.

The Dallas Cowboys were sold to Arkansas oil-and-gas explorer Jerry Jones, who fired coach Tom Landry and gladly let club-builder Tex Schramm go.

Ch-ch-ch-changes.

Each of the last four Super Bowl champions experienced upheaval as well, perhaps none so much as the Chicago Bears, champions of 1985, who continued to lose critical players from their glory years. Linebacker Otis Wilson and cornerback Mike Richardson, both of whom were Plan B free agents, went to the Raiders, the haven for all great old players. Both were eventually cut. But the most traumatic departure for the Windy City faithful was that of outspoken quarterback Jim McMahon to the San Diego Chargers.

In Chicago in this decade, you have either been for McMahon or against him. So on Aug. 17, when the team announced that it was trading him, the city bared its soul. The Bears were either: 1) trading the heart of their team and their only proven quarterback for no apparent reason; or 2) making a commonsense move, because McMahon was so often hurt. Whichever, the die was cast, and McMahon was dealt to San Diego for a future draft choice. McMahon was glad to be rid of the Bears. In San Diego, he thought, he would run the

Chicago defensive end Richard Dent (left) shared a smile with McMahon and son Sean after the game.

11

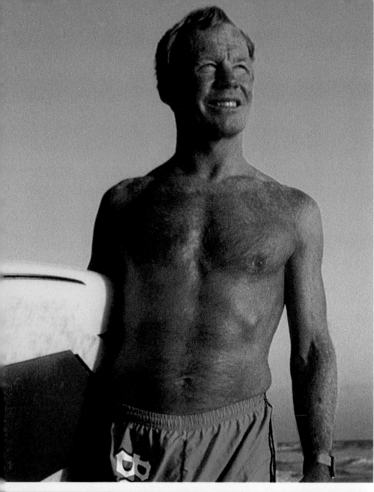

offense his way and not have to look over his shoulder at coach Mike Ditka, the madman who tried to crush his independence in Chicago.

It was a dark and emotional night when the Bears hosted San Diego in a preseason game a scant 48 hours after the trade. McMahon played very little for the Chargers, completing just one of three passes in San Diego's 24-7 romp. But the Soldier Field crowd was in a frenzy anyway, booing Ditka lustily, while McMahon got spontaneous ovations every time he waved to the stands. From his box atop the stadium, the architect of the Bears, vice-president for player personnel Bill Tobin, looked at his team and at the scene and spoke a truth that every great team faces up to sooner or later.

"We want to win this year," Tobin said. "But we also have to play football in 1990, 1991 and 1992. I realize we've lost Walter Payton, Willie Gault, Wilber Marshall, Mike Richardson and now McMahon. You're saying goodbye to a lot of greatness. But you don't win if you don't look to the future."

Down in the locker room, Mike Singletary said that the Bears had to adjust to life in this very malleable sport. Things stay the same for about four or five games—max—and then there's an injury or a contract dispute or another injury or a slump. Or success. Singletary has an eagle eye about these things. He's the best middle linebacker in football, maybe the best in the game since Dick Butkus. Singletary knows why teams win. He thought, entering the season, that Chicago would have a difficult time of it but still believed that his team could win everything again.

"My goodness," he said, pondering the McMahon deal, "life goes on. In my heart, I love Jim McMahon. I love what he's done for everybody in this room. I hope someday after we finish playing, I get to sit down at Thanksgiving with him and some of the other guys who've left this team. But not now. Now, I want to go to the Super Bowl and beat the hell out of these people. That's our business."

East of Chicago, the winds of change were blowing too. The New York Giants, champions of 1986, were leaderless after defensive rudders George Martin, Harry Carson and Jim Burt retired and Kenny Hill was waived. They also missed running back Joe Morris, their rushing game since 1984. He broke his foot in the final preseason game and would be lost for the season. They missed an offensive line too: Four of the five starters in the Super Bowl unit had retired, been released or were injured entering the regular season. "You can't stay still in football and be successful,"

Away from the Redskins pressure, Beathard had time for his favorite avocation: surfing.

Parcells, according to one Giant, was a more active coach than ever.

preached coach Bill Parcells of the Giants. "We've got to move on with this team." The youthful Giants' training camp seemed to invigorate Parcells. "He's coaching more now than anytime since I've been with the team. He's revitalized," said one veteran, who dates back to the Giants' Super Bowl season.

For the Washington Redskins, champions of 1987, change meant struggling to cope without quarterback Doug Williams, who was lost to off-season back surgery, and without running back Timmy Smith, who had been ineffective since gaining 204 yards against the Broncos in Super Bowl XXII. After Washington chose to leave him unprotected under Plan B, Smith signed as a free agent with San Diego and was later released. But the biggest gap at the Redskins' training camp in Carlisle, Pa., was created by the departure of general manager Bobby Beathard, who left for a sabbatical from the game in May. Beathard, one of the brightest minds in football, was always wheeling and dealing to get a veteran gap-plugger here and an extra draft pick there, but he'd had enough of the Redskins pressure. So off he went, to live in a beach house in Southern California and work part-time as an NFL analyst for NBC Sports. "In a way I kind of feel guilty, because I'm not doing anything," Beathard said, looking out at the ocean six weeks before the season started. "But in a way I say, 'God, this is great!' All my friends in football say, 'God, you're lucky.' "

Beathard's last acts—dealing on draft day for two skilled running backs, Earnest Byner and Gerald Riggs—bolstered Washington but left the team uncertain about its prospects entering the season.

West of Chicago, the San Francisco 49ers, champions of 1988, were also coping with a major loss, that of their Univac computer, a.k.a. Bill Walsh, the mastermind who led the club to three Super Bowl titles in his 10 seasons as head coach. Walsh retired from coaching on Jan. 26, after the third title, but he was retained to run the front office and to continue to shape the team. Then he stunned the Niners and the sport in mid-July by jumping ship to work for NBC as its top color analyst on NFL games. "I needed a new challenge," Walsh said. The 49ers needed stability, so they elevated defensive coordinator George Seifert, a nice guy who had been a head coach only at tiny Westminster College and at Cornell, to Walsh's job.

Ch-ch-ch-changes.

The shelf life of a championship team in football seems so short. Could one of the champions rise to the top again? If not, then who would be the new great team? Cincinnati, perhaps, except the Bengals had to worry about the strength of quarterback Boomer Esiason's throwing shoulder. Or maybe up-and-coming Minnesota or Philadelphia or the Rams, all of whom had wonderfully young nuclei, with talented players like the Eagles' Randall Cunningham.

Which teams would rise, and which would fall? Parcells has an answer for such questions. "That's why they play the games," he says.

And the games began.

Philadelphia's Cunningham eyed a top-tier finish for the Eagles.

Whole Lotta Shakin' Going On

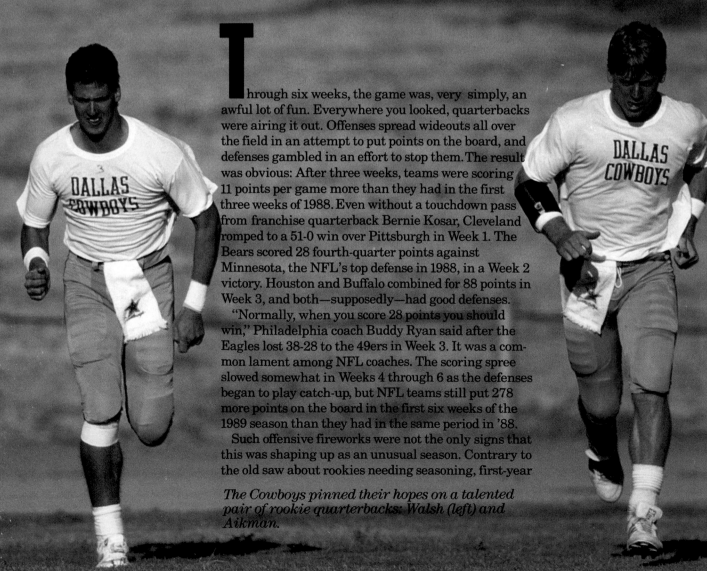

Through six weeks, the game was, very simply, an awful lot of fun. Everywhere you looked, quarterbacks were airing it out. Offenses spread wideouts all over the field in an attempt to put points on the board, and defenses gambled in an effort to stop them. The result was obvious: After three weeks, teams were scoring 11 points per game more than they had in the first three weeks of 1988. Even without a touchdown pass from franchise quarterback Bernie Kosar, Cleveland romped to a 51-0 win over Pittsburgh in Week 1. The Bears scored 28 fourth-quarter points against Minnesota, the NFL's top defense in 1988, in a Week 2 victory. Houston and Buffalo combined for 88 points in Week 3, and both—supposedly—had good defenses.

"Normally, when you score 28 points you should win," Philadelphia coach Buddy Ryan said after the Eagles lost 38-28 to the 49ers in Week 3. It was a common lament among NFL coaches. The scoring spree slowed somewhat in Weeks 4 through 6 as the defenses began to play catch-up, but NFL teams still put 278 more points on the board in the first six weeks of the 1989 season than they had in the same period in '88.

Such offensive fireworks were not the only signs that this was shaping up as an unusual season. Contrary to the old saw about rookies needing seasoning, first-year

The Cowboys pinned their hopes on a talented pair of rookie quarterbacks: Walsh (left) and Aikman.

Receivers like high-flying Eagle Cris Carter were having a field day in the early going.

impact players abounded, as coaches started 18 rookies on opening day. The most exciting emerging players were on offense. Dallas rookie quarterback Troy Aikman, suffering through the Cowboy reconstruction, proved his worth with a strong arm and mobile legs before he got hurt and gave way to the other capable rookie quarterback in Dallas, Steve Walsh. Detroit running back Barry Sanders electrified everyone who saw him. "I don't know if he signed for $9 million for one year or $9 million for five. Whatever it is, he's worth it," said Lawrence Taylor of the Giants, after watching Sanders gain 57 yards on the ground and 96 more in pass receptions against his team in Week 2.

The most scintillating defensive newcomer was Deion (Prime Time) Sanders, a cornerback and return specialist for Atlanta. The limo he took to and from games was bigger than owner Rankin Smith's, but maybe he deserved it. On his first official play, Sanders ran a punt back 68 yards for a touchdown in the opening week against the Rams.

Normalcy wasn't in evidence off the field either. Dallas was 0-5 when Jones and new coach Jimmy Johnson decided to forsake the present for the future, trading running back Herschel Walker to Minnesota for a package of players and draft picks. Three days later, in one of the season's most dramatic moments, Walker rushed for 148 yards against the Packers the first time he put on Viking colors. "Herschelmania!" hollered some guy in section 108 of the Metrodome in the middle of Walker's debut.

SUDDEN IMPACT: The Rookies Roll

Just how great was the impact of those first-year phenoms? By season's end, they had contributed 32,539 yards in total offense, an increase of over 26% from the rookie crop of the previous season. Here is a look at the top ten rookie contributors as well as the relevant totals for 1988 and '89.

TOP TEN ROOKIES	Total	Rushing	Receiving	Passing	Return
1. Troy Aikman, QB, Cowboys	2,051	—	—	2,051	—
2. Dave Meggett, RB, Giants	1,607	117	531		1,159
3. Eric Metcalf, RB, Browns	1,760	633	397		
4. Barry Sanders, RB, Lions	1,752	1,470	282		
5. James Dixon, DB, Cowboys	1,689	30			
6. Rodney Peete, QB, Lions	1,627	148			
7. Bobby Humphrey, RB, Broncos	1,410	1,151			
8. Steve Walsh, QB, Cowboys	1,387	16			
9. Billy Joe Tolliver, QB, Chargers	1,099	2			
10. Keith Jones, WR, Falcons	1,033	202			
SEASON TOTALS					
1988	25,806	6,462			
1989	32,539	7,923			
Percentage change	+26.1	+22.6			

First Quarter
Key Games

Oldies But Goodies

After six weeks, three teams had emerged from the parity-muddled standings to stake claims as the best outfit in the game: the San Francisco 49ers, the Denver Broncos and the New York Giants, all former Super Bowl teams led by proven veterans. Meanwhile, preseason darlings like the Houston Oilers and the Minnesota Vikings, who were expected to knock the establishment on its ear, sank beneath the weight of those rosy predictions, plodding along near the .500 mark. Three games told the tale of why the Broncos, the 49ers and the Giants were leading the pack.

Denver 28, Buffalo 14—Week 2, at Buffalo. This looked to be a Bills' walkover. The Broncos had never played well on the road, and despite firing defensive coordinator Joe Collier at the end of the '88 season, they still had a reputation as a weak-kneed defensive team. This was the defense, after all, that had allowed 81 points and 1,001 yards in two straight Super Bowl losses. Buffalo, on the other hand, was playing in front of its home crowd for the first time in 1989 and was alleged to be a powerhouse, picked by many to go to the Super Bowl.

But Denver's new defensive coordinator, Wade Phillips, hadn't been idle. He installed a simpler

San Francisco 38, Philadelphia 28—Week 3, at Philadelphia. The 49ers hadn't been this euphoric since—well, since winning Super Bowl XXIII the previous January against Cincinnati, when Joe Montana threw a last-minute winning touchdown pass to John Taylor. As the seconds ticked down against the Eagles, San Francisco owner Eddie DeBartolo Jr. got a little misty standing in the end zone. "I'm prouder of them right now than I was at the Super Bowl," DeBartolo said. "God, they're spunky. I love this team."

With slightly more than eight minutes remaining, his outlook had been a bit less sanguine. The Eagles were leading by 11 points. Montana had been sacked seven times. The Niners' running game had been held to eight yards. Their special teams had turned the ball over twice, leading to 14 Eagle points.

Then came another in a long line of Montana Miracles. Montana simply stole this game and turned it into a personal highlight film, throwing three touchdown passes to lead the 49ers back in the fourth quarter. "You relish being in those situations," said the typically blasé Montana, who completed 25 of 34 passes for 428 yards and five touchdowns overall. In the fourth quarter alone—perhaps the best of his 11-year career—Montana completed 11 of 12 passes for 227 yards, including touchdown passes of 70, 8, 24 and 33 yards to wide receiver John Taylor, fullback Tom Rathman, tight end Brent Jones and wide receiver Jerry Rice, respectively. Making Montana's performance even more remarkable was the pressure he faced all afternoon from a gritty Eagle defense that hounded him from sideline to sideline, much of the dogging coming from defensive end Reggie White, who sacked Montana three times.

Eagle quarterback Randall Cunningham had a good day too, throwing for 192 yards and eluding everyone in red. But it wasn't his best day. When San Francisco took a 31-28 lead with 3:17 left, Cunningham got a chance for his own fabulous finish. He threw to fullback Heath Sherman for 17 yards and ran for three more himself. Next, he tried a seven-yard flareout to running back Keith Byars, but the ball bounced off Byars's hands and into the arms of Niner safety Ronnie Lott. Game, Set, Match.

Montana (16) hooked up with John Taylor (82) for a 36-yard gain on the go-ahead drive.

Vicious sacks like this one by White couldn't stop the amazing Montana: He still threw for five touchdowns.

New York Giants 20, Washington 17—Week 6, at New Jersey. "I guess old Parcells wasn't too conservative today, was he?" asked the coach of the Giants after this one. If talk-show slings and arrows ever found their mark, Bill Parcells long ago would have been wounded from head to toe by the callers who rip him for being such a staid football tactician. But against the Redskins in New Jersey, Parcells gambled three times on fourth down. Each time the gamble worked, and each time the success led to Giants' points, 17 of their 20 on the day. "It just goes to show you," said Giants quarterback Phil Simms, "that Bill Parcells will do what it takes to win."

This game also showed that the Giants weren't ready to fall back into mediocrity after two nonplayoff seasons since the Super Bowl win, and it showed the considerable skills still left in the 31-year-old Ottis Anderson, who gained 101 yards on 25 carries to record his first 100-yard day since 1985. "I can't play," Anderson chided reporters afterward. "I'm an old man. Don't you know that by now?"

In fact, Anderson looked anything but old. In the fourth quarter, he barreled down the sideline for 20 yards—the last 10 with defenders draped around his neck—to set up the 12-yard touchdown pass from Simms to tight end Mark Bavaro that put the Giants in the lead 13-10. Four-and-a-half minutes later, he picked up the first down in a fourth-and-one situation to keep the game-winning drive alive. Simms followed with another touchdown strike, this one to Odessa Turner.

It was a big win for the entire team and especially for Parcells, who gambled not only in this game, but also with the Giants' offensive line, a reconstructed unit that averaged just 1.8 years of NFL experience as a group. Perhaps it's time to remove the conservative rap and recognize Parcells for the terrific coach he is.

One other thing to recognize: the Giants, the Broncos and the 49ers all proved without a doubt that a team with a core of talent doesn't have to suffer a Cowboy-like rebuilding period in order to stay successful. Not, that is, if management is willing to embrace football's law of constant flux rather than to resist it.

Simms, who threw two touchdown passes, praised his gambling coach after the game.

 Anderson showed that there's still some life in those aging legs.

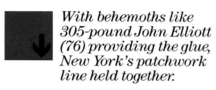 With behemoths like 305-pound John Elliott (76) providing the glue, New York's patchwork line held together.

First Quarter
Week 1
Memorable Moments

STANDINGS

AFC EAST	W	L	T	Pct	PF	PA
Buffalo	1	0	0	1.000	27	24
New England	1	0	0	1.000	27	24
Indianapolis	0	1	0	.000	24	30
Miami	0	1	0	.000	24	27
N.Y. Jets	0	1	0	.000	24	27

AFC CENTRAL	W	L	T	Pct	PF	PA
Cleveland	1	0	0	1.000	51	0
Cincinnati	0	1	0	.000	14	17
Houston	0	1	0	.000	7	38
Pittsburgh	0	1	0	.000	0	51

AFC WEST	W	L	T	Pct	PF	PA
Denver	1	0	0	1.000	34	20
L.A. Raiders	1	0	0	1.000	40	14
Kansas City	0	1	0	.000	20	34
San Diego	0	1	0	.000	14	40
Seattle	0	1	0	.000	7	31

NFC EAST	W	L	T	Pct	PF	PA
Philadelphia	1	0	0	1.000	31	7
Phoenix	1	0	0	1.000	16	13
N.Y. Giants	1	0	0	1.000	27	24
Dallas	0	1	0	.000	0	28
Washington	0	1	0	.000	24	27

NFC CENTRAL	W	L	T	Pct	PF	PA
Chicago	1	0	0	1.000	17	14
Minnesota	1	0	0	1.000	38	7
Tampa Bay	1	0	0	1.000	23	21
Detroit	0	1	0	.000	13	16
Green Bay	0	1	0	.000	21	23

NFC WEST	W	L	T	Pct	PF	PA
L.A. Rams	1	0	0	1.000	31	21
New Orleans	1	0	0	1.000	28	0
San Francisco	1	0	0	1.000	30	24
Atlanta	0	1	0	.000	21	31

RESULTS

Chicago 17, Cincinnati 14
Philadelphia 31, Seattle 7
Minnesota 38, Houston 7
San Francisco 30, Indianapolis 24
Phoenix 16, Detroit 13
Denver 34, Kansas City 20
L.A. Raiders 40, San Diego 14
Buffalo 27, Miami 24
New England 27, N.Y. Jets 24
Cleveland 51, Pittsburgh 0
New Orleans 28, Dallas 0
Tampa Bay 23, Green Bay 21
L.A. Rams 31, Atlanta 21
N.Y. Giants 27, Washington 24 (Monday night)

 With his team down by 11 points and less than three minutes left, Buffalo quarterback Jim Kelly went to work against the Dolphins, hitting Flip Johnson with a 26-yard strike for one touchdown and then completing the comeback with a two-yard touchdown dive for the 27-24 victory.

Deion Sanders, in his first official play for Atlanta, electrified the Falcon faithful with a 68-yard punt return for a touchdown against the Rams. It was certainly a Prime Time performance, but Atlanta still lost, 31-21.

Defensive tackle Dan Hampton celebrated one of his two sacks of Cincinnati quarterback Boomer Esiason in Chicago's 17-14 win. Hampton had much cause for celebration: He also deflected two passes, blocked a field goal and made a key tackle in a fourth-and-inches situation.

David Grayson, linebacker, Cleveland. *As long as Grayson had been playing football, he had never scored twice in a game, not even as a kid in California. But that's exactly what he did in the Browns' season-opening 51-0 rout of Pittsburgh in Three Rivers Stadium. In fact, one could make the case that Grayson was the man most responsible for sending the Steelers to their worst loss in franchise history. First he gobbled up a first-quarter fumble by Tim Worley. That led to a 27-yard field goal by Matt Bahr for a 10-0 Browns lead. Then, still in the first quarter, he stripped the ball from Steeler wide receiver Louis Lipps and galloped 28 yards to put his team in front 17-0. Without those two plays, who knows how the course of the game might have gone? Sadly for the Steelers, it went steadily downhill, with Grayson's 14-yard touchdown on a third-quarter interception mere icing on the cake.*

How rare is a two-TD day for a linebacker? Consider this: Teammate Clay Matthews has played 12 seasons, totaling 169 games. And he has two career touchdowns. "I never thought about something like this before," Grayson said. He should savor the thought; it may never happen again.

23

Week 2

➤ Ram wide receiver Henry Ellard hovered in mid-air while waiting for a pass from quarterback Jim Everett. Ellard's numbers were sky-high too: 12 catches for 230 yards and three touchdowns in L.A.'s 31-17 win over the Colts.

➤ A rare sight in pro football: Eagle coach Buddy Ryan was carried off the field after Philadelphia's wild 42-37 win over Washington. The game seemed to be securely in the Redskins' grasp late in the fourth quarter, but a fumble by Washington's Gerald Riggs was scooped up by Eagle linebacker Al Harris and then lateraled to safety Wes Hopkins, who ran 77 yards to set up the game-winning score.

STANDINGS

AFC EAST	W	L	T	Pct	PF	PA
Buffalo	1	1	0	.500	41	52
Miami	1	1	0	.500	48	37
New England	1	1	0	.500	37	48
Indianapolis	0	2	0	.000	41	61
N.Y. Jets	0	2	0	.000	48	65

AFC CENTRAL	W	L	T	Pct	PF	PA
Cleveland	2	0	0	1.000	89	24
Cincinnati	1	1	0	.500	55	27
Houston	1	1	0	.500	41	65
Pittsburgh	0	2	0	.000	10	92

AFC WEST	W	L	T	Pct	PF	PA
Denver	2	0	0	1.000	62	34
Kansas City	1	1	0	.500	44	53
L.A. Raiders	1	1	0	.500	59	38
San Diego	0	2	0	.000	41	74
Seattle	0	2	0	.000	31	65

NFC EAST	W	L	T	Pct	PF	PA
N.Y. Giants	2	0	0	1.000	51	38
Philadelphia	2	0	0	1.000	73	44
Phoenix	2	0	0	1.000	50	37
Dallas	0	2	0	.000	21	55
Washington	0	2	0	.000	61	69

NFC CENTRAL	W	L	T	Pct	PF	PA
Chicago	2	0	0	1.000	55	21
Green Bay	1	1	0	.500	56	57
Minnesota	1	1	0	.500	45	45
Tampa Bay	1	1	0	.500	39	41
Detroit	0	2	0	.000	27	40

NFC WEST	W	L	T	Pct	PF	PA
L.A. Rams	2	0	0	1.000	62	38
San Francisco	2	0	0	1.000	50	40
Atlanta	1	1	0	.500	48	52
New Orleans	1	1	0	.500	62	35

RESULTS

Philadelphia 42, Washington 37
L.A. Rams 31, Indianapolis 17
Chicago 38, Minnesota 7
Houston 34, San Diego 27
N.Y. Giants 24, Detroit 14
San Francisco 20, Tampa Bay 16
Cleveland 38, N.Y. Jets 24
Phoenix 34, Seattle 24
Green Bay 35, New Orleans 34
Miami 24, New England 10
Kansas City 24, L.A. Raiders 19
Cincinnati 41, Pittsburgh 10
Atlanta 27, Dallas 21
Denver 28, Buffalo 14 (Monday night)

In spite of pressure from the likes of Cowboy defensive end Ed Jones, Atlanta quarterback Chris Miller completed 21 of 29 passes for 255 yards to bring his team back from a 21-10 half-time deficit. The Falcons erupted for 17 unanswered points in the second half to pull out the 27-21 victory.

Miami quarterback Dan Marino threw three touchdown passes in the Dolphins' 24-10 win over New England to give him 200 for his career. He reached that mark in just his 89th game, faster than any other quarterback in NFL history. Who's next on the list? Below are the best of the rest:

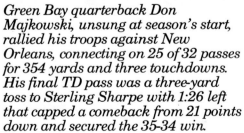

Green Bay quarterback Don Majkowski, unsung at season's start, rallied his troops against New Orleans, connecting on 25 of 32 passes for 354 yards and three touchdowns. His final TD pass was a three-yard toss to Sterling Sharpe with 1:26 left that capped a comeback from 21 points down and secured the 35-34 win.

	FIRST SEASON	DATE OF 200TH TD	GAMES FOR 200TH TD	PASSES FOR 200TH TD	CAREER TD PASSES
Johnny Unitas	1956	10/31/65	121	*3,040	290
Fran Tarkenton . .	1961	11/29/70	137	*3,329	342
Dan Fouts	1973	11/18/84	143	4,245	254
John Hadl	1962	12/ 3/72	152	*3,558	244
Len Dawson	1957	10/18/71	153	*2,756	239
Sonny Jurgensen . .	1957	10/26/69	156	*3,239	255
Terry Bradshaw . . .	1970	11/21/82	161	3,737	212
Y.A. Tittle	1950	12/15/63	164	*3,517	212
Roman Gabriel . . .	1962	11/21/76	167	4,406	201
John Brodie	1957	12/19/71	180	*4,170	214

*Estimated; pass totals at conclusion of the games in which 200th TD was achieved.

Jet quarterback Ken O'Brien had his usual field day against Miami, completing 27 of 37 passes for 329 yards and three touchdowns, including an 11-yard scoring strike to Roger Vick with 1:29 left for the margin of victory in the 40-33 win.

STANDINGS

AFC EAST	W	L	T	Pct	PF	PA
Buffalo	2	1	0	.667	88	93
Indianapolis	1	2	0	.333	54	70
Miami	1	2	0	.333	81	77
New England	1	2	0	.333	40	72
N.Y. Jets	1	2	0	.333	88	98

AFC CENTRAL	W	L	T	Pct	PF	PA
Cincinnati	2	1	0	.667	76	41
Cleveland	2	1	0	.667	103	45
Houston	1	2	0	.333	82	112
Pittsburgh	1	2	0	.333	37	106

AFC WEST	W	L	T	Pct	PF	PA
Denver	3	0	0	1.000	93	55
Kansas City	1	2	0	.333	50	74
L.A. Raiders	1	2	0	.333	80	69
San Diego	1	2	0	.333	62	80
Seattle	1	2	0	.333	55	68

NFC EAST	W	L	T	Pct	PF	PA
N.Y. Giants	3	0	0	1.000	86	45
Philadelphia	2	1	0	.667	101	82
Phoenix	2	1	0	.667	57	72
Washington	1	2	0	.333	91	76
Dallas	0	3	0	.000	28	85

NFC CENTRAL	W	L	T	Pct	PF	PA
Chicago	3	0	0	1.000	102	48
Tampa Bay	2	1	0	.667	59	51
Green Bay	1	2	0	.333	94	98
Minnesota	1	2	0	.333	59	72
Detroit	0	3	0	.000	54	87

NFC WEST	W	L	T	Pct	PF	PA
L.A. Rams	3	0	0	1.000	103	76
San Francisco	3	0	0	1.000	88	68
Atlanta	1	2	0	.333	57	65
New Orleans	1	2	0	.333	72	55

RESULTS

Buffalo 47, Houston 41, OT
San Francisco 38, Philadelphia 28
Tampa Bay 20, New Orleans 10
N.Y. Giants 35, Phoenix 7
Pittsburgh 27, Minnesota 14
Washington 30, Dallas 7
N.Y. Jets 40, Miami 33
San Diego 21, Kansas City 6
L.A. Rams 41, Green Bay 38
Chicago 47, Detroit 27
Denver 31, L.A. Raiders 21
Seattle 24, New England 3
Indianapolis 13, Atlanta 9
Cincinnati 21, Cleveland 14 (Monday night)

Tampa Bay wide receiver Mark Carrier burst past the Saints secondary for one of his five catches for 120 yards in the Bucs' 20-10 upset win over New Orleans.

When Liz Taylor showed up with Dallas owner Jerry Jones for the Washington game, the crowd went wild. So, apparently, did referee Pat Haggerty, who asked her to call the pregame coin toss, in violation of the rule allowing the visiting team to make the call. Washington protested and was granted another toss.

Eric Ball, running back, Cincinnati. *Great story. The Bengals are this penurious organization run absolutely down to the bone with the league's smallest office staff and most spartan facilities. In the 1989 NFL draft, it was their turn to make a selection late in the first round. They liked Ball, a running back from UCLA, but they didn't like him well enough to spend huge first-round money on him. So Cincinnati took an offer from Atlanta to swap draft choices—Atlanta threw in two more picks—and were still able to get Ball eight picks later, near the top of the second round. The club saved $360,000 or so in bonus money, and they still got the guy they wanted.*

Fast forward to Week 3 of the season, eight days after stalwart back Ickey Woods tore up his knee, sidelining him for the season. On national TV, playing against Cleveland—the Bengals' hated AFC Central rivals— Ball rushed 18 times for 78 yards to help his team to an important 21-14 victory. Alas, he never made it into the end zone, so he didn't get to shuffle.

 With tackles like this, Pittsburgh's Tim Johnson (78) and Gregg Carr helped to hold Viking running back D.J. Dozier to just 12 yards on six carries in the Steelers' 27-14 upset victory. After yielding 520 yards and 41 points in Week 2 against Cincinnati, the Steelers limited Minnesota to just 258 offensive yards.

STANDINGS

AFC EAST	W	L	T	Pct	PF	PA
Buffalo	3	1	0	.750	119	103
Indianapolis	2	2	0	.500	71	80
Miami	1	3	0	.250	88	116
New England	1	3	0	.250	50	103
N.Y. Jets	1	3	0	.250	98	115

AFC CENTRAL	W	L	T	Pct	PF	PA
Cincinnati	3	1	0	.750	97	58
Cleveland	3	1	0	.750	119	58
Houston	2	2	0	.500	121	119
Pittsburgh	2	2	0	.500	60	109

AFC WEST	W	L	T	Pct	PF	PA
Denver	3	1	0	.750	106	71
San Diego	2	2	0	.500	86	93
Seattle	2	2	0	.500	79	88
Kansas City	1	3	0	.250	67	95
L.A. Raiders	1	3	0	.250	100	93

NFC EAST	W	L	T	Pct	PF	PA
N.Y. Giants	4	0	0	1.000	116	58
Philadelphia	2	2	0	.500	114	109
Phoenix	2	2	0	.500	70	96
Washington	2	2	0	.500	107	90
Dallas	0	4	0	.000	41	115

NFC CENTRAL	W	L	T	Pct	PF	PA
Chicago	4	0	0	1.000	129	61
Green Bay	2	2	0	.500	117	119
Minnesota	2	2	0	.500	76	75
Tampa Bay	2	2	0	.500	62	68
Detroit	0	4	0	.000	57	110

NFC WEST	W	L	T	Pct	PF	PA
L.A. Rams	4	0	0	1.000	116	88
San Francisco	3	1	0	.750	100	81
Atlanta	1	3	0	.250	78	88
New Orleans	1	3	0	.250	86	72

RESULTS

Cleveland 16, Denver 13
L.A. Rams 13, San Francisco 12
N.Y. Giants 30, Dallas 13
Washington 16, New Orleans 14
Cincinnati 21, Kansas City 17
Indianapolis 17, N.Y. Jets 10
Pittsburgh 23, Detroit 3
Houston 39, Miami 7
Minnesota 17, Tampa Bay 3
Seattle 24, L.A. Raiders 20
Buffalo 31, New England 10
San Diego 24, Phoenix 13
Green Bay 23, Atlanta 21
Chicago 27, Philadelphia 13 (Monday night)

When 37-year-old center Mike Webster (left) and 38-year-old quarterback Ron Jaworski started for the Chiefs against the Bengals, they became the oldest quarterback-center combo in more than a decade. Cincinnati won anyway, 21-17.

Ram coach John Robinson ranted on the sidelines during the 49er game. Later his ranting would turn to raving—about his team—after Mike Lansford kicked a 26-yard field goal with two seconds left to win the game 13-12.

Packer quarterback Don Majkowski staged another stirring comeback against the Falcons, this time leading his team back from a 21-6 deficit with 17 unanswered points in the fourth quarter to pull out the 23-21 victory. Majkowski completed 12 of 18 passes in the second half, including a 23-yard toss to Perry Kemp that led to the game-winning 22-yard field goal by Chris Jacke with 1:42 remaining.

This 48-yard field goal, kicked by Cleveland's Matt Bahr with time running out, beat the Broncos 16-13. Earlier in the fourth quarter, the game had been delayed when referee Tom Dooley decided to switch ends to escape the shower of batteries, dog biscuits and eggs thrown by Cleveland's rowdy fans who inhabit the end zone seats known as the Dawg Pound. Bahr, who got a tail wind out of the switch, claimed that the wind was no factor in his winning kick. Denver coach Dan Reeves disagreed.

Week 5

Tampa Bay's Vinny Testaverde aired it out against Chicago, connecting on 22 of 36 passes for 269 yards and three touchdowns in the 42-35 win. The victory was the first for the Bucs against the Bears since 1983.

STANDINGS

AFC EAST	W	L	T	Pct	PF	PA
Buffalo	3	2	0	.600	133	140
Indianapolis	3	2	0	.600	108	94
Miami	2	3	0	.400	101	126
New England	2	3	0	.400	73	116
N.Y. Jets	1	4	0	.200	105	127

AFC CENTRAL	W	L	T	Pct	PF	PA
Cincinnati	4	1	0	.800	123	74
Cleveland	3	2	0	.600	129	71
Houston	2	3	0	.400	134	142
Pittsburgh	2	3	0	.400	76	135

AFC WEST	W	L	T	Pct	PF	PA
Denver	4	1	0	.800	122	81
Kansas City	2	3	0	.400	87	111
L.A. Raiders	2	3	0	.400	114	100
San Diego	2	3	0	.400	96	109
Seattle	2	3	0	.400	95	108

NFC EAST	W	L	T	Pct	PF	PA
N.Y. Giants	4	1	0	.800	135	79
Philadelphia	3	2	0	.600	135	128
Washington	3	2	0	.600	137	118
Phoenix	2	3	0	.400	98	126
Dallas	0	5	0	.000	54	146

NFC CENTRAL	W	L	T	Pct	PF	PA
Chicago	4	1	0	.800	164	103
Green Bay	3	2	0	.600	148	132
Minnesota	3	2	0	.600	100	92
Tampa Bay	3	2	0	.600	104	103
Detroit	0	5	0	.000	74	134

NFC WEST	W	L	T	Pct	PF	PA
L.A. Rams	5	0	0	1.000	142	102
San Francisco	4	1	0	.800	124	101
Atlanta	1	4	0	.200	92	114
New Orleans	1	4	0	.200	106	95

RESULTS

Washington 30, Phoenix 28
Tampa Bay 42, Chicago 35
Philadelphia 21, N.Y. Giants 19
San Francisco 24, New Orleans 20
Kansas City 20, Seattle 16
L.A. Rams 26, Atlanta 14
Denver 16, San Diego 10
Cincinnati 26, Pittsburgh 16
Minnesota 24, Detroit 17
Green Bay 31, Dallas 13
Miami 13, Cleveland 10, OT
Indianapolis 37, Buffalo 14
New England 23, Houston 13
L.A. Raiders 14, N.Y. Jets 7 (Monday night)

Cincinnati's James Brooks swept around end for one of his two touchdowns in the Bengals' 26-16 victory over Pittsburgh. Brooks carried 17 times for 127 yards on the day.

 Raider coach Art Shell got an 87-yard interception return from cornerback Eddie Anderson for a 14-7 victory over the Jets in his first game as head coach. Shell's appointment made him the first black head coach in the NFL's modern era.

Redskins running back Earnest Byner, acquired from Cleveland in the off-season, paid his first real dividend to his new team in a 30-28 win over Phoenix, running for 100 yards and grabbing five passes for 71 yards more through the air.

The Giants defense kept Philadelphia's Keith Byars out of the end zone on this goal line stand, but they couldn't stop quarterback Randall Cunningham, who scored two touchdowns to lead the Eagles to a 21-19 comeback win.

Week 6

 Houston's Warren Moon exposed the weakness of Chicago's once-vaunted defense, throwing for 317 yards and two touchdowns in a 33-28 Oiler victory. Moon also ran for a score, one of two unanswered touchdowns by Houston in the last four minutes of the game.

STANDINGS

AFC EAST	W	L	T	Pct	PF	PA
Buffalo	4	2	0	.667	156	160
Indianapolis	3	3	0	.500	111	108
Miami	3	3	0	.500	121	139
New England	2	4	0	.333	88	132
N.Y. Jets	1	5	0	.167	119	158

AFC CENTRAL	W	L	T	Pct	PF	PA
Cincinnati	4	2	0	.667	136	94
Cleveland	3	3	0	.500	136	88
Houston	3	3	0	.500	167	170
Pittsburgh	3	3	0	.500	93	142

AFC WEST	W	L	T	Pct	PF	PA
Denver	5	1	0	.833	136	84
L.A. Raiders	3	3	0	.500	134	114
Seattle	3	3	0	.500	112	124
Kansas City	2	4	0	.333	101	131
San Diego	2	4	0	.333	112	126

NFC EAST	W	L	T	Pct	PF	PA
N.Y. Giants	5	1	0	.833	155	96
Philadelphia	4	2	0	.667	152	133
Washington	3	3	0	.500	154	138
Phoenix	2	4	0	.333	103	143
Dallas	0	6	0	.000	68	177

NFC CENTRAL	W	L	T	Pct	PF	PA
Chicago	4	2	0	.667	192	136
Minnesota	4	2	0	.667	126	106
Green Bay	3	3	0	.500	162	158
Tampa Bay	3	3	0	.500	120	120
Detroit	1	5	0	.167	91	150

NFC WEST	W	L	T	Pct	PF	PA
L.A. Rams	5	1	0	.833	162	125
San Francisco	5	1	0	.833	155	115
Atlanta	2	4	0	.333	108	129
New Orleans	2	4	0	.333	135	109

RESULTS

Minnesota 26, Green Bay 14
Denver 14, Indianapolis 3
Houston 33, Chicago 28
Miami 20, Cincinnati 13
N.Y. Giants 20, Washington 17
Detroit 17, Tampa Bay 16
San Francisco 31, Dallas 14
Pittsburgh 17, Cleveland 7
Seattle 17, San Diego 16
New Orleans 29, N.Y. Jets 14
L.A. Raiders 20, Kansas City 14
Philadelphia 17, Phoenix 5
Atlanta 16, New England 15
Buffalo 23, L.A. Rams 20 (Monday night)

Herschel Walker made his first appearance in a Viking uniform a sensational one, bursting through and around the Packer defense for 148 yards on 18 carries. A cry of "Herschelmania" could be heard in the Metrodome, and Minnesota fans began thinking Super Bowl.

 Bo Jackson, late of baseball's Kansas City Royals, made many of his former fans unhappy in his season debut for the Raiders, rushing for 85 yards on 11 carries against the Kansas City Chiefs. The unkindest cut was a 45-yard gallop in the fourth quarter that set up the game-winning score in L.A.'s 20-14 victory.

Frank Reich, quarterback, Buffalo. *Best known as the best man at college roommate Boomer Esiason's wedding, Reich became a free agent at the end of the 1988 season. Truth be told, the Bills didn't care if he stayed or left the team. In the off-season, such luminaries as Steve Slayden, Mike Norseth and Brent Pease were signed as reserve quarterbacks. Not Reich. Even worse, the Bills told him that if he wanted to come back, he would have to accept a cut in his 1988 salary. These aren't exactly big confidence builders for a guy.*

But when Buffalo quarterback Jim Kelly went down with a separated shoulder in Week 5, backup Reich stepped in and won three games in a row. His shining hour came on Monday Night Football *against the Rams in Week 6. Trailing 20-16 with 1:22 left, Reich engineered one of the finer drives of the season, connecting with Thurman Thomas for gains of 17 and 15 yards, with Ronnie Harmon for 14 more and finally with Andre Reed on an eight-yard pass with 16 seconds left that gave the Bills the 23-20 victory. "It's like a fairy tale," Reich said. Midnight came for this Cinderella in Week 9, when Kelly's return sent Reich back to the bench.*

SECOND QUARTER:
Weeks 7-12

Pete's Farewell Parity

With interest piqued by Pete's Parity, fans—in all sizes, shapes and mental states—turned out in record numbers.

A few days before Pete Rozelle officially left office, he was asked about his major accomplishments as commissioner. One of his first responses: "Close, competitive games."

The Prince of Parity, the King of Kloseness, maybe that's how Rozelle should be remembered. Year after year, he strived to make games close by applying blatantly socialist principles to the National Football League. Many people thought this made the game mediocre. Many people thought this made the game boring. But many people clearly love it. Because, after 12 weeks of the 1989 season, the league's TV ratings were up on two of the three networks, and the average attendance was nearly 61,000 fans a game. The fact of the matter is that the Rozelle rules have kept relatively bad teams contending for the playoffs into late November, insuring higher attendance figures, better TV ratings and more money in the 1990 television contract negotiations. Who can argue with that?

"Here's the bottom line," said Mike Brown, Cincin-

nati's assistant general manager. "If the teams in markets the size of Cincinnati can't remain competitive with teams in New York and Los Angeles, the whole league will suffer."

Rozelle certainly didn't orchestrate it, but the race to replace him was every bit as competitive as the league he has fostered. On Oct. 27, the day after Rozelle's successor was elected during an owners' meeting in Cleveland, new commissioner Paul Tagliabue sat at a corner table in one of Washington's poshest restaurants. Looking every bit the D.C. corporate lawyer that he is, or rather was, he was talking about how close the vote to approve him had been and how uncertain he had been of the outcome.

The night before the vote, league counsel Jay Moyer called Tagliabue at his Bethesda, Md., home. "If it happens tomorrow," Moyer told Tagliabue, "it won't happen fast. Sleep late." So Tagliabue did. And what happened? The unexpected, of course. Tagliabue was shaving the next morning, after sleeping until almost nine, when Rozelle called from Cleveland. "Here are three flights," Rozelle said, ticking off the flight information. "Try to make one of them." Simple as that.

That night, home from Cleveland and the bustle of the day, Tagliabue found 33 messages on the answering machine at his house. On the phone when he walked in was an overseas operator. "You better take this one, Dad," his daughter Emily told him. "It's Ronald Reagan. It's the third time he's called for you tonight."

What a difference a day makes. Before his election, Tagliabue had been an anonymous guy in Washington, who regularly rode the subway to work. Now he would have hired cars and drivers and a life in the public eye.

"I'll lose my privacy, which I don't like," he said that day in the restaurant. "And I'll miss practicing law, which I really happen to like. But this is a fun game. I think it'll be a good job."

Perhaps, but Tagliabue will certainly have his share of headaches. On Nov. 7, the players' union, in a move designed to foster free agency, announced plans to decertify, meaning it would no longer be the bargaining agent for NFL players. Ever since the old bargaining agreement expired in August 1987, the league has been intent on getting a new one, and this would only delay that into the '90s. There was the new television contract to be negotiated as well, and Tagliabue also had to worry about the mounting number of collegians who wanted to enter the NFL draft before their college eligibility had expired. Problems enough? More would follow.

For the moment, though, Tagliabue could sit back and take delight in his going-away gift from Rozelle: a weekly package of squeakers, nail-biters and fantastic finishes as the league careened its way toward the playoffs. In Weeks 7 through 12 of the NFL's 70th season, the little guys rose up and the big guys fell down.

But no one fell too far.

The Steelers lost their first two games in '89 by 82 points, then won four of six. The Rams won their first five, then lost four straight. Buffalo lost top-rated AFC quarterback Jim Kelly, won three straight with a quarterback (Frank Reich) nobody wanted in Plan B last winter, then got Kelly back and lost to 2-6 Atlanta. Five weeks after the Browns won by 51 at Pittsburgh, the Steelers won by 10 at Cleveland. Dallas, the worst team, won by 10 at Washington. Washington won by two at New Orleans. New Orleans won by 19 at the

Tagliabue had better stay in shape; he'll need his strength for the many tasks that lie ahead.

Rams. The Rams won by one over San Francisco, the league's best team. Voilá: Dallas should beat San Francisco by 32. Hey, the way things go in this league, we would barely do a double take at that score.

Need we mention that pesky P word again? In the year that Parity Pete leaves the game, it's only fitting that parity is at an alltime high. After 12 games, 15 teams were bunched in the standings with 5, 6 or 7 wins and all but four teams still had a shot at the play-offs. Steelers equal Skins. Packers equal Bears. In New England, if you don't like the weather, wait two hours, and it will change. In Pittsburgh, if you don't like the Steelers, wait two weeks, and *they* will change.

"What an unbelievable year," said the 1988 executive of the year, Buffalo general manager Bill Polian. "I turn 47 in December, but this season my stomach is 116 and aging geometrically."

Through 12 weeks of the season, the NFL appeared headed for its fourth straight season in which at least 47% of the games were decided by a touchdown or less. "I can't remember the last time I was in a game that was over in the third quarter," said Patriots guard Sean Farrell. The entire decade has been marked by parity, but it has been turned up a notch or two in the last year and a half.

Why? First of all, the scheduling system has changed. The NFL has always tried to pit weak-versus-weak and strong-versus-strong in the early going so as to keep as many teams as possible in the playoff pic-ture for as long as possible. But in 1987, for the first time, the league went from giving a division's first- and fourth-place finishers comparable schedules and the second- and third-place finishers comparable sched-ules to making the first-place team play the toughest schedule, the second-place team play the next-toughest schedule, and so on. What that meant in practice is that the Steelers, who won only five games in 1988, rather than getting a carbon copy of the Super Bowl Bengals' schedule, got a much easier deal, playing opponents like San Diego, New England and the Jets (combined 1988 record: 23-24-1), while Cincinnati got Indianapolis, Buffalo and Seattle (30-18). The results were obvious: After 12 weeks, both the Steelers and the Bengals were in wild-card competition.

The Plan B free-agency system is the second new wrinkle, serving to distribute marginal players to needy teams; the Raiders and the Dolphins both got desperately needed linebacker help, and both were con-tending for wild-card spots. The rich get poor and the poor get richer. Call it Rozelle's Law.

Other spurs to parity have evolved over time. Scout-ing—endless, redundant scouting—has become stan-dard throughout the league. Two years ago, Buffalo scouted, interviewed or worked out defensive tackle Pierce Holt of Angelo (Texas) State eight times—and then didn't draft him. It's been 14 years since the league moved the draft from January to April, a crit-ical change that gave every club the opportunity to spend three months quadruple-checking the heights, weights and speeds of those small-college prospects in Nebraska. We're just now seeing the full effect of the later draft, because only now are virtually all of the

players in the league the result of the new system. "It used to be," said former Dallas president Tex Schramm, "that the good organizations were ready to draft in January, and the others weren't. After the first round, I'd always see four, five, six of our players still on the board, and we'd get one in the second round. But teams have so much time to scout now that nobody can make a really big mistake. I think it hurt us."

Another cause of the current competitiveness is a set of rules—most of which have been instituted since 1978—that aid pass receivers and pass blockers. Desper-ate offenses can catch up more easily now. In Week 11, New England trailed Buffalo by 11 in the fourth quar-ter, scored 20 points in the last 7:45 and won by nine.

The simple truth may also be that the bad teams just aren't as bad as they used to be. New Orleans presi-dent Jim Finks points out that with no expansion for 13 years and no competing league for four years, teams naturally are going to be facing fewer patsies on their schedule. The Bucs and the Seahawks of today are a far cry from their former expansion selves. Here's what perhaps the five worst teams in the league did in Week 9: Dallas won at previously 4-4 Washington; the Jets won at 3-5 New England; San Diego, at home, beat 6-2 Philadelphia; Atlanta, at home, beat 6-2 Buffalo; and Detroit led or was tied at 4-4 Houston for 44 min-

Home Run Baker performed some of his quick-strike magic in a 20-13 Giants win over Phoenix in Week 9.

utes before losing by four. Five "terrible" teams went 4-1.

Finally, it's just a tougher business today. There's very little cronyism left in the game. Coaches now hire the best motivators and teachers as their assistants; in the '50s and '60s, friendships and good connections often determined the staff makeup. In Pittsburgh, under the direction of club president Dan Rooney, coach Chuck Noll replaced almost his entire defensive staff after the '88 season.

Of course there are always the cynics, like Dallas cornerback Everson Walls, who think the current parity is the result of the mediocre talent in the league these days. "Nowadays you've got fewer young guys who are impact players," Walls says. Wait a minute. Wake up, Everson. Nowadays you've got passing-down sack spe-

cialists like Seattle's Rufus Porter wreaking havoc and fourth wideouts like the Giants' Stephen Baker, who are home run threats on every pattern. Ten years ago one quarterback finished the season with a passer rating over 85. After nine weeks of 1989 play, nine quarterbacks were over 85. The talent is there. Look at the bad teams. Ken O'Brien handing off to Freeman McNeil and throwing to Al Toon is an easy day for an opponent? Defending against Rodney Peete and Barry Sanders is a piece of cake?

The end result was clear in the chummy standings: After 12 weeks, the first- and fourth-place teams in the AFC Central were 7-4-1 and 6-6, respectively; the first- and fourth-place teams in the NFC Central were 7-5 and 5-7, respectively. Parity prevailed.

"Will somebody tell me what's wrong with close, competitive games?" general manager George Young of the Giants harrumphs. "That's our business. Since when did 'blowout' become such a great word? Fans don't want blowouts. They want close games. And that's what we're giving them."

39

The parity parade was in full swing in the second quarter, as NFL outcomes became as unpredictable as the events in Eastern Europe. The following four games left observers around the league shaking their heads and uttering the '89 motto: Go figure.

Green Bay 14, Chicago 13—

Week 9, at Green Bay. Welcome to controversy, Commissioner Tagliabue. Sixteen hours into his new job, Tagliabue watched on the evening highlight shows as the Packers used the most controversial instant-replay call in the four-year history of the system to catapult themselves into the NFL playoff race.

The Pack led from almost the outset until the third quarter, when Chicago quarterback Jim Harbaugh finally got his troops in gear. First he hit tight end James Thornton for a 22-yard gain. Then, in the game's biggest play to that point, he connected with wideout Dennis Gentry, who scampered up the left sideline for 46 yards. Four plays later, fullback Brad Muster dived across from the two-yard line to give the Bears a 13-7 lead with 3:03 left in the third quarter.

That's how it stayed until late in the game, when Green Bay quarterback Don Majkowski, already enjoying a season of dreams, began one of his patented last-minute drives. He hit wide receiver Perry Kemp for 26 yards. Four plays later, he hit tight end Ed West for 17 more. With 49 seconds to play, the Packers had a fourth-and-goal on the Bears' 14-yard line.

Majkowski took the snap from center Blair Bush and jogged right. And jogged right, and jogged right, and looked into the end zone, and approached the line of scrimmage, and looked pressure and Bear defensive end Trace Armstrong in the face and didn't flinch. Right at the 14, Majkowski slung a bullet into the end zone. Green Bay wide receiver Sterling Sharpe cradled it. Touchdown.

The Packers were going nuts until someone noticed the yellow flag that had fluttered out of line judge Jim Quirk's pocket on the far sidelines. Quirk said Majkowski had gone over the line of scrimmage before throwing the winning pass to Sharpe. No TD. But replay official Bill Parkinson wanted to review the play. Four minutes passed. "I was just thinking to myself, These refs are going to have a hard time getting out of here if they don't call it a touchdown," Packer linebacker Tim Harris said. Parkinson did overturn the call and award the touchdown, and the game, to Green Bay. This despite the fact that the replay, which allows calls to be changed only when there's indisputable evidence of an error, didn't provide indisputable evidence.

The Bears seethed. "I really think what they ought to do is just get a couple of computer programmers, and let them play the game on videotape," said Chicago linebacker Ron Rivera. "Or they could get 11 robots and put jerseys on them, and let them play."

No man is an island, but Majkowski certainly looked like one as he awaited the replay official's decision.

Green Bay was a joyous Pack until someone noticed the flag on the play.

Sharpe calmly jogged out of the end zone after scoring what appeared to be the game-winning touchdown.

Kansas City 10, Cleveland 10

Kansas City 10, Cleveland 10—Week 11, at Cleveland. In some ways, this was Kansas City's coming-out party. For weeks, teams had known the Chiefs were good. In fact, in Weeks 9 and 10, against Seattle and Denver, the Chiefs, with their sixth defensive coordinator (Bill Cowher) in the last six seasons, allowed just 129 and 213 yards, respectively. Over one 17-quarter span, the defense yielded just one touchdown. "It's been incredible, learning that many defenses in that many years," said Chiefs safety Deron Cherry, who has had to learn them all. "Finally, I think we've got a system we'll stay with for a while."

On this frigid day on the lousy grass of Cleveland Stadium, the Chiefs actually blew a gimme win. The Browns took a 3-0 lead on a Matt Bahr field goal in the second quarter that was set up by cornerback Mark Harper's interception of a Steve DeBerg pass. Kansas City went in front in the third quarter when Browns running back Mike Oliphant lost the handle after a smashing hit from Chiefs defensive end Neil Smith, who gobbled up the loose ball and returned it three yards for a touchdown. Eric Metcalf answered for Cleveland with a one-yard scoring run in the third quarter, but Kansas City kicker Nick Lowery tied it on a 41-yard field goal with 3:48 remaining in regulation.

Then things got hairy. With four seconds left, Lowery missed a 45-yard field goal attempt. Wide to the right. O.K., even though the guy *is* the second most accurate kicker in NFL history, he can't make them all. But there was a flag on the play. Offsides, Browns. Lowery got another chance, this time from a very makeable 39 yards. Again, he missed. Had enough? Not quite. Lowery got *another* chance with seven seconds left in overtime. This time he came up short on a 47-yard attempt. Strike Three. You're out. Game tied.

It was a tough moment for Lowery, but for the Chiefs the game was a victory of sorts. After all, they proved that the Browns weren't the only defensive powerhouse on the block. Cleveland had played tough, holding Christian Okoye—Kansas City's fullback and resident Mack truck—to only 40 yards on 21 carries. But Kansas City had hung in there and should have won. There's consolation in that—and hope for the future.

Kansas City's Dan Saleaumua, who had eight solo tackles, used strong-arm tactics to stop Metcalf (21) in the third quarter.

The agony of de feet: Lowery crumpled to the ground after missing in overtime.

Oliphant's third-quarter fumble led to Smith's touchdown and Kansas City's only lead of the day.

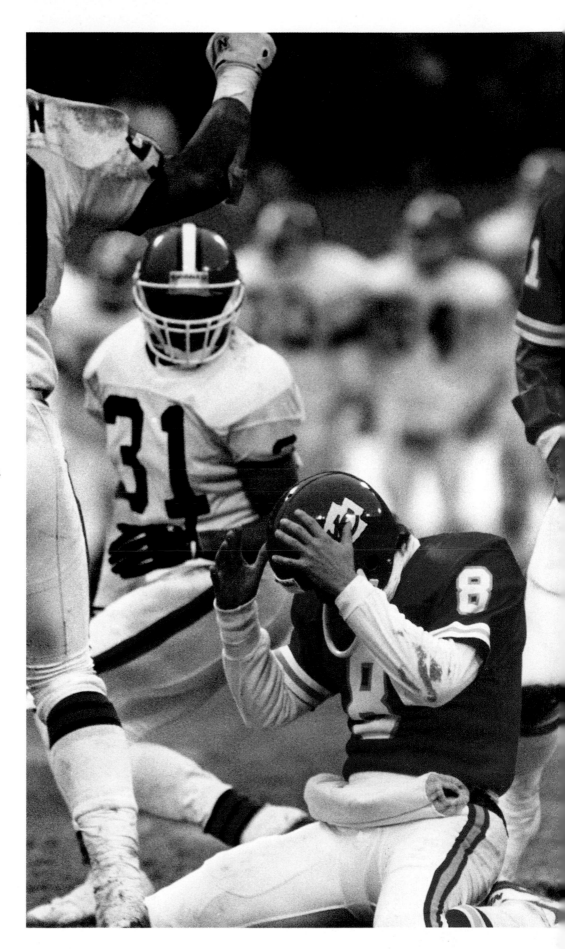

Pittsbugh 34, Miami 14—Week 12, at Miami. Parity reared its confusing head again, this time in a raging rainstorm. In the first 12 minutes of the game, when it was raining only moderately, the Dolphins, playing much like the Dolphins of the mid-80s, scored on a one-yard run by rookie running back Sammie Smith and a 66-yard pass from Dan Marino to Mark Clayton. It looked like the Dolphins, 7-4 entering the game and locked in a dogfight in the AFC East, would get the win they needed to keep pace with the Bills, while the Steelers, with only the slimmest of playoff hopes at 5-6, would be all but eliminated.

"Then," Pittsburgh cornerback Dwayne Woodruff said, "the skies opened."

In the second quarter alone it rained two inches. Water cascaded from the upper deck at Joe Robbie Stadium in torrents to the lower deck and in turn poured onto the field as if from an open faucet. The stadium has a state-of-the-art drainage system, but even it couldn't handle this downpour. The rain turned out to be the great equalizer for Pittsburgh. The Steelers sloshed to a Merrill Hoge one-yard touchdown run midway through the second quarter and, on the next Miami possession, scored one of the strangest touchdowns of the year. Smith took a handoff from Marino at the Miami 23 and just plain dropped the ball, which lay in a puddle for a couple of microseconds before the aptly named Carnell Lake, a Pittsburgh safety, swooped in from the right side to pick it up. As he was being downed, Lake lateraled the ball to Woodruff, who splish-splashed 21 yards for the tying touchdown. "That turned the tide," said Lake, metaphorically.

Indeed. Aided by more Miami miscues—the Dolphins lost three fumbles and had two passes picked off overall—the Steelers turned the game into a rout, getting two Gary Anderson field goals and two more Hoge touchdown runs to extend their lead to 20 points by the end of the third quarter. Pittsburgh running back Tim Worley, the seventh pick in the '89 draft, seemed to thrive in the slop, running for 95 yards on 22 carries, while Miami's Marino seemed to wilt, passing for only 128 yards before leaving the game in the third quarter with a slightly separated shoulder. The Dolphins just weren't used to playing in this stuff. In Pittsburgh, the autumn can get ugly, and the Steelers coped.

Recall that the Steelers were embarrassed 92-10 in their first two games of the season. Now, by gosh, they had won six of their last 10 and, at 6-6, still had a prayer for a wild-card berth. Strange days in this weird league.

 Even a torrential downpour couldn't douse the fiery spirit of Pittsburgh quarterback Bubby Brister.

 Smith's touchdown dive in the early going bode well for Miami, but after the deluge, he was left high and dry.

 While the Dolphins played like landlubbers, Pittsburgh's Rod Woodson seemed right at home in the slop.

Buffalo 24, Cincinnati 7—Week 12, at Buffalo.

"The crowd was the 12th man," Cincinnati linebacker Reggie Williams said after 80,074 yelled themselves silly in Rich Stadium. It was the same way the previous year, when the Bengals twice beat Buffalo in tight games at Riverfront Stadium, one of them for the AFC championship. The crowd was into it, and the Bills were too. The night before the game, coach Marv Levy showed a highlight film of great Cincinnati moments from the '88 season—kind of a friendly in-your-face to his players. The message got across. "I've never seen this team so ready to play a game," Buffalo nosetackle Fred Smerlas said.

The Bills won because they ran 47 times for 228 yards against a team that had been tough against the run in seasons past. It wasn't on this day. Buffalo's Thurman Thomas rushed 26 times for 100 yards, and former Bengal Larry Kinnebrew rushed 15 times for 66 yards. And Bills quarterback Jim Kelly, who would have big problems in December, closed November with a three-touchdown day to turn the game into a rout and provide the Buffalo fans with some sweet revenge

for the AFC title loss.

Bills kicker Scott Norwood started the scoring with a 24-yard field goal after a drive that would set the tone for the game, with Kelly connecting on several key passes and Thomas and Kinnebrew each contributing key 12-yard runs. More of the same led to a 19-yard touchdown strike from Kelly to Andre Reed in the second quarter. Cincinnati's James Brooks fumbled early in the third quarter, and Kelly followed quickly with another touchdown, this one on a 42-yard completion to running back Ronnie Harmon. Bills 17, Bengals 0. Kelly's final touchdown toss—a one-yarder to tight end Butch Rolle for his first catch of the season—was academic.

The Buffalo defense deserves some credit for this win too. They were a feisty bunch against Cincinnati, holding Bengal quarterback Boomer Esiason to just 11 completions in 26 attempts for a measly 136 yards. It was a balanced, team effort that seemed to presage a powerful Bills surge toward the playoffs. But, as we know, things are rarely what they seem in the NFL these days.

Kelly's three-touchdown day gave no hint of the troubles he would have in December.

There's more than one way to skin a Bengal: Kinnebrew (28) bowled over defenders while Thomas (34) dashed from a Cincinnati posse.

Second Quarter
Week 7
Memorable Moments

STANDINGS

AFC EAST	W	L	T	Pct	PF	PA
Buffalo	5	2	0	.714	190	163
Indianapolis	4	3	0	.571	134	120
Miami	4	3	0	.571	144	159
New England	2	5	0	.286	108	169
N.Y. Jets	1	6	0	.143	122	192

AFC CENTRAL	W	L	T	Pct	PF	PA
Cincinnati	4	3	0	.571	148	117
Cleveland	4	3	0	.571	163	95
Houston	4	3	0	.571	194	170
Pittsburgh	3	4	0	.429	93	169

AFC WEST	W	L	T	Pct	PF	PA
Denver	6	1	0	.857	160	105
Kansas City	3	4	0	.429	137	159
L.A. Raiders	3	4	0	.429	141	124
Seattle	3	4	0	.429	133	148
San Diego	2	5	0	.286	125	146

NFC EAST	W	L	T	Pct	PF	PA
N.Y. Giants	6	1	0	.857	175	109
Philadelphia	5	2	0	.714	162	140
Washington	4	3	0	.571	186	166
Phoenix	3	4	0	.429	137	163
Dallas	0	7	0	.000	96	213

NFC CENTRAL	W	L	T	Pct	PF	PA
Minnesota	5	2	0	.714	146	113
Chicago	4	3	0	.571	199	163
Green Bay	3	4	0	.429	182	181
Tampa Bay	3	4	0	.429	148	152
Detroit	1	6	0	.143	98	170

NFC WEST	W	L	T	Pct	PF	PA
San Francisco	6	1	0	.857	192	135
L.A. Rams	5	2	0	.714	183	165
New Orleans	3	4	0	.429	175	130
Atlanta	2	5	0	.286	128	163

RESULTS

Denver 24, Seattle 21, OT
San Francisco 37, New England 20
New Orleans 40, L.A. Rams 21
N.Y. Giants 20, San Diego 13
Philadelphia 10, L.A. Raiders 7
Phoenix 34, Atlanta 20
Houston 27, Pittsburgh 0
Indianapolis 23, Cincinnati 12
Miami 23, Green Bay 20
Minnesota 20, Detroit 7
Washington 32, Tampa Bay 28
Kansas City 36, Dallas 28
Buffalo 34, N.Y. Jets 3
Cleveland 27, Chicago 7 (Monday night)

Denver quarterback John Elway staved off the Seahawks by passing for 344 yards and two touchdowns, including a 54-yard scoring toss to Vance Johnson to tie the game with 2:19 left. The Broncos won the game in overtime, 24-21, on a 27-yard David Treadwell field goal.

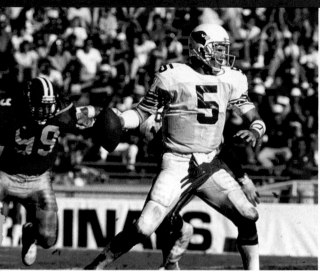

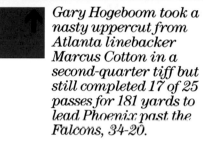

Gary Hogeboom took a nasty uppercut from Atlanta linebacker Marcus Cotton in a second-quarter tiff but still completed 17 of 25 passes for 181 yards to lead Phoenix past the Falcons, 34-20.

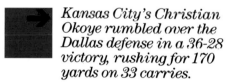

Kansas City's Christian Okoye rumbled over the Dallas defense in a 36-28 victory, rushing for 170 yards on 33 carries.

Eric Dickerson, who complained that he got no respect from the media and the fans, surely got some from the Bengals as he ran for 152 punishing yards in a 23-12 Colts' win.

Week 8

STANDINGS

AFC EAST	W	L	T	Pct	PF	PA
Buffalo	6	2	0	.750	221	180
Indianapolis	4	4	0	.500	154	143
Miami	4	4	0	.500	161	190
New England	3	5	0	.375	131	189
N.Y. Jets	1	7	0	.125	132	215

AFC CENTRAL	W	L	T	Pct	PF	PA
Cincinnati	5	3	0	.625	204	140
Cleveland	5	3	0	.625	191	112
Houston	4	4	0	.500	211	198
Pittsburgh	4	4	0	.500	116	186

AFC WEST	W	L	T	Pct	PF	PA
Denver	6	2	0	.750	184	133
L.A. Raiders	4	4	0	.500	178	148
Seattle	4	4	0	.500	143	155
Kansas City	3	5	0	.375	154	182
San Diego	2	6	0	.250	132	156

NFC EAST	W	L	T	Pct	PF	PA
N.Y. Giants	7	1	0	.875	199	123
Philadelphia	6	2	0	.750	190	164
Phoenix	4	4	0	.500	156	173
Washington	4	4	0	.500	210	203
Dallas	0	8	0	.000	106	232

NFC CENTRAL	W	L	T	Pct	PF	PA
Chicago	5	3	0	.625	219	173
Minnesota	5	3	0	.625	160	137
Green Bay	4	4	0	.500	205	201
Tampa Bay	3	5	0	.375	171	208
Detroit	1	7	0	.125	118	193

NFC WEST	W	L	T	Pct	PF	PA
San Francisco	7	1	0	.875	215	145
L.A. Rams	5	3	0	.625	193	185
New Orleans	4	4	0	.500	195	143
Atlanta	2	6	0	.250	141	183

RESULTS

Chicago 20, L.A. Rams 10
Philadelphia 28, Denver 24
Seattle 10, San Diego 7
New England 23, Indianapolis 20, OT
New Orleans 20, Atlanta 13
Phoenix 19, Dallas 10
Pittsburgh 23, Kansas City 17
Green Bay 23, Detroit 20, OT
Cleveland 28, Houston 17
Cincinnati 56, Tampa Bay 23
Buffalo 31, Miami 17
L.A. Raiders 37, Washington 24
San Francisco 23, N.Y. Jets 10
N.Y. Giants 24, Minnesota 14 (Monday night)

Chicago's Wendell Davis couldn't hold on to this one, but he did grab two passes for 49 yards in the Bears' 20-10 win over the Rams. The toothless Bears would win only one more game the rest of the way.

Keith Byars squirted through the Denver defense for 93 yards and two touchdowns, including the game-winner with 5:25 left, as the Eagles pulled out a 28-24 victory. Philadelphia rushed for 215 yards in the game.

Eddie Anderson (33) jarred the ball loose from Washington's Earnest Byner as Scott Davis (70) closed in for the kill during L.A.'s 37-24 thrashing of the Redskins. Anderson also had two key interceptions in the victory.

Steve Grogan, one of a revolving quartet of New England quarterbacks, went solo in the second half against Indianapolis, completing 20 of 28 passes for 248 yards and a touchdown in a 23-20 win. He continued to shine in overtime, driving his team 54 yards to get into position for Greg Davis's 51-yard game-winning field goal.

Eric Metcalf contributed 126 all-purpose yards in the Browns' 28-17 defeat of Houston, including a 32-yard option pass to Reggie Langhorne for the game-clinching touchdown in the fourth quarter. The Browns used a series of gimmick plays, including a flea-flicker and a reverse, to score all their points in the second half.

STANDINGS

AFC EAST	W	L	T	Pct	PF	PA
Buffalo	6	3	0	.667	249	210
Miami	5	4	0	.556	180	203
Indianapolis	4	5	0	.444	167	162
New England	3	6	0	.333	157	216
N.Y. Jets	2	7	0	.222	159	241

AFC CENTRAL	W	L	T	Pct	PF	PA
Cleveland	6	3	0	.667	233	143
Cincinnati	5	4	0	.556	211	168
Houston	5	4	0	.556	246	229
Pittsburgh	4	5	0	.444	123	220

AFC WEST	W	L	T	Pct	PF	PA
Denver	7	2	0	.778	218	140
L.A. Raiders	5	4	0	.556	206	155
Kansas City	4	5	0	.444	174	192
Seattle	4	5	0	.444	153	175
San Diego	3	6	0	.333	152	173

NFC EAST	W	L	T	Pct	PF	PA
N.Y. Giants	8	1	0	.889	219	136
Philadelphia	6	3	0	.667	207	184
Phoenix	4	5	0	.444	169	193
Washington	4	5	0	.444	213	216
Dallas	1	8	0	.111	119	235

NFC CENTRAL	W	L	T	Pct	PF	PA
Minnesota	6	3	0	.667	183	158
Chicago	5	4	0	.556	232	187
Green Bay	5	4	0	.556	219	214
Tampa Bay	3	6	0	.333	202	250
Detroit	1	8	0	.111	149	228

NFC WEST	W	L	T	Pct	PF	PA
San Francisco	8	1	0	.889	246	158
L.A. Rams	5	4	0	.556	214	208
New Orleans	4	5	0	.444	208	174
Atlanta	3	6	0	.333	171	211

RESULTS

Minnesota 23, L.A. Rams 21, OT
Green Bay 14, Chicago 13
Atlanta 30, Buffalo 28
Houston 35, Detroit 31
Cleveland 42, Tampa Bay 31
Dallas 13, Washington 3
Miami 19, Indianapolis 13
L.A. Raiders 28, Cincinnati 7
San Diego 20, Philadelphia 17
N.Y. Giants 20, Phoenix 13
Denver 34, Pittsburgh 7
N.Y. Jets 27, New England 26
Kansas City 20, Seattle 10
San Francisco 31, New Orleans 13
(Monday night)

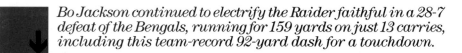

It was a wild finish in Buffalo as the Falcons and the Bills combined for 17 points in the final 82 seconds of play. Atlanta quarterback Chris Miller (12) had the last laugh, connecting with Stacey Bailey for 41 yards to set up Paul McFadden's 50-yard field goal with two seconds left for the 30-28 upset win.

Bo Jackson continued to electrify the Raider faithful in a 28-7 defeat of the Bengals, running for 159 yards on just 13 carries, including this team-record 92-yard dash for a touchdown.

Ken O'Brien provided Jet fans with a brief respite from their season-long gloom as he led New York past New England, 27-26. O'Brien completed 22 of 29 passes for 386 yards and two touchdowns.

Rich Karlis, kicker, Minnesota Vikings. *Karlis (13) had been the Broncos' Super Bowl kicker twice this decade, but he had fallen on hard times in 1988, missing 13 field goal tries. The Broncos balked when he insisted on a raise, choosing to waive him in early September. Four weeks later, Karlis signed as a free agent with the Vikings. In Week 9 against Denver, Karlis showed his new team just how valuable he is and sent a message to the Broncos as well.*

Karlis became the first kicker in NFL history to make seven field goals in seven attempts in a single game. Only one kicker had made seven before in a game: Jim Bakken of St. Louis, in 1967. Bakken missed two that day. Karlis was good from 20, 24, 22, 25, 29, 36 and 40, including the game-tying kick with eight seconds left in the fourth quarter of a 23-21 overtime win. "I used to read Jim Bakken's instructional booklet on how to kick field goals when I was a kid," Karlis said. Oddly enough, Karlis was nervous going into the game, because he didn't kick well in pregame warmups. "I was all over the place," he said. What counts, though, is when it counts. Seven for seven isn't bad, especially for a guy whose team didn't want him in September.

Eight weeks of frustration finally came to an end as the Cowboys beat the Redskins 13-3 for their first win of the season. Paul Palmer, who was picked up on waivers from Detroit after Week 6, ran for 110 yards on 18 carries.

Darth Vader in the NFL? No, it's Jim McMahon getting ready to launch one against the Eagles. McMahon threw for 264 yards and two touchdowns to lead the Chargers to a 20-17 victory.

The Giants, at 8-1, figured to cruise against the 5-4 Rams, but nobody told Jim Everett, who completed 23 of 33 passes—including a team-record 18 in a row at one point—for 295 yards and two touchdowns as Los Angeles made it look easy against New York, 31-10.

STANDINGS

AFC EAST	W	L	T	Pct	PF	PA
Buffalo	7	3	0	.700	279	217
Miami	6	4	0	.600	211	226
Indianapolis	4	6	0	.400	174	192
New England	3	7	0	.300	181	244
N.Y. Jets	2	8	0	.200	182	272

AFC CENTRAL	W	L	T	Pct	PF	PA
Cleveland	7	3	0	.700	250	150
Houston	6	4	0	.600	272	253
Cincinnati	5	5	0	.500	235	194
Pittsburgh	4	6	0	.400	123	240

AFC WEST	W	L	T	Pct	PF	PA
Denver	8	2	0	.800	234	153
L.A. Raiders	5	5	0	.500	218	169
Kansas City	4	6	0	.400	187	208
San Diego	4	6	0	.400	166	185
Seattle	4	6	0	.400	160	192

NFC EAST	W	L	T	Pct	PF	PA
N.Y. Giants	8	2	0	.800	229	167
Philadelphia	6	4	0	.600	210	194
Phoenix	5	5	0	.500	193	213
Washington	5	5	0	.500	223	219
Dallas	1	9	0	.100	139	259

NFC CENTRAL	W	L	T	Pct	PF	PA
Minnesota	7	3	0	.700	207	168
Chicago	6	4	0	.600	252	187
Green Bay	5	5	0	.500	241	245
Tampa Bay	3	7	0	.300	212	274
Detroit	2	8	0	.200	180	250

NFC WEST	W	L	T	Pct	PF	PA
San Francisco	9	1	0	.900	291	161
L.A. Rams	6	4	0	.600	245	218
New Orleans	5	5	0	.500	236	198
Atlanta	3	7	0	.300	174	256

RESULTS

L.A. Rams 31, N.Y. Giants 10
Chicago 20, Pittsburgh 0
New Orleans 28, New England 24
San Francisco 45, Atlanta 3
Detroit 31, Green Bay 22
Phoenix 24, Dallas 20
Miami 31, N.Y. Jets 23
Cleveland 17, Seattle 7
Washington 10, Philadelphia 3
Denver 16, Kansas City 13
Minnesota 24, Tampa Bay 10
Buffalo 30, Indianapolis 7
San Diego 14, L.A. Raiders 12
Houston 26, Cincinnati 24 (Monday night)

 In spite of double-teams and blatant holds like this one by Tampa Bay's Tom McHale, Keith Millard (75) still sacked Vinny Testaverde twice in the Vikings' 24-10 win.

 Thurman Thomas galloped for 127 yards on 29 carries as the Bills romped over the Colts 30-7 to avenge a loss earlier in the season to their AFC East rivals.

 Cardinals quarterback Tom Tupa came off the bench to complete 14 of 22 second-half passes for 245 yards and two touchdowns in a 24-20 comeback win over the Cowboys.

Boomer Esiason had a field day against Detroit, completing 30 of 39 passes for 399 yards and three touchdowns in a 42-7 blowout. Apparently the loss was therapeutic for the Lions—they would win their next five games.

STANDINGS

AFC EAST	W	L	T	Pct	PF	PA
Buffalo	7	4	0	.636	303	250
Miami	7	4	0	.636	228	240
Indianapolis	5	6	0	.455	201	202
New England	4	7	0	.364	214	268
N.Y. Jets	2	9	0	.182	192	299

AFC CENTRAL	W	L	T	Pct	PF	PA
Cleveland	7	3	1	.682	260	160
Houston	7	4	0	.636	295	260
Cincinnati	6	5	0	.545	277	201
Pittsburgh	5	6	0	.455	143	257

AFC WEST	W	L	T	Pct	PF	PA
Denver	9	2	0	.818	248	163
L.A. Raiders	5	6	0	.455	225	192
Kansas City	4	6	1	.409	197	218
San Diego	4	7	0	.364	183	205
Seattle	4	7	0	.364	163	207

NFC EAST	W	L	T	Pct	PF	PA
N.Y. Giants	9	2	0	.818	244	170
Philadelphia	7	4	0	.636	220	203
Phoenix	5	6	0	.455	207	250
Washington	5	6	0	.455	233	233
Dallas	1	10	0	.091	153	276

NFC CENTRAL	W	L	T	Pct	PF	PA
Minnesota	7	4	0	.636	216	178
Chicago	6	5	0	.545	283	219
Green Bay	6	5	0	.545	262	262
Tampa Bay	4	7	0	.364	244	305
Detroit	2	9	0	.182	187	292

NFC WEST	W	L	T	Pct	PF	PA
San Francisco	9	2	0	.818	308	182
L.A. Rams	7	4	0	.636	282	232
New Orleans	6	5	0	.545	262	215
Atlanta	3	8	0	.273	191	282

RESULTS

Philadelphia 10, Minnesota 9
Tampa Bay 32, Chicago 31
Indianapolis 27, N.Y. Jets 10
Cincinnati 42, Detroit 7
Green Bay 21, San Francisco 17
Houston 23; L.A. Raiders 7
L.A. Rams 37, Phoenix 14
N.Y. Giants 15, Seattle 3
New England 33, Buffalo 24
New Orleans 26, Atlanta 17
Miami 17, Dallas 14
Kansas City 10, Cleveland 10, OT
Pittsburgh 20, San Diego 17
Denver 14, Washington 10 (Monday night)

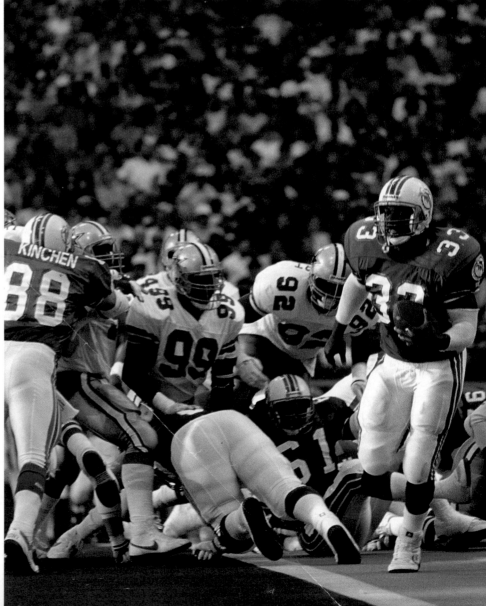

New England's John Stephens, who started slowly in '89 due to an injury, hit high gear against Buffalo, running for 126 yards on 23 carries and gaining 76 yards receiving in a 33-24 win. New England scored 20 unanswered points in the fourth quarter, the last 10 coming after Bills turnovers.

An unsuspecting Chris Miller looked downfield while a thundering Pat Swilling closed in for the kill. Swilling had a dominant day: 3 1/2 sacks and six solo tackles as the Saints swamped the Falcons 26-17.

Sammie Smith swept in for the go-ahead touchdown in Miami's 17-14 come-from-behind win over Dallas. The Dolphins got their other touchdown on a 48-yard Hail Mary pass from Dan Marino to Andre Brown as time expired in the first half. Ironically, Brown played his collegiate football at Miami under Dallas coach Jimmy Johnson.

 Green Bay's Sterling Sharpe caught the Minnesota defense lying down on this nine-yard touchdown toss from Don Majkowski that put the Pack in front in the fourth quarter. Sharpe had 10 catches for 157 yards in the 20-19 win.

STANDINGS

AFC EAST	W	L	T	Pct	PF	PA
Buffalo	8	4	0	.667	327	257
Miami	7	5	0	.583	242	274
Indianapolis	6	6	0	.500	211	208
New England	4	8	0	.333	235	292
N.Y. Jets	3	9	0	.250	219	306

AFC CENTRAL	W	L	T	Pct	PF	PA
Cleveland	7	4	1	.625	270	173
Houston	7	5	0	.583	295	294
Cincinnati	6	6	0	.500	284	225
Pittsburgh	6	6	0	.500	177	271

AFC WEST	W	L	T	Pct	PF	PA
Denver	10	2	0	.833	289	177
L.A. Raiders	6	6	0	.500	249	213
Kansas City	5	6	1	.458	231	218
San Diego	4	8	0	.333	189	215
Seattle	4	8	0	.333	177	248

NFC EAST	W	L	T	Pct	PF	PA
N.Y. Giants	9	3	0	.750	268	204
Philadelphia	8	4	0	.667	247	203
Washington	6	6	0	.500	271	247
Phoenix	5	7	0	.417	220	264
Dallas	1	11	0	.083	153	303

NFC CENTRAL	W	L	T	Pct	PF	PA
Green Bay	7	5	0	.583	282	281
Minnesota	7	5	0	.583	235	198
Chicago	6	6	0	.500	297	257
Tampa Bay	5	7	0	.417	258	318
Detroit	3	9	0	.250	200	302

NFC WEST	W	L	T	Pct	PF	PA
San Francisco	10	2	0	.833	342	206
L.A. Rams	8	4	0	.667	302	249
New Orleans	6	6	0	.500	279	235
Atlanta	3	9	0	.250	198	309

RESULTS

Detroit 13, Cleveland 10
Philadelphia 27, Dallas 0
Washington 38, Chicago 14
Tampa Bay 14, Phoenix 13
L.A. Raiders 24, New England 21
Indianapolis 10, San Diego 6
N.Y. Jets 27, Atlanta 7
Kansas City 34, Houston 0
Denver 41, Seattle 14
Green Bay 20, Minnesota 19
Buffalo, 24, Cincinnati 7
Pittsburgh 34, Miami 14
L.A. Rams 20, New Orleans 17, OT
San Francisco 34, N.Y. Giants 24 (Monday night)

Sudden "★"

Willie (Flipper) Anderson, wide receiver, Los Angeles Rams. *In a Week 12 game at New Orleans, Anderson did his best imitation of Lou Gehrig replacing Wally Pipp. With star Ram wideout Henry Ellard on the bench with a pulled hamstring muscle, the Rams looked to Anderson most of the night, and he responded by setting an NFL record. Anderson, a second-round pick from UCLA in 1988, was having a good night early in the fourth quarter. He had caught six passes for 141 yards, and the Rams were trailing the Saints 17-3. Then all heck broke loose in the Ram offense. Anderson caught seven balls for 155 yards in the last 10 minutes of regulation as the Rams tied the score at 17, and in overtime, he added two more catches to put the Rams in position for the game-winning field goal by Mike Lansford. "Flipper put on the greatest performance I've ever seen by a receiver," said Ram coach John Robinson. The end result: 15 receptions for a league-record 336 yards. "I really can't say how I feel," Anderson said. "Maybe it'll sink in when I see my name in the record book."*

Anderson is part of the baby boom the Rams are hoping will make them the NFL's team of the '90s. They will certainly have a wondrously young offensive unit entering the decade: their quarterback (Jim Everett), their two wide receivers after Ellard (Anderson, Aaron Cox) and their running back group (Robert Delpino, Gaston Green, Cleveland Gary) are all 27 or younger.

The Bears' late-season hibernation began, as the Redskins stuffed Neal Anderson and the Chicago offense, holding Anderson to 27 yards on 13 carries and the Bears to a paltry 191 offensive yards overall. Washington's Mark Rypien threw for 401 yards and four touchdowns in the 38-14 victory.

Chiefs quarterback Steve DeBerg helped begin Kansas City's late-season surge with a 224-yard, one-touchdown day in a 34-0 thumping of the Oilers.

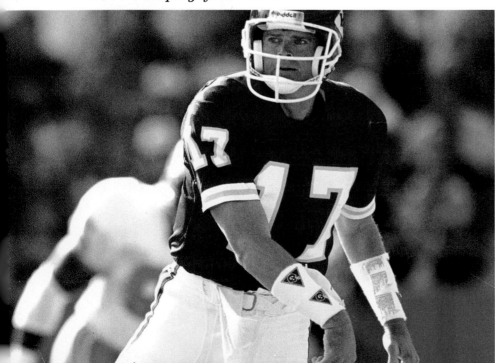

Luis Zendejas, kicker, Dallas Cowboys. *How weird. A journeyman kicker becomes, if not a star, at least a celebrity of sorts. In Week 12, on Thanksgiving Day, the Eagles played in Dallas, and Zendejas, an ex-Eagle, was convinced that Philadelphia coach Buddy Ryan was out to get him. "There's a bounty out on me," Zendejas told his best Dallas friend, punter Mike Saxon, before the game. Zendejas said he was warned by several former Philadelphia teammates and by Eagle special teams coach Al Roberts that there was a bounty of $200 for any Eagle who knocked Zendejas out of the game.*

Sure enough, Eagle rookie Jessie Small ran straight for Zendejas on the Dallas kickoff beginning the second half and lunged at the kicker's legs. Zendejas tried to stop Small with his head and got the wind knocked out of him. Disoriented, he had to be helped off the field on wobbly legs. Ryan denied Zendejas's charge and the league found no conclusive evidence of wrongdoing, but Zendejas later claimed to have a tape of a phone conversation in which Roberts told him about the bounty. Zendejas has yet to produce the tape. Stay tuned.

THIRD QUARTER
Weeks 13-16

The Meek Begin To Roar

The big, bad Bear was eating—no, attacking—a baked potato with nothing on it, a salad with garbonzo beans and a large glass of water. It was four hours before the Chicago Bears would play at Washington in a game crucial to their playoff hopes, and coach Mike Ditka was wolfing down one of those think-thin meals that his doctor had forced on him after his heart attack a year earlier.

The Bears were struggling mightily at 6-5, trying to recapture a fragment of their greatness, but Ditka hadn't given up. "We're as good as we were last year," Ditka said. "Our record isn't. The reason is, other teams have gotten better. But if you ask me if I'm proud of this team, I am."

Seven hours later, with his team in ruins after a 38-14 shredding by the Redskins, Ditka reconsidered. "We stink," Ditka said. "We are absolutely an atrocious football team at this point. We have to play the rest of our games, but there's no question in my mind that we will be fortunate to win one game."

He was right. The Bears finished the season without another victory, dropping their last six games. As we look back on 1989, we will surely remember how parity played foul with the Bears, who fell to earth with a nasty thud and finished 6-10; and how it played fair with the Packers, who finished 10-6, and with the Lions, who won their last five. And what of Pittsburgh, which lost its first two games by a combined 82 points, then wound up in the playoffs after going 9-5 the rest of the way?

Toothless Bears

Everyone knows the Bears took a mauling in '89. But just how bad was the damage? Really bad. With their overall defensive ranking falling from second in the league to 24th, the Bears ceased to intimidate anyone. Here are the ugly numbers.

	1988	1989
Win-Loss Record	12-4	6-10
Average Yards Allowed	272.5	358.1
Total Points Allowed	215	377
Points Allowed Per Game	13.4	23.6
Defensive Rank Overall	2	24
Ranking vs. Rush	11	15
Ranking vs. Pass	9	24

The meek may soon inherit the NFL earth. But oh, how the mighty have already fallen.

The Bears had been up for so long that you knew the fall, when it came, would be ugly. It was. Two losses to Tampa Bay. Two losses to Green Bay. A loss to Detroit. "We're a member of the pack," Bears center Jay Hilgenberg said. "We don't intimidate anybody anymore. You can see it." Echoed Tampa Bay linebacker Kevin Murphy: "People are putting the image of the big, bad Bears out of their minds."

The reasons for this sea change were obvious. In the past, the Bears had manhandled the rest of the world

As Chicago's woes mounted, Ditka became a growling Bear.

with their pressure defense and ferocious pass rush, surely one of the best of all time. But injuries and age caught up to the rushers, forcing Chicago to replace All-Pros Dan Hampton, Otis Wilson and Wilber Marshall with Trace Armstrong, John Roper and Ron Rivera. Nice touch of youth there, but forget dominance. The Bears still had Richard Dent, a tenacious pass rusher in his heyday, but there were games in '89 when he simply didn't show up. Against the Redskins, Dent had zero tackles and zero sacks.

The Bears had an embarrassing season, but all is not lost. They have loaded up with quality youth in the past five or six drafts and have five picks in the first three rounds of 1990's. What Ditka needs to do with this crop of players is what he did with his previous crop: toughen them mentally. "Sometimes I wonder,

How do you get the importance of the moment across? That's a never-ending struggle. How do you make them aware that there might not be another time, that there might not be another chance? Who knows? You might be out in the yard the next year," he said. That was a harsh reality the Bears hadn't experienced for almost a decade, but they were having to face it now.

As the Bears took a turn for the worse, two other teams in the NFC Central—the Packers and the Lions—righted themselves after a prolonged period as divisional doormats. The Packers scripted the feel-good story of the year, as they scratched and fought their way to a 10-6 record and came within a whisker of winning their division. The last time they had won 10 games was in 1972, when Dan Devine coached them to a brief respite from the post-Lombardi gloom. Only a Viking win over the Bengals in the final week of the '89 regular season robbed the Packers of a trip to the playoffs. It was a disappointing finish for a team that had captured the imagination of the country with its dramatic style of play. Look at these sound bites from the Packer year for an illustration of why, in midseason, the Green Bay faithful started calling their team the Cardiac Pack:
* Weeks 1 through 4: Lost by two, won by one, lost by three, won by two.
* Weeks 7 through 9: Lost by three, won by three, won by one.
* Weeks 11 through 13: Won by four, won by one, won by one.
* Record in games decided by four points or less: 7-3.
* Percentage of victories in which the Packers trailed in the fourth quarter: 50

"I've hunted bears, I've killed bears and once I even wrestled a bear," said Packer linebacker Brian Noble after the Pack had beaten the Bears in Green Bay, breaking an eight-game Packer losing streak against Chicago. "Now I can finally say I've beaten the Bears."

Green Bay worked miracles all season long with their pressure-loving young quarterback, Don Majkowski, throwing for a league-high 4,318 yards, and with their sack-happy linebacker, Tim Harris, keying the defense. "It wasn't luck," said Lindy Infante, named coach of the year by the Associated Press after the season. "If you do it once, it's luck. These guys did it over and over again."

So did Detroit in the last month of the season. The Lions began the year with the Silver Stretch, a catchy nickname for a gimmicky attack pioneered by offensive assistant Mouse Davis in his days as a head coach at Portland State and in the USFL. The Silver Stretch, more commonly known as the run-and-shoot, features four wide receivers, no tight end and one running back. Its most critical component is a mobile quarterback capable of rolling out, pitching the ball with ease and throwing well-timed passes on the run. Both Rodney Peete and backup Bob Gagliano proved up to the task, but Detroit's wide receivers spent much of the first part of the year dropping balls, missing eight at Tampa Bay alone. Once they got the hang of the offense and began hanging on to the football—and once Barry Sanders began to show what a wonderful talent he is—the Lions became a tough team to beat.

Beginning on Thanksgiving Day, Detroit ran off five straight victories to close the season, including impressive wins over Cleveland, New Orleans and Chicago. Sanders kept getting stronger as the year wore on, finishing with 1,470 rushing yards, more than any player in 1989 except for Christian Okoye of the Chiefs, who gained 10 yards more but had 90 additional carries. "There's still room for improvement," said coach Wayne Fontes, "but I think anybody can see how much progress we've made here. It shows how far you can go if you believe." This is a team to be reckoned with in the '90s.

The most unlikely story of the year? Easy. The rise of the Steelers. After they got demolished in their first two games, a very composed Pittsburgh coach, Chuck Noll, walked into the interview area and said: "Either the Super Bowl team comes out of our division, or we are very bad. One or the other." He was wrong on both counts, but his no-panic manner helped revitalize this team. "He shouldn't be coach of the year," said Cleveland VP Ernie Accorsi. "He ought to be coach of the decade." The Steelers made the playoffs on the last Monday night of the season, when Cincinnati lost at Minnesota—the same game that eliminated the Packers—handing Pittsburgh the second wild-card spot in the AFC. Then the Steelers went to Houston and beat the Oilers in overtime on a 50-yard Gary Anderson field goal. The next stop was Denver, where the Steelers lost, 24-23, when rookie Mark Stock dropped a very catchable ball with two minutes to go, and flustered quarterback Bubby Brister fumbled away a shotgun snap from center. But how 'bout those Steelers? With strong running from rookie Tim Worley (770 yards on the season) and third-year fullback Merril Hoge (220 yards in Pittsburgh's two playoff games) and fiery leadership from Brister, the Steelers are looking good. "They're going to continue to grow," said Noll. "They grew in all manner this year. They endured some tough stuff."

When the Bears go 6-10 and the Steelers go 9-7, as happened in 1989, one thing becomes very clear for 1990 and all future years in the NFL.

You've heard it before. It starts with: *On any given Sunday....*

Third Quarter Key Games The Good, The Bad, The Ugly

As the regular season careened through its final weeks, several games made clear just how much the league topography had changed, as longtime patsies began to rise from the depths and teams on top began to fall. And, lest we forget the NFL's time-honored tradition of sportsmanship, there was Sam Wyche to remind us that, good or bad, there are still some things that you just don't do.

Los Angeles Rams 35, Dallas 31—Week 13, at Dallas. "We're going to be good before too long," Dallas coach Jimmy Johnson said in October, when the Cowboys gave up Herschel Walker to acquire most of the draft picks in the lifetime of Minnesota general manager Mike Lynn. And at times, in spite of winning only one game, they didn't look too bad. This game was one of their better performances.

The Rams came to Dallas with an 8-4 record, two games behind San Francisco in the NFC West and fighting for a wild-card spot in the playoffs. Dallas was 1-11 and counting the quarters until vacation. Expected outcome? A Ram rout. Which is what seemed to be developing when Los Angeles sped to a 21-10 lead midway through the third quarter, thanks largely to two Jim Everett touchdown throws: a one-yarder to Damone Johnson in the first quarter and an 18-yarder to Aaron Cox in the third.

Suddenly, the Cowboys began to show some toughness, a trait they will need in abundance over the next season or two. First they foiled a fake Ram punt late in the third quarter, and then Troy Aikman, who will be a marvelous NFL quarterback if he survives physically, tossed a 35-yard scoring pass to James Dixon. Rams, 21-17. On L.A.'s next possession, Everett made his only mistake of the day by throwing an interception to Dallas safety Ray Horton. The Cowboys responded with a 59-yard drive that featured a 19-yard Aikman scramble and concluded with a five-yard scoring pass from Aikman to Steve Folsom. Dallas, 24-21. The Rams' Ron Brown fumbled the ensuing kickoff, Dallas recovered at the L.A. two-yard line and Aikman threw his third touchdown pass in seven minutes, this one to Bernard Ford. Dallas, 31-21.

That's how it was with five minutes to go and Dallas in possession of the ball. But, as his opponents have learned, Jim Everett is a master of the quick-strike comeback. The previous week, in a 20-17 win over New Orleans, he threw two touchdown passes in the final three minutes of regulation to tie the game, then drove his team into position for the game-winning field goal in overtime. He got his chance this time when Cowboy fullback Daryl Johnston fumbled the ball away at the Dallas 44. It took Everett just two plays to score, this time on a 39-yard pass to the penitent Brown. The Rams stopped Dallas on the next series, and Everett had the game won 10 seconds past the two-minute warning, on a 23-yard TD pass to Aaron Cox. Final score: Rams 35, Cowboys 31. Dallas scares. Rams win. Aikman shows promise, Everett shows fulfillment. If the Rams had lost this game, they wouldn't have made the playoffs. "I'd hate to be facing Jim Everett now, the way he's playing," said Ram linebacker Kevin Greene. They may say that about Aikman someday.

 Johnston's fumble gave Everett his chance for a fantastic finish.

 Cox sprinted for the winning touchdown with 1:50 left.

 Jack Del Rio (55) and the Dallas defense kept the Rams off balance through most of the second half.

 Singletary was singing the praises of the elusive Sanders after the game.

 Gagliano scrambled 14 yards for the Lions' first touchdown.

Detroit 27, Chicago 17—Week 14, at Chicago. It was six years and 10 straight losses to the Bears in coming, but the Lions aren't the old Lions anymore. And the Bears most certainly aren't the old Bears. "The past is the past," said Detroit linebacker Chris Spielman. Indeed. After the Bears went up 3-0 in the first quarter, Detroit surged in front 14-3 on solid drives of 74 and 81 yards against the once-proud Bears defense. All-world rookie running back Barry Sanders figured prominently in both touchdowns, acting as a decoy on quarterback Bob Gagliano's 14-yard run for the first score and running the ball in himself for the second score on an 18-yard scamper that had several Bears grabbing at empty air. The Lions would never trail after that.

More than any other game during the season, this one marked the renaissance of the Lions, proving for sure that they were starting to get good. And more than any other person, Sanders is the one responsible. His day: 120 rushing yards, 39 receiving yards, 59 yards on kickoff returns. He touched the ball 31 times.

He gained 218 all-purpose yards. By the third quarter, the Bears were within seven, at 17-10, but Sanders and the Lions were still in full gear. In the middle of a 72-yard drive, Sanders caught a 19-yard pass from Gagliano. At the end of the drive, he slashed three yards for the touchdown that put the game out of reach and the Bears out of playoff contention. It was the end of a proud run for Chicago, which had won five consecutive NFC Central titles.

After the game, the Bears were marveling at Sanders's talent. "You'd step one way, and he'd go the other way," said Chicago linebacker Mike Singletary, who has seen a host of terrific runners during his nine years in the league. Even Walter Payton, just a spectator now, was in awe, describing Sanders as "better than I was."

For the Lions, the game was like a festive coming-out party, announcing to the world the arrival of a new contender. Detroit would go on to win their next two games to extend their season-ending winning streak to five, but it wasn't enough to overcome their 2-9 start and propel them into the playoffs. Still, the future looks bright for this young group of Lions. "We're a team to be reckoned with now," coach Wayne Fontes said. "It's about time we got the Bears off our backs."

Cincinnati 61, Houston 7

Cincinnati 61, Houston 7—Week 15, at Cincinnati. This is a game that will haunt Sam Wyche for the rest of his career, even though the Bengals won it and kept their slim playoff hopes alive. Because of uncomplimentary things Houston coach Jerry Glanville had said about the Bengals and because Wyche thought Glanville, in general, to be an idiot, Wyche ignored the unwritten rule in coaching—and in most of polite society—that says you never run up the score on an opponent. Never kick a man when he's down. Be gracious in victory. Wyche violated them all with an in-your-face series of coaching decisions that would have made Gengis Khan blush.

First the game, which wasn't much to speak of after

the Bengals exploded for three touchdowns in the first quarter on two passes from Boomer Esiason to Eddie Brown and a 14-yard run by James Brooks. Cincinnati would score another 31 points before Houston got on the board, as everyone in a Bengal uniform had a field day. Esiason completed 20 of 27 passes for 326 yards and four touchdowns. His backup, Erik Wilhelm, threw for 76 yards and a fifth touchdown. Eric Ball ran for 86 yards and a touchdown. Tim McGee had six catches for 147 yards, Brown had six for 107. By the time the day was through, Cincinnati had run up 584 yards in total offense, handing the Oilers their worst defeat in franchise history.

As the scoring mounted, Wyche began his display of

poor sportsmanship. After it was 45-0, he had the Bengals attempt two onside kicks. With 21 seconds left, the Bengals stopped the clock so Jim Breech could kick a 30-yard field goal. Long after the outcome was beyond any doubt, Esiason and Wilhelm continued to throw on first down. If there was one coaching bush-league act in 1989, it was Wyche's in this game. "Mass murderers have been gentler with their victims," wrote *The Houston Chronicle*'s Ed Fowler.

Afterward, Wyche was without shame. Listen to Wyche on the game: "We were going for their jugular, and we weren't going to reset our heel either. We don't like this team, and we don't like their people. When you have a chance to do this, you do it. I wish the game was five quarters, so we could have hit triple digits." Wyche on the Oilers: "This is the dumbest football team, the most stupid, undisciplined team. It's just ridiculous." Wyche on Glanville: "Honest to goodness, he's probably the biggest phony in football." Sheesh. Said Houston defensive end Sean Jones: "It's a damn shame they beat us, and the questions involve why they ran up the score instead of the way they kicked our butts."

Glanville may have left the Oilers, but his players remain. They won't forget this game.

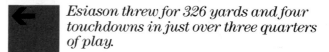

Wyche could barely restrain his glee as the score mounted.

Esiason threw for 326 yards and four touchdowns in just over three quarters of play.

James Brooks celebrated his 14-yard run for the Bengals' second score; six more touchdowns would follow.

Third Quarter
Week 13
Memorable Moments

STANDINGS

AFC EAST	W	L	T	Pct	PF	PA
Buffalo	8	5	0	.615	343	274
Miami	7	6	0	.538	263	300
Indianapolis	6	7	0	.462	227	230
New England	5	8	0	.385	257	308
N.Y. Jets	4	9	0	.308	239	323

AFC CENTRAL	W	L	T	Pct	PF	PA
Houston	8	5	0	.615	318	310
Cleveland	7	5	1	.577	270	194
Cincinnati	7	6	0	.538	305	225
Pittsburgh	6	7	0	.462	193	294

AFC WEST	W	L	T	Pct	PF	PA
Denver	10	3	0	.769	302	193
L.A. Raiders	7	6	0	.538	265	226
Kansas City	6	6	1	.500	257	239
Seattle	5	8	0	.385	194	264
San Diego	4	9	0	.308	206	235

NFC EAST	W	L	T	Pct	PF	PA
N.Y. Giants	9	4	0	.692	285	228
Philadelphia	9	4	0	.692	271	220
Washington	7	6	0	.538	300	257
Phoenix	5	8	0	.385	230	293
Dallas	1	12	0	.077	184	338

NFC CENTRAL	W	L	T	Pct	PF	PA
Green Bay	8	5	0	.615	299	297
Minnesota	8	5	0	.615	262	214
Chicago	6	7	0	.462	313	284
Tampa Bay	5	8	0	.385	274	335
Detroit	4	9	0	.308	221	316

NFC WEST	W	L	T	Pct	PF	PA
San Francisco	11	2	0	.846	365	216
L.A. Rams	9	4	0	.692	337	280
New Orleans	6	7	0	.462	293	256
Atlanta	3	10	0	.231	208	332

RESULTS
Philadelphia 24, N.Y. Giants 17
Cincinnati 21, Cleveland 0
Green Bay 17, Tampa Bay 16
Houston 23, Pittsburgh 16
San Francisco 23, Atlanta 10
Minnesota 27, Chicago 16
Washington 29, Phoenix 10
N.Y. Jets 20, San Diego 17
L.A. Rams 35, Dallas 31
Detroit 21, New Orleans 14
L.A. Raiders 16, Denver 13, OT
Kansas City 26, Miami 21
New England 22, Indianapolis 16
Seattle 17, Buffalo 16 (Monday night)

After the Giants tied the game at 17 and then pinned the Eagles on their own two-yard line, they seemed ready to take charge. But this 91-yard punt by quarterback Randall Cunningham led to a Giants fumble and a two-yard TD dive by Philadelphia's Keith Byars for the 24-17 Eagle win.

Raider tight end Mike Dyal made a fingertip grab, then shook off two Denver defenders en route to a 67-yard game-tying touchdown in the fourth quarter. Dyal also starred in overtime, making two critical catches to help set up Jeff Jaeger's 26-yard field goal for the 16-13 upset victory.

New England's John Stephens was unstoppable in a 22-16 defeat of the Colts, running for 124 yards and scoring the game-winning touchdown with 25 seconds left.

→ *Rookie Andre Rison raised his arms in triumph after his 51-yard TD catch put the Colts in front of the Browns 7-0. But he would have to wait until OT to really celebrate, when teammate Mike Prior made a 58-yard interception return for the 23-17 win.*

STANDINGS

AFC EAST	W	L	T	Pct	PF	PA
Buffalo	8	6	0	.571	362	296
Miami	8	6	0	.571	294	310
Indianapolis	7	7	0	.500	250	247
New England	5	9	0	.357	267	339
N.Y. Jets	4	10	0	.286	239	336

AFC CENTRAL	W	L	T	Pct	PF	PA
Houston	9	5	0	.643	338	327
Cleveland	7	6	1	.536	287	217
Cincinnati	7	7	0	.500	322	249
Pittsburgh	7	7	0	.500	206	294

AFC WEST	W	L	T	Pct	PF	PA
Denver	10	4	0	.714	309	207
L.A. Raiders	8	6	0	.571	281	240
Kansas City	7	6	1	.536	278	242
Seattle	6	8	0	.429	218	281
San Diego	4	10	0	.286	227	261

NFC EAST	W	L	T	Pct	PF	PA
N.Y. Giants	10	4	0	.714	299	235
Philadelphia	10	4	0	.714	291	230
Washington	8	6	0	.571	326	278
Phoenix	5	9	0	.357	244	309
Dallas	1	13	0	.071	194	358

NFC CENTRAL	W	L	T	Pct	PF	PA
Minnesota	9	5	0	.643	305	231
Green Bay	8	6	0	.571	302	318
Chicago	6	8	0	.429	330	311
Tampa Bay	5	9	0	.357	291	355
Detroit	5	9	0	.357	248	333

NFC WEST	W	L	T	Pct	PF	PA
San Francisco	12	2	0	.857	395	243
L.A. Rams	9	5	0	.643	364	310
New Orleans	7	7	0	.500	315	275
Atlanta	3	11	0	.214	225	375

RESULTS

N.Y. Giants 14, Denver 7
New Orleans 22, Buffalo 19
Kansas City 21, Green Bay 3
Detroit 27, Chicago 17
Washington 26, San Diego 21
Philadelphia 20, Dallas 10
Indianapolis 23, Cleveland 17, OT
L.A. Raiders 16, Phoenix 14
Pittsburgh 13, N.Y. Jets 0
Houston 20, Tampa Bay 17
Seattle 24, Cincinnati 17
Miami 31, New England 10
Minnesota 43, Atlanta 17
San Francisco 30, L.A. Rams 27 (Monday night)

Sudden "★"

John Taylor, wide receiver, San Francisco. *Only three NFL players in 1989 caught more touchdown passes than Taylor's 10: teammate Jerry Rice (17), Green Bay's Sterling Sharpe (12) and Philadelphia's Cris Carter (11). Taylor is quite content to live in Rice's shadow, even though he caught the winning touchdown in Super Bowl XXIII against Cincinnati and had a 1,077-yard receiving season in 1989. Taylor got a huge chunk of those yards against the Rams in Week 14, when he* gained a team-record 286 yards on 11 catches in a comeback 30-27 win by the 49ers.

What made his performance against L.A. particularly noteworthy was this: No player in the 70-season history of the league, until this Monday night, had ever scored two touchdowns of more than 90 yards in a game. Taylor did just that, taking two short slant patterns over the middle and turning them into 92- and 95-yard touchdown receptions.

The 49ers' p.r. staff had to practically drag Taylor to an interview room after the game, because he doesn't like to talk to the press. He's painfully shy, and he's also embarrassed by his substance-abuse suspension in 1988. This is what he quietly told the assembled media that night: "I caught the ball and followed my blocking. It felt good, but it could have been anyone else."

"Yup," Rice said with a smile after the game, "I'm just a blocking receiver now."

 History in the making: Seattle's Steve Largent caught this 10-yard bullet from quarterback Dave Krieg for his 100th touchdown reception, moving him past Don Hutson into first place on the alltime NFL list. Largent also had a key 33-yard catch in the fourth quarter drive that provided the margin of victory in the Seahawks' 24-17 win.

Sudden "★"

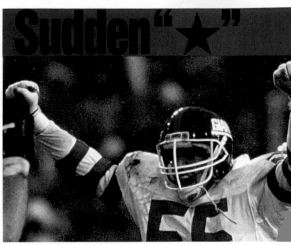

Gary Reasons, linebacker, Giants. *It was the hit every player dreams of, the sort of crushing, highlight-film, game-turning hit people will remember for years. The situation: Giants 14, Denver 0, Broncos at New York's one-yard line, third quarter, fourth-and-goal. Denver decided to go for the touchdown, because New York's defense had been so stifling. Who knows how many more chances the Broncos would have to score? The Giants put nine men at the line of scrimmage, with inside linebackers Reasons and Steve DeOssie a couple of yards behind. Denver quarterback John Elway took the snap and handed the ball to running back Bobby Humphrey. Reasons, about six yards away, took a flying leap over the bodies blocking each other near the goal line. His shoulder pads met Humphrey's helmet, which was rocketing toward the goal line. WHAP! The padded earpiece from the left side of Humphrey's helmet went frisbeeing 10 feet up in the air. Humphrey crumpled at the two, fortunately uninjured. Reasons exulted. The Giants won 14-7. "It's the kind of hit you think about making your whole career," said Reasons. Make no mistake about the significance of the hit. The Giants finished the season 12-4, a single game ahead of Philadelphia in the NFC East. The equation is simple: No win against Denver, no division title.*

Everything went right for Denver in a 37-0 drubbing of Phoenix, including rookie running back Bobby Humphrey's first NFL pass completion, which went to Melvin Bratton for a 17-yard touchdown in the third quarter.

STANDINGS

AFC EAST	W	L	T	Pct	PF	PA
Buffalo	8	7	0	.533	372	317
Indianapolis	8	7	0	.533	292	260
Miami	8	7	0	.533	307	352
New England	5	10	0	.333	277	367
N.Y. Jets	4	11	0	.267	253	374

AFC CENTRAL	W	L	T	Pct	PF	PA
Houston	9	6	0	.600	345	388
Cleveland	8	6	1	.567	310	234
Cincinnati	8	7	0	.553	383	256
Pittsburgh	8	7	0	.553	234	304

AFC WEST	W	L	T	Pct	PF	PA
Denver	11	4	0	.733	346	207
L.A. Raiders	8	7	0	.553	298	263
Kansas City	7	7	1	.500	291	262
Seattle	7	8	0	.467	241	298
San Diego	5	10	0	.333	247	274

NFC EAST	W	L	T	Pct	PF	PA
N.Y. Giants	11	4	0	.733	314	235
Philadelphia	10	5	0	.667	311	260
Washington	9	6	0	.600	357	308
Phoenix	5	10	0	.333	244	346
Dallas	1	14	0	.067	194	373

NFC CENTRAL	W	L	T	Pct	PF	PA
Green Bay	9	6	0	.600	342	346
Minnesota	9	6	0	.600	322	254
Chicago	6	9	0	.400	358	351
Detroit	6	9	0	.400	281	340
Tampa Bay	5	10	0	.333	298	388

NFC WEST	W	L	T	Pct	PF	PA
San Francisco	13	2	0	.867	416	253
L.A. Rams	10	5	0	.667	402	324
New Orleans	8	7	0	.553	345	295
Atlanta	3	12	0	.200	255	406

RESULTS

N.Y. Giants 15, Dallas 0
Denver 37, Phoenix 0
Cincinnati 61, Houston 7
Cleveland 23, Minnesota 17, OT
Indianapolis 42, Miami 13
San Francisco 21, Buffalo 10
Green Bay 40, Chicago 28
L.A. Rams 38, N.Y. Jets 14
Detroit 33, Tampa Bay 7
Washington 31, Atlanta 30
San Diego 20, Kansas City 13
Pittsburgh 28, New England 10
Seattle 23, L.A. Raiders 17
New Orleans 30, Philadelphia 20 (Monday night)

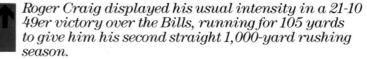

Roger Craig displayed his usual intensity in a 21-10 49er victory over the Bills, running for 105 yards to give him his second straight 1,000-yard rushing season.

Seattle's Melvin Jenkins (left) stopped the Raiders' Bo Jackson on the first of Jackson's two consecutive tries at the end zone in the first quarter. Los Angeles was forced to take a field goal and ended up losing 23-17 as Seahawk fullback John L. Williams caught 12 passes for 129 yards.

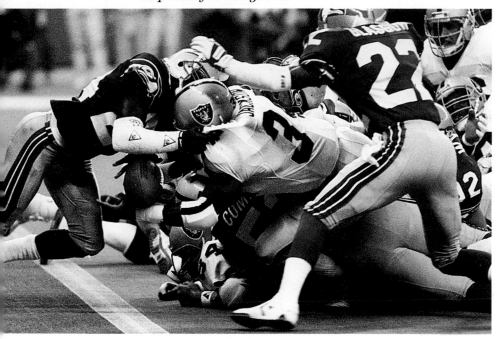

The Giants' Steve DeOssie (99) went over the top to make a goal line stop of the Cowboys' Broderick Sargent in the fourth quarter of New York's 15-0 defeat of Dallas. It was the third straight game in which New York had completed a successful goal line stand.

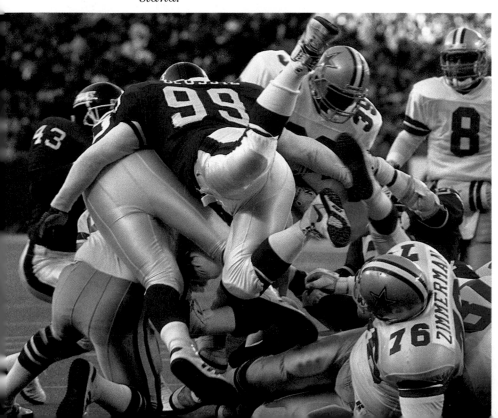

Marion Butts, running back, San Diego. *Butts, the AFC's 10th leading rusher in 1989, weighs 248 pounds and started only three games at Florida State. A dozen years ago, he might have been overlooked by the pro scouts. But with the expanded scouting systems employed today, clubs are able to look for players whose college production may have been skimpy but whose physical skills show promise. That was the case with Butts, whom the Chargers gambled on in the seventh round of the '89 draft.*

The ingredients for a big rushing performance were there against the Chiefs. It was a bad day in Kansas City for passing—windy and bitterly cold. San Diego's quarterback situation, with an inconsistent Jim McMahon and a wet-behind-the-ears Billy Joe Tolliver, also argued against the pass. So what could they do? Ask Butts to run the ball— which he did, a team-record 39 times for 176 yards as the Chargers knocked off Kansas City 20-13. In the second half alone, Butts ran 24 times for 112 yards against a defense that hadn't allowed a rusher to exceed 85 yards in '89.

"It's a very glorious moment for me," said Butts. "The coaches gave me the chance, and I did the best I could."

77

Saints quarterback John Fourcade scampered around the Colts' Harvey Armstrong for a few of the 30 yards he gained on five carries in New Orleans' 41-6 demolition of the Colts. Fourcade also completed 21 of 28 passes for 291 yards and two TDs.

FINAL STANDINGS

AFC EAST	W	L	T	Pct	PF	PA
Buffalo	9	7	0	.563	409	317
Indianapolis	8	8	0	.500	298	301
Miami	8	8	0	.500	331	379
New England	5	11	0	.313	297	391
N.Y. Jets	4	12	0	.250	253	411

AFC CENTRAL	W	L	T	Pct	PF	PA
Cleveland	9	6	1	.594	334	254
Houston	9	7	0	.563	365	412
Pittsburgh	9	7	0	.563	265	326
Cincinnati	8	8	0	.500	404	285

AFC WEST	W	L	T	Pct	PF	PA
Denver	11	5	0	.688	362	226
Kansas City	8	7	1	.531	318	286
L.A. Raiders	8	8	0	.500	315	297
Seattle	7	9	0	.438	241	327
San Diego	6	10	0	.375	266	290

NFC EAST	W	L	T	Pct	PF	PA
N.Y. Giants	12	4	0	.750	348	252
Philadelphia	11	5	0	.688	342	274
Washington	10	6	0	.625	386	308
Phoenix	5	11	0	.313	258	377
Dallas	1	15	0	.063	204	393

NFC CENTRAL	W	L	T	Pct	PF	PA
Minnesota	10	6	0	.625	351	275
Green Bay	10	6	0	.625	362	356
Detroit	7	9	0	.438	312	364
Chicago	6	10	0	.375	358	377
Tampa Bay	5	11	0	.313	320	419

NFC WEST	W	L	T	Pct	PF	PA
San Francisco	14	2	0	.875	442	253
L.A. Rams	11	5	0	.688	426	344
New Orleans	9	7	0	.563	386	301
Atlanta	3	13	0	.188	279	437

WEEK 16 RESULTS

Cleveland 24, Houston 20
Buffalo 37, N.Y. Jets 0
Washington 29, Seattle 0
New Orleans 41, Indianapolis 6
Pittsburgh 31, Tampa Bay 22
N.Y. Giants 34, L.A. Raiders 17
Kansas City 27, Miami 24
Philadelphia 31, Phoenix 14
L.A. Rams 24, New England 20
San Francisco 26, Chicago 0
Detroit 31, Atlanta 24
San Diego 19, Denver 16
Green Bay 20, Dallas 10
Minnesota 29, Cincinnati 21 (Monday night)

Happiness is an upset victory: Delirious Charger Chris Bahr was hoisted off his feet after kicking a 45-yard field goal as time expired to beat the Broncos, 19-16.

The Rams' Greg Bell had an awesome day against the Patriots, rolling up 210 yards on 26 carries, including a three-yard plunge with 1:55 left for the game-winning score. The 24-23 win guaranteed the Rams a wild-card playoff spot.

FOURTH QUARTER

Playoffs & Super Bowl

Who's The Fairest Of Them All?

Let us, for a moment, put aside Montana Mania, Holmgren Hysteria and Rice Revelry. Let's look at the *real* reason why the San Francisco 49ers have become such a talent-deep and dominant team, and why they whipped through the playoffs and won their fourth world title in nine years. The reason? Simple. Telephones.

In 1985, Bill Walsh, then the guru of this franchise, wanted a wide receiver named Jerry Rice from little Mississippi Valley State in itty-bitty Itta Bena, Miss. So Walsh picked up the phone a few times, talked to the New England people and ended up trading the 49ers' low first and second-round picks for the Patriots' first pick, which was in the middle of the first round. The 49ers got Rice. The Patriots got Trevor Matich and Ben Thomas. Need we say more?

That was just a warmup for Walsh. In 1986, he was in on so many draft-day conversations that the telephone must have taken root in his ear. In seven hours, Walsh made six trades. He didn't like the quality of players high in the draft, but he did like the third- and fourth-round quality, so he started trading down in the first round, and down in the second round, and down some more. He finished with what Giants coach Bill Parcells called "the smartest draft I've ever seen," ending up with three third- and three fourth-round picks.

Love those WATS lines.

The acquisition of Rice was a coup for Walsh.

Here's what the 49ers got from all those '86 picks:

* Third round—Fullback Tom Rathman, cornerback Tim McKyer, wide receiver John Taylor.

* Fourth round—Outside linebacker Charles Haley, tackle Steve Wallace, defensive tackle Kevin Fagan.

Four of those players started in Super Bowl XXIV. McKyer, who deflected two passes in the Super Bowl, would have started had his bad-mouthing of the 49ers not gotten in the way in midseason. Wallace was a part-time starter all season long.

The point here is this: The 49ers have great players and great management and great coaching and great blahblahblah—the football world will worship at their altar for some time to come—but they also have great savvy about personnel. Look at the guys who fit into their system. Rathman had never been a receiver, but he led NFC backs with 73 receptions in 1989. Taylor was strictly a background receiver until one night in Anaheim last December, when he became the first player in history to catch two touchdown passes of more than 90 yards in an NFL game. Tight end Brent Jones came to the 49ers as an unwanted free agent, and ended up catching a touchdown pass in each of the 49ers' three postseason games.

Of course, we won't think of the telephones and the deals and the drafts when we think of this postseason. We will think of one of the most awesome playoff performances in the 70-year history of the league.

San Francisco outscored the opposition (Minnesota, the Rams, Denver) 126-26. Average winning playoff margin: 33.3 points per game.

At halftime of the three games, the 49ers were up 27-3, 21-3 and 27-3.

Joe Montana threw 11 playoff touchdowns and no interceptions.

The Achilles' heel of the 49ers, it was said before the playoffs, was the offensive line. In the three games, Montana was sacked once—a cheap, zero-yard sack in the Super Bowl when Montana was chased out of bounds.

"Now," said running back Roger Craig, when it was all over, "we can be mentioned in the same breath as the Pittsburgh Steelers, the Miami Dolphins and the Green Bay Packers."

One of the shames of today's overcoverage of pro sports is that every champion is instantly analyzed and compared with the champions of the past. Victories cannot stand alone. They have to be lauded as better than somebody else's victory or demeaned as not as good. San Francisco received the same treatment; with the ink barely dry on the Super Bowl stories, the 49ers were being compared with the best teams ever.

In this case, given the mockery that San Francisco made of the playoffs, the analysis is justified. Most football experts would concede that the three most consistently excellent teams in NFL history were the Browns of the '50s, the Packers of the '60s and the Steelers of the '70s. Let's look at each team in their most dominating season and compare them with the 49ers of 1989.

In 1954, Cleveland beat Detroit 56-10 to win the second of three championships that the Browns would win in the '50s; the team would also win seven conference titles. Otto Graham's touch passes to Dante Lavelli were the league's best offensive weapon then, and Paul Brown's Browns had the league's stingiest defense, allowing just 13.5 points per game. There were no playoff games in those days; the Eastern Conference winner faced the Western Conference winner the week after the regular season ended to decide the league champion. So it's impossible to compare a playoff run of today with a Browns' late-season march of the '50s. Cleveland, however, did lose at home to Detroit, the western champion, in the final week of the regular season.

In 1962, Green Bay was probably at its best—in the midst of a string of five NFL championships in seven years. The Packers had an overpowering offense, led by fullback Jim Taylor's 19 touchdowns, and a Ray Nitschke defense that just crushed people. The Packers went 13-1, winning by an average score of 30-11. Again, there were no playoff games then except the championship, which the Packers won in New York over the Giants 16-7. The Pack's biggest conference rival that year was Detroit. They played twice, with Green Bay winning by two at home and losing by 12 on the road.

In 1978, Pittsburgh won its third of four Super Bowls in six seasons. Finally, the Steelers were a well-balanced team offensively, with quarterback Terry Bradshaw using Lynn Swann and John Stallworth to take the offensive pressure off tailback Franco Harris. No defense was better. The Steelers blew through the regular season with a 14-2 record. In the playoffs, they beat Denver 33-10 and Houston 34-5 before hanging on to beat Dallas 35-31.

In 1989, San Francisco won its fourth title in nine seasons. The 49ers went 17-2 including the playoffs, with perhaps the most impressive stat of all being their record away from Candlestick Park: 10-0. This was a poised team led by veterans and given a new zest by all the young players drafted in the mid-80s. In the playoffs, they beat Minnesota by 28, the Rams by 27 and Denver by 45. They had to call off the dogs in each game. Clearly, the margin could have been worse each time.

One final exclamation point to the 49ers' late-decade success. San Francisco played six playoff games after the '88 and '89 seasons. They went 6-0. The average score of those games: 49ers 35, Foes 9.

So who's your best team ever? It's still an academic, unanswerable question. But it's clear, at the very least, that this 49er team will have to be in the argument for as long as football is played. ∎

Pittsburgh 26, Houston 23—Five minutes earlier, Gary Anderson's size 6½ right shoe had left 250-pound men sprawled face first on the Houston Astrodome carpet, some in anguish, some in joy. Now, Anderson was on the phone, feeling equal parts anguish and joy himself.

Doug Anderson, 59, Gary's soccer coach, rugby coach, field goal instructor, agent, counselor and father, lay dying in San Diego, and both the son and the father knew it. Last fall, Doug became ill with a rare lung disease, known as Wegener's granulomatosis, and has not beaten it. He was home from the hospital, no better, propped up in front of the television, unable to speak more than a word or so at a time.

Around him were his two daughters, Beverley and Lauren, his other two sons, Sean and Terence, his wife, Pat, and her parents, all hoping Gary might make his day. "These last few days have been the roughest of all," said Sean. "But we haven't given up hope."

Nearly 3½ minutes into overtime of the Pittsburgh Steelers' AFC wild-card game with the Houston Oilers, it was so far, so good for Gary: His 3-for-3 day in field goals had kept the Steelers in the game, and now, with the score tied 23-23, he was staring at one of the most monstrous chances in his life, a 50-yarder that would send the ugliest girl at the NFL's playoff dance, Pittsburgh, on to the next fiesta. Pittsburgh, which hadn't been anywhere but on the couch at this time of year since 1984, came in dead last in the NFL in offense and 19th in defense. The Steelers made it to Houston thanks to four teams' losses in the last week of regular-season play and their own 31-22 win over Tampa Bay. This was a team that started the year by setting a new record for turf ingested: It lost its first two games by a total of 92-10. "All our fans wanted to know was who would be the Number 1 pick in the draft," says Pittsburgh tackle Tunch Ilkin.

Those fans also wanted to know when the Steeler management would fill out the big pink slip for the Human Ice Sculpture, Pittsburgh coach Chuck Noll. In 1988, hadn't he gone 5-11, the Steelers' worst record in 19 years? And wasn't this season's start just the first 15 minutes of a bad rerun? And weren't the '90s a time for a fresh start? Things got so bad that Pittsburgh president Dan Rooney gave Noll the dreaded "pep" talk. "I didn't think we needed it," says Noll, who, had he been standing on the deck of the Titanic, would have wondered what was the big deal with all the dinghies.

In fact, Noll just plain refused to acknowledge that the Steeler ship was sinking, and so it never did. He stayed the course, kept teaching his young team, never changed expression, won five out of his last six games, and suddenly found himself in the playoffs coaching one of the hottest teams in the league.

He was fortunate to draw Houston in the first round, a team that two weeks before had been 9-5, only to be blown out by Cincinnati 61-7 and then kicked out of its sure-thing AFC Central title by Cleveland. A team coached—and soon not to be coached—by Jerry (There's Trouble In) Glanville.

And so it was that these NFL escalators passed each other, one going up and the other going down. Pittsburgh led 16-9 in the fourth quarter, 10 of its points having come from the foot of Anderson and six on Noll's first-quarter fourth-and-one call from the Houston nine that tailback Tim Worley bull-rushed into a touchdown. But Oiler quarterback Warren Moon started to click. He hit Ernest Givins with an impeccable 18-yard touchdown pass on a crossing pattern to tie the score at 16. Then Moon hit Givins for

the 11th time in the game, with a nine-yard beauty that gave Houston a 23-16 lead with 6:02 left.

How would Bayou Bubby Brister respond? No problem. All Brister did was go 82 yards in 11 plays, the last a handoff to the unknown soldier, Merril Hoge, who scored from one yard out to tie the game with 46 tiny ticks left.

Hello, overtime. Hello, last great game of the 1980s. Pittsburgh wins the toss, goes nowhere, punts badly, and Houston takes over at the Steeler 45. Oh, geez. The Steeler 45? Moon, who had been going through Pittsburgh like a USAir connection, needed only, what, 15 yards for a field goal? He could get that with a cup of decaf in his right hand. Jerry, call your accountant. Tell him everything will be all right.

On the first play, Moon handed the ball to Lorenzo White, who took it wide, got run over by a speeding train known as cornerback Rod Woodson, coughed up the ball and watched Woodson pounce on it. "This is a sellout game," Woodson said later. "If you don't sell out your body now and go flying in at somebody, you'll never do it."

Anderson's moment had arrived.

"Lots of money riding on that kick," Anderson said afterward. "Lots of pressure." And none of it meant nearly as much to him as did that one silent TV viewer in San Diego.

Houston called a timeout to let Anderson squirm, and Ilkin wandered over to him and said, "If there's one guy in the world I'd like to have kicking this kick for us, it's you." Anderson smiled.

"I had all kinds of confidence he was going to make it," said Brister. "Then I looked up at the scoreboard and it said, 'Gary Anderson has not attempted a kick from 50 yards or more this year.' And I thought, Oh, God."

When the kick went up, all Noll could think was, Thank goodness for the dome. Everybody kicks a little longer indoors, and this boot was plenty long. And plenty good. "That thing would've gone from 60," said Brister.

For the Anderson family, the kick gave them a moment as bittersweet as any could be. "We were all crying," says Sean. "Even my dad."

And so, five minutes after his field goal, with players whooping it up all around him and his own tears not helping much, Gary called his old coach.

"Dad?" said Gary. "Dad, I did it for you." ■

LOS ANGELES RAMS 21, PHILADELPHIA 7—

Pro football's newest hero is a white-haired, pink-faced chap who resembles your grocer and once coached swimming at Albion College. Fritz Shurmur, the 57-year-old defensive coordinator of the Los Angeles Rams, looks as if he should be telling housewives, "Please, don't squeeze the Charmin."

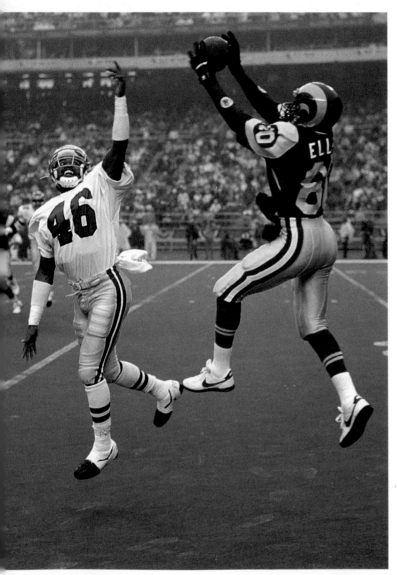

Ellard scampered into the end zone with this Everett toss on the Rams' first possession.

In an age when defensive coaches scream "Attack!" and pound the table so hard it splinters, Shurmur rolled the clock back for the Rams' NFC wild-card playoff game in Philadelphia. He plunked his team into a defense that was all the rage when people were carrying anti-Vietnam War signs. Zone. Pure zone. Nothing but zone.

"Never played a single snap of man-to-man, not one," said Shurmur proudly after his lie-back-and-stop-it defense had befuddled quarterback Randall Cunningham and the rest of coach Buddy Ryan's Eagles, holding them to a single touchdown in L.A.'s 21-7 victory. "We never rushed more than four people. We didn't blitz once."

O.K., let's look at this zone thing, the object of which is not to send the quarterback running for his life but to confuse him. Zone defenses have been around since the 1950s, but no one made a big deal of them. Then in the '80s along came Ryan and his "46" defense, which he pioneered when he was defensive coordinator in Chicago. Attacking the quarterback became the manly way to go. The big gamble. Fans loved it.

There remained a few fuddy-duddies who mumbled into their beer and stuck to basic zones. Shurmur was one. He became the Rams' defensive coordinator in '83, and though his defense never led the league, his team usually made the playoffs. "Sound" was the word people used to describe the Ram defense.

Coming into the Philly game, the Ram defense ranked 21st, and it was dead last against the pass. Shurmur tried to explain that two of his key performers, linebackers Fred Strickland and Larry Kelm, had been injured much of the season and that a lot of the passing yardage was given up after opponents had fallen behind and were forced to throw. Yeah, sure. Nice old guy. Let's not be too tough on him.

The day before the game, the Rams took a look at the gray Philadelphia sky, shivered under a cold drizzle and promptly went indoors, into the Eagles' practice bubble. This gave the Philly faithful a laugh. L.A. beach boys. Ram coach John Robinson wasn't worried. He knew he had big-play potential in his quarterback, Jim Everett, who had enjoyed the 10th-most-prolific passing season in NFL history, and serious deep threats in his wideouts, Henry Ellard and Flipper Anderson. The Eagles' gambling defense was built around a relentless front four, which piled up

Everett's two first-quarter touchdown passes were all that Los Angeles would need.

the sacks, knocked the ball loose and provided field position for Cunningham.

How to stop Cunningham? The Rams' defensive line was hurting, with tackles Doug Reed and Bill Hawkins on injured reserve. Only four linemen would dress for the game. To keep the big guys fresh for Philly's ground game, which had become surprisingly effective late in the season, Shurmur thought up a new wrinkle. Pull the linemen on long-yardage passing downs and rush only linebackers. And that's what L.A. did—from left to right: Kevin Greene, rookie George Bethune, Strickland and Brett Faryniarz.

The first half of the opening quarter couldn't have been scripted any better for L.A. The Rams' initial two possessions produced 14 points, the first score coming on a 39-yard pass to Ellard, the second set up by a 30-yarder to Ellard. Meanwhile, Cunningham was having big problems. First three possessions: three downs and out. Fourth possession: interception. Net passing yardage for the quarter: -15.

The Philadelphia defense took hold after that. Jerome Brown, the 295-pound right tackle, was just about uncontrollable, sacking Everett once and spilling running back Greg Bell twice for losses. But everyone kept waiting for Philly's offense to do something. "The thing about having four linebackers on the rush is that they're more agile and can cut off Cunningham's scrambling," said Shurmur. "And the thing about all that zone is that everyone's always facing Cunningham and seeing what he does. No one's back is turned."

The score remained 14-0 in favor of L.A. until Philly scored early in the fourth quarter. The Eagles stopped the Rams on their next two possessions, but the offense remained ineffective. Then Philly's defense cracked. The front four had come into the game weary and bruised from a pressure-filled season. "Reggie White and Mike Pitts have knee sprains," Brown had said before the game. "Clyde Simmons is just wore out. I've got two bad knees and a shoulder that will have to be operated on after the season. We've just got to piece it together."

With a little more than three minutes left, Bell broke a 54-yard run, down to the 10, and punched it in on two more carries. The hunt was over. Cunningham had filled the air with dink passes but never got anything going downfield. He had scrambled six times for 39 yards, but he had started to run a lot more times, only to change his mind. "He was running around, pulling up and then throwing, but that's not his game," said Ram linebacker Mel Owens. "Randall's normally a one-looker. If he doesn't see what he likes, he goes. He can't pull up and deliver the ball with a soft touch, like Joe Montana can."

"Buddy got on me all week to run more," said Cunningham, "but if I get hurt in the beginning of the game, then where are we? The way they played their zone, well, I never saw that on film. You can dink and dunk all day, but you have to make big plays, and we didn't have them. The way they played those zones, it was like they knew we couldn't go deep—and we couldn't. No excuses."

"Please say this about the Rams," said Ron Heller, the Eagles' right tackle. "They have real class. No cheap shots, no talking. The two guys I played against, Greene and Shawn Miller, I have nothing but respect for. They're just a well-coached team." ∎

DENVER 24, PITTSBURGH 23—Happiness is being a TV repairman in Cleveland in the aftermath of this nail-biter. Can you imagine? Just think how many shoes, bricks, bottles, remote-control clickers and clam dip bowls went through Cleveland picture tubes as Denver used luck, pluck and a seeing-eye extra point to beat the Pittsburgh Steelers.

And to think that Cleveland was within one point of staying home and hosting upstart Pittsburgh, which outplayed Denver left, right, up, down and everywhere but on the scoreboard. "The best team did not win today," said the Steelers' 230-pound running back, Merril (as in *barrel*) Hoge, and he might be right. Using Hoge's impossibly gritty performance and the shoot-me-because-I'm-not-gonna-die will of quarterback Bubby Brister, the slower, younger, talent-poorer Steelers came *thisclose* to pulling off the upset of the year.

The Steelers arrived in Colorado as 10-point underdogs, wearing their 9-7 regular-season record—worst among the playoff teams—like a tattoo. They were outscored by 61 points during the year and outgained in every game but three. This team was Cinderella, working the ballroom in a burlap strapless.

And here was Denver, 11-5, the first team in the NFL to clinch a division crown and an odds-on favorite to spend the last week in January eating jambalaya in New Orleans. "It's going to come down to you and Bubby," Bronco coach Dan Reeves told quarterback John Elway before the game. Wait a minute. John Elway versus Bubby Brister? Beef Wellington versus Spam?

But Reeves was right. Denver had a Bubby blister right from the coin flip. Before the Broncos could clear their throat, Brister had staked the Iron City to a 10-0 lead after a seven-yard touchdown run by Hoge (as in *dodge*). Hoge not only became the first anybody to run for 100 yards against Denver this season, but

he also did it in the first half. How can a slow-footed fullback from Pocatello, Idaho, go for two straight 100-yard games in the first two playoff games of his life? Maybe the secret is in his locker back at Three Rivers Stadium—it's Franco Harris's old one.

The Broncos finally got in the game midway through the second quarter with six points from Melvin Bratton's one-yard back dive, but David Treadwell's PAT attempt was blocked by Aaron Jones. Well, kind of blocked. "All I heard was two thumps, my foot kicking it and somebody blocking it," said Treadwell.

Said Jones, "It hit my hand. I thought I had it blocked." But the ball belly flopped a foot over the crossbar and died happily on the other side. Jones had a gnawing in his stomach. "I had that *feeling* that we might need that," he said.

Brister came back with a little buttonhook TD pass to Louis Lipps six minutes later, and the worms were eating the fish 17-7, with 26 seconds to go before halftime. But before the gun could sound, Denver got

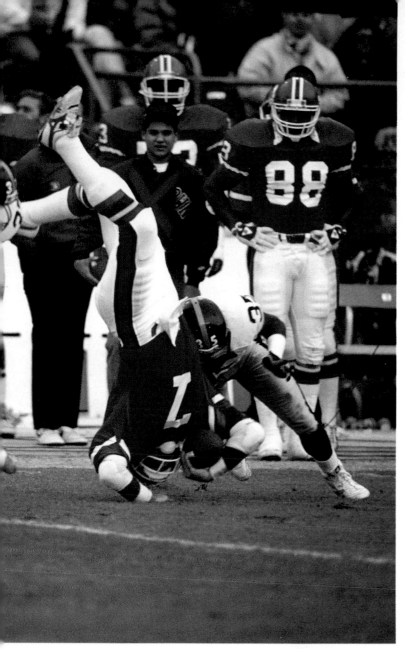

lenburg nearly put a forearm through Brister's forehead, but Bayou Bubby wouldn't leave the game. He was so woozy that in one huddle his outlandish play call prompted his teammates to stand up, look questioningly at the sideline and call timeout. *Whaddaya mean, run to the Buick and I'll fake it to you?*

Hoge was so drop-dead tired in the fourth quarter that on one occasion Brister literally picked him up and dragged him back to the huddle. Pittsburgh was playing on nothing but guts and memory. And it was working. Still, there was an itchy feeling on the Steeler sideline. "When we were getting our threes, we should've been getting sixes," said Hoge.

And now Pittsburgh had left a window for Elway: 7:06 and 71 yards to go. Done. Elway found regular-season MIA Mark Jackson on an 18-yard sideline pattern. Then, with a second-and-inches, he handed off to running back Bobby Humphrey, who pitched the ball back to Elway, who launched the ball "into rightfield" (he's a former Yankee, remember) and Johnson's diving catch gave Denver a first down on the Steeler 26. From there, Reeves called Humphrey's number four straight times and Bratton's twice. Bratton's one-yard dive and Treadwell's one-thump extra point put the home team ahead by one.

Uh-oh, still 2:20 to play. Brister, for one, liked the look of things. But Stock dropped a cinch 20-yard gain on first down, and Brister had to throw the ball away on second. That left third-and-desperate. By now, the 75,868 fans were making a din you could hear in the back bowls at Vail. Worse, Brister was working with a new center—exhausted starter Dermontti Dawson had left the game on account of not getting enough air into his lungs—the 45-second clock was down to :01 and as hard as Brister stamped his foot for the snap, it wouldn't come. When he turned his head away for just a moment to look at the clock, the ball arrived, bounced off his ankle, through Hoge's fingers and into the welcoming embrace of Denver safety Randy Robbins. *Cleveland Suicide Prevention Line. Can you hold?*

Pittsburgh's locker room felt like anything but a loser's. "I think America woke up today," said Hoge. "Nobody gave us much respect. Ten-point underdog? That's ridiculous. We showed we're a good team."

Meanwhile, safety Dennis Smith approached Elway in the Bronco locker room with his own message. "You're still the man around here," Smith told him. "I don't care what anybody says. You're the man, and you always will be the man."

For Elway, who has suffered a season of controversy and booing—it was his worst statistical campaign since his rookie year—Smith's words meant more than any piece of bronze or polished silver. "To hear it from a teammate," he said, "that meant a lot." ■

back in it on two bits of pure Rocky Mountain mother-lode luck. Elway hooked up with Ricky Nattiel for 15 yards, even though replays showed that the ball took a little hop off Nattiel's chest, onto the grass and back into his arms. That's when Treadwell ricocheted one in off the left upright to make it 17-10. "Ugly but effective," he said.

Until then, the Steelers had stopped Elway the only way anybody knows how: They kept him standing on the sideline with his helmet off. He only had the ball on four possessions. Sooner or later, however, Elway will throw a spiral through your heart, and he did it not two minutes into the second half with a 37-yard vector to Vance Johnson that tied the game 17-17.

Brister answered that tit with two tats, driving for two consecutive field goals to put Pittsburgh in front 23-17. Along the way, he threw to guys nobody had ever heard of—Mark Stock, for instance—and let Hoge make like Red Grange (final numbers: 120 yards running, 60 catching). The Steelers seemed bulletproof. At one point, Bronco linebacker Karl Meck-

CLEVELAND 34, BUFFALO 30—A lot of people figured this playoff game between teams from look-alike Lake Erie industrial towns would be low scoring, defense dominated. Your mill workers against ours in a no-wrenches-barred brawl in the muck. After all, during the regular season, the AFC Central-champion Cleveland Browns had allowed only 254 points, the second fewest in the conference; had intercepted an AFC-high 27 passes; and had set a team record of 45 sacks. The AFC East-champion Buffalo Bills had struggled some on defense in 1989, but they had shut out the New York Jets 37-0 in their regular-season finale and would be starting brute defensive end Bruce Smith and bloodthirsty linebackers Shane Conlan and Cornelius Bennett together for only the fourth time in this injury-plagued season. What's more, the game would be played in Cleveland. That usually meant ice and mud and a swirling wind cold enough to freeze the whiskers on the Dawg Pound mutts.

So what happened? The weather was comparatively balmy (33°), the wind was calm and the gridiron was as dry as a Milk-Bone. In celebration of the favorable playing conditions, the offenses went wild. The final score was 34-30 in Cleveland's favor, even though Buffalo piled up 453 yards to the Browns' 325. Cleveland won because quarterback Bernie Kosar converted 20 of 29 passes for 235 yards and three touchdowns and threw no interceptions; because 230-pound running back Kevin Mack, who spent 33 days in jail for cocaine possession, had a game-high 62 yards; and because wide receiver Webster Slaughter got help from his Light Time shoes, the spray-painted Day-Glo wheels that he and a number of other Browns wear.

Most of all, though, the Browns won because the Bills' passing attack faltered at the end of the game. On second down from the Cleveland 11 with 14 seconds left, Buffalo running back Ronnie Harmon dropped a pass from his quarterback, Jim Kelly, in the end zone. On the next play Kelly saw running back Thurman Thomas break open on the goal line, but his throw was intercepted by linebacker Clay Matthews, and the whole stadium sighed with relief.

"It was one of those games in which it looked like the last team to have the ball would win," said the Browns' first-year coach, Bud Carson.

Matthews was so ecstatic over his interception that he fell flat on his back while trying to spike the ball. Recovering nicely, he held the ball aloft for the bel-

lowing and barking fans as he started for the tunnel. Then he stopped and heaved the ball into the stands. It hit the facade on the second deck, right next to the BIL-JAC DOG FOOD sign, and dropped into the rabid masses. Arf, arf, this pigskin's for you, Cleveland!

The game was so entertaining, with three lead changes and four fourth-down attempts—three of which were successful—that you could almost forget how vital the outcome was for both teams. Of course, the winner would move to the AFC Championship Game, but more important than that, the game would determine which team was in an ascent and which was in a slide.

Both had better records last season. Buffalo was 12-4 in 1988 and was picked by many NFL observers to make the Super Bowl this year. But after winning only one of their final four games, the Bills finished at 9-7. This fade brought out the best in their personalities. Kelly blamed some of the Bills for screwing up. Thomas then took it upon himself to defend his teammates and blamed Kelly for screwing up. After a

began to question everything from first-year offensive coordinator Marc Trestman's game plans to Kosar's sore elbow to Carson's suitability to be a head coach. Players grumbled too.

Carson persevered too, and the Browns won their last two games, against the Minnesota Vikings and the Houston Oilers, to win the division crown by half a game. Good thing, because Carson had made it pretty clear he didn't want to hit the road again.

The Bills struck first, on a 72-yard touchdown pass from Kelly to wide receiver Andre Reed 10 minutes into the game. Cleveland's Matt Bahr had already tried a 45-yard field goal but had missed to the right when he slipped in sand that had been spotted around the field to soak up water. He connected on another 45-yarder from almost the same spot at the end of the first quarter, however, and the Browns added a TD early in the second period on a 52-yard bomb from Kosar to Slaughter.

Buffalo answered with a 33-yard Kelly-to-James Lofton scoring pass, which put the Bills in front 14-10. Kosar then hit tight end Ron Middleton with a three-yard touchdown pass, and the Browns led 17-14 at the half.

The Browns took a 31-21 advantage into the fourth quarter following a 44-yard touchdown pass from Kosar to Slaughter, a six-yard Kelly-to-Thomas scoring toss and a 90-yard kickoff return by Metcalf for a TD.

Kelly, who was masterful, completing 28 passes in 54 attempts for 404 yards and four touchdowns, brought the Bills to within four points, 34-30, with an eight-play, 77-yard scoring drive that consumed less than three minutes. He didn't use a timeout, and got the score on a three-yard pass to Thomas with four minutes to go. Thomas would catch 13 passes for 150 yards and two touchdowns and run 10 times for 27 yards. None of that would matter, however. Buffalo kicker Scott Norwood slipped in the sand and kicked the extra-point attempt into a teammate's back, making a field goal useless to the Bills. "I felt real bad for him," said Bahr of Norwood. "The field has bitten so many people."

Kelly's final drive was stopped by Matthews's interception with three seconds remaining, and Buffalo fans were left to wonder about what might have been. For the woofing Cleveland faithful, the victory provided redemption for all those infamous ill-fated losses. But would they be barking or bawling after the Denver game? ■

joint Kelly-Thomas press conference on Dec. 14, ostensibly to bury the hatchet, Kelly said he would no longer talk to the media. Said coach Marv Levy of the search for where to pin the blame, "This team is drowning in analysis."

Nosetackle Fred Smerlas had said of his team's blown games, of which he figured there were five, "When you keep cutting your own throat, eventually you run out of blood."

But sutures were again called for after this defeat. Both Harmon and Thomas accused Kelly of holding the ball too long before passing on the Bills' last two plays. Kelly would not comment on what he said to his two teammates.

Cleveland's story was remarkably similar. The Browns were 10-6 in 1988 and 9-6-1 in '89, though most people thought Cleveland should have improved with the addition of speedy rookie running back Eric Metcalf and the development of defensive tackle Michael Dean Perry. But the Browns stumbled, winning only two of their final six games, and critics

SAN FRANCISCO 41, MINNESOTA 13—The San Francisco 49ers have served notice to any unbelievers who might conceivably remain. Give Joe Montana time to throw, and his performance will approach perfection.

One half was all the Niners needed to dispose of the Minnesota Vikings and qualify for the NFC championship. The final score read 41-13, but the game was over by halftime. At that point, San Francisco led 27-3 and had treated the 64,585 fans at sold-out Candlestick Park to a remarkable show of offensive football.

There had never been anything like it at this level of competition and against this caliber of opponent—the No. 1-rated defensive team in football. The 49ers had six possessions in the first half, not counting a one-play kneel by Montana at the end, and they scored four touchdowns. The other two times, they drove to the nine and fumbled, and to the 14 and missed a field goal.

The halftime numbers looked like final stats. Montana completed 13 of 16 passes for 210 yards and four touchdowns, and the three incompletes came on two drops and a throwaway. Roger Craig rushed 95 yards on 11 carries. Jerry Rice made five catches for 112 yards and two touchdowns. The offense gained 10 yards a play and piled up 320 yards. The Vikings had held 13 regular-season opponents to less than that for an entire game. "Awesome, just awesome," said Minnesota defensive coordinator Floyd Peters. "We were in shock."

"What was your game plan?" he was asked.

"Didn't look like there was one, did it?" he said.

The odd thing was that, early on, the game had the look of an upset. After a 58-yard return on the opening kickoff from Terrence Flagler, San Francisco ran a four-play minidrive then coughed up that fumble on the nine. The Vikes responded by launching a seven-minute, painstaking field goal drive to go ahead 3-0. Then the fun started.

Second series: Montana to Rice, 72 yards for a score on a play that started as a five-yard hook pass. "The defense went into shock after that," said Peters. "Nobody stepped forward to make a big play. It was a total collapse."

Third series: 29-yard run by Craig down to the Minnesota 33, after Montana had connected with Rice on a 12-yard slant-in that was so perfectly timed, so quick and decisive, that the pass looked like a telephone wire stretched between quarterback and receiver. "One second, one and a half at most," Terry Bradshaw, who was doing the game for CBS-TV, said later. "No way in the world you can stop that pass when the timing is so perfect."

San Francisco's second scoring series ended with a touchdown pass to tight end Brent Jones in the same corner of the end zone where Dwight Clark had made his famous catch against the Dallas Cowboys in the '82 NFC Championship Game. The play was a near replica of Clark's game-winner: cut left, break right, Montana delivering the ball just as the receiver is being chased out of the end zone.

The Niners used everybody in that first half, from tight end Jamie Williams, a little-used Plan B free agent picked up from the Houston Oilers, to wide receiver Mike Sherrard, the former Dallas wideout who was activated the week before the game, after having missed all of the 1987, '88 and '89 seasons recovering from a broken leg. "They're running so many people in and out," Giants director of pro personnel Tim Rooney said at halftime, "that Peters can't run his defense. They're so concerned about people they've never seen."

It was utter annihilation. But here are the most revealing stats: Minnesota, which finished the regular season one sack short of the NFL record of 72, got no sacks; end Chris Doleman, tackle Keith Millard, tackle Henry Thomas and end Al Noga—the finest front four in the business—had a cumulative six tackles and three assists.

San Francisco's offensive line was the platform from which Montana launched all those pretty, well-timed passes. It was magnificent. "We blocked them the way a field goal team would block," said center Jesse Sapolu. "We blocked gaps instead of individual men. Each man was responsible for a gap, and we had to read the scheme together. We all had to be on the same page. If one guy broke down, the scheme wouldn't work.

"They're always stunting and looping. They stunt themselves into big plays. They're so quick, they get into those gaps and get their sacks and big losses on running plays. So we had to beat them to the gap."

Millard, Minnesota's quickest inside rusher, got most of the double-team treatment, though not all of it. Sapolu was responsible for making the line calls, such as which way the double-teams would shift—the first man fills the gap, the second zeros in on the defender. On pass plays, a call of "Minnesota" meant the line double-teamed left; "Viking" meant it double-teamed right. Then there were the run calls, and dummy calls to keep the Viking defenders guessing.

Everything worked. The offensive line performed like a precision drill team.

Offensive line coach Bobb McKittrick, who designed most of these schemes, rubbed his eyes in disbelief as he watched the carnage. "I mean, you expect some things to work," he said, "but never in my wildest dreams did I expect anything like this. During the week I'd be sitting in the hot tub and I'd be thinking, What if they line up this way, can my guys make an adjustment? And I'd jot something down. Then it would work."

"The way they played today," said Minnesota center Kirk Lowdermilk, "no one can touch them. They'll walk into the Super Bowl. I'll tell you what the real difference was between the two teams. We thought we could win. They knew they were going to win. That was the story." ■

Craig ran for 95 yards in the first half alone.

LOS ANGELES 19, NEW YORK 13—The day before the Los Angeles Rams met the New York Giants in their NFC semifinal playoff game, the Rams jogged onto the field at Giants Stadium just after noon. What followed was not a practice but a frolic. The defensive linemen snuck up behind the offensive linemen, whacked their fannies and ran for cover. Quarterback Jim Everett told a kid standing on the sideline to go deep, and he hit him with a bomb. A security guy with a worried look approached coach John Robinson and asked if he should clear the place of spectators. "Nah, let 'em stay," said Robinson. "It's a fun day."

Then the Rams took a bus back to their hotel to complete their rigorous afternoon of training. They lay on their beds, watched TV between naps and ordered room service when they felt up to it. "We're loving this," said linebacker Kevin Greene, as he watched the Buffalo Bills duel the Cleveland Browns. "We're so loose. We've got a playful nature as a team, and it stems from Coach Robinson. He sets down one rule above all: Have fun. Have fun—as long as you get your work done, which we do—and you'll play well."

Nice game plan, coach. The next day Los Angeles continued its unlikely frolic through the Eastern time zone with a 19-13 overtime win, which ended with some Robinson-inspired fun. On the fourth play of OT, the Rams were on the New York 30-yard line with a first down. Almost everybody in the stadium

The beaten Collins (25) could only get a piece of Anderson as he streaked by with the game-winner.

expected L.A. to wham running back Greg Bell up the gut three times to set up a 40-yard Mike Lansford field goal try.

Accordingly, New York threw an eight-man front at the Rams, which left cornerback Mark Collins one-on-one with wideout Flipper Anderson. Collins futilely bumped Anderson two yards off the line. Then Anderson raced unhindered to the right corner of the end zone. Quarterback Jim Everett threw a perfect rainbow to Anderson, six inches beyond Collins's grasp. Anderson caught the ball, and he didn't stop running until he'd stuffed it into his locker.

What a bitter loss it was for the Giants, who had overachieved throughout 1989 to win the NFC East with a 12-4 record. A walk through their locker room shows just how far they've come, and how quickly. Gone are Harry Carson and Jim Burt and many other starters from the team that won the Super Bowl in 1987. In their place are youngsters like Dave Meggett, Greg Jackson and Reyna Thompson. "When we ended last season, I knew that group had taken us as far as we could go," said Giants coach Bill Parcells early last week. "That same group would have been 7-9 or 8-8 this year, and we'd just have put off rebuilding a year."

So the game would be a matchup between the loose and quick-strike Californians and the men on a mission from New Jersey who had to do everything right. And they did—for 28 minutes. Lawrence Taylor cut off two Los Angeles drives with jarring sacks of Everett, and running back Ottis Anderson, who finished with a season-high 120 yards, rushed for 24 and 36 yards, respectively, on the Giants' first two drives. Both ended in field goals by Raul Allegre, and New York headed toward halftime ahead 6-0.

Then Everett began being Everett. The Giants, conservative to a fault all season, had the lead and the ball on their own nine-yard line with 1:45 to go in the half. This time Parcells uncharacteristically tried to get more. "What are we doing?" said one befuddled New York player as his team kept attacking. Five plays into the drive, Simms threw the ball right at L.A. cornerback Jerry Gray. It ricocheted off Gray's hands to safety Michael Stewart, who returned it 29 yards to the Giants' 20. Bang! Everett to Anderson at the goal line, and the Rams led 7-6 at halftime.

Robinson's light-and-lively mind immediately went to work. "I try to give the players something visual at halftime," said Robinson later. "So I told them that

was our rope-a-dope half. They were Ali, and they kept letting the Giants hit 'em and hit 'em. I told them it was our time to hit back."

The Rams would have the ball six more times. Each time they would get into Giants territory. It was only a matter of time, it seemed, before they would win.

But the Giants didn't fall easily. Anderson finished an 82-yard drive with a two-yard TD run late in the third quarter to put New York ahead 13-7. Then the Rams chipped away and chipped away, tying the score with two Lansford field goals in the fourth quarter.

The only leftover from Los Angeles's 1980 Super Bowl team, tackle Jackie Slater, made the next important decision. "Heads," he said when referee Bob McElwee threw the coin up before overtime. Heads it was.

After passing for a pair of first downs in OT, Everett sent Anderson on a deep slant, and as Anderson dived for the ball, cornerback Sheldon White dived on his back. The play was close. Field judge Bernie Kukar called it interference on White. The Giants called it many things, among them, an uncatchable football. "Superman couldn't have caught that," said White.

With a first down at the New York 25, Robinson planned to shove Bell up the middle for three plays and then let Lansford try to win the game. But Slater got whistled for a false start, sending the ball back to the 30. So Robinson sent in play 8-44, which calls for Anderson and Henry Ellard, who caught eight passes for 125 yards, to line up way wide on opposite sides and try to attract single coverage. Tight end Pete Holohan is the safety valve. The Rams got what they wanted. For the first time all afternoon, Collins, who had been playing well off the line of scrimmage, tried to bump Anderson at the line.

"I was glad he bumped me," said Anderson. "He can only touch me for five yards, then it's a footrace. I like my chances in a footrace with anybody."

After Anderson made the catch, he kept going, through the end zone, past an army of photographers and into the bowels of the stadium. He took a right into the Ram locker room and was still bouncing with glee 15 seconds later, when his best friend, Ram wideout Aaron Cox, crashed in and tackled him to the floor, bruising Anderson's jaw. A playful pileup ensued.

Were the Rams having fun yet? They certainly were. But the killjoy 49ers were laying in wait. ∎

DENVER 37, CLEVELAND 21—Okay, we'll soon be starting construction on the Joe Montana wing of the Pro Football Hall of Fame. But while we're at it, maybe somebody should start dusting off a shelf back near the broom closet for Denver Bronco quarterback John Elway. What else are we going to do with Elway? He continues doing his impression of the Energizer bunny. He keeps going and going and going....

He especially keeps going to Super Bowls. In fact, this game sent Elway to his third in four years, thanks to his jaw-dropping performance at Denver's Mile High Stadium, where he beat the Cleveland Browns with a contortionist's throws and a cat burglar's feet, 37-21, to win the AFC title.

Forget about the game for a moment. In the week preceding the latest renewal of this testy rivalry, people were talking about The Box, The Sox and, of course, The Ox.

The Ox was Cleveland coach Bud Carson's and owner Art Modell's worry that there wasn't enough oxygen at Mile High Stadium. Team doctors had advised that the less exposure the Browns had to Denver's thin air, the better it would be for them. So new NFL commissioner Paul Tagliabue agreed to let the Browns arrive one day before the game instead of the required two. The Browns also hoped to avoid the kind of Dawg-hounding the Broncos got at their Cleveland hotel from rabid fans three years ago. "They tried to take advantage of a rookie commissioner," said a ticked-off Reeves, "and he fell for it."

Modell decided to further tweak his hosts by refusing to sit in Denver's visiting owner's luxury box, calling it a "disgrace" and choosing to pay $5,000 to rent a different luxury box.

Then came The Sox. Denver receiver Vance Johnson painted a Frank-buster symbol on his practice hose—the jersey number 31, worn by Browns cornerback Frank Minnifield, with a slash through it. Elway isn't fond of Minnifield either. "He walks around and acts cool before the game," said Elway. "He's like a bad rash," said Denver receiver Michael Young, who would have a career day, with two catches for 123 yards and a touchdown. "He holds more than any defensive back in the league."

Sadly, Sunday came and a game had to be played. Sadly, Cleveland quarterback Bernie Kosar had to

Sore-armed entering the game, Kosar suffered more abuse from the Denver defense, which sacked him four times.

Elway's happy feet had already danced 25 yards when Kyle Kramer got a grip.

play in it. Kosar wasn't ready for a game; Kosar was ready for a gurney. He had a sore throwing elbow, a rubber brace on the index finger of his throwing hand, a sore throwing shoulder and a staph infection in his throwing arm. Other than that, he was 100%.

Remember, this is a guy whose passes don't look too good with five fingers. Kosar started 1 for 8 for three yards in the first 18 minutes. He had tried to patch together a throwing motion out of his Blue Cross bag of tricks, but nothing was working. "He said he was all right," said Carson, "but, hell, Bernie always says he's all right."

Denver took a 3-0 lead late in the first quarter on David Treadwell's 29-yard field goal and should have had more. On the Broncos' first possession of the game, they looked at a first-and-goal from the two and came away with zilch when tailback Bobby Humphrey fumbled Elway's broken-play pitch, after having been stopped twice on plunges up the middle.

But then came Elway's revenge on Minnifield. Minnifield tried to jam Young at the line and got jammed himself, stumbling and falling flat on his face. Elway rolled right, with linebacker Clay Matthews on his heels, and heaved the ball off the wrong foot, sidearm, from here to Colorado Springs, for a 70-yard touchdown. "I guess Frank was pretty quiet today, wasn't he?" said Elway afterward.

At halftime, Denver led 10-0, but even one-armed, Kosar can be a bandit. He opened the second half by finding wide receiver Brian Brennan on a zigzag pattern, 27-yard touchdown to make the score 10-7. Why should the Broncos have covered Brennan? He hadn't scored in his last 30 games.

Elway answered Kosar's strike with a touchdown of his own, a perfect spiral as soft as a baby's blanket to tight end Orson Mobley, who was in for the injured Pat Kelly, who had been in for the injured Clarence Kay. "Can you believe it, a touch pass!" said Elway, making fun of writers who say he possesses no such thing.

After Denver got the ball back less than a minute later, forgotten halfback Sammy Winder (two touchdowns after replacing Humphrey, who left with broken ribs) scored on a seven-yard, USC-style sweep, and Denver led 24-7. You could hear Denverites thinking up excuses not to go to Super Bowl parties all over town.

But the Browns chose not to go away quietly. Two minutes and seven seconds later, Kosar hit Mr. Touchdown, Brennan, who made a marvelous diving catch in the end zone. Barely two minutes after that, Cleveland scored again, off a fumble by Denver running back Melvin Bratton and a two-yard touchdown run around left end by Tim Manoa. Uh-oh, 24-21.

"I could just see it," said Elway, conjuring up a twist on past meetings between these two teams. "The Drive. The Fumble. The Comeback."

The forgotten Winder wound up for a joyful spike after his second touchdown.

Wrong. Meet The Throw. On third-and-10 from his own 43, in the most important Denver drive of the day, with the momentum seeping out of the stadium, Elway spun away from the relentless Cleveland rush—if Montana had Elway's offensive line, he would be a life insurance salesman by now—fled to his left, chose not to visit with Browns defensive end Al (Bubba) Baker, who was eager to speak with him, saw only one receiver even remotely lonely and threw the ball on the run, across his body at least 25 yards east-to-west and another 20 north-to-south, over the hungry digits of—guess who?—Minnifield and into the hands of Johnson. Two plays later, Elway connected with Winder for a 39-yard touchdown, on which Winder eluded two tacklers, one of whom was —you guessed it—Minnifield.

Kosar was intercepted on each of the Browns' next two possessions, Treadwell added two more field goals, of 34 and 31 yards, and the Broncos started to think about making their dinner reservations at Antoine's in New Orleans.

"You tell me how he does it," said Denver quarterbacks coach Mike Shanahan of Elway's performance. "How can he be running left, his toe pointed the wrong way, and still throw it the opposite direction and drop it with perfect touch? *That's* coaching."

People say he doesn't win the big ones, but if Mr. and Mrs. Montana had never had Little Joe, wouldn't Elway have been the quarterback of the 1980s? Even Elway admitted this was his best game of the season —he completed 20 of 36 for 385 yards and three TDs— perhaps because, as he had said earlier in the week, "this is the biggest game of my life."

As the Broncos ran off the field after their victory, they were surprised to find Reeves standing in the hallway leading to the locker room, beaming and yelling at them to turn around. "Let's go back out and say thank you to the fans," he said.

And so, just as the multitudes were trying to remember where they had parked their cars, out came their heroes again, all of them, in a frolicking Don't Worry, Be Happy lap that featured thrown footballs, Arsenio Hall whoop-fists and semi-strip shows.

Elway, for his part, took off his two wristbands and two elbow pads and, one by one, threw them into the stands.

Save 'em, Bronco fans. This guy is going to be famous. ∎

youngest of five sons of Manita Carter, his doting
mother. His father, Nate, left when Anthony was six.
Most of Carter's seven sisters and brothers and 24
nieces and nephews live nearby, well within maximum
effective gossiping range. Little Gnat, as Anthony was
once called, astounded his family by playing first for
Michigan, then for the USFL's Michigan Panthers and
Oakland Invaders, and, since 1985, for the Vikings.
But Carter didn't merely play. He won championships,
changed thinking, jump-started leagues and caught
touchdowns from Ann Arbor to Sweden. With a victory
in the Rose Bowl during his college years and a championship in the USFL as a pro, Carter has won everything but one thing.

"I want that ring. I need that sucker," he says of the
Super Bowl symbol that has thus far eluded him.

Looking at Carter, you would not think that a realistic goal. At 5'11", he hardly has the long limbs normally associated with the NFL's most gifted receivers.
Over the years his playing weight has fluctuated
between 155 and 170 pounds. He jogs with an uneven,
flat-footed gait. "I've always said that if the good Lord
put anybody on earth to play football it was AC,"
Viking coach Jerry Burns has said. "He just forgot to
give him a body."

A body would only get in the way. When Carter sees
a pass, his stride smooths out, speeds up and lengthens
to nearly three yards. He walks with a clomp, but he
runs like liquid. For Carter, it is the smooth stride that
enables him to make instantaneous changes of direc-

*Anthony loves spending time with Manita and
the Carter clan.*

tion. Mix in his discipline while running routes, his
absolute concentration, his fearlessness and his confidence in his ability to finesse the defender, and you
understand why he is separate from the pack.

Carter is a master of all the field's dimensions. He
runs over the middle, dancing dangerously beneath
the linebackers. He excels at quick outs and curls, and
he makes the deep turn-ins in front of maniacal safe-
ties. But it is in the third dimension, midair, that
Carter plays alone.

"He can adjust to the football like no one I've ever
seen; that's what makes him great," says Bo
Schembechler, who coached Carter at the University of
Michigan. "Bad balls, balls over the wrong shoulder,
balls that shouldn't be caught don't matter. He catches
them." Schembechler pauses, then adds, "Carter is the
greatest athlete I've ever coached."

The Minnesota faithful are certainly convinced. In
his five seasons with the Vikings, Carter has averaged
18.4 yards on 256 catches for 32 touchdowns. He set the
Vikings' season record with 1,225 receiving yards in
1988, the first Viking in seven years to surpass 1,000
yards. His numbers were down somewhat in '89—a fact
that led Carter and others to complain about the uni-
maginative Minnesota offense—but he still caught 65
passes for 1,066 yards. With fans and critics alike clam-
oring for a more exciting approach after the Vikings'

111

quick exit in the '89 playoffs, look for Carter to have a big year in '90.

That would certainly please Carter and his wife of six years, Ortancis, known as Tan, a former Riviera Beach councilwoman and the force behind the travel agency she and Anthony own in a Palm Beach Gardens minimall. The two met eight years ago, when Carter was at Michigan. Tan is "thirtysomething," as she says, her husband's senior by nearly a decade. She had two daughters, Tara and Nikki, when she married AC. Both are in college now. She used to have to smile bravely through family gatherings, deflecting or ignoring the chance comment. Now she's an accepted member of Carter's giant extended clan.

To his family and most of his neighbors, Carter is someone to look up to. "People don't look at the big picture," says Carter. "You've got to know the right angles. Most people miss them. That's why I stay in Riviera Beach. If I leave, if I don't get the ring, who does everybody look to then? It's my job to show them how it's done." ∎

RANDALL CUNNINGHAM

Philadelphia quarterback Randall Cunningham is, quite simply, amazing. Not only does he run, kick (he's the Eagles' backup punter), pass, decimate NFL defenses, own an option on Philadelphia's inkwells and airwaves, play catch one-handed, get booed and get cheered, but he also manages to make coach Buddy Ryan treat him with a deference normally reserved for the legends of the game.

"The Boss doesn't have anything to prove around here," says Ryan, calling Cunningham something that Ryan never deigned to call Bears coach Mike Ditka when Ryan worked in Chicago. "First of all, he's the best athlete to ever play the position. Sammy Baugh might be right there with him. I hope Randall can win like Sammy. But Randall could probably lead the league in punting. He's the best runner in the league, and if you can't see he can throw the football, I won't waste my time with you. I heard some of that black crap: 'Move him to wide receiver, move him to defensive back.' I don't hear those voices too much anymore. I call him the Boss so the other guys can hear it. It's his offense. I want him to realize that. So there's nobody around here who's going to have any problem with Randall being the Boss. I say so. Hell, it's my team."

That commitment is just fine with Cunningham. "I've been given the talent to run and throw and kick. The way Buddy has built me up, the pressure's definitely on me. I'd rather it be on me than on Buddy. He's a good old man, and if you pass his psychology test, he'll be on your side forever."

Cunningham's versatility makes him seem like several players rolled into one.

Thus far Cunningham, 27, has passed every test that Ryan, and the rest of the league for that matter, has thrown at him. In '88, he threw for 24 touchdowns and set Eagle records for attempts (560), completions (301) and passing yardage (3,808). His 624 yards rushing made him the team's top runner for the second year in a row. All told, Cunningham either passed or ran for 75% of Philadelphia's offensive yardage in 1988. It was that kind of performance that persuaded the Eagles to give Cunningham a whopping five-year, $17 million

Randall loved dearly, died in November, a victim of cancer. The following spring, Tony Gilbert, a friend who worked out with Randall and his brother Bruce near the Cunningham home in Santa Barbara, also died of cancer. Gilbert was a triple jumper and hurdler at Michigan State. "During a workout before Tony died," says Bruce, "Randall threw a ball from one end of the field to the other and Tony dove in the end zone and caught it. He came back, breathing hard, and said 'Randall, one of these days you are going to be the best quarterback in the NFL.' Randall didn't forget." The following November, Randall's father, Samuel, died of congestive heart failure.

His personal travails notwithstanding, Cunningham won the starting job in the second game of his sophomore season. Over the next three years he became only the third quarterback in NCAA history (the other two are John Elway of Stanford and Doug Flutie of Boston College) to throw for 2,500 yards in three consecutive seasons. In 1985 he became Philadelphia's second pick in the NFL draft.

Cunningham's family now consists of his three brothers, Bruce, Anthony and former Patriots running back Sam, and his mother's sister Nettie Hyde, an influential figure in Randall's life since childhood. Randall still calls his Aunt Nettie regularly. "I am a link for Randall, yes," she says. "He loved his mother so. Once he was mad about something, a bad game, and he shouted at me. I told him to please remember who he was talking to. I know you're hurt but please don't raise your voice to me. I tell him to make himself proud. Make the memory of his parents proud, make me and his brothers proud, but make himself proud first." ■

REGGIE WHITE

Each Sunday, Reggie White lines up at defensive left end for the Philadelphia Eagles and prepares to meet disaster. It can come in any number of ways: a 300-pound tackle flying down the line of scrimmage at him from the blind side, or a 240-pound fullback delivering a cut block, or just a jumble of bodies—teammates and opponents alike—falling across the back of his legs. "Getting caught in the wash," the players call it.

The bigger the star, the bigger the target he is for the special mayhem devised to stop him. And no star is bigger than the 6'5", 285-pound White. In the living room of his house, which he shares with his wife, Sara, and their two small children in Sewell, N.J., are 12 Eagle game balls. In Philadelphia's press book, under Honors Received by Eagles in 1988, White has 17 mentions, including his third consecutive start in the Pro Bowl. In an SI poll conducted during the 1989 sea-

contract extension early in the '89 season. How did Cunningham react to his newfound wealth? He had perhaps his finest game as a pro in a stirring come-from-behind win over Washington, throwing for 447 yards and five touchdowns. In the ensuing weeks, he went on to have another fine season, leading the Eagles again in rushing—with 621 yards—and throwing for 21 touchdowns and 3,400 yards to account for more than 75% of Philadelphia's '89 offensive output.

Those kinds of accomplishments were hardly in Cunningham's mind eight years earlier when he suffered through a difficult freshman year at the University of Nevada- Las Vegas. His mother, Mabel, whom son, in which NFL players were asked to choose the best defensive player in the league, the 27-year-old White was named on 38% of the ballots, more than three times as many as any other performer.

Oh, White gets paid very well to put everything on the line each Sunday—$6.1 million for four years, under the terms of the contract he signed last August. But his career could be ended in the blink of an eye. All he needs to avoid catastrophe are eyes everywhere, an uncanny feel for where danger is coming from and the ability to avoid it an instant before it arrives.

Case in point: Oct. 8, 1989, the Eagles versus the New York Giants on a cloudy, cool day in Philadelphia's Veterans Stadium. Two Giants—245-pound tight end Mark Bavaro and 275-pound tackle Doug Riesenberg—would occupy White most of the game. Plus, on occasion the Giants would line up three tight ends on White's side.

"In high school and college you're taught to hit the ground on a double team," says White. "Here you're expected to take it on. I get double-teamed on every play, so I expect it. Sacks are great, and they get you elected to the Pro Bowl. But I've always felt that a great defensive lineman has to play the run and the pass equally well."

Eyes on the prize:
White sets his sights for John Elway.

White takes great pride in the 133 tackles he made in '88—96 of them unassisted—to go along with his league-leading 18 sacks. Last season his sacks were down to 11 but, in spite of the double-teaming, his solo tackles still totaled an impressive 79.

White got his first sack of the Giants game on New York's second series. He sprinted past Riesenberg, with a right-arm rip and a shoulder slap with his left hand. Both moves were performed with the speed of a featherweight throwing a combination. White circled in from a wide-angle rush, leaning to his inside like a cyclist going around a velodrome, and swooped down on Giants quarterback Phil Simms before the ball could be released.

That one play demonstrated the essence of what makes White superior: power, hand-eye coordination and speed. He has been clocked by the Eagles at 4.69 in the 40. That's more speed than a 285-pound man should be allowed to have.

Watching the tapes of his amazing grace and dexterity in avoiding injury, White sees nothing unusual: "You don't say to yourself, 'Gee, that one could have ended my career.' I only thought about that once, when I saw Joe Theismann's [career-ending leg] injury on TV. That really scared me more than anything. For a few weeks I couldn't get it out of my mind. You say, 'God, that could happen to me.' "

God. It's not a word White uses lightly. He's an ordained Baptist minister. He has preached since he was 17 in more than 100 churches. His mother, Thelma Collier, says that when he was 12 he wanted to be two things: a football player and a minister. White says his idol while growing up in Chattanooga was a preacher named Reverend Ferguson.

"A white minister in an all-black church," he says. "Reverend Ferguson was the greatest man of God I ever saw. He had a way with kids and teaching. I always wanted to be a Christian, but I never knew how. He said that understanding was the first thing I had to know."

White tithes to two churches, one in Tennessee and one in New Jersey. "Some players find this hard to understand," he says. "They ask me, 'Your really do that?' I say, 'Yeah, I have to give it back to the Lord.' They say, 'That's a lot of money, man.' "

"I believe that I've been blessed with physical ability in order to gain a platform to preach the gospel. A lot of people look at athletes as role models, and to be successful as an athlete, I've got to do what I do, hard but fair. That's the only reason I'm playing the game."

When the grades for the Giants game were given out by the Philly coaches, White got a 92. Clyde Simmons, the defensive right end, was high man with a 96. But the marks didn't take into consideration the fact that White had fought off two, sometimes three blockers. "No, I don't grade that," says Dale Haupt, Philadelphia's defensive line coach. "Reggie expects it. Special people get special treatment." ■

Hampton's injuries in '89 had him playing the blues.

DAN HAMPTON

Defensive tackle Dan Hampton of the Chicago Bears knows about pain. In his 32 years, he has broken 15 bones, received some 300 stitches and undergone ten arthroscopic operations—five on each knee—including two after a season-ending injury against Philadelphia on October 2. To lessen the burning under the right kneecap, he maneuvers down stairs sideways, always stepping with the left foot first. "I can feel cold fronts moving in," he says. "Willard Scott takes a backseat to me."

Eight of his fingers are misshapen from fractures, dislocations and torn tendons. He can't fully extend either hand. Because of his aching back, says his wife, Terry, Dan watches television from the living room floor, flat on his back with his legs elevated on a chair. She often catches him squishing his knees for signs of fluid. On his worst mornings she has to dress him. "He'll sit on the side of the bed, and I'll know he can't do it," says Terry. "He won't have to ask." Despite the injuries and operations, Hampton had missed only ten games before the 1989 season.

Pride and a love for the game have kept him going, earning Hampton four trips to the Pro Bowl and making him the league's most consistently excellent defensive player of the 1980s. A 6'5", 275-pound bull of a pass rusher, Hampton was the one Chicago player on whom opposing offensive coordinators focused their game plans. No offensive lineman could block him alone. He had the tremendous reflexes and quickness and the unusual ability to move with equal effectiveness to the right or left. His absence for much of the 1989 season cost the Bears dearly: Before his injury they were 4-0; after, they sank to 2-10. "I don't want to get into comparing him," says Buddy Ryan, the coach of the Philadelphia Eagles and the former defensive coordinator of the Bears, "but nobody has played

115

tackle better than Hampton. And surely no one has played it with more heart. Dan's my hero."

Hampton was born in Oklahoma City, but when he was five, his parents, Robert and Joan, moved the family to a 40-acre farm in Cabot, Ark. (pop. 6,168), 22 miles northeast of Little Rock. One July day in 1969, when he was 12, Dan was climbing a large elm tree in the front yard. When he grabbed a rotten branch, it broke and he fell 30 feet to the ground, smashing his left heel and breaking his right ankle and left wrist. Sixty percent of Hampton's heel was removed, and the rest had to be pieced together with pins. The doctors said that the breaks might distort his growth—he now has scoliosis of the lower spine—and that he would probably have a hard time walking. For five depressing months Hampton was confined to a wheelchair.

Dan's life was just coming back together when, a few days before Christmas 1970, he learned that his father had kidney cancer. "I always felt deep in my heart he wasn't going to die," says Dan. "But by February you could tell he wasn't doing good. He couldn't get out of bed, so we watched TV together and talked. It was hard for me to be around him. I loved him so much."

Robert died in April at the age of 38. He left the family about $30,000 in savings and insurance, which soon was gone, forcing Joan to work as a waitress and cook at a truck stop six days a week. Dan felt lost. Ron Mayton, a math teacher and assistant football coach, took an interest in Dan, urging him to try out for the Jacksonville High football team. For months Dan resisted Mayton's pleas. So Mayton made Dan a promise: "If you come out, I'll help you get a college scholarship." True to Mayton's word, Hampton's dominant play earned him a free ride to Arkansas. The next prediction from Mayton, dispensed before Dan's junior year as a Razorback, was equally on the mark: "Build your stats and kick some butt, and you'll play in the NFL someday."

A year and a half later—after stepping on a scale for NFL scouts with a 10-pound weight hidden in his jock-strap to bring him up to 254—Hampton became the Bears' first choice and the fourth overall in the 1979 draft. In the spring of '83, Dan and Terry, who had been living year-round in Chicago, moved home, back to Cabot. They bought a dilapidated dairy farm and that summer added a sprawling, white stucco, four-bedroom house that Hampton lovingly calls Disgraceland.

Hampton will spend his days there during the off season, tending his cows, calves and his favorite play-pal, a 2,100-pound bull named Sig. Many friends are urging him to retire, but the smart money says he'll return for another shot at football. "The only thing certain in life is death and taxes," he says. "And I've already paid a lot of taxes. You only live once, but if you do it right the first time, you won't wish for a second chance. When I go, I'll be smiling. I've already cut a big swath through a whole bunch of life." ∎

...& Flakes

The Characters Of The Game

DEION SANDERS

About the jewelry. Or as Deion Sanders pronounces it with an obvious bow to the only vowels not deserving enough to make it into his glorious first name, the "juray."

Discount.

Yeah, really. The juray is off-the-cuff, wholesale, deep discount. But you didn't really think that Sanders just strolled in and picked up those twined dollar signs and crosses and initials and whoknowswhatelse the circumference of cantaloupes after breakfast at Tiffany's, did you?

In the matter of juray, his mama don't dance and his baby don't rock and roll. Carolyn Chambers, the striking Florida A&M graduate with whom Deion lives, couldn't care less about all those golden ropes, wrist manacles and knuckle knockers weighing down her boy. And the other woman in his life? "That glitzed-up stuff?" says Sanders's mother, Connie Knight. "He knows better than to wear that junk around me. He only likes to flash that mess for the pictures."

In June 1989, Sanders's contract talks with Atlanta stalled with the parties only about, oh, $7.5 million apart. So it's a wonder that only 10 weeks later the Falcons were able to bring themselves to pay the defensive back $4.4 million over four years. And it's even more of a wonder that 24 hours after slugging a home run in Seattle on Tuesday, Sept. 5, Sanders could strike out, high-five his Yankee teammates goodbye inside the visitors' dugout on Wednesday, fly the red-cornea to Atlanta on Thursday morning and then, on Sunday, run back a punt 68 yards for a touchdown against the Rams five minutes and 31 seconds into the first pro football game he had ever played.

In his first season, Sanders also intercepted five passes, anchored Atlanta's kickoff unit and was con-

According to Connie, Sanders only flashes his "juray" for the cameras.

sistently among the NFC leaders in punt and kickoff returns. His remarkable speed—at Florida State, Sanders was once timed in pads at a stunning 4.21 for the 40-yard dash—even got a rise out of then Falcon coach, Marion Campbell, who resigned with four weeks left in the season. "A real doer. I like this guy," he said. "He's a takeaway guy, a weapon."

Just as important, surely by now any fool for juray must realize that Deion Sanders has turned into one of the greatest self-hypes on the planet. Of course, he's an act. Of course, he's two people. He's even got two languages, street and smart. On this point, Deion is right-on.

"All my life I be the man," he says. "I've been in the spotlight at every level. It's just a bigger spotlight. I learned the system in college. How do you think defensive backs get attention? They don't pay nobody to be humble. I'm a businessman now, and the product is me. Prime Time."

Privately, at home—a new $500,000 pink-stucco Mediterranean-style house in a subdivision cut out of the cow fields of suburban Alpharetta, Ga.—with his shades off and his terrific teeth gleaming, Sanders is a child wondering if the neighbors will complain that he had a satellite dish constructed in the backyard woods.

This from the same fellow who pretty much spit on propriety at Florida State. Sanders set records in Tallahassee for on-field trash talk. He also established himself as one of the most versatile college athletes of this or any other age. The 6-foot, 185-pounder was a two-time All-America, and as a senior he led the country in punt runbacks, with a 15.2-yard average, and won the Thorpe Award as the nation's best defensive back. He once played in a Metro Conference tournament baseball game, ran to the track to help win a relay race while still wearing his baseball pants, then raced back to the diamond in time to get the hit that won the second game of the doubleheader.

Given his obnoxious, thundering-rap rep, Sanders has bent over backward to ingratiate himself with his teammates on the Falcons, as he did with the Yankees. The punt return for a touchdown right out of the box helped. His gifts of Gucci watches to the 10 other Falcons on the return squad didn't hurt his cause either.

Early in the season, Sanders volunteered to play wide receiver if it would get him more playing time. Jim Hanifan, the interim head coach after Campbell's departure, is the freethinker who, as coach of the St. Louis Cardinals in 1981, played the versatile Roy Green at both cornerback and wide receiver. "I hate to say it, because this guy hasn't even learned defense yet," said Hanifan, "but hell, yes, Deion could do both."

Forget whether Atlanta loves him or hates him or can't live without him. Or even if the NFL is really ready for Prime Time. The question may be, How would pro football like two of Deion Sanders? ■

118

Harris looks more like an NBA power forward than an NFL linebacker.

TIM HARRIS

Scene from the third play of Tim Harris's first NFL start, in Cleveland on Oct. 19, 1986: Harris, an outside linebacker for the Green Bay Packers, has just steamrolled over the Browns' Pro Bowl tight end, Ozzie Newsome, and after the play, as he stands over Newsome, Harris screams, "Gonna be a looong day, Ozzie! I can't believe it! Veteran like you getting beat by a rookie! A rookie, Ozzie! Woooohoooo!"

Scene from pregame warmups in Milwaukee, Oct. 1, 1989: Harris walks up to Atlanta Falcon center Jamie Dukes, who he played against in college, and says, "I'm going to be your worst nightmare today." Harris smiles when he says this, but he is serious. By the end of the first half, Harris has three sacks—he finishes the game with four and is named the NFC Defensive Player of the Week—as the surprising Packers notch their second of three victories in the first five weeks.

If something other than the ignorance of his fellow players kept Harris from being voted to the Pro Bowl until the '89 season, it must have been his age, which is now 25, or his mouth, which is big. It certainly hasn't been his performance—he finished the '89 season with 19½ sacks, second best in the league—or his body, which is a chiseled 6'5½" and 250 pounds, a tad taller and heavier than today's typical outside linebacker. He looks more like an NBA power forward, but with slightly thinner legs. Those legs enable him, as he will readily tell you, to run all day.

But the first thing you notice about Harris is his mouth. "He must lead the league in talking," says his teammate and close friend, safety Kenny Stills. Harris might even lead the league in talking about talking. "I do it," he says at his home in Green Bay, which he shares with his wife, Barbara, and 21-month-old daughter, Marissa, "because I've been doing it all my life and because I think it gets people off their game."

It takes more than a little woofing to throw Harris off his game. In his never-ending quest for the most direct route to the quarterback, he may line up on either side of the field or sometimes even over the center—anywhere that will allow him to use his exceptional speed and nifty moves to dance around the bulky linemen facing him. Defensive plays are called by defensive coordinator Hank Bullough; about a third of the time they include the words Tim Defense, which means Harris is free to line up wherever he likes.

Understand that Harris isn't much of a student of the game, and he has always hated watching football—or any other sport—on TV. Harris and Barbara join several other Packers and their spouses on Monday night for poker and *Monday Night Football*. "I'm always saying, 'Turn that thing off,' or 'Change the channel,'" says Harris. "To me, it's boring."

But Harris has loved *playing* football since he was 10.

"I remember one play in '88," says Bears center Jay Hilgenberg. "Harris lined up over me on a pass play, and we threw to [wide receiver] Dennis Gentry. I'm trying to hold on to Harris as Gentry gets the ball, but he gets away, runs 20 yards downfield and catches Gentry from behind. Then he gets up and starts screaming, 'I'm all over the place! You can't stop me! You can't catch me!' He's just having fun out there. I know a lot of guys on my team will get ticked off at me for saying this, but I have tremendous respect for him. He's a great player. People just don't know it yet."

Harris isn't sure where his energy comes from, but he's had it ever since his childhood in Birmingham. "I hated being inside, hated doing nothing," he says. "I'd come in when it got dark. My neighbors used to say, 'Look at Tim. He never gets tired.' I used to hate it in nursery school when we had to go down for our naps. I hated naps. I would listen to the older kids out playing and listen to the ticks on the clock, waiting for the end of naptime."

At Woodlawn High in Birmingham, Harris worried about the fact that college scouts were not watching him play much. So before his senior year, the family sent him to live with his mother's sister's family in Memphis and attend Catholic High, where Harris quickly attracted the interest he was seeking. He spurned football scholarships to UCLA, Ole Miss and Tennessee and a basketball scholarship to Nebraska to stay in Memphis and play at Memphis State, where he made a school-record 47 career solo tackles for lost yardage. The Packers chose him in the fourth round of the 1986 draft and last August signed him to a two-year $1.185 million contract that will keep Harris in Green Bay at least through next season. Don't be surprised if he stays for a decade or so.

Which means that Green Bay should be an uncharacteristically noisy place in the '90s. "The country will know about Tim Harris soon," says Packer coach Lindy Infante. And if it's slow in coming, Harris will just take matters into his own mouth. ∎

KEITH MILLARD

If you ask Keith Millard about his outstanding 1989 season with the Minnesota Vikings, he'll tell you that he got by with a little help from his friends. In fact, he did a lot more than get by, finishing the season with 18 sacks—third best in the league and more than any defensive tackle has had since they began keeping the statistic in '82. "I'm just one of the good players here," he says modestly.

We'll give that to him. Technically. Certainly being surrounded by the likes of linemates Chris Doleman, Al Noga and Henry Thomas hasn't hurt him, but it is

Millard's son Dustin keeps in close touch as Dad meets his public.

a tribute to his greatness that opponents often select him, over his talented linemates, to double-team. The result of such tactics frequently is a sack for one of his teammates. By season's end, the Vikings had recorded 71 sacks, just one less than the NFL record set by the Bears in 1984. Much of the credit must go to Millard's ability to tie up more than one blocker at a time.

Defensive coordinator Floyd Peters agrees: "He's a great player. He allows us to do so many more things because he's so quick and active. But when they start doubling him on every play, it makes our other guys great players too."

Millard has an aggressive, you-can't-stop-me attitude best exemplified by what he told a police officer after his arrest for disorderly conduct at a Mankato, Minn., hotel the day before training camp opened in 1986. "My arms," he said, "are more powerful than your gun." It's a posture that gets him into trouble—on and off the field. Since coming to the Vikings in 1985, he

has been embroiled in a series of scrapes with the law, one of which involved drunken driving and the kicking in of a police vehicle door in March 1989. For that transgression, Millard was required to perform 200 hours of community service, complete two years of counseling and pay a fine of $1,071 for damages to the car. Today, he claims that a more moderate approach has solved his temper problems and lessened the off-field antics but just six days before the 1990 Pro Bowl, he was again arrested for drunken driving.

His fiery temperament has been a liability in his football career as well. As he told *The Los Angeles Times* in 1988: "I'd be in the locker room talking and getting people fired up and firing myself up, I'd be walking around, pacing the carpet, doing whatever. Then in pregame warmups, I'd be out there smacking guys around, doing anything I could to stay fired up. Hell, by the second quarter I was so burned out, I couldn't get anything going. I'd get frustrated and tend to get a little overemotional on the sideline." Now, there's allegedly a calmer Millard roaming the field; he even uses breathing exercises to stay relaxed and preserve his strength for the long haul.

Millard's '89 accomplishments testify to the value of a more moderate approach. In Week 5, he had three sacks against Detroit. In Week 6, against Green Bay, he had four. Eight days, seven sacks. Only seven other defensive tackles or nosetackles had seven sacks or more for the entire season.

After the Green Bay game, the 6'6", 260-pound Millard was asked what it was that made him so good. "Luck," he said, reiterating his self-effacing assessment. "Really. I'm on the right team. The whole defensive line is playing well. Somebody has to come free, and it's just been me."

"He is getting better and growing by leaps and bounds," says Minnesota general manager Mike Lynn. "You wonder how really great he can be. If he continues improving, he'll end up MVP in the league."

It's been a strange ascent to greatness for Millard, who five seasons ago was under fire from Bud Grant, then the Vikings' coach. In 1985, after playing a 17-game schedule with Jacksonville of the United States Football League, a tired Millard jumped to the Vikings, where Grant immediately installed him as a starting defensive end in his 3-4 scheme. After the season, Grant, unhappy with Millard's lackluster play, complained in the press that Millard was too slow. It was a charge that stung Millard deeply. He was determined to prove that fatigue—and not a lack of innate speed—was the cause of his mediocre season.

In 1986, Peters came from the Cardinals to be Minnesota's defensive coordinator and he brought the 4-3 defense with him. With a three-man front, the down linemen rarely get sacks—their job consists of trying to tie up the opponent's offensive line and open the way for the blitzing linebackers to get to the quarterback. In the 4-3, offensive lines have four defensive linemen with which to contend, making it harder to keep them all in check. Thinking Millard too slow for a defensive end, Peters moved him to a defensive tackle spot. To everyone's surprise, Millard appeared lightning quick in training camp, producing a ferocious inside pass rush. The Vikings were so pleased that they decided to keep him at tackle, a move that has paid dividends ever since. It is also a major reason why Millard decided to stay in Minnesota and accept a three-year, $2.5 million contract in September of '89 rather than to seek free-agency offers elsewhere. "I love being where I am," he says. "Plus, I didn't want to go somewhere and have them move me to defensive end."

Where *should* Millard play? The answer, like the punch line to the joke about the giant gorilla, is very simple: Wherever he wants. ∎

JERRY GLANVILLE

The quips come in sudden spasms. "When I was born," says Jerry Glanville, the controversial ex-coach of the Houston Oilers, "the doctor looked at me and spanked my mom." On a 300-pound player he cut during training camp: "This guy was so fat it looked like someone sat in his lap and didn't leave." On why he would never own a horse: "I don't want to keep anything that eats while I'm sleeping, including a wife."

Glanville never debunks a story. "My life is partly truth, partly fiction," he says. "I guess you could say it's a contradiction." Glanville didn't come up with that line. Kris Kristofferson did. Glanville thinks Kristofferson is one of the three great poets of the 20th century. The other two are the late folk singer Harry Chapin and country balladeer Jerry Jeff Walker.

"Jerry Jeff is one of my top assistants," Glanville says. After a defeat, Walker consoles Glanville on his car CD player. "The man with the big hat is buying," Glanville sings along in a strong but not necessarily musical voice, "so drink up while the drinking is free."

Glanville had been an NFL assistant for 12 years when the Oilers promoted him to head coach late in the 1985 season. In the four years before he took over, Houston had gone 1-8, 2-14, 3-13 and 5-11. "When I got here in '84, we had the nicest guys in the NFL," he says. "Their mamas loved 'em. Their daddies loved 'em. But they wouldn't hit if you handed 'em sticks."

Glanville re-created the Oilers in his own brash image. They became known as the Bad Boys, the Astrodome as the House of Pain. "Jerry teaches us to expect everything but fear nothing," said linebacker Robert Lyles early in the '89 season. "If the sucker's moving, our goal is to get 11 guys on him. Put the flag up. Surrender. He's dead. It's over. He's a landmark. It's hit, crunch and burn." Houston went 9-6 in 1987 and made the playoffs for the first time since '80. In '88, the Oilers were 10-6 in the regular season but lost to the Buffalo Bills in the second round of the playoffs.

Then, in '89, the team stumbled to 9-7, losing three of its last five games and falling to the Cleveland Browns in the first round of the playoffs. Suddenly, the outspoken darling of Houston became a liability and the animosity between Glanville and the Oiler brass, always simmering under the surface, reached full boil. Just one week after the playoff loss, Glanville was gone, allegedly by mutual agreement between himself and owner Bud Adams.

The press conference to announce the decision was oddly free of rancor. Adams, choked with emotion, praised Glanville's contributions to the city of Houston, informed the assembled reporters of Glanville's departure and then, fighting back tears, warmly hugged Glanville and his wife, Brenda. A subdued

121

The man in black got gunned down in Houston.

Glanville expressed his wish to remain lifelong friends with Adams. A strange firing indeed. Just one week later, Glanville was hired as the new head coach of the Atlanta Falcons.

A compact 5′9″, 175 pounds, Glanville turned 48 on Oct. 14, but he looks 10 years younger—well, maybe five. He's renowned for appearing on the sidelines in black. He screams around downtown Houston in a black-on-black Corvette and a 1950 Mercury, which he calls "my James Dean special." A replica of a Tennessee license plate on the front of the 'vette reads 1-Elvis. Glanville insists that Elvis "is alive and living in Grand Rapids, Michigan." He knows this because he read it in a supermarket tabloid. Glanville believes everything he reads that isn't about him.

Before a 1988 preseason game in Memphis, Glanville left a pass for Elvis at the Liberty Bowl's will-call window. The King never picked it up, but Glanville enjoyed the attention that the gesture attracted. Later in the season he left passes to Oiler games for Buddy Holly in Dallas, James Dean in Indianapolis, Loni Anderson in Cincinnati and the Phantom of the Opera at the Meadowlands. "People think I'm crazy," Glanville says, "but I don't have to be. If I can convince them I may be, then I've accomplished all I want."

For all his loudmouthing, Glanville doesn't talk much about his speeches to church groups, his fight to reopen an inner-city boys' club or his work with runaways, drug addicts and the homeless. During his tenure with the Oilers, he visited the children's wards of Houston hospitals every Wednesday morning, practicing his bedside manner on cancer patients and quadriplegics, not just kids in for tonsillectomies. "Jerry would come in the middle of the night if I asked him," says Jim Alcorn, chaplain of St. Luke's Episcopal Hospital. "He has incredible compassion toward these kids. He finds a way to touch them."

Perhaps that compassion stems from Glanville's awareness of just how tenuous life can be. "You know what NFL really stands for?" he asked prophetically, several months before his firing. "Not For Long." He reached behind his office desk and grabbed a recent group photo of NFL coaches. "Six of us get fired every year," he said. "I'm in an elite fighter-pilot group. I know one day I'm not coming back, but I go out anyway. And one day I'll say, My god, they got me, too." ∎

Hellos...
The NFL's Latest Sensations

CHRISTIAN OKOYE

At 28, Christian Okoye still calls his father, who lives seven time zones away in Enugu, Nigeria, for advice. "He is a very wise man who knows what is right," says Okoye, the extraordinary third-year running back for the Kansas City Chiefs.

Once a month, Okoye writes his family to describe his life in America. "It is a country with very many opportunities, but those opportunities are often mis-used," he says in a clipped, British-sounding accent. "I would say to each American, 'If you can, go to Africa. There, people live life. They appreciate life every day.'"

Okoye finished his phenomenal 1989 season as the league leader in rushes (370) and rushing yards (1,480). But his 1989 wages—$215,000—amount to about one-seventh of the salary of the Indianapolis Colts' Eric Dickerson. Okoye doesn't complain. "Man does not live by money alone," he says. "If you can eat and raise children and live comfortably and give help to people who need it, that is good."

Is this guy's act for real?

"I guarantee it's real," says K.C. quarterback Ron Jaworski. "He's such a good guy. We just love him."

Okoye seems too good to be true on the field as well. Six years after he first touched a football at Azusa Pacific, an NAIA school where he had enrolled with a partial scholarship as a track and field athlete, Okoye has become the most dangerous runner in the NFL. To understand why, consider these two factors:

1) He weighs as much (260 pounds) as Chiefs center Mike Webster.

2) He runs as fast (a 4.48 40) as San Francisco 49er wide receiver Jerry Rice.

Okoye tells young Americans to appreciate their "very many opportunities."

In addition, he has the right coach this year. Marty Schottenheimer, who took over in Kansas City in January 1989, believes in the rushing game as much as any coach in the league. He also inherited an offensive line that was one of the NFL's hidden gems. It averages 6'5" and 287 pounds, and its members love to run-block, something that the Chiefs' game plan largely avoided in recent years. A healthy Okoye might have changed that, but a variety of injuries limited Okoye to just 1,133 yards in his first two seasons, including a paltry 473 yards in '88, when he was forced to sit out seven games.

The suddenness of Okoye's rise in 1989 was breathtaking. A neck injury kept him from having a single carry in K.C.'s exhibition games, and he got just five in a season-opening loss at Denver. Over the next eight games, however, he averaged 26 carries and 114 yards. Impressive figures, especially considering that no K.C. back had exceeded 110 yards in a game since 1981. "I would have to say it is quite amazing," says Okoye.

Okoye is still learning, of course. He runs too upright; defenders get too many open shots at him, and even though they generally bounce off, the hits take a toll. Okoye also needs to protect the ball better in traffic; he fumbled seven times last season. He needs to hit holes more precisely and quickly. And he needs to become a better receiver; he had only two catches for the year. However, those improvements will come with time. "Some things in football you learn as a junior high or high school player," says Chiefs president and general manager Carl Peterson. "But you've got to realize he never was one."

In high school, at the Uwani Secondary School in Enugu, Okoye became a discus thrower, and he says that if he had not decided to come to the U.S. to study and be a track and field athlete, he would probably be coaching track at the school today. The first time he picked up a football, he tried to play catch but couldn't figure out how to handle the ball. Okoye made the Azusa Pacific football team in 1984, and in '86 he led all collegians in rushing yards per game, with 186.7. In the '87 draft, K.C. gave up second- and fourth-round choices to move up 11 spots in the second round, where it claimed the unpolished Okoye.

"You try to think of who he reminds you of," says Webster, who has been in the league for 16 years. "Earl Campbell is the only guy who comes to mind. But he was 35 pounds lighter than Christian, and Christian is probably faster. Look at how Christian is built. The guy ought to be blocking for me."

Okoye's confidence is growing, but opponents still taunt him and try to break his concentration. "Sometimes the other players cuss me out and say bad words," he says. "Or they'll say things like, 'Not today! Not today!' Silly things. But it is nothing. After the game everyone shakes hands, and all is forgotten. I do not hate them. There is no one I do not like.

"But," he adds, "I do like to beat them." ∎

DERRICK THOMAS

You're walking through the Kansas City Chiefs' parking lot at Arrowhead Stadium, and you come to a license plate you can't quite figure out. Football players are fond of vanity plates, but this one seems to be covered with gibberish.

ISAKQBS. That's what it says.

Then you get it: I sack quarterbacks. This car belongs to Derrick Thomas, the man who was named Defensive Rookie of the Year by the Associated Press, the man who was voted to the Pro Bowl by his peers, the man who led all first-year players in 1989 with 10 sacks—more than either Cornelius Bennett (8.5) or Lawrence Taylor (9.5) had in their rookie seasons. The Man, period. "As far as my expectations," Thomas says "I don't think there's anything I can't do."

"My best job as a coach," says Chiefs defensive coordinator Bill Cowher, "is to leave Derrick alone."

Which, oddly enough, is something that Thomas has grown quite accustomed to in his 23 years. Born out of wedlock to a teenage mother he never got a chance to know, Thomas was raised poor on Miami's south side, where Christmas sometimes came without gifts. Most of his values he learned from his aunt, Annie Adams, who became Derrick's surrogate parent after his world was shattered by his father's apparent death in Vietnam, the victim of a military strategy called, ironically, Operation Linebacker. It was part of Richard Nixon's tactic of massive bombing that he hoped, incorrectly, would bring about a speedy end to the war. On December 17, 1972, Air Force Captain Robert Thomas and his B-52 crew were shot out of the sky. Concerned for the safety of his men, Thomas parachuted out of the plane last before it exploded into flame. The crew, except for Thomas, survived and returned home. Thomas was listed as missing in action until 1980, when the Air Force declared him legally dead. There was a memorial service, but Thomas still wonders whether his father might be alive.

Derrick was almost six years old when his father's plane went down. For years afterward, he suffered the fate of a fatherless boy in a troubled part of town, getting into several minor scrapes with the law before a stint in a school for problem teenagers helped to straighten him out and give him an interest in sports. Soon he was a football star at South Miami High and then at the University of Alabama, where he won the Butkus trophy in his senior season as the nation's finest linebacker. Nearly five months later, he was selected by the Kansas City Chiefs, the fourth choice overall in the '89 draft.

Now he talks of opening his own boys' home after he

The memory of his father is Thomas's greatest inspiration.

leaves football. But most of all, he wants to live up to his father's memory. "He's a great inspiration," Derrick says. "Everything he set out to accomplish he accomplished. He graduated with honors from high school, he graduated at the head of his class in ROTC and he graduated with honors from Tennessee State. He ran track. He did it all."

And, Derrick adds: "I think he'd be proud of me."

Thomas's teammates and coaches certainly would agree. It's too early to gauge just how good he is, but Thomas shows signs of being very good indeed. Blessed with a 6'3", 234-pound frame, Thomas also has that exceptionally quick first step that outside pass-rushers need. In Week 2 against the Raiders, he had seven tackles and 2½ sacks, numbers that earned him AFC Defensive Player of the Week honors. But Thomas still wasn't a complete player. It took him 10 or 12 games before he fully understood the Kansas City defense and began giving the Chiefs the outside passrusher and run-stuffer combination that they haven't had since the '60s and early '70s, when they had the best linebackers in football.

"I'm going to keep coming," he says. "If the opposition doesn't come as hard as I do, they'll be in serious trouble."

Thomas has had his share of trouble. Now he's ready to make some. ■

DON MAJKOWSKI

In 1987, an option quarterback from Virginia named Don Majkowski was slated to be a midround draft choice. When he complained of shoulder soreness in workouts, his value plummeted even further. Then came draft day and Majkowski watched while his name went uncalled through round after round after round. Finally, in the 10th round, after 254 other players had been picked, Majkowski was selected by the Green Bay Packers, who were desperately seeking a quarterback to improve on the ho-hum performance of incumbent Randy Wright. Tenth rounders, like beggars, can't be choosers, so Majkowski was happy to sign with the Pack at a salary of $65,000, with a $10,000 bonus up front. From such humble beginnings emerged the Majik Man, the master of the quick-strike comeback and the NFL's most engaging new star.

His first two seasons hardly suggested such storybook celebrity. Majkowski got a shot to win the starting job in his rookie season, and again in 1988. He played in 20 games. He completed 50% of his passes. He threw 14 touchdown passes and 14 interceptions. His quarterback ratings hovered in the mid-60's. He was mediocre.

In the last game of the '88 season, Majkowski

brought the Pack back with two touchdown passes to beat the Phoenix Cardinals 26-17 in Tempe. They were the two most important passes of his career, because if the Packers had lost, they would have tied the Dallas Cowboys for the worst record in the league and thus would have had the first pick in the draft. Welcome to Lombardi Land for UCLA quarterback Troy Aikman. But the win kept that from happening and condemned Aikman to an indefinite period of servitude in Dallas.

Losing Aikman didn't prevent Green Bay from showing its supreme confidence in Majkowski by spending a third-round pick in the 1989 draft on a bright kid from Duke named Anthony Dilweg, a talented quarterback prospect for the future. Nor did it keep them from trying to meet their *present* needs by endeavoring—and failing—to sign free-agent Gary Hogeboom, who chose to go to Phoenix. They probably would have taken Steve Walsh from Miami too if Dallas hadn't taken him first in the Supplemental Draft.

The fact of the matter was that Lindy Infante, who took over the Green Bay coaching reins in 1988, wasn't sure that Majkowski was the man to run the show. Infante had been the offensive coordinator in Cincinnati who designed the cerebral passing system that got the Bengals into the '82 Super Bowl. His offense places a premium on quick decisions and split-second timing. Athletes didn't impress Infante. He was looking for brains. "In the off-season he told me something I never forgot," says Majkowski. "He said, 'I want you to be a manipulator, not a gunslinger.' So I became a student. I was in here every day, looking at film."

The student learned his lessons well. In '89, Majkowski went out and had a Pro Bowl season. He threw an NFL-high 599 passes (average: 37 per game) for an NFL-high 4,318 yards, the ninth most prolific season ever. He engineered upsets over the Bears in Week 9 and the 49ers in Week 11; he led his team to five wins in which the Packers trailed in the fourth quarter. "If Montana was the quarterback of the '80s, Majkowski might be the quarterback of the '90s," says Chicago coach Mike Ditka.

The kid proved that he had the brains Infante was looking for, but he also had something else—hunger. "Ever since I was six years old, the only thing I wanted to be was an NFL quarterback," he says. "Every place I've been, I was like a big secret. I always had confidence in myself, but no one else did. Maybe if I'd been a warm-weather quarterback or played in a passing sytem, it would have been easier."

He played high school ball in Depew in the upper New York State snowbelt. As a senior he broke his hand in two places, and the colleges said, See ya. "Syracuse suggested that I spend a year at Fork Union [Va.] Military Academy, so I went there and my father paid for it," says Majkowski. "Then Syracuse forgot about me. I wound up at Virginia. I was a good option quarterback, and you know where option QBs get drafted—in the 10th round."

Infante (left) wasn't sure that Majkowski was the quarterback he wanted but '89 made him a believer.

Infante says Majkowski's success has come from his dedication to learning the system, which calls for a complex set of reads and adjustments on the go, not only for Majkowski, but also for all five receivers. Center Blair Bush says the key to Majkowski's ability to bring the team from behind is his "almost maniacal competitiveness in football, darts, anything he can beat you at. He never feels we're out of a game, and it has rubbed off on everyone."

"He scares the death out of me," Minnesota defensive tackle Keith Millard says. "Every time he gets the ball, he's a threat to do something big. From watching film on him, you see he gets the ball off like Elway and he's a threat to run. Playing him, you don't breathe easy until he's down."

Assuming the Packers can keep their talented star in the fold, there should be labored breathing in the Green Bay vicinity for years to come. ∎

ART SHELL

Gene Upshaw has been fond of Art Shell since the day they met in July 1968 at the opening of the Oakland Raiders' training camp. Through the years, the friendship between the outspoken guard and the quiet, gentle tackle grew. In private moments over cold beers, Upshaw and Shell shared secrets and private dreams. Upshaw hoped one day to be a politician; Shell wanted to be a football coach. And they both longed to be elected to the Football Hall of Fame.

By 1987, their dreams started becoming reality. Upshaw, who by then was the executive director of the NFL Players Association, was enshrined in the Hall of Fame. Last summer it was Shell's turn. Then, on Oct. 3, Shell became the NFL's first black head coach in 64 years when he was named coach of the Los Angeles Raiders. The league's only other black head coach was

Fritz Pollard, who handled the Hammond (Ind.) Pros from 1923 to '25.

"I've been pinching myself ever since I heard," Upshaw told Shell over the telephone after the news was announced. "I'm so happy." Shell was choked with emotion. "I can't believe it, Gene," he said softly. "All those plans we made so many years ago have actually come true."

Standing 6'5" and weighing more than 300 pounds, Shell was an intimidating presence with the physical skills to dominate his opponents. But his most impressive trait, as a player and later as a coach, was his habit of close observation. "John Madden taught me about the game of people," says Shell, who at 43 is the youngest head coach in the NFL. "I learned that you have to understand each individual, when to push his buttons and when not to. From Tom Flores [who coached the Raiders from 1979 to '87] I learned patience. He was a quiet, stoic leader. Mike Shanahan [whom Upshaw replaced] was one of the most organized people I ever met."

The Raiders, who had chafed under Shanahan's tight reign, became one big, happy family under Upshaw. From the beginning, Upshaw set about the task of reconstructing his players' psyches and training them to feel like the Raiders of yesteryear, when they were the NFL's nastiest, most feared bunch. His work bore fruit with astonishing quickness: With Upshaw at the helm, the Raiders, who had lost three of four under Shanahan, won seven of their last 12 games and were in playoff contention until the season's final week.

Learning to be tough and to persevere has been a theme throughout Shell's life. The eldest of five children, he grew up in the Daniel Jenkins Project in Charleston, S.C. Fortunately for Upshaw, the project was safe, friendly and filled with devout Baptists who kept watchful eyes on their children as well as those of their neighbors. Doors were never locked. "I enjoyed my childhood," says Shell. "I didn't want for a meal or toys. I had what I wanted—an extended family."

His mother, Gertrude, died of a heart attack when Shell was only 15, causing Arthur Sr. to gather his five children and make them a promise. "I will raise you all," he said. "Being a family is the most important thing."

"Art was his father's heart," says Eugene Graves, Shell's basketball coach at Bonds-Wilson High, where Art was all-state in both basketball and football before accepting a football scholarship to Maryland State. "He always talked about Art. He was so proud of him."

On Jan. 24, 1989, Shell learned he had been elected to the Hall of Fame. A half hour later, his sister Eartha phoned to say their father had suffered a stroke. Shell spoke to his father the next morning. "I told him to hang in there tough, that I loved him so much," says Shell. Arthur Sr., 67, died late the next day. His final wish was that the family stay close.

Shell tried to make his players feel like the Raiders of yesteryear.

Shell took the death hard. "I didn't get to see him before he closed his eyes," he says. "He died an hour before my plane landed. I went straight to the hospital and sat in the room with him by myself. I reflected on my life. I know I made him happy."

Before the Chiefs game in the Coliseum last season, less than two weeks after being named the Raiders' new coach, Shell was presented with his Hall of Fame ring. As Upshaw watched his best friend, he was in a reflective mood. "In the early years I didn't think Art would be a pioneer," he said. "Lately I was worried that it would get to the point where he would be too old to be a head coach. Maybe I shouldn't have. There's one thing that Art and I have learned over the years: You shouldn't be afraid to dream, because you can wake up and find out it's a reality." ∎

BARRY SANDERS

Two weeks before the 1989 draft, Detroit coach Wayne Fontes visited Stillwater, Okla., to watch a workout of Oklahoma State running back Barry Sanders. Afterward, he was totally candid about his assessment: This was the kid he wanted. The Lions would be picking third, and the first two selections, Troy Aikman (to Dallas) and Tony Mandarich (to Green Bay) were virtually done deals. Fontes's buddies in the football business told him not to get too excited about Sanders. After all, he was only 5'8".

"Records were made to be broken," Fontes said, "and this kid is going to break a lot of records."

Fontes must be feeling pretty good these days about his powers of prognostication, because before the '89 season was done, Sanders had rushed for more yardage than any running back—rookie or otherwise—in Lion history. Along the way, he became the impact rookie of the season, an almost unanimous choice as rookie of the year. As the season progressed, the Lions fiddled with their pass-dominated run-and-shoot offense, while Sanders burned the league, running for 1,057 yards in the last nine weeks alone to finish with 1,470, just 10 less than league-leader Christian Okoye of Kansas City, who had 90 more carries. His 5.3 yards per rushing attempt was tops among NFC running backs. Even more impressive than his personal numbers was his effect on the Lions, who had gone 4-12 in 1988 but finished at 7-9 in '89, including a snazzy five-game winning streak at the end of the season. Sanders, almost by himself, made the future very, very bright for a franchise that has seen nothing but darkness for a generation.

"He's better than I ever was," Walter Payton said after watching him run.

"I thought he had silicone on his jersey, he bounced off us so easy," said Minnesota defensive tackle Keith Millard after Sanders ran for 99 yards against the Vikings.

"I was born to be an athlete," Sanders says simply.

That may be true of Sanders's nature, but his nurture involved a lot more than sports. Sanders grew up in a modest, three-bedroom house in Wichita, the youngest son in a family of three boys and eight girls born to William, a carpenter and roofer, and Shirley, a registered nurse. From his father, Barry learned discipline and the value of a dollar. It was William who pressed Barry to leave Oklahoma State after his junior year and head for the lucrative NFL hills. From his mother, he learned about God and the value of faith. It was Shirley who took him to the Paradise Baptist Church, the lucky institution that has already received more than $200,000 from Barry's five-year $9.5 million contract with Detroit. From both his parents, Barry learned to be humble. The lesson was clear: Don't brag. Don't put others down. Don't gloat.

When the Heisman spotlight shone on Sanders in 1988, the world was amazed at this modest young man, who actually said that he wanted USC's Rodney Peete to win because he, Sanders, didn't want the attention. When the voters ignored his advice and gave him the Heisman anyway, Sanders lent the trophy to a restaurant called Georgio's, a local hangout where William often drinks his morning coffee.

Sanders is a walking contradiction to the old axiom that money changes people, because his newfound wealth has not altered him a whit. Throughout his rookie season, he was as unassuming as ever, giving away all the gifts and trinkets he got for being player of the game, the week, the month—whatever—to his teammates. When he scored, he invariably handed the ball to the nearest official. When was the last time you saw that happen in this age of look-at-me football?

This is the type of professional we have here: Late in

Sanders is a rare commodity:
a superstar without ego.

the season, HBO approached Sanders about appearing in an episode of the "First and 10" series, a fictional, but allegedly realistic, drama about pro football. "They wanted me to play a drunk person," Sanders says, "and I wouldn't do it." Of course not. It just wouldn't be right.

On the field, Sanders's instincts are just as sure. What Fontes's skeptical pals might have discovered, if they had looked past his height, is that Sanders also possesses 37-inch thighs and a 41-inch vertical leap, both of which give him a strength and explosiveness that more than make up for his lack of stature. He also has an elusiveness—and let's not start the comparisons in earnest just yet—that reminds a lot of football people of Payton. "Anybody can run straight or through a wide hole," Sanders says. "But I think it takes someone special to make people miss. It's almost something that came naturally, but I've developed it."

That's as close to a boast as Sanders will make—but he couldn't even let that statement stand without adding a self-deprecating explanation: "I was smaller than everybody else. I didn't want to take a pounding." ■

Good guy Steve enjoys life with his high school sweetheart.

...& Goodbyes

The Departing Greats

STEVE LARGENT

Seattle wide receiver Steve Largent had just broken the last NFL record left for him to break by making his 100th career touchdown reception at Cincinnati on Dec. 10. This is what he did after the game: He took off his jersey and handed it to Seattle play-by-play man Pete Gross, a collector of sports memorabilia who is stricken with stomach cancer. "I admire you," Largent told a choked-up Gross. Then he flew 4½ hours back to Seattle, got some sleep and was up at 7:30 to vanpool his four kids and four others to the Heritage Christian School in Bothell, Wash. Two weeks later, after the final game of his 14-year NFL career, Largent was at a benefit in downtown Seattle, signing some 750 autographs at $10 a hit, with every dime going to Seattle's homeless.

"He's an ordinary guy who's always played hard and sought perfection," Seattle general manager Tom Flores says. "People like Steve Largent don't exist, except in Walt Disney movies."

Indeed. One rated G, of course. The kind it's safe to take the whole family to see. Can't you picture it? Audiences would mist over as Largent stands at the altar in 1974, reciting his marriage vows to Terry, his high school sweetheart whom he met in Latin class. Knowing smiles would abound as a naive Largent, convinced his NFL career is over before it has even begun, packs up his U-Haul to head home to Tulsa after the Houston Oilers put him on waivers in 1976—only to wind up in Seattle when the Oilers trade him to the Seahawks for an eighth-round draft pick. There wouldn't be a dry eye in the house as Largent talks about his son Kramer, who was born in 1985 with spina bifida, a birth defect that has left Kramer able to walk only short distances without the use of crutches. After a difficult period of adjustment, Largent expresses profound respect for his son and for his positive outlook on life. Moviegoers would swell with admiration as Largent's growing compassion motivates him to make phone calls to terminally ill children and host fund-raising events for the homeless. Finally, there would be the catch against Cincinnati that added an exclamation point to an already record-studded career. Could anyone in the theater complain they didn't get their money's worth?

Certainly you'll get no complaints from anyone who ever saw Largent perform on the football field. After all, he finished his final injury-plagued season with solid holds on all the major career receiving records in the NFL. His 819 catches are 69 ahead of retired Charlie Joiner in second place. His 13,089 yards receiving is 943 ahead of Joiner. His 177 consecutive games with at least one pass reception is 27 ahead of the stopped streak of Ozzie Newsome. Not bad for a guy once described by the Raiders' Lester Hayes as "a Caucasian Clydesdale." He might even have lengthened his leads had he not fallen on an unpadded sliding pit in Week 1 at Philadelphia, cracking his elbow and putting him out of action for six weeks.

Regrets? None, even though those six games missed due to injury in '89 were two more than he had missed in his entire career to that point. He says he would be foolish to have any qualms. "Don't feel sorry for me," he said. "That would be like feeling sorry for Donald Trump if he had his wallet lifted or Leona Helmsley if she had her purse snatched."

During his layoff, Largent wasn't allowed to practice with the Seahawks because of NFL rules, which say that injured players can't practice with the team for six weeks after being placed on the injured-reserve list. So Largent got the Seattle practice schedule every day, went off by himself to a nearby field and duplicated as best he could the grind his teammates were experiencing. "His energy level is unbelievable," says Seattle coach Chuck Knox. "He only knows one way, and that's full-speed, all the time." Knox and his staff keep a statistic called the HN. "It stands for 'Hit no one.' It means, when a receiver goes down the field and isn't the primary receiver, does he hit anyone and knock them out of the play? Steve's always great in that category."

At the beginning of the season, Largent was asked why he just couldn't walk away from the game, why at age 35 he was still going out there to get concussed a couple of times a year. The $1.3 million a year helps, to be sure. But his place in the record books was more compelling. This is what he said: "If I quit now, it would haunt me for the rest of my life. Physically, it is a battle now. I don't regret the decision to play this year, but I also know retirement at the end of the season is the best decision I could make."

Canton and the Pro Football Hall of Fame await Largent's arrival in 1995. But first he has things to do: a few more vanpools, a few more appearances, a few more acts of kindness. ■

Rozelle was a commissioner for all.

PETE ROZELLE

In 1960, the National Football League owners met in Miami Beach to elect a new commissioner. The logical candidate was Paul Brown, the respected and innovative coach. But Brown wasn't interested—he didn't want to move to New York—and the league didn't have another solid candidate it could push through the membership.

On the ninth day of commissionerlock, Brown and Wellington Mara, the president of the New York Giants, met the Los Angeles Rams' general manager, Pete Rozelle, by the pool at the old Kenilworth Hotel. They asked him if, for the good of the league, he would accept being advanced as a compromise candidate. "I was stunned," Rozelle says. "I knew Wellington barely well enough to say 'Hi' to. I said, 'I'm only 32, 33 years old. You people have mentioned Supreme Court justices [as candidates].'"

Brown said to Rozelle: "Don't worry. You'll grow into the job."

Prophetic words. As impossible as the job became in the '80s, there couldn't have been a better man for it than Rozelle. The founder of the rival USFL, David Dixon, calls him brilliant. His bitterest rival, Raider owner Al Davis, calls him a great commissioner. But 30 years after his ascension, he's gone. For only one reason, really. Simply put, he is tired. Tired of his bickering owners, tired of the lawsuits with rival leagues and rival owners, tired of football being more business than sport. Of course, that development was unavoidable. Says noted agent Leigh Steinberg: "Given the tumult of the world, it's amazing that things have gone as smoothly as they have in the NFL. I think Rozelle is a big reason. He pioneered the role of the aggressive, creative commissioner."

"He is like all of us in football," former Dallas president Tex Schramm says. "We weren't born with legal backgrounds, but we sure had to learn."

But it would be a sad legacy if Rozelle were remembered as the man who dragged football into the courtroom. Litigation always accompanies successful enterprises. Lots of litigation accompanies wildly successful ones. Football ranks among the latter. In 1984, as the game soared to new heights of popularity, CBS and the New York Times surveyed Americans and asked them to name their favorite sport. Football, 53% replied. Baseball, said 18%.

Much of this success, it can be argued, was inevitable. Football on Sunday in the '60s and '70s became a living-room fixture as ubiquitous as the family couch. It probably would have prospered with Oliver Hardy as commissioner. But football hasn't just prospered. Rozelle very early on saw the importance of television to the sport, and he courted the networks warmly, getting the first of several highly lucrative television contracts in 1962. But just as significant as the money itself was how it was to be divided. Is there any better illustration of Rozelle's negotiating skills than the owners' acceptance of his contention that the pie should be split evenly? That the team in New York, a city 100 times the size of Green Bay, should receive the same proceeds from the deal as the Packers? The man was egalitarian down to his last NFL dime, and if there's one way we should remember him, it is as a commissioner for all.

Even his rivals. Just after Rozelle stunned the owners in March 1989 by tearfully announcing his resignation at a league meeting, he walked from the podium toward the door. He was intercepted by Davis, the man who had battled with him so frequently over the years. Davis hugged him warmly. Remember that hug—it says more about the man than any lawsuit. ■

Awards

The Outstanding & Outrageous

Peter King selects his faves and knaves from the season past.

Most Valuable Player: Don Majkowski, QB, Green Bay. Strange, because the quarterback of the year in the NFL, in anyone's book, had to be Joe Montana. But think of the 49ers without Montana. They're still okay, a 10- or 11-win team at least. Think of the Pack without the Majik Man and his 599 passes and his 27 touchdowns and his game-winning scramble at San Francisco. They're 4-12. Maybe.

Offensive Player of the Year: Joe Montana, QB, San Francisco. Anyone who sets the alltime passer-rating record, throws only eight interceptions, carries his team to a 10-0 road record, wins his third Super Bowl MVP award and doesn't even brag once has our vote.

Rookie of the Year: Barry Sanders, RB, Detroit. He missed one game and parts of two others with a hip pointer, and still he finished with 1,470 yards, just 10 yards out of the league lead. And boy, was he exciting. What fun he'll be to watch in the '90s, especially with the improving Lions.

Defensive Player of the Year: Dennis Smith, SS, Denver. The heck with this bend-but-don't-break stuff of the Denver past. In Smith, first-year defensive coordinator Wade Phillips had a big enforcer of a safety, and the Broncos had a defense again. Sure, they got burned in the Super Bowl, but they still got there—that's more than 26 other NFL teams can say.

Coach of the Year: Gene Stallings, Phoenix. By the midpoint of the season, 14 starters had missed at least one game due to injury, and that didn't include Neil Lomax, the quarterback who left the Cards with an arthritic hip before the season began. Still, the Cards were a game out of a wild-card berth after 10 weeks. Stallings was fired a week later, and Phoenix went on to lose its last five games, while Stallings landed on his feet: He was hired as head coach by the University of Alabama in February. With apologies to Chuck Noll, Stallings had to make do with even less.

The Personal Hygiene Award: To San Diego quarterback Jim McMahon. After refusing to answer questions he considered negative, McMahon blew his nose on the shoulder of a persistent reporter. "There's an answer for you," quipped the witty McMahon.

The Ain't That America Award: To Philadelphia special-teams coach Al Roberts. Former Eagle kicker Luis Zendejas claimed that he had a tape of Roberts saying there was a bounty put out on Zendejas by the Eagles, prompting an angry Roberts to deny the charge and say: "Luis is going to pay. I'm going to own a Mexican restaurant. I'm going to name it 'The Bounty.' Suing people is the name of the game in America."

The Front-Office Decision of the Year: To Indianapolis GM Jimmy Irsay. He overpaid to get rookie wide receiver Andre Rison signed in May 1989 (five years, $2.9 million), but it got Rison to camp on time and enabled him to learn the Indy offense, while other rookies struggled. "Sometimes you have to take risks to get things done," Irsay said. Good risk. Rison was the most productive rookie receiver in '89.

The Let Them Start Too Tall Award: To Dallas coach Jimmy Johnson, who reversed his decision to remove Dallas defensive tackle and team fixture Ed (Too Tall) Jones from the starting lineup in Week 8 after the Cowboy offices received 200 negative phone calls on the move. "If the fans want Ed to start, he'll start," Johnson said.

The Don't Mess with Bill Award: To Buffalo GM Bill Polian. After a December barrage of public and media criticism of the Bills' offense, Polian lashed out at detractors of his quarterback, offensive coordinator and coach: "Jim Kelly's still the quarterback and Ted Marchibroda's still the offensive coordinator and Marv Levy's still the head coach. And if you don't like it, get out of town!"

The (in Hindsight) Bad Front-Office Decision of the Year: To Minnesota GM Mike Lynn. He surrendered, among other things, his first-round draft choices in the next three drafts to get Herschel Walker. "If we get to the Super Bowl while Herschel Walker's a member of this team, it's a good trade," Lynn said. The Vikings never fit Walker into their offense, the team barely won the NFC Central and the 49ers booted Walker and the Vikings out of the playoffs in the first round.

133

The Blood Is Thicker than Water Award: To Cleveland rookie Eric Metcalf, whose diminutive size and all-purpose abilities made him the spitting image of his old man, Terry, who was an All-Pro with the Cardinals in the '70s.

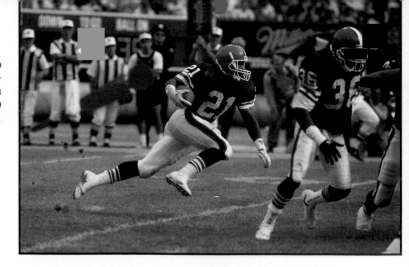

The Grace Under Pressure Award: To Denver's John Elway, who suffered through a season of heavy criticism from all quarters but still got his team to the Super Bowl. Even after the disastrous defeat in New Orleans, Elway carried himself well, refusing to indulge in the kind of backbiting that so typified the league in '89.

The Singin' In The Rain Award: To the drenched but indomitable Dolphin cheerleaders who kept their poise in spite of a deluge of Biblical proportions during the Pittsburgh game.

The He Ain't Heavy, He's My Teammate Award: To 330-pound William (Refrigerator) Perry of the Bears, 275-pound Darryl Grant of the Redskins and 275-pound Lomas Brown of the Lions, all of whom prove that, in the NFL anyway, fat is still tons of fun.

The Hair-Brained Award: To Washington's Greg Manusky and an unidentified Ram fan, both of whom felt compelled to shave their heads to resemble their team logos.

The Just Happy To Be Here Award: To New Orleans linebacker Rickey Jackson. A few hours after the Saints' season-opening win over Dallas, Jackson lost control of his sports car on a Louisiana country road, skidded several hundred feet and plowed into a truck. He missed only two games in spite of having various facial bones reconstructed.

All-Pro Team

WR—Jerry Rice, S.F., Mark Carrier, T.B.
TE—Pete Holohan, Rams
T—John Alt, K.C., Jim Lachey, Wash.
G—Tom Newberry, Rams, Steve Wisniewski, Raiders
C—Jim Sweeney, Jets
QB—Joe Montana, S.F.
RB—Barry Sanders, Det., Christian Okoye, K.C.

DE—Reggie White, Phi., Chris Doleman, Minn.
DT—Keith Millard, Minn.
NT—Jerry Ball, Det.
OLB—Tim Harris, G.B., Leslie O'Neal, S.D.
ILB—Mike Singletary, Chi., Sam Mills, N.O.
CB—Gill Byrd, S.D., Frank Minnifield, Cle.
SS—Dennis Smith, Den.
FS—Steve Atwater, Den.

K—Eddie Murray, Det.
P—Sean Landeta, Giants
KR—Mel Gray, Det.
PR—Walter Stanley, Det.
Special Teams Players—Robert Delpino, Rams; Reyna Thompson, Giants; Toby Caston, Det.

All-Rookie Team

WR—Andre Rison, Ind., Shawn Collins, Atl.
TE—Jimmie Johnson, Wash.
T—Andy Heck, Sea., Kevin Haverdink, N.O.
G—Steve Wisniewski, Raiders, Joe Wolf, Phoe.
C—Courtney Hall, S.D.
QB—Troy Aikman, Dall.
RB—Barry Sanders, Det., Bobby Humphrey, Den.

DE—Burt Grossman, S.D., Trace Armstrong, Chi.
DT—Tracy Rocker, Wash.
NT—Glenn Montgomery, Hou.
OLB—Derrick Thomas, K.C., John Roper, Chi.
ILB—Jerry Olsavsky, Pitt., Eric Hill, Phoe.
CB—Donnell Woolford, Chi., Deion Sanders, Atl.
SS—Myron Guyton, Giants
FS—Steve Atwater, Den.

K—Chris Jacke, G.B.
P—Chris Mohr, T.B.
KR—Eric Metcalf, Cle.
PR—Dave Meggett, Giants

Overtime
A Look At The Season & Decade Ahead

It probably won't happen this way. At least we think it won't. But can anyone say what the '90s will be like in this unpredictable sport? Here's one version, year by year, of what we might see:

1990—The San Francisco 49ers become the first team since Lombardi's Packers to win three consecutive championships, beating Denver 65-10 in the Super Bowl. Joe Montana, who had signed a new deal before the season, signs a new $4 million-a-year contract. "I want to play until the year 2000," he says... Bo Jackson retires after signing a four-year, $17 million contract with the Kansas City Royals... Barry Sanders sets the all-time rushing record with 2,222 yards. The Lions make the playoffs. The Giants, Vikings and Browns don't... Jerry Glanville is fired as head coach in Atlanta. Minnesota hires him.

1991—The 49ers win their fourth Super Bowl in a row, crushing the Broncos 75-10. Montana throws seven touchdown passes, all in the first half, and owner Eddie DeBartolo signs Montana to a new $5 million-a-year contract after the season... Offensive coordinator Mike Holmgren finally leaves the 49ers to be the head coach in San Diego... DeBartolo names Montana offensive coordinator and says he'll still play quarterback... Attendance hits record high of 62,000 per game, and TV ratings are going through the roof... Commissioner Paul Tagliabue resigns to run for president... Jerry Glanville is fired as head coach in Minnesota. Chicago hires him.

1992—The 49ers win their fifth straight Super Bowl, beating Denver 85-10. Montana, offered a $6 million-per-year contract after the game, refuses when news comes in from San Francisco that mayor Art Agnos has been recalled, and Montana has been elected mayor of the city in a massive write-in campaign... Tagliabue shocks America by winning the New Hampshire Republican primary, but he weakens steadily from there. Campaign chairman Pete Rozelle convinces Tagliabue to accept front-runner Dan Quayle's vice-presidential offer. The Quayle-Tagliabue ticket wins the narrowest election in history. "I demand instant replay—er, a recount," says loser Lloyd Bentson... Barry Sanders rushes for a league-record 2,525 yards and buys the Detroit Lions from William Clay Ford... Jerry Glanville is fired as head coach in Chicago. Washington hires him.

1993—The 49ers don't win the Super Bowl because there is none. A strike shuts down the sport. The players, unhappy with the $776,700 average salary, say they won't return until the league raises the minimum salary to $500,000... New commissioner Al Davis moves the league office to Oakland when he gets a better deal on a building lease... Jerry Rice retires from football, bored because there are no games. Montana immediately names Rice deputy mayor... Jerry Glanville is fired as head coach in Washington. Buffalo hires him.

1994—Under the NFL's new free-agency system, the richest men sign the most players. DeBartolo signs Barry Sanders, who in turn sells the Lions to Bo Schembechler, who in turn resigns as the president of the Detroit Tigers, who in turn replace Schembechler with Bill Laimbeer, who in turn quits the Detroit Pistons. DeBartolo also signs free-agents Randall Cunningham, Flipper Anderson and Derrick Thomas... Montana is elected governor of California, edging out Clint Eastwood. Montana names Rice as his lieutenant governor... The NFL expands to Charlotte and St. Louis, where Walter Payton becomes the league's first black owner. He immediately hires Jerry Glanville, who had been fired as head coach in Buffalo, as the St. Louis Rivermen's head coach... Commissioner Davis moves the league office to Sacramento. "What can I say? Sometimes I get restless," Davis says.

1995—After two months in Sacramento, commissioner Davis becomes unhappy with the coffee service at the NFL office and moves the league headquarters to Irwindale, Calif... The NFL signs a new TV deal, netting each franchise $40 million in TV revenue annually. A nightly game of the week begins, with Monday night on ABC, Tuesday night on NBC, Wednesday night on CBS, Thursday night on Fox, Friday night on HBO and Saturday night on TBS. A new Saturday morning game of the week begins on Nickelodeon... In Super Bowl XXIX in the new 140,000-seat LoboDome in Albuquerque, Charlotte beats Denver 95-10... Jerry Glanville is fired as head coach in St. Louis. Seattle hires him.

1996—New Denver owner John Elway, after the club's seventh straight AFC Championship, forfeits

Super Bowl XXX at the TarheelDome in Raleigh. "We didn't want to get beat 105-10," Elway says... At a tearful press conference, Davis announces the return of the NFL office to Oakland. "I feel a loyalty to the people of Oakland," he says... The NFL goes to court to prevent high school seniors from entering the draft. But an Amarillo high school senior, William Robert (Billy Bob) Tucker wins the suit and is the first-round draft choice of the 49ers. DeBartolo signs him to a five-year, $10 million deal... The ticket of Montana and Rice sweeps through the primaries and beats the Tagliabue-Modell ticket for the presidency... Jerry Glanville is fired as head coach in Seattle. Detroit hires him.

1997—President Montana and First Lady Jennifer Montana host Mikhail and Raisa Gorbachev at Super Bowl XXXI at the PotatoDome in Boise. The Gorbachevs, through an interpreter, are shocked at the outcome. "When will Mr. Elway fire Mr. Reeves?" Mikhail asks Joe in the midst of the 115-10 St. Louis blowout of Denver. Dan Reeves falls to 0-10 in Super Bowls... The NFL expands to Prague, Rio de Janeiro, Beijing and Sydney. "We wanted to be able to have games of the week at all different hours of the day to maximize our TV revenue," says TV committee chairperson Ivana Trump... Jerry Glanville is fired as head coach of Detroit. The Canberra Koalas hire him.

1998—At the BrezhnevDome in Moscow, the Broncos lose Super Bowl XXXII to Beijing 125-10. "I guess we need to make some defensive changes," coach Reeves says... Donald Trump buys the Giants for $4 billion and moves them to a domed stadium underneath Trump Tower in Manhattan. The city woos him with promises of running water, free subway tokens and the fur-salon concession... Al Davis moves the league office to a new building on the grounds of the razed L.A. Coliseum... Jerry Glanville is fired as head coach of Canberra. Houston hires him.

1999—The country is in a major recession. DeBartolo brings back embattled President Montana to quarterback the team once more. Montana, 43, beats Denver 135-10 in Super Bowl XXXIII at the NutmegDome in Hartford... Young succeeds Montana as president... NFL owners Hunt, McCaskey and Trump stage a bloodless coup at the NFL offices in Los Angeles, and Davis is ousted. Davis flees to the Papal Nuncio in Panama City. The NFL office returns to New York. Owners enter the new decade without a commissioner, after holding 21 fruitless meetings to elect one... Jerry Glanville is fired in Houston. No one hires him as head coach. He joins The Bum Phillips Home For Wayward Oiler Coaches as a camp counselor.

2000—In a compromise move, Joe Montana is elected commissioner. Rice is named league president... The Denver franchise moves to Pueblo. Reeves stays on as coach despite massive picketing all over Colorado... Pueblo loses Super Bowl XXXIV at the HulaDome in Maui 144-10 to Prague... Al Davis moves to a fortress-like home in Homestead, Fla., where Gene Upshaw, Art Shell and Jim Otto are on 24-hour guard... Jerry Glanville is fired as camp counselor. "I am retiring from everything," Glanville says. There are celebratory parades all over Texas... The league expands to 64 teams, with at least two in every time zone. "This way," Ivana Trump says, "we can be on TV every hour of every day."

Now seriously folks.

The '90s will begin as the age of the athlete and finish as the age of brute strength. This is why: In football today, we're seeing great athletes flourish on defense, as the Lawrence Taylors and Charles Haleys and Cornelius Bennetts defy double-teams and find ways to slip through and smash quarterbacks. This trend will become more pronounced in the early part of the decade, because colleges will continue to put their best athletes on defense. "You might even see the creation of a new term for the type of player who can rush, back up the line and cover," Indianapolis coach Ron Meyer says. "He'd do for the NFL what Magic Johnson did for the NBA. Who envisioned a 6'9" guard in basketball 25 years ago?"

This trend will change NFL offenses. The beauty of Joe Montana and Boomer Esiason throwing slant patterns to the ultraquick wide receivers will be blunted by increasing injuries to quarterbacks and increasing pressure from defensive lines and linebacker groups. By the middle of the decade, we're going to have a bunch of quick and mobile quarterbacks scrambling to find time and receivers. We're also going to be inundated with big backs playing basic football as a means to lessen the impact of the multipurpose linebackers. Colleges will shift their talent to the offensive side of the ball. The time of games will go down drastically because teams will run so much. Miami linebacker Rick Graf says the game of the '90s "will be big guys running into each other as hard as they can, with no technique, just trying to run the ball, control it. It'll be smash-mouth football, and the fans will love it."

TV coverage will expand. By the middle of the decade, we'll be seeing weekly games on Sunday, Monday and Thursday nights. The revenues are just too enormous for the league to ignore, particularly with the owners unable to keep a cap on salaries. Sunday afternoons won't contain the best football anymore. The real marquee games will happen in prime time, almost exclusively.

The league will also expand, probably by four teams. Orlando has a new direct flight to Tokyo, new movie studios and a Disney empire that continues to grow every year. Charlotte has a sports-starved region and is surrounded by six middle-level TV markets. Sacramento, two hours from terrific winter sports in Nevada, 90 minutes from gambling and 90 minutes from the Bay Area, is hell-bent for baseball and football franchises—so much so that the city is building sports stadiums without the promise of teams. Baltimore, St. Louis and Memphis had all better come up with some legitimate financial incentives if they hope to compete for today's NFL owner.

But none of this will have much effect on 1990, which should be a season with only minimal shocks.

The league is on the verge of crowning some new stars. The best back in the game will be Barry Sanders. He should lead the Lions, who finished 1989 with five straight wins, into the playoffs. If he does, he'll be the MVP. Jim Everett will emerge as the leading quarterback contender to the Montana throne, with competition from Don Majkowski, who wasn't a fluke in his starry Green Bay season of '89. The best receivers, early in the decade, will be Flipper Anderson of the Rams, Tim McGee of the Bengals and Brian Blades of Seattle.

New names. New teams. Here's our early view of the 1990 season:

Philadelphia wins the **NFC East** not because of its own superior play but because of the transition game being played by the Giants 95 miles up I-95. The Eagles need to find a deep threat for legend-in-his-own-mind Randall Cunningham, but their defense is good enough to hold off everyone in the division. *New York's* two best players, Phil Simms (34) and Lawrence Taylor (31), are a year older and as irreplaceable as ever—facts that make a potential training-camp holdout by Taylor and the ongoing organizational doubt about Simms very dangerous. But the Giants have the ingredients (running game, pass defense) to be threats. The departure of Bobby Beathard enters year two in *Washington,* leaving no one to badger Joe Gibbs into playing younger guys. Now he's being forced to. Look for tight end Jimmie Johnson to emerge in a big way in 1990 and for the passing game to keep the 'Skins contenders. It's hopeless, at the moment, for *Phoenix* and *Dallas.* Joe Bugel, the new Cards coach, is one of the nicest guys in the game. But he's a running game coach. You can't run it 45 times a game outdoors in Arizona's 90° weather. Bugel ought to feel the heat from the fans and from owner Bill Bidwill by late September. Dallas will eventually be good. But not now. It will take a couple of years for the Cowboys to turn their jillion draft choices into competent players. But they've already got the genuine item—Troy Aikman—at the most important position. There's hope, Cowboy freaks.

In the **NFC Central,** *Detroit* will be the surprise team of the league. Barry Sanders will prove that neither Herschel Walker nor Neal Anderson is the best back in the division, and Sanders, with more pass-receiving responsibility in the run-and-shoot offense, will emerge as the best back in football. The Lions are solid up the middle on defense, with nosetackle Jerry Ball, inside linebacker Chris Spielman and

safety Bennie Blades forming a good nucleus for the '90s. The most overrated fact of 1989 was *Green Bay's* signing of 20 Plan B free agents and how it turned the Pack into a contender. The heck it did. Don Majkowski did. And Sterling Sharpe and Tim Harris and Brent Fullwood. The test is whether they can do it again. They will, contending for the division title into Week 16. *Minnesota* and *Chicago,* the division's dominant teams in the '80s, are both sliding. The Vikings, football's unhappiest team, will continue struggling to make Walker a dominant player. If they don't, their Super Bowl dream is probably shot. The Bears have a brighter picture, with some talented youth. But the key question in Chicago will be: Can the players get along with Mike Ditka? There's a groundswell of dislike in the locker room for the big bad Bear right now. *Tampa Bay* is not a bad team. Honest. But the Bucs are missing a running game and a pass rush. You just can't win in the NFL by rushing for 3.7 yards a carry and getting just two sacks a game.

The *49ers,* in the **NFC West,** seem destined to win for as long as they care to. Their biggest foe is inside their team, not outside it. Can they get motivated again? Count on it. If not, *Los Angeles* is ready. How many years in a row do we have to say this? The Rams are the NFC's second-best team. Unfortunately for them, they're also the NFC West's second-best team. In *New Orleans,* the Saints may be marching out. They never were as good as the 49ers, and now they're not as good as the Rams. Jim Mora may have taken them as far as they can go, and if Bobby Hebert continues to be a dissatisfied and underachieving quarterback, mediocrity might not be far behind. Jerry Glanville takes over in *Atlanta,* which is another sign—a bad one—that the Smith family is still running the Falcon show. This team had better get an offensive brain and some people to catch Chris Miller's passes, or it's going to be another endless autumn in Georgia.

Buffalo will win the **AFC East** in spite of itself. The Bills are the NFL's version of the Brat Pack, with trillionaire quarterback Jim Kelly the envy of his own locker room and defensive keystones Bruce Smith and Cornelius Bennett too often breaking away from team football to do their own things. But there's no one around to beat the Bills. The *Jets* will be a good team before long. Bruce Coslet is an excellent young coach, but the Jets' most important new addition might be Larry Beightol, who comes from San Diego to tutor a porous offensive line. If the line gives Johnny Hector some holes and Ken O'Brien some time, we're looking at Cincinnati East in a hurry with this team. *Miami* is always a threat with Dan Marino, of course, but the running game they tried so hard to establish last year with the brittle Sammie Smith never got going. Smith is just not a durable 16-game NFL back. And the Plan B-fortified defense isn't pressure-packed enough to create consistent havoc. *Indianapolis* is falling. This is a crucial year for coach Ron Meyer. He has a perenially dissatisfied superback in Eric Dickerson, who never knows on Tuesday how he'll feel on Wednesday. He also doesn't have a quarterback. The job clock ran out on *New England's* Raymond Berry in February and the reins were handed over to 63-year-old Rod Rust for a quick fix. The Patriots will still finish last, despite the return of linebacker Andre Tippett, who missed 1989 with a torn pectoral muscle. If owner Victor Kiam ran his shaver company the way he runs the Pats, millions of Americans would still be using straight razors. The man doesn't know what it takes to build a football team.

Despite the loss to the Jets of underappreciated offensive coordinator Coslet—"It's like losing my right arm," says Boomer Esiason—*Cincinnati* is the most talented team in the **AFC Central** and is mature enough to win the conference. The Bengals will get Ickey Woods back from the knee injury that forced him to miss almost all of 1989. Look for Sam Wyche to return to the close-to-the-vest running-oriented attack that had the Bengals roaring near the close of 1988. Bud Carson redesigned the coaching staff in *Cleveland*. He'll be happy to discover that Bernie Kosar won't miss the security blanket of dismissed offensive coordinator Marc Trestman. Kosar is an unusually mature guy who will do fine with Zeke Bratkowski as his teacher. The Browns will miss the Super Bowl again, though, because of an aging defense with only one great player: tackle Michael Dean Perry. The Steelers made *Pittsburgh* proud last season by winning the wild-card game in Houston and nearly winning a divisional playoff game in Denver. This is a decent team with a fine young secondary and offensive backfield. But the pass rush will do in the Steelers. They had only 31 sacks in '89. In *Houston*, new coach Jack Pardee will open up the offense, which should please Warren Moon. But the Oilers need a great linebacker and some corners. Isn't it about time they traded one of their talented backs—Allen Pinkett or Mike Rozier or Alonzo Highsmith or Lorenzo White—for some defense? Come on, make a deal!

The **AFC West**, annually, is the toughest division to predict. Why? Because there hasn't been a great team in the division since the Raiders started declining six or seven years ago. The Broncos have been in three recent Super Bowls, but they haven't been a great team. This year, the door is wide open for *Kansas City*. The Chiefs led the league with 559 rushes last year, which might seem like a silly stat. But think of what it means: The Chiefs were running the ball a lot—35 times a game—and hence were hanging on to the ball a lot. So they were keeping the defense off the field and limiting the opposition's possessions and opportunities to score. Monster back Christian

Okoye is healthy, and the defense, bolstered by bright young coordinator Bill Cowher, is rising. *Denver* must recover from the nightmare of Super Bowl XXIV, which won't be easy. Defensive coordinator Wade Phillips, who is capable of good patchwork, must adjust better and more innovatively against great offenses. It wouldn't hurt to have a pass rusher and some corners either. The Chargers should bring some life to *San Diego*, if only with the addition of new GM Bobby Beathard. It'll take a year or so, but Beathard will have this team on top of the division eventually. First coach Dan Henning is going to have to make a quarterback out of Billy Joe Tolliver, which isn't impossible. Tolliver is a red-headed Phil Simms of 10 years ago; he even has the same number. The *Raiders*—wherever they may be playing in the future—had better have a few good drafts. Art Shell can't do it on Raiderness and emotion alone. He might have to do it without Bo Jackson, who may opt for baseball soon. *Seattle* had a million problems, but the team will never be totally moribund as long as it plays in the Kingdome. Anyone could win four games a year there, it's so loud and intimidating. The Seahawks do have a promising quarterback, Kelly Stouffer, and an exciting young wide receiver, Brian Blades. But the lines are getting too old. It's time to rebuild.

So much for the regular season. What about the playoffs? In the NFC, the 49ers, Lions and Eagles should win their divisions, with the Rams beating the Packers in one wild-card game and the Eagles defeating the Vikings in the other. The 49ers should beat Los Angeles in a NFC Championship Game rematch.

In the AFC—what a crystal-ball job this is—Buffalo, Cincinnati and Kansas City look like division winners, with Cleveland finally beating Denver in one wild-card game and Kansas City beating the surprising Jets in the other. The Bengals should beat the Chiefs for the conference title.

The Super Bowl? It's threepeat time for the Niners, who continue to amaze the football world in Tampa by winning their third straight Super Bowl.

Arguments, please. There's plenty of time for them. ■

139

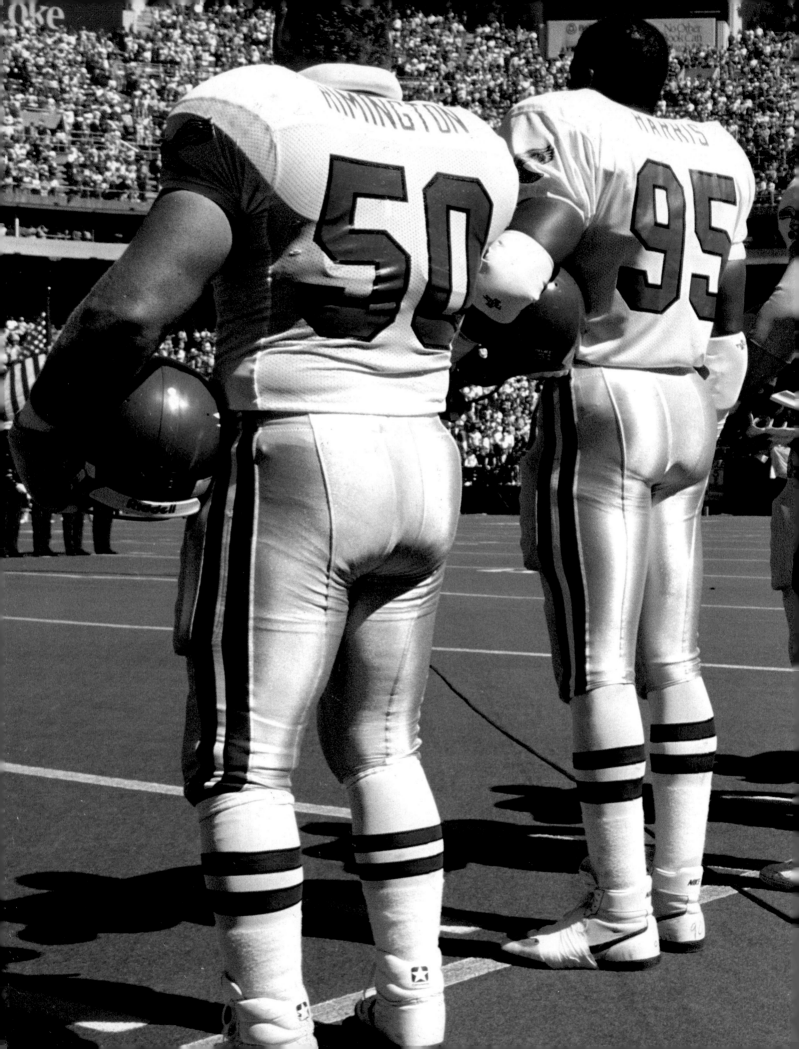

APPENDIX

Game Summaries

Week One

STANDINGS

AFC EAST	W	L	T	Pct	PF	PA
Buffalo	1	0	0	1.000	27	24
New England	1	0	0	1.000	27	24
Indianapolis	0	1	0	.000	24	30
Miami	0	1	0	.000	24	27
N.Y. Jets	0	1	0	.000	24	27

AFC CENTRAL	W	L	T	Pct	PF	PA
Cleveland	1	0	0	1.000	51	0
Cincinnati	0	1	0	.000	14	17
Houston	0	1	0	.000	7	38
Pittsburgh	0	1	0	.000	0	51

AFC WEST	W	L	T	Pct	PF	PA
Denver	1	0	0	1.000	34	20
L.A. Raiders	1	0	0	1.000	40	14
Kansas City	0	1	0	.000	20	34
San Diego	0	1	0	.000	14	40
Seattle	0	1	0	.000	7	31

NFC EAST	W	L	T	Pct	PF	PA
Philadelphia	1	0	0	1.000	31	7
Phoenix	1	0	0	1.000	16	13
N.Y. Giants	1	0	0	1.000	27	24
Dallas	0	1	0	.000	0	28
Washington	0	1	0	.000	24	27

NFC CENTRAL	W	L	T	Pct	PF	PA
Chicago	1	0	0	1.000	17	14
Minnesota	1	0	0	1.000	38	7
Tampa Bay	1	0	0	1.000	23	21
Detroit	0	1	0	.000	13	16
Green Bay	0	1	0	.000	21	23

NFC WEST	W	L	T	Pct	PF	PA
L.A. Rams	1	0	0	1.000	31	21
New Orleans	1	0	0	1.000	28	0
San Francisco	1	0	0	1.000	30	24
Atlanta	0	1	0	.000	21	31

RESULTS

Chicago 17, Cincinnati 14
Philadelphia 31, Seattle 7
Minnesota 38, Houston 7
San Francisco 30, Indianapolis 24
Phoenix 16, Detroit 13
Denver 34, Kansas City 20
L.A. Raiders 40, San Diego 14
Buffalo 27, Miami 24
New England 27, N.Y. Jets 24
Cleveland 51, Pittsburgh 0
New Orleans 28, Dallas 0
Tampa Bay 23, Green Bay 21
L.A. Rams 31, Atlanta 21
N.Y. Giants 27, Washington 24 (Monday night)

SUNDAY, SEPTEMBER 10

Chicago 17, Cincinnati 14—At Soldier Field. After facing early-game boos from the Chicago faithful, Bears quarterback Mike Tomczak redeemed himself by leading a 95-yard fourth-quarter TD drive, culminating in a 20-yard strike to tight end James Thornton that put Chicago in front with 4:54 remaining. Running back Neal Anderson ran for a career-high 146 yards on 21 carries, and tackle Dan Hampton had an outstanding day on defense with two deflected passes, a blocked field goal, two sacks and a key tackle of Bengal running back Ickey Woods in a critical fourth-and-inches situation.

Cincinnati	7	0	7	0	—	14
Chicago	0	7	3	7	—	17

Cin — Brooks 4 pass from Esiason (Gallery kick)
Chi — Tomczak 11 run (Butler Kick)
Cin — Woods 5 run (Gallery kick)
Chi — FG Butler 29
Chi — Thornton 20 pass from Tomczak (Butler kick)
A: 64,730 T: 3:13

Philadelphia 31, Seattle 7—At Veterans Stadium. The Eagles dominated the Seahawks from the opening kickoff as Philadelphia quarterback Randall Cunningham threw for two touchdowns and no interceptions, wide receiver Mike Quick grabbed six passes for 140 yards and the Eagle defense harried Seattle quarterback Dave Krieg into a 15-for-34 day.

Seattle	7	0	0	0	—	7
Philadelphia	7	10	7	7	—	31

Phi — Toney 1 run (Zendejas kick)
Sea — Largent 23 pass from Krieg (Johnson kick)
Phi — FG Zendejas 24
Phi — Carter 8 pass from Cunningham (Zendejas kick)
Phi — Quick 8 pass from Cunningham (Zendejas kick)
Phi — Everett 30 interception return (Zendejas kick)
A: 64,287 T: 3:17

Minnesota 38, Houston 7—At the Metrodome. Viking wide receiver Anthony Carter showed no signs of rust after missing the entire preseason as a holdout, grabbing seven passes for 123 yards and a touchdown. The Minnesota defense stifled the Oilers all day, sacking quarterback Warren Moon seven times, limiting him to 69 passing yards and holding Houston to just 104 offensive yards overall.

Houston	7	0	0	0	—	7
Minnesota	14	10	7	7	—	38

Hou — Highsmith 1 run (Zendejas kick)
Minn — Carter 32 pass from Wilson (Garcia kick)
Minn — Jordan 2 pass from Wilson (Garcia kick)
Minn — Fenney 1 run (Garcia kick)
Minn — FG Garcia 35
Minn — Fenney 3 run (Garcia kick)
Minn — Anderson 2 run (Garcia kick)
A: 54,015 T: 3:06

San Francisco 30, Indianapolis 24—At the Hoosier Dome. It was a game of firsts as the 49ers won their first game for new head coach George Seifert and Colt running back Eric Dickerson ran for 106 yards to become the first player to pass the 10,000-yard rushing mark in only 91 games. San Francisco's Roger Craig rushed for 131 yards on 24 carries, and wide receiver Jerry Rice caught six passes for 163 yards, including a key 58-yard touchdown toss from quarterback Joe Montana.

San Francisco	3	10	10	7	—	30
Indianapolis	3	7	0	14	—	24

S.F. — FG Cofer 38
Ind — FG Biasucci 31
S.F. — Craig 1 run (Cofer kick)
Ind — Brooks 22 pass from Chandler (Biasucci kick)
S.F. — FG Cofer 26
S.F. — Craig 4 run (Cofer kick)
S.F. — FG Cofer 31
Ind — Chandler 1 run (Biasucci kick)
S.F. — Rice 58 pass from Montana (Cofer kick)
Ind — Bentley recovered blocked punt in end zone (Biasucci kick)
A: 60,111 T:3:13

Phoenix 16, Detroit 13—At the Silverdome. The regular-season debut of the Lions' "Silver Stretch" run-and-shoot offense was a limited success, with recently signed first-round draft choice Barry Sanders rushing for 71 yards on nine carries in just more than a quarter of play. But in the end the outcome was determined by Cardinals quarterback Gary Hogeboom (21 of 35 passes for 264 yards) and kicker Al Del Greco, who booted the game-winning 33-yard field goal with 13 seconds remaining in the fourth quarter.

Phoenix	0	6	0	10	—	16
Detroit	3	0	7	3	—	13

7Det — FG Murray 30
Phoe — FG Del Greco 29
Phoe — FG Del Greco 23
Det — Sanders 3 run (Murray kick)
Phoe — Green 15 pass from Hogeboom (Del Greco kick)
Det — FG Murray 23
Phoe — FG Del Greco 33
A: 36,735 T:2:58

Denver 34, Kansas City 20—At Mile High Stadium. The Broncos, with 17 new roster players, scored 17 unanswered points in the first 8:30 of play and never looked back en route to a win over the Chiefs, who were competing with 18 new roster players. Twenty-four of Denver's points came as a result of Chiefs turnovers.

Kansas City	0	10	3	7	—	20
Denver	17	0	7	10	—	34

Den — FG Treadwell 41
Den — Braxton 34 interception return (Treadwell kick)
Den — Winder 2 run (Treadwell kick)
K.C. — FG Lowery 41
K.C. — Gamble 1 run (Lowery kick)
K.C. — FG Lowery 23
Den — Sewell 9 pass from Elway (Treadwell kick)
Den — FG Treadwell 29
K.C. — Carson 5 pass from DeBerg (Lowery kick)
Den — Robbins 18 interception return (Treadwell kick)
A: 74,284 T: 2:53

L.A. Raiders 40, San Diego 14—At Memorial Coliseum. The Raiders rebounded from a winless preseason with a thumping of the Chargers, but the victory was costly as Los Angeles wide receiver Tim Brown tore ligaments in his left knee—he would miss the entire season—and quarterback Jay Schroeder was knocked out of the game with a slightly separated collarbone. Backup QB Steve Beuerlein filled in well, completing 15 of 22 passes for 206 yards and two TDs. The debut of Charger QB Jim McMahon was less than spectacular: he completed only seven of 18 passes and was replaced early in the third quarter.

San Diego	7	0	7	0	—	14
Los Angeles	7	14	7	12	—	40

L.A. — Mueller 26 pass from Schroeder (Jaeger kick)
S.D. — Butts 50 run (Bahr kick)
L.A. — Fernandez 4 pass from Beuerlein (Jaeger kick)
L.A. — Allen 1 run (Jaeger kick)
L.A. — Gault 39 pass from Beuerlein (Jaeger kick)
S.D. — Butts 1 run (Bahr kick)
L.A. — FG Jaeger 22
L.A. — Safety, Floyd tackled in end zone
L.A. — Mueller 1 run (Jaeger kick)
A: 40,237 T: 3:03

Buffalo 27, Miami 24—At Joe Robbie Stadium. Bills quarterback Jim Kelly dived across the goal line as time expired to pull out a come-from-behind victory for Buffalo. Kelly, who had hit wide receiver Flip Johnson with a 26-yard TD pass to bring the Bills within four points with 2:50 to play, saw an opening up the middle after taking the snap in the shotgun formation.

Buffalo	3	0	10	14	—	27
Miami	0	10	7	7	—	24

Buff — FG Norwood 34
Mia — Stradford 1 run (Stoyanovich kick)
Mia — FG Stoyanovich 29
Buff — Kinnebrew 2 run (Norwood kick)
Mia — Logan 2 blocked punt return (Stoyanovich kick)
Buff — FG Norwood 37
Mia — Brown 8 pass from Marino (Stoyanovich kick)
Buff — Johnson 26 pass from Kelly (Norwood kick)
Buff — Kelly 2 run (Norwood kick)
A: 54,541 T: 3:19

New England 27, N.Y. Jets 24—At Giants Stadium. After completely dominating the Jets during the first half, the Patriots squandered a 21-point lead in the second half and needed a four-yard TD plunge by running back Reggie Dupard with 1:55 remaining to win the game. New York seemed to have the game won with 3:33 to play when the Pats failed to get a first down on fourth-and-one on the Jets four-yard line. But New England's defense forced New York to punt and Patriots QB Tony Eason (15 of 23 for 273 yards, 2 TDs) marched his team back into scoring position.

New England	7	14	0	6	—	27
New York	0	0	17	7	—	24

N.E. — Fryar 20 pass from Eason (Davis kick)
N.E. — Morgan 30 pass from Eason (Davis kick)
N.E. — Stephens 1 run (Davis kick)
N.Y. — Vick 1 pass from O'Brien (Leahy kick)
N.Y. — FG Leahy 40
N.Y. — Prokop 17 run (Leahy kick)
N.Y. — Townsell 48 pass from O'Brien (Leahy kick)
N.E. — Dupard 4 run (kick failed)
A: 64,541 T: 2:59

Cleveland 51, Pittsburgh 0—At Three Rivers Stadium. The Steelers suffered their worst loss in franchise history as the Browns held Pittsburgh to just five first downs and 53 yards overall, sacking Steeler QB Bubby Brister six times. Cleveland was greatly aided by Pittsburgh's eight turnovers, including three fumbles by first-round draft pick Tim Worley.

Cleveland	17	13	14	7	—	51
Pittsburgh	0	0	0	0	—	0

Cle — Matthews 3 fumble return (Bahr kick)
Cle — FG Bahr 27
Cle — Grayson 28 fumble return (Bahr kick)
Cle — FG Bahr 20
Cle — Manoa 3 run (Bahr kick)
Cle — FG Bahr 27
Cle — Manoa 2 run (Bahr kick)
Cle — Grayson 14 interception return (Bahr kick)
Cle — Oliphant 21 run (Bahr kick)
A: 57,928 T: 3:10

New Orleans 28, Dallas 0—At the Superdome. The Saints ruined the debut of Dallas coach Jimmy Johnson by shutting out the Cowboys for only the fourth time in Dallas franchise history. Using a conservative ball-control offense, New Orleans ate up the clock with first-half TD drives of 74 and 73 yards, sparked by the rushing of Dalton Hilliard (22 carries for 83 yards). Dallas QB Troy Aikman, making his first regular-season start, was held to 180 yards passing, and running back Herschel Walker gained only 10 yards on eight carries.

Dallas	0	0	0	0	—	0
New Orleans	7	14	0	7	—	28

N.O. — Hilliard 4 run (Andersen kick)
N.O. — Heyward 1 run (Andersen kick)
N.O. — Shepard 56 punt return (Andersen kick)
N.O. — Frazier 1 run (Andersen kick)
A: 66,977 T: 3:12

Tampa Bay 23, Green Bay 21—At Lambeau Field. Tampa Bay defensive back Mark Robinson made a key interception, his second of the game, on his own eight-yard line with 5:32 remaining to seal the victory for the Bucs. QB Vinny Testaverde had a near perfect afternoon for Tampa Bay, completing 22 of 27 passes for 205 yards, one TD and no inteceptions.

Tampa Bay	0	20	3	0	—	23
Green Bay	7	0	7	7	—	21

G.B. — Fullwood 3 run (Jacke kick)
T.B. — Tate 2 run (Igwebuike kick)
T.B. — Tate 1 run (Igwebuike kick)
T.B. — Howard 9 pass from Testaverde (kick failed)
G.B. — West 11 pass from Majkowski (Jacke kick)
T.B. — FG Igwebuike 52
G.B. — Bland recovery of fumble in end zone (Jacke kick)
A: 55,650 T: 2:47

L.A. Rams 31, Atlanta 21—At Fulton County Stadium. The Rams got strong performances from QB Jim Everett (14 for 25, 206 yards, one TD) and running back Greg Bell (26 carries for 128 yards) to overcome the pesky Falcons. The newly signed Deion Sanders, late of baseball's New York Yankees, returned his first NFL punt reception for a 68-yard TD to put Atlanta in front 7-0, but Everett answered by completing a 46-yard Hail Mary TD pass to Henry Ellard at the close of the first half.

Los Angeles	3	14	7	7	—	31
Atlanta	7	7	0	7	—	21

Atl — Sanders 68 punt return (McFadden kick)
L.A. — FG Lansford 23
L.A. — Bell 2 run (Lansford kick)
Atl — Dixon 53 pass from Miller (McFadden kick)
L.A. — Ellard 46 pass from Everett (Lansford kick)
L.A. — Everett 13 run (Lansford kick)
L.A. — Bell 8 run (Lansford kick)
Atl — Haynes 33 pass from Miller (McFadden kick)
A: 38,708 T: 2:57

MONDAY, SEPTEMBER 11

N.Y. Giants 27, Washington 24—At RFK Stadium. Giants kicker Raul Allegre booted a 32-yard field goal to tie the game with 2:17 remaining and a monster 52-yarder to win it as time expired. The Giants, led by the rejuvenated Ottis Anderson (93 yards on 23 carries), had to overcome an outstanding performance from Washington quarterback Mark Rypien, who completed 22 of 32 passes for 349 yards and two TDs.

N.Y. Giants	7	7	0	13	—	27
Washington	0	3	7	14	—	24

N.Y. — Turner 30 pass from Simms (Allegre kick)
N.Y. — Meggett 62 pass from Simms (Allegre kick)
Wash — FG Lohmiller 24
Wash — Sanders 48 pass from Rypien (Lohmiller kick)
N.Y. — Anderson 14 run (Allegre kick)
Wash — Monk 6 pass from Rypien (Lohmiller kick)
Wash — Coleman 24 interception return (Lohmiller kick)
N.Y. — FG Allegre 32
N.Y. — FG Allegre 52
A: 54,160 T: 3:03

STANDINGS

AFC EAST	W	L	T	Pct	PF	PA
Buffalo	1	1	0	.500	41	52
Miami	1	1	0	.500	48	37
New England	1	1	0	.500	37	48
Indianapolis	0	2	0	.000	41	61
N.Y. Jets	0	2	0	.000	48	65

AFC CENTRAL	W	L	T	Pct	PF	PA
Cleveland	2	0	0	1.000	89	24
Cincinnati	1	1	0	.500	55	27
Houston	1	1	0	.500	41	65
Pittsburgh	0	2	0	.000	10	92

AFC WEST	W	L	T	Pct	PF	PA
Denver	2	0	0	1.000	62	34
Kansas City	1	1	0	.500	44	53
L.A. Raiders	1	1	0	.500	59	38
San Diego	0	2	0	.000	41	74
Seattle	0	2	0	.000	31	65

NFC EAST	W	L	T	Pct	PF	PA
N.Y. Giants	2	0	0	1.000	51	38
Philadelphia	2	0	0	1.000	73	44
Phoenix	2	0	0	1.000	50	37
Dallas	0	2	0	.000	21	55
Washington	0	2	0	.000	61	69

NFC CENTRAL	W	L	T	Pct	PF	PA
Chicago	2	0	0	1.000	55	21
Green Bay	1	1	0	.500	56	57
Minnesota	1	1	0	.500	45	45
Tampa Bay	1	1	0	.500	39	41
Detroit	0	2	0	.000	27	40

NFC WEST	W	L	T	Pct	PF	PA
L.A. Rams	2	0	0	1.000	62	38
San Francisco	2	0	0	1.000	50	40
Atlanta	1	1	0	.500	48	52
New Orleans	1	1	0	.500	62	35

RESULTS

Philadelphia 42, Washington 37
L.A. Rams 31, Indianapolis 17
Chicago 38, Minnesota 7
Houston 34, San Diego 27
N.Y. Giants 24, Detroit 14
San Francisco 20, Tampa Bay 16
Cleveland 38, N.Y. Jets 24
Phoenix 34, Seattle 24
Green Bay 35, New Orleans 34
Miami 24, New England 10
Kansas City 24, L.A. Raiders 19
Cincinnati 41, Pittsburgh 10
Atlanta 27, Dallas 21
Denver 28, Buffalo 14 (Monday night)

SUNDAY, SEPTEMBER 17

Philadelphia 42, Washington 37—At RFK Stadium. The Eagles came back from a 20-point deficit behind quarterback Randall Cunningham, who completed 34 of 46 passes (12 to tight end Keith Jackson) for 447 yards and five TDs. The comeback seemed doomed when Redskins running back Gerald Riggs, who had 221 yards on the day, burst 56 yards up the sideline to give Washington the ball on the Philadelphia 22-yard line with 1:35 remaining and the Redskins in front by two. But three plays later Riggs fumbled the ball to Eagles linebacker Al Harris, who handed off to safety Wes Hopkins, who raced 77 yards to the Washington four. Cunningham concluded matters by tossing a four-yard lob to Jackson for the winning TD with 52 seconds left.

Philadelphia	7	7	7	21	—	42
Washington	20	10	0	7	—	37

Wash — Clark 80 pass from Rypien (kick failed)
Wash — Riggs 41 run (Lohmiller kick)
Wash — Byner 11 pass from Rypien (Lohmiller kick)
Phi — Jackson 17 pass from Cunningham (Zendejas kick)
Wash — Clark 5 pass from Rypien (Lohmiller kick)
Phi — Toney 3 run (Zendejas kick)
Wash — FG Lohmiller 25
Phi — Jackson 5 pass from Cunningham (Zendejas kick)
Phi — Carter 5 pass from Cunningham (Zendejas kick)
Wash — Monk 43 pass from Rypien (Lohmiller kick)
Phi — Quick 2 pass from Cunningham (Zendejas kick)
Phi — Jackson 4 pass from Cunningham (Zendejas kick)
A: 53,493 T: 3:25

L.A. Rams 31, Indianapolis 17—At Anaheim Stadium. QB Jim Everett (28 of 35 for 368 yards, including a team-record 14 completions in a row) and wide receiver Henry Ellard (12 catches for 230 yards) connected on three TD passes to power the Rams and more than compensate for the performance of Colts running back Eric Dickerson (116 yards on 21 carries), who was playing for the first time against the team that traded him in 1987.

Indianapolis	3	14	0	0	—	17
Los Angeles	10	7	7	7	—	31

L.A. — FG Lansford 40
Ind — FG Biasucci 19
L.A. — Ellard 29 pass from Everett (Lansford kick)
Ind — Verdin 82 pass from Chandler (Biasucci kick)
Ind — Dickerson 2 run (Biasucci kick)
L.A. — Ellard 17 pass from Everett (Lansford kick)
L.A. — Ellard 6 pass from Everett (Lansford kick)
L.A. — Bell 2 run (Lansford kick)
A: 63,995 T: 2:58

Chicago 38, Minnesota 7—At Soldier Field. The Bears exploded for four touchdowns in the fourth quarter, including two by RB Neal Anderson, who also scored in the first quarter on a pass from QB Mike Tomczak. The Chicago defense limited the Vikings to just 67 yards on the ground and intercepted Minnesota QB Wade Wilson four times.

Minnesota	0	7	0	0	—	7
Chicago	7	3	0	28	—	38

Chi — Anderson 24 pass from Tomczak (Butler kick)
Minn — Gustafson 4 pass from Wilson (Garcia kick)
Chi — FG Butler 40
Chi — Anderson 2 run (Butler kick)
Chi — Anderson 13 run (Butler kick)
Chi — Stinson 29 interception return (Butler kick)
Chi — Green 37 run (Butler kick)
A: 66,475 T: 3:17

Houston 34, San Diego 27—At Jack Murphy Stadium. A valiant effort by Charger QB Jim McMahon was not enough to overcome his team's mistakes as the Oilers converted four San Diego turnovers into 24 points. It appeared that McMahon, who completed 27 of 45 passes for a career-high 389 yards, would have a final crack at a comeback when the Chargers recovered an onside kick with less than a minute left. But the officials ruled that the ball had been touched by the Chargers before it had traveled the requisite 10 yards.

Houston	3	17	14	0	—	34
San Diego	7	7	0	13	—	27

Hou — FG Zendejas 24
S.D. — A. Miller 63 pass from McMahon (Bahr kick)
S.D. — Butts 1 run (Bahr kick)
Hou — Givins 14 pass from Moon (Zendejas kick)
Hou — Moon 1 run (Zendejas kick)
Hou — FG Zendejas 32
Hou — Hill 5 pass from Moon (Zendejas kick)
Hou — Highsmith 16 run (Zendejas kick)
S.D. — Butts 1 run (pass failed)
S.D. — A. Miller 10 pass from McMahon (Bahr kick)
A: 42,013 T: 3:38

N.Y. Giants 24, Detroit 14—At Giants Stadium. After a listless first half, the Giants caught fire, scoring 21 second-half points and forcing the Lions into four fourth-quarter turnovers. QB Phil Simms (20 of 26 for 218 yards and two TDs) and RB Ottis Anderson (85 yards and one TD) led the comeback. Detroit got fine performances from QB Bob Gagliano (21 of 31 for 344 yards) and wide receiver Richard Johnson (nine catches for 172 yards), neither of whom played organized football last season.

Detroit	0	7	7	0	—	14
New York	3	0	14	7	—	24

N.Y. — FG Allegre 49
Det — Johnson 71 pass from Gagliano (Murray kick)
Det — Sanders 4 run (Murray kick)
N.Y. — Anderson 11 run (Allegre kick)
N.Y. — Turner 9 pass from Simms (Allegre kick)
N.Y. — Bavaro 24 pass from Simms (Allegre kick)
A: 76,021 T: 2:57

San Francisco 20, Tampa Bay 16—At Tampa Stadium. The 49ers needed a four-yard TD run by quarterback Joe Montana with 40 seconds remaining to pull out the victory. The Bucs, who held San Francisco to just 63 yards rushing, had gone ahead 16-13 with 3:25 left on a TD pass from Vinny Testaverde to Mark Carrier, but Montana, who hit 25 of 39 passes for 266 yards, brought his team back with a 70-yard game-winning drive.

San Francisco	0	6	0	14	—	20
Tampa Bay	3	0	6	7	—	16

T.B. — FG Igwebuike 23
S.F. — FG Cofer 47
S.F. — FG Cofer 32
T.B. — FG Igwebuike 44
T.B. — FG Igwebuike 37
S.F. — Rice 2 pass from Montana (Cofer kick)
T.B. — Carrier 18 pass from Testaverde (Igwebuike kick)
S.F. — Montana 4 run (Cofer kick)
A: 64,087 T: 3:25

Cleveland 38, N.Y. Jets 24—At Cleveland Stadium. The Browns overcame a first half marked by mistakes, blocked passes and a sluggish offense, scoring on three of their first four second-half possessions to subdue the stubborn Jets. Cleveland quarterback Bernie Kosar threw for 196 yards and three TDs while New York QB Ken O'Brien saw his fine day (24 of 43 passes for 270 yards) ruined by four interceptions.

New York	0	7	10	7	—	24
Cleveland	0	14	14	10	—	38

N.Y. — Vick 39 run (Leahy kick)
Cle — Slaughter 35 pass from Kosar (Bahr kick)
Cle — Gash 36 interception return (Bahr kick)
N.Y. — Townsell 49 pass from O'Brien (Leahy kick)
Cle — Manoa 6 pass from Kosar (Bahr kick)
N.Y. — FG Leahy 36
Cle — Jones 9 run (Bahr kick)
N.Y. — McNeil 1 run (Leahy kick)
Cle — Newsome 4 pass from Kosar (Bahr kick)
Cle — FG Bahr 21
A: 73,516 T: 3:35

Phoenix 34, Seattle 24—At the Kingdome. The renaissance of Gary Hogeboom continued as the Phoenix quarterback had another great day, completing 18 of 24 passes for 298 yards and four touchdowns. Three of the TD tosses went to wide receiver Roy Green, who grabbed eight passes for 166 yards on the afternoon.

Phoenix	13	0	7	14	—	34
Seattle	0	7	7	10	—	24

Phoe — Green 51 pass from Hogeboom (kick failed)
Phoe — Jordan 1 run (Del Greco kick)
Sea — Skansi 3 pass from Krieg (Johnson kick)
Phoe — Smith 25 pass from Hogeboom (Del Greco kick)
Sea — Skansi 17 pass from Krieg (Johnson kick)
Phoe — Green 6 pass from Hogeboom (Del Greco kick)
Sea — FG Johnson 39
Phoe — Green 59 pass from Hogeboom (Del Greco kick)
Sea — Blades 5 pass from Krieg (Johnson kick)
A: 60,444 T: 3:12

Green Bay 35, New Orleans 34—At Lambeau Field. The Packers staked the Saints to a 21-point lead, then stormed back to win behind brilliant performances by unsung quarterback Don Majkowski, who threw for three TDs and 354 yards, and running back Brent Fullwood, who ran for two TDs and 125 yards. Majkowski, who connected on 25 of 32 passes, including a team-record 18 in a row in the second half, hit Sterling Sharpe for the game-winner with 1:26 left.

New Orleans	14	10	0	10	—	34
Green Bay	0	7	14	14	—	35

N.O. — Hill 32 pass from Hebert (Andersen kick)
N.O. — Hilliard 3 run (Andersen kick)
N.O. — Brenner 1 pass from Hebert (Andersen kick)
G.B. — Fullwood 1 run (Jacke kick)
N.O. — FG Andersen 38
G.B. — Fullwood 4 run (Jacke kick)
G.B. — West 3 pass from Majkowski (Jacke kick)
N.O. — Hill 24 pass from Hebert (Andersen kick)
G.B. — West 17 pass from Majkowski (Jacke kick)
N.O. — FG Andersen 32
G.B. — Sharpe 3 pass from Majkowski (Jacke kick)
A: 55,809 T: 3:06

Miami 24, New England 10—At Sullivan Stadium. The Dolphins scored 24 unanswered points in the first half in an easy victory over the Patriots. For the 14th consecutive game, the Miami offensive line did not allow a sack against quarterback Dan Marino, who threw three TD passes to give him 200 for his career in just his 89th game, the fastest any quarterback has ever reached that mark. Patriots wide receiver Stanley Morgan caught six passes for 88 yards to become the seventh player in NFL history to gain 10,000 yards receiving.

Miami	17	7	0	0	—	24
New England	0	0	3	7	—	10

Mia — Clayton 15 pass from Marino (Stoyanovich kick)
Mia — Jensen 16 pass from Marino (Stoyanovich kick)
Mia — FG Stoyanovich 31
Mia — Jensen 10 pass from Marino (Stoyanovich kick)
N.E. — FG Davis 28
N.E. — Dykes 6 pass from Eason (Davis kick)
A: 57,043 T: 2:55

Kansas City 24, L.A. Raiders 19—At Arrowhead Stadium. The Chiefs defense held Los Angeles to just three second-half points, and Kansas City running back Christian Okoye plunged across from the one-yard line to score the winning touchdown in the fourth quarter. The stars of the game were Okoye, who carried 27 times for 95 yards, and rookie linebacker and first-round draft choice Derrick Thomas, who registered 2½ sacks.

Los Angeles	6	10	3	0	—	19
Kansas City	7	10	0	7	—	24

L.A. — Fernandez 25 pass from Schroeder (kick failed)
K.C. — Dressel 49 pass from DeBerg (Lowery kick)
L.A. — Junkin 3 pass from Schroeder (Jaeger kick)
K.C. — FG Lowery 47
L.A. — FG Jaeger 39
K.C. — Okoye 8 run (Lowery kick)
L.A. — FG Jaeger 40
K.C. — Okoye 1 run (Lowery kick)
A: 71,741 T: 3:10

Cincinnati 41, Pittsburgh 10—At Riverfront Stadium. The once-mighty Steelers continued to struggle as division-rival Cincinnati rolled up 520 yards in total offense, sacked Pittsburgh quarterback Bubby Brister six times and thoroughly dominated the game. Bengal QB Boomer Esiason completed 16 of 27 passes for 328 yards, and James Brooks ran for 113 yards on 20 carries.

Pittsburgh	3	0	7	0	—	10
Cincinnati	3	17	7	14	—	41

Cin — FG Gallery 26
Pitt — FG Anderson 38
Cin — Brown 27 pass from Esiason (Gallery kick)
Cin — FG Gallery 47
Cin — Woods 1 run (Gallery kick)
Pitt — Hill 7 pass from Brister (Anderson kick)
Cin — Jennings 1 run (Gallery kick)
Cin — Brooks 2 run (Gallery kick)
Cin — Jennings 43 pass from Esiason (Gallery kick)
A: 53,885 T: 3:19

Atlanta 27, Dallas 21—At Fulton County Stadium. In the first half, the Cowboys seemed to have it all together, rolling up 263 yards and an 11-point lead, with Herschel Walker (85 yards on 23 carries for the day) dominating on the ground and quarterback Troy Aikman connecting through the air. But the second half was a different story as Falcon QB Chris Miller, who completed 21 of 29 passes for 255 yards, brought his team back with 17 unanswered points to pull out the victory.

Dallas	14	7	0	0	—	21
Atlanta	7	3	10	7	—	27

Dall — Irvin 65 pass from Aikman (Ruzek kick)
Atl — Butler 29 fumble return (McFadden kick)
Dall — Walker 4 run (Ruzek kick)
Atl — FG McFadden 28
Dall — Walker 20 run (Ruzek kick)
Atl — FG McFadden 38
Atl — Flowers 1 run (McFadden kick)
Atl — Settle 4 run (McFadden kick)
A: 55,825 T: 3:04

MONDAY, SEPTEMBER 18

Denver 28, Buffalo 14—At Rich Stadium. The Bills' attempt to stage another last-quarter rally was thwarted by the heroics of Bronco quarterback John Elway, who scrambled for 31 yards to keep a Denver drive going late in the fourth quarter. One play later, rookie running back Bobby Humphrey (76 yards on 10 carries) dashed across from the five to put the game out of reach. The victory spoiled a fine performance by Bills wide receiver Andre Reed, who grabbed 13 passes for 157 yards.

Denver	5	13	3	7	—	28
Buffalo	0	0	7	7	—	14

Den — Safety, Mueller tackled in end zone
Den — FG Treadwell 22
Den — FG Treadwell 33
Den — Johnson 9 pass from Elway (Treadwell kick)
Den — FG Treadwell 46
Den — FG Treadwell 24
Buff — Kinnebrew 1 run (Norwood kick)
Buff — Harmon 20 pass from Kelly (Norwood kick)
Den — Humphrey 5 run (Treadwell kick)
A: 78,176 T: 3:35

Week Three

STANDINGS

AFC EAST	W	L	T	Pct	PF	PA
Buffalo	2	1	0	.667	88	93
Indianapolis	1	2	0	.333	54	70
Miami	1	2	0	.333	81	77
New England	1	2	0	.333	40	72
N.Y. Jets	1	2	0	.333	88	98

AFC CENTRAL	W	L	T	Pct	PF	PA
Cincinnati	2	1	0	.667	76	41
Cleveland	2	1	0	.667	103	45
Houston	1	2	0	.333	82	112
Pittsburgh	1	2	0	.333	37	106

AFC WEST	W	L	T	Pct	PF	PA
Denver	3	0	0	1.000	93	55
Kansas City	1	2	0	.333	50	74
L.A. Raiders	1	2	0	.333	80	69
San Diego	1	2	0	.333	62	80
Seattle	1	2	0	.333	55	68

NFC EAST	W	L	T	Pct	PF	PA
N.Y. Giants	3	0	0	1.000	86	45
Philadelphia	2	1	0	.667	101	82
Phoenix	2	1	0	.667	57	72
Washington	1	2	0	.333	91	76
Dallas	0	3	0	.000	28	85

NFC CENTRAL	W	L	T	Pct	PF	PA
Chicago	3	0	0	1.000	102	48
Tampa Bay	2	1	0	.667	59	51
Green Bay	1	2	0	.333	94	98
Minnesota	1	2	0	.333	59	72
Detroit	0	3	0	.000	54	87

NFC WEST	W	L	T	Pct	PF	PA
L.A. Rams	3	0	0	1.000	103	76
San Francisco	3	0	0	1.000	88	68
Atlanta	1	2	0	.333	57	65
New Orleans	1	2	0	.333	72	55

RESULTS

Buffalo 47, Houston 41, OT
San Francisco 38, Philadelphia 28
Tampa Bay 20, New Orleans 10
N.Y. Giants 35, Phoenix 7
Pittsburgh 27, Minnesota 14
Washington 30, Dallas 7
N.Y. Jets 40, Miami 33
San Diego 21, Kansas City 6
L.A. Rams 41, Green Bay 38
Chicago 47, Detroit 27
Denver 31, L.A. Raiders 21
Seattle 24, New England 3
Indianapolis 13, Atlanta 9
Cincinnati 21, Cleveland 14 (Monday night)

SUNDAY, SEPTEMBER 24

Buffalo 47, Houston 41—At the Astrodome. It took five touchdown passes from Bills quarterback Jim Kelly to subdue the stubborn Oilers in a game that saw a combined 701 yards passing from Kelly (17 of 29 passes for 363 yards, 290 in the second half) and Houston quarterback Warren Moon (28 of 42 for 338 yards). After tying the game on a 52-yard field goal by kicker Tony Zendejas with :03 remaining in regulation, the Oilers appeared to have the game won on their first drive in overtime, but Zendejas missed a 37-yarder to give the Bills new life. Kelly then led his team on a 79-yard drive, capped by a 28-yard TD pass to wide receiver Andre Reed for the win.

Buffalo	10	10	7	14	6	—	47OT
Houston	7	3	14	17	0	—	41

Buff — FG Norwood 43
Hou — Moon 1 run (Zendejas kick)
Buff — Thomas 6 pass from Kelly (Norwood kick)
Buff — FG Norwood 26
Hou — FG Zendejas 26
Buff — Kelso 76 blocked field goal return (Norwood kick)
Buff — Beebe 63 pass from Kelly (Norwood kick)
Hou — Highsmith 4 run (Zendejas kick)
Hou — Dishman 7 blocked punt return (Zendejas kick)
Buff — Reed 78 pass from Kelly (Norwood kick)
Hou — Givins 26 pass from Moon (Zendejas kick)
Hou — White 1 run (Zendejas kick)
Buff — Thomas 26 pass from Kelly (Norwood kick)
Hou — FG Zendejas 52
Buff — Reed 28 pass from Kelly
A: 57,278 T: 3:57

San Francisco 38, Philadelphia 28—At Veterans Stadium. Quarterback Joe Montana had one of the greatest days in his illustrious career, completing 25 of 34 passes for 428 yards and five touchdowns to lead the 49ers back from an 11-point fourth-quarter deficit. Montana had a better than average day in the fourth quarter alone, completing 11 of 12 passes for 227 yards and four TDs. Jerry Rice was Montana's favorite target, grabbing six passes for 164 yards and two TDs.

San Francisco	7	3	0	28	—	38
Philadelphia	9	3	6	10	—	28

S.F. — Rice 68 pass from Montana (Cofer kick)
Phi — Sherman 2 run (Zendejas kick)
Phi — Safety, Montana tackled in end zone by Harris
Phi — FG Zendejas 35
S.F. — FG Cofer 32
Phi — FG Zendejas 25
Phi — FG Zendejas 44
Phi — FG Zendejas 20
S.F. — Taylor 70 pass from Montana (Cofer kick)
Phi — Giles 3 pass from Cunningham (Zendejas kick)
S.F. — Rathman 8 pass from Montana (Cofer kick)
S.F. — Jones 25 pass from Montana (Cofer kick)
S.F. — Rice 33 pass from Montana (Cofer kick)
A: 66,042 T: 3:20

Tampa Bay 20, New Orleans 10—At Tampa Stadium. The Bucs continued to surprise, limiting the Saints to a touchdown by running back Dalton Hilliard on the opening drive and a field goal by Morten Andersen in the second quarter. Both New Orleans QBs, starter Bobby Hebert and backup John Fourcade, were knocked out of the game, with Hebert forced to return to action with one tooth missing and another cracked after Fourcade went down with a sprained ankle and knee.

New Orleans	7	3	0	0	—	10
Tampa Bay	0	10	7	3	—	20

N.O. — Hilliard 1 run (Andersen kick)
T.B. — FG Igwebuike 34
T.B. — Hall 11 pass from Testaverde (Igwebuike kick)
N.O. — FG Andersen 33
T.B. — Tate 5 run (Igwebuike kick)
T.B. — FG Igwebuike 37
A: 44,053 T: 3:15

N.Y. Giants 35, Phoenix 7—At Giants Stadium. New York's defense rose up against the Cardinals, limiting them to 65 yards rushing and intercepting quarterback Gary Hogeboom four times. The 31-year old Ottis Anderson gained 98 yards on 21 carries for the Giants and Raul Allegre converted four of five field goal attempts.

Phoenix	0	0	0	7	—	7
New York	14	6	5	10	—	35

N.Y. — Baker 39 pass from Simms (Allegre kick)
N.Y. — Kinard 58 interception return (Allegre kick)
N.Y. — FG Allegre 22
N.Y. — FG Allegre 38
N.Y. — FG Allegre 32
N.Y. — Safety, Hogeboom tackled in end zone by Reasons
N.Y. — Anderson 36 run (Allegre kick)
N.Y. — FG Allegre 32
Phoe — Smith 21 pass from Hogeboom (Del Greco kick)
A: 75,742 T: 3:00

Pittsburgh 27, Minnesota 14—At Three Rivers Stadium. The Steelers rebounded from disastrous defeats in their first two games to upset the heavily favored Vikings. After yielding 520 yards and 41 points to Cincinnati the previous week, Pittsburgh limited Minnesota to just 258 yards and sacked the Viking quarterbacks five times.

Minnesota	7	7	0	0	—	14
Pittsburgh	7	14	0	6	—	27

Pitt — Mularkey 15 pass from Brister (G.Anderson kick)
Minn — Wilson 1 run (Garcia kick)
Pitt — Worley 8 run (Anderson kick)
Minn — Thomas 27 fumble return (Garcia kick)
Pitt — Hoge 2 run (Anderson kick)
Pitt — FG Anderson 38
Pitt — FG Anderson 44
A: 50,744 T: 3:02

Washington 30, Dallas 7—At Texas Stadium. The hapless Cowboys continued their slide, running their record to 0-3. With Washington's Gerald Riggs sidelined by a bruised chest in the second half, the rushing duties fell to Jamie Morris, who gained 100 yards on 26 carries. Dallas rookie quarterback Troy Aikman had a forgettable day, completing only six of 21 passes for 83 yards and two interceptions before being replaced by fellow rookie Steve Walsh, who also had two passes picked off.

Washington	14	3	3	10	—	30
Dallas	7	0	0	0	—	7

Wash — Walton 29 interception return (Lohmiller kick)
Dall — Jeffcoat 77 fumble return (Ruzek kick)
Wash — Byner 12 run (Lohmiller kick)
Wash — FG Lohmiller 26
Wash — FG Lohmiller 37
Wash — Morris 12 run (Lohmiller kick)
Wash — FG Lohmiller 33
A: 53,200 T: 3:17

N.Y. Jets 40, Miami 33—At Joe Robbie Stadium. Their previous six meetings had produced an average of 70 points per game, so it was no surprise when the season's first contest between the Jets and the Dolphins produced more offensive fireworks. Miami quarterback Dan Marino and New York's Ken O'Brien engaged in yet another aerial duel, with Marino completing 33 of 55 attempts for 427 yards and three TDs and O'Brien connecting on 27 of 37 for 329 yards and three TDs, including 10 completions to wide receiver Al Toon.

New York	3	9	7	21	—	40
Miami	7	13	10	3	—	33

N.Y. — FG Leahy 32
Mia — Edmunds 8 pass from Marino (Stoyanovich kick)
Mia — Edmunds 19 pass from Jensen (kick failed)
N.Y. — Radachowsky 78 blocked field goal return (Leahy kick)
N.Y. — Safety, punt snapped out of end zone
Mia — Banks 43 pass from Marino (Stoyanovich kick)
Mia — FG Stoyanovich 21
N.Y. — Toon 37 pass from O'Brien (Leahy kick)
Mia — Clayton 14 pass from Marino (Stoyanovich kick)
N.Y. — Hector 23 pass from O'Brien (Leahy kick)
Mia — FG Stoyanovich 20
N.Y. — Hector 1 run (Leahy kick)
N.Y. — Vick 11 pass from O'Brien (Leahy kick)
A: 65,908 T: 3:19

San Diego 21, Kansas City 6—At Jack Murphy Stadium. The Chargers stifled the Chiefs and quarterback Steve DeBerg, sacking him three times and picking off five of his passes. On offense, San Diego ate up the clock with a ground game sparked by the running of Rod Bernstine, who had 73 yards on five carries, and Marion Butts, who had 62 on 15.

Kansas City	3	3	0	0	—	6
San Diego	7	0	7	7	—	21

S.D. — Spencer 9 run (Bahr kick)
K.C. — FG Lowery 23
K.C. — FG Lowery 31
S.D. — Bernstine 1 pass from McMahon (Bahr kick)
S.D. — Bernstine 32 run (Bahr kick)
A: 40,128 T: 2:46

L.A. Rams 41, Green Bay 38—At Anaheim Stadium. Running back Greg Bell had a career-high 221 yards to power the Rams, who led by 31 points at the half but just barely avoided being overtaken by the suddenly dangerous Packers. Green Bay quarterback Don Majkowski completed 25 of 43 passes for 335 yards, but was undone by three interceptions and a key fourth-quarter fumble by Brent Fullwood in the Rams' end zone.

Green Bay	0	7	21	10	—	38
Los Angeles	10	28	0	3	—	41

L.A. — FG Lansford 39
L.A. — Bell 1 run (Lansford kick)
G.B. — Majkowski 8 run (Jacke kick)
L.A. — McGee 4 pass from Everett (Lansford kick)
L.A. — Newsome 81 interception return (Lansford kick)
L.A. — Bell 45 run (Lansford kick)
L.A. — Johnson 4 pass from Everett (Lansford kick)
G.B. — Sharpe 18 pass from Majkowski (Jacke kick)
G.B. — Fullwood 11 run (Jacke kick)
G.B. — West 1 pass from Majkowski (Jacke kick)
G.B. — FG Jacke 43
L.A. — FG Lansford 45
G.B. — Fullwood 1 run (Jacke kick)
A: 57,701 T: 3:28

Chicago 47, Detroit 27—At the Silverdome. Bears quarterback Mike Tomczak completed four passes of more than 40 yards en route to a career-high 302-yard day, while running back Neal Anderson added 116 yards on the ground, including a 53-yard touchdown run in the third quarter. Rookie sensation Barry Sanders continued to be the one bright spot for the 0-3 Lions, rushing for 126 yards on 18 carries.

Chicago	10	10	13	14	—	47
Detroit	0	13	7	7	—	27

Chi — FG Butler 21
Chi — Muster 6 run (Butler kick)
Det — Sanders 3 run (Murray kick)
Chi — McKinnon 40 pass from Tomczak (Butler kick)
Det — FG Murray 40
Chi — FG Butler 22
Det — FG Murray 48
Chi — Anderson 53 run (Butler kick)
Det — Gagliano 1 run (Murray kick)
Chi — FG Butler 25
Chi — FG Butler 32
Chi — Muster 3 pass from Tomczak (Butler kick)
Chi — Harbaugh 1 run (Butler kick)
Det — Gagliano 1 run (Murray kick)
A: 71,418 T: 3:05

Denver 31, L.A. Raiders 21—At Mile High Stadium. Trailing 28-0 at the half, the Raiders almost closed the gap in the fourth quarter, but their sixth turnover of the game, with 3:23 left, put the Broncos in position for the clinching field goal. L.A.'s Jay Schroeder completed 15 of 28 passes for 290 yards, but his three interceptions and three fumbles were costly.

Los Angeles	0	0	7	14	—	21
Denver	21	7	0	3	—	31

Den — Elway 29 run (Treadwell kick)
Den — Alexander 1 run (Treadwell kick)
Den — Jackson 46 pass from Elway (Treadwell kick)
Den — Jackson 11 pass from Elway (Treadwell kick)
L.A. — Washington 22 interception return (Jaeger kick)
L.A. — Fernandez 75 pass from Schroeder (Jaeger kick)
L.A. — King 15 fumble return (Jaeger kick)
Den — FG Treadwell 38
A: 75,754 T: 3:11

Seattle 24, New England 3—At Sullivan Stadium. Seahawk quarterback Dave Krieg threw three touchdown passes in the second quarter, running backs Curt Warner and John L. Williams combined for 129 yards on the ground and Seattle's defense held the Patriots to just 219 yards in total offense in an easy victory.

Seattle	0	21	3	0	—	24
New England	3	0	0	0	—	3

N.E. — FG Davis 35
Sea — Clark 27 pass from Krieg (Johnson kick)
Sea — Skansi 19 pass from Krieg (Johnson kick)
Sea — Williams 10 pass from Krieg (Johnson kick)
Sea — FG Johnson 23
A: 48,025 T: 2:53

Indianapolis 13, Atlanta 9—At the Hoosier Dome. The Colts, trailing 9-0 in the third quarter, shut down the Falcon offense and produced just enough firepower of their own to pull out the victory. Both starting quarterbacks were knocked out of the game, Atlanta's Chris Miller with bruised ribs and Indianapolis's Chris Chandler with torn ligaments in his left knee. The key play was made by Colt defensive end Ezra Johnson, who sacked Miller in the third quarter, forcing the fumble that led to Indianapolis's lone touchdown of the day.

Atlanta	3	3	3	0	—	9
Indianapolis	0	0	6	7	—	13

Atl — FG McFadden 19
Atl — FG McFadden 34
Atl — FG McFadden 27
Ind — FG Biasucci 25
Ind — FG Biasucci 29
Ind — Trudeau 1 run (Biasucci kick)
A: 57,816 T: 3:02

MONDAY, SEPTEMBER 25

Cincinnati 21, Cleveland 14—At Riverfront Stadium. The Bengals stopped the Browns twice inside their own 10-yard line in the fourth quarter to hang on for the victory over their cross-state rival. Cincinnati quarterback Boomer Esiason threw three touchdowns out of the Bengals' no-huddle offense, and rookie Eric Ball ran for 78 yards on 18 carries.

Cleveland	0	14	0	0	—	14
Cincinnati	0	14	7	0	—	21

Cin — Holman 8 pass from Esiason (Gallery kick)
Cle — Metcalf 5 pass from Kosar (Bahr kick)
Cin — Holman 16 pass from Esiason (Gallery kick)
Cle — Manoa 6 pass from Kosar (Bahr kick)
Cin — Brooks 19 pass from Esiason (Gallery kick)
A: 55,996 T: 3:10

STANDINGS

AFC EAST	W	L	T	Pct	PF	PA
Buffalo	3	1	0	.750	119	103
Indianapolis	2	2	0	.500	71	80
Miami	1	3	0	.250	88	116
New England	1	3	0	.250	50	103
N.Y. Jets	1	3	0	.250	98	115

AFC CENTRAL	W	L	T	Pct	PF	PA
Cincinnati	3	1	0	.750	97	58
Cleveland	3	1	0	.750	119	58
Houston	2	2	0	.500	121	119
Pittsburgh	2	2	0	.500	60	109

AFC WEST	W	L	T	Pct	PF	PA
Denver	3	1	0	.750	106	71
San Diego	2	2	0	.500	86	93
Seattle	2	2	0	.500	79	88
Kansas City	1	3	0	.250	67	95
L.A. Raiders	1	3	0	.250	100	93

NFC EAST	W	L	T	Pct	PF	PA
N.Y. Giants	4	0	0	1.000	116	58
Philadelphia	2	2	0	.500	114	109
Phoenix	2	2	0	.500	70	96
Washington	2	2	0	.500	107	90
Dallas	0	4	0	.000	41	115

NFC CENTRAL	W	L	T	Pct	PF	PA
Chicago	4	0	0	1.000	129	61
Green Bay	2	2	0	.500	117	119
Minnesota	2	2	0	.500	76	75
Tampa Bay	2	2	0	.500	62	68
Detroit	0	4	0	.000	57	110

NFC WEST	W	L	T	Pct	PF	PA
L.A. Rams	4	0	0	1.000	116	88
San Francisco	3	1	0	.750	100	81
Atlanta	1	3	0	.250	78	88
New Orleans	1	3	0	.250	86	72

RESULTS

Cleveland 16, Denver 13
L.A. Rams 13, San Francisco 12
N.Y. Giants 30, Dallas 13
Washington 16, New Orleans 14
Cincinnati 21, Kansas City 17
Indianapolis 17, N.Y. Jets 10
Pittsburgh 23, Detroit 3
Houston 39, Miami 7
Minnesota 17, Tampa Bay 3
Seattle 24, L.A. Raiders 20
Buffalo 31, New England 10
San Diego 24, Phoenix 13
Green Bay 23, Atlanta 21
Chicago 27, Philadelphia 13 (Monday night)

SUNDAY, OCTOBER 1

Cleveland 16, Denver 13—At Cleveland Stadium. After Cleveland fans in the east end zone, known as the "Dawg Pound," pelted the Broncos and the officials with batteries, dog biscuits and eggs, referee Tom Dooley decided to switch end zones for the final quarter, arousing the ire of Denver coach Dan Reeves, whose team was forced to play the final 12:31 against the wind. The defensive contest, decided on a 48-yard field goal by Matt Bahr (he claimed the wind was no factor) with no time left, seemed to be in Denver's grasp when the Broncos drove to the Cleveland eight-yard line with 1:49 left and the game tied at 13. But running back Sammy Winder fumbled the ball away and Browns quarterback Bernie Kosar led his team into position for the game-winning field goal.

Denver	0	3	3	7	—	13
Cleveland	7	3	3	3	—	16

Cle — Slaughter 9 pass from Kosar (Bahr kick)
Den — FG Treadwell 21
Cle — FG Bahr 36
Cle — FG Bahr 48
Den — FG Treadwell 26
Den — Johnson 7 pass from Elway (Treadwell kick)
Cle — FG Bahr 48
A: 78,637 T: 3:13

L.A. Rams 13, San Francisco 12—At Candlestick Park. Ram kicker Mike Lansford booted a 26-yard field goal with two seconds left to give Los Angeles the win in a hard-fought defensive contest. The single turnover of the game, a fumble by 49er running back Tom Rathman on the L.A. 20-yard line late in the fourth quarter, proved decisive when Ram quarterback Jim Everett drove his team 72 yards on nine plays to get into field-goal range for the winning kick. The key play was a 31-yard completion to tight end Pete Holohan.

Los Angeles	3	7	0	3	—	13
San Francisco	6	3	0	3	—	12

S.F. — FG Cofer 26
L.A. — FG Lansford 40
S.F. — FG Cofer 32
L.A. — Anderson 65 pass from Everett (Lansford kick)
S.F. — FG Cofer 41
S.F. — FG Cofer 17
L.A. — FG Lansford 26
A: 64,250 T: 3:00

N.Y. Giants 30, Dallas 13—At Texas Stadium. The Giants (4-0) and Cowboys (0-4) continued in opposite directions in the NFC East as New York held Dallas to a single fourth-quarter touchdown. More disturbing than the loss of the game for the Cowboys was the loss of rookie quarterback Troy Aikman, who fractured his left index finger, an injury that would sideline him for five weeks. Fellow rookie Steve Walsh was effective in relief, completing 13 of 24 passes for 190 yards, much of it on short passes to Herschel Walker, who picked up 85 yards on nine catches.

New York	3	17	7	3	—	30
Dallas	0	6	0	7	—	13

N.Y. — FG Allegre 37
Dall — FG Ruzek 19
N.Y. — Anderson 1 run (Allegre kick)
Dall — FG Ruzek 33
N.Y. — Meggett 33 pass from Simms (Allegre kick)
N.Y. — FG Allegre 32
N.Y. — Bavaro 13 pass from Simms (Allegre kick)
N.Y. — FG Allegre 27
Dall — Walker 27 pass from Walsh (Ruzek kick)
A: 51,785 T: 2:59

Washington 16, New Orleans 14—At the Superdome. The Saints used stubborn defense and just enough offense to build a 14-3 halftime lead, then allowed turnovers and missed opportunities to cost them the game. Key miscues included a fumble by punt returner Derrick Shepard that gave the Redskins field position for the decisive 18-yard field goal and a subsequent missed field goal by the normally sure-footed Morten Andersen. Saints quarterback Bobby Hebert had a good day in defeat, completing 16 of 25 passes for 259 yards.

Washington	3	0	10	3	—	16
New Orleans	7	7	0	0	—	14

Wash — FG Lohmiller 48
N.O. — Hill 11 pass from Hebert (Andersen kick)
N.O. — Hilliard 3 run (Andersen kick)
Wash — FG Lohmiller 19
Wash — Riggs 9 run (Lohmiller kick)
Wash — FG Lohmiller 18
A: 46,358 T: 2:59

Cincinnati 21, Kansas City 17—At Arrowhead Stadium. Linebacker Leon White stripped the ball from Chiefs running back Christian Okoye and ran 22 yards for the game-winning TD in the fourth quarter to give Cincinnati its first victory in Arrowhead Stadium since 1980. QB Boomer Esiason, expected to sit out the game with an ankle sprain, was forced into action when backup Turk Schonert went down with an ankle sprain of his own on the opening series. Chiefs QB Ron Jaworski, starting in place of the ineffective Steve DeBerg, completed 14 of 28 passes for 163 yards but was intercepted four times.

Cincinnati	0	14	0	7	—	21
Kansas City	3	14	0	0	—	17

K.C. — FG Lowery 23
K.C. — Okoye 11 run (Lowery kick)
Cin — McGee 40 pass from Esiason (Gallery kick)
K.C. — Thomas 5 pass from Jaworski (Lowery kick)
Cin — Ball 2 run (Gallery kick)
Cin — White 22 fumble return (Gallery kick)
A: 60,165 T: 3:26

Indianapolis 17, N.Y. Jets 10—At Giants Stadium. The game began disastrously for the Colts, who had two apparent touchdowns nullified by the officials on the opening drive, then watched helplessly as Jet free safety Erik McMillan picked off a Jack Trudeau pass and ran it 92 yards for a TD. But Trudeau bounced back in the second half, completing 10 of 16 passes for 156 yards and a touchdown, Clarence Verdin made an electrifying 49-yard punt return for another TD and the Indianapolis defense shut the Jets down completely.

Indianapolis	0	0	7	10	—	17
New York	7	3	0	0	—	10

N.Y. — McMillan 92 interception return (Leahy kick)
N.Y. — FG Leahy 26
Ind — Brooks 55 pass from Trudeau (Biasucci kick)
Ind — FG Biasucci 38
Ind Verdin 49 punt return (Biasucci kick)
A: 65,542 T: 3:02

Pittsburgh 23, Detroit 3—At the Silverdome. The surprising resurgence of the Steelers continued as Pittsburgh took advantage of four Lion turnovers to score all their points, while limiting Detroit to just 18 yards rushing. Quarterback Bubby Brister survived seven sacks to complete 21 of 27 passes for 267 yards, including a team-record 15 in a row, and seven completions to wide receiver Louis Lipps for 126 yards. Lion rookie QB Rodney Peete, in his first NFL start, completed 15 of 30 passes for 160 yards before being benched but was hurt by his receivers, who dropped six passes.

Pittsburgh	0	10	7	6	—	23
Detroit	3	0	0	0	—	3

Det — FG Murray 37
Pitt — Lipps 48 pass from Brister (Anderson kick)
Pitt — FG Anderson 20
Pitt — Carter 1 run
Pitt — Wallace 2 run (pass failed)
A: 43,804 T: 3:30

Houston 39, Miami 7—At the Astrodome. Oiler quarterback Warren Moon connected on 19 of 23 passing attempts for 254 yards and two touchdowns, while his Dolphin counterpart Dan Marino completed 11 of 29 attempts for just 103 yards, a career low. Running back Lorenzo White gained 97 yards on 17 carries and the Oiler defense, burned for five touchdowns by Buffalo QB Jim Kelly the previous week, held the Dolphins to just 160 total yards.

Miami	0	0	0	7	—	7
Houston	2	17	6	14	—	39

Hou — Safety, Roby fumble out of end zone
Hou — FG Zendejas 32
Hou — Highsmith 3 run (Zendejas kick)
Hou — Pinkett 2 pass from Moon (Zendejas kick)
Hou — FG Zendejas 40
Hou — FG Zendejas 32
Hou — Duncan 25 pass from Moon (Zendejas kick)
Hou — Pinkett 10 run (Zendejas kick)
Mia — Logan 97 kickoff return (Stoyanovich kick)
A: 53,326 T: 3:06

Minnesota 17, Tampa Bay 3—At the Metrodome. The Viking defense carried the day, holding the Bucs to just 158 yards in total offense and harassing quarterback Vinny Testaverde into a 6-for-23 performance, his worst as a pro. Minnesota quarterback Tommy Kramer completed 18 of 32 passes for 190 yards and two TDs but was intercepted twice.

Tampa Bay	0	3	0	0	—	3
Minnesota	0	10	7	0	—	17

Minn — Carter 12 pass from Kramer (Karlis kick)
Minn — FG Karlis 20
T.B. — FG Igwebuike 44
Minn — Lewis 28 pass from Kramer (Karlis kick)
A: 54,817 T: 3:00

Seattle 24, L.A. Raiders 20—At Memorial Coliseum. The Seahawks, trailing by 10 points after the third quarter, woke up in the fourth to score two touchdowns and pull out the win. Seattle quarterback Dave Krieg, in spite of being sacked four times, completed 22 of 31 passes for 227 yards and two TDs, while Curt Warner rushed for 102 yards on 21 carries. The winning touchdown came on a 19-yard strike from Krieg to wide receiver Brian Blades.

Seattle	7	0	0	17	—	24
Los Angeles	0	10	7	3	—	20

Sea — Williams 14 pass from Krieg (Johnson kick)
L.A. — FG Jaeger 45
L.A. — Washington 37 fumble return (Jaeger kick)
L.A. — Fernandez 36 pass from Schroeder (Jaeger kick)
Sea — Warner 6 run (Johnson kick)
Sea — Blades 19 pass from Krieg (Johnson kick)
L.A. — FG Jaeger 28
Sea — FG Johnson 48
A: 44,319 T: 3:07

Buffalo 31, New England 10—At Rich Stadium. Bills quarterback Jim Kelly made the most of his completions against the Patriots, connecting on 12 of 17 passes for 278 yards and three TDs. Patriots QB Doug Flutie, starting in place of the ineffective Tony Eason, was less productive, completing just three of 12 passes for 28 yards in the first half and 15 of 41 overall for 176 yards. Running back Thurman Thomas gained 105 yards on 21 carries for the Bills.

New England	3	0	7	0	—	10
Buffalo	7	17	0	7	—	31

N.E. — FG Davis 35
Buff — Thomas 4 run (Norwood kick)
Buff — McKeller 39 pass from Kelly (Norwood kick)
Buff — Metzelaars 8 pass from Kelly (Norwood kick)
Buff — FG Norwood 36
N.E. — Jones 20 pass from Flutie (Davis kick)
Buff — Thomas 74 pass from Kelly (Norwood kick)
A: 78,921 T: 3:13

San Diego 24, Phoenix 13—At Sun Devil Stadium. The Chargers exploded for 17 points in the fourth quarter to overtake the Cardinals. Just more than a minute after running back Marion Butts scored the go-ahead TD on a two-yard plunge early in the fourth quarter, linebacker Billy Ray Smith scooped up a fumble by Phoenix running back Earl Ferrell and ran 15 yards for a second score to put San Diego ahead by eight. Charger QB Jim McMahon completed 15 of 23 passes for 188 yards.

San Diego	0	0	7	17	—	24
Phoenix	0	3	10	0	—	13

Phoe — FG Del Greco 36
Phoe — FG Del Greco 33
S.D. — Miller 16 pass from McMahon (Bahr kick)
Phoe — Green 59 pass from Hogeboom (Del Greco kick)
S.D. — Butts 2 run (Bahr kick)
S.D. — Smith 15 fumble return (Bahr kick)
S.D. — FG Bahr 37
A: 44,201 T: 3:15

Green Bay 23, Atlanta 21—At Milwaukee County Stadium. The Packers staged another stirring comeback victory, this time scoring 17 points in the fourth quarter to overcome a 21-6 Falcon lead. Unheralded quarterback Don Majkowski was the spark plug again, completing 12 of 18 passes in the second half, including a critical 23-yard completion to wide receiver Perry Kemp that led to the game-winning 22-yard field goal by Chris Jacke with 1:42 remaining. Falcon QB Hugh Millen completed 20 of 28 passes for 294 yards, but his interception with 1:13 to go sealed the win for Green Bay.

Atlanta	7	7	7	0	—	21
Green Bay	0	6	0	17	—	23

Atl — Beckman 3 pass from Millen (McFadden kick)
G.B. — FG Jacke 35
Atl — Settle 1 run (McFadden kick)
G.B. — FG Jacke 52
Atl — Lang 10 run (McFadden kick)
G.B. — Sharpe 5 fumble return (Jacke kick)
G.B. — Fontenot 37 pass from Majkowski (Jacke kick)
G.B. — FG Jacke 22
A: 54,647 T: 3:07

MONDAY, OCTOBER 2

Chicago 27, Philadelphia 13—At Soldier Field. Bears quarterback Mike Tomczak continued to silence his critics, hitting 24 of 38 passing attempts for 266 yards and three touchdowns. The Eagles, dominated by Chicago in the first half, revived in the second, but turnovers (six overall), dropped passes and missed opportunities prevented a comeback. Philadelphia QB Randall Cunningham threw a team-record 62 passes, completing 32 for 401 yards, but his four interceptions proved costly.

Philadelphia	0	0	3	10	—	13
Chicago	0	13	7	7	—	27

Chi — McKinnon 14 pass from Tomczak (Butler kick)
Chi — Suhey 1 pass from Tomczak (kick failed)
Phi — FG Zendejas 47
Chi — Anderson 2 run (Butler kick)
Phi — Garrity 24 pass from Cunningham (Zendejas kick)
Phi — FG Zendejas 19
Chi — Thornton 36 pass from Tomczak (Butler kick)
A: 66,625 T: 3:28

Week Five

STANDINGS

AFC EAST	W	L	T	Pct	PF	PA
Buffalo	3	2	0	.600	133	140
Indianapolis	3	2	0	.600	108	94
Miami	2	3	0	.400	101	126
New England	2	3	0	.400	73	116
N.Y. Jets	1	4	0	.200	105	127
AFC CENTRAL	**W**	**L**	**T**	**Pct**	**PF**	**PA**
Cincinnati	4	1	0	.800	123	74
Cleveland	3	2	0	.600	129	71
Houston	2	3	0	.400	134	142
Pittsburgh	2	3	0	.400	76	135
AFC WEST	**W**	**L**	**T**	**Pct**	**PF**	**PA**
Denver	4	1	0	.800	122	81
Kansas City	2	3	0	.400	87	111
L.A. Raiders	2	3	0	.400	114	100
San Diego	2	3	0	.400	96	109
Seattle	2	3	0	.400	95	108
NFC EAST	**W**	**L**	**T**	**Pct**	**PF**	**PA**
N.Y. Giants	4	1	0	.800	135	79
Philadelphia	3	2	0	.600	135	128
Washington	3	2	0	.600	137	118
Phoenix	2	3	0	.400	98	126
Dallas	0	5	0	.000	54	146
NFC CENTRAL	**W**	**L**	**T**	**Pct**	**PF**	**PA**
Chicago	4	1	0	.800	164	103
Green Bay	3	2	0	.600	148	132
Minnesota	3	2	0	.600	100	92
Tampa Bay	3	2	0	.600	104	103
Detroit	0	5	0	.000	74	134
NFC WEST	**W**	**L**	**T**	**Pct**	**PF**	**PA**
L.A. Rams	5	0	0	1.000	142	102
San Francisco	4	1	0	.800	124	101
Atlanta	1	4	0	.200	92	114
New Orleans	1	4	0	.200	106	95

RESULTS

Washington 30, Phoenix 28
Tampa Bay 42, Chicago 35
Philadelphia 21, N.Y. Giants 19
San Francisco 24, New Orleans 20
Kansas City 20, Seattle 16
L.A. Rams 26, Atlanta 14
Denver 16, San Diego 10
Cincinnati 26, Pittsburgh 16
Minnesota 24, Detroit 17
Green Bay 31, Dallas 13
Miami 13, Cleveland 10, OT
Indianapolis 37, Buffalo 14
New England 23, Houston 13
L.A. Raiders 14, N.Y. Jets 7 (Monday night)

SUNDAY, OCTOBER 8

Washington 30, Phoenix 28—At RFK Stadium. The Redskins' off-season trade for running back Earnest Byner paid its first substantial dividend of the season as Byner carried 14 times for 100 yards and grabbed five passes for 71 yards more. Trailing 21-13 at the end of the third quarter, Washington scored 17 unanswered points in the fourth quarter, only to watch the Cardinals respond with a touchdown to draw within two with 14 seconds left. Phoenix recovered the ensuing onsides kick but ran out of time before getting into field goal range. The Redskins' Mark Rypien completed 23 of 42 passes for 333 yards and three TDs. Phoenix's J.T. Smith caught eight passes for 114 yards and three TDs.

Phoenix	0	14	7	7	—	28
Washington	10	3	0	17	—	30

Wash — FG Lohmiller 22
Wash — Byner 2 pass from Rypien (Lohmiller kick)
Wash — FG Lohmiller 32
Phoe — Smith 7 pass from Hogeboom (Del Greco kick)
Phoe — Smith 20 pass from Hogeboom (Del Greco kick)
Phoe — Ferrell 44 run (Del Greco kick)
Wash — FG Lohmiller 37
Wash — Monk 12 pass from Rypien (Lohmiller kick)
Wash — Clark 23 pass from Rypien (Lohmiller kick)
Phoe — Smith 17 pass from Hogeboom (Del Greco kick)
A: 53,335 T: 3:25

Tampa Bay 42, Chicago 35—At Tampa Stadium. The Bucs converted two Bears turnovers into early touchdowns and quarterback Vinny Testaverde completed 22 of 36 passes for 269 yards and three touchdowns to lead Tampa Bay to its first win against Chicago since 1983. Tampa Bay's Lars Tate carried 18 times for 112 yards and two TDs, while Neal Anderson had 86 yards and three TDs for Chicago.

Chicago	0	14	7	14	—	35
Tampa Bay	14	14	0	14	—	42

T.B. — Carrier 11 pass from Testaverde (Igwebuike kick)
T.B. — Howard 1 run (Igwebuike kick)
T.B. — Harris 3 pass from Testaverde (Igwebuike kick)
Chi — Anderson 5 run (Butler kick)
T.B. — Hill 22 pass from Testaverde (Igwebuike kick)
Chi — Anderson 1 run (Butler kick)
Chi — Sanders 16 pass from Tomczak (Butler kick)
T.B. — Tate 16 run (Igwebuike kick)
T.B. — Tate 4 run (Mohr run)
Chi — Harbaugh 26 run (Butler kick)
Chi — Anderson 1 run (Butler kick)
A: 72,077 T: 3:21

Philadelphia 21, N.Y. Giants 19—At Veterans Stadium. Eagle quarterback Randall Cunningham connected on only 10 of 24 passes for 106 yards, but he performed well in the clutch, running for two touchdowns and completing several key passes in the game-winning drive late in the fourth quarter. The Giants were victimized by mistakes, including two interference calls that led to Eagle touchdowns and an interception with less than two minutes left thrown by quarterback Phil Simms.

New York	3	10	0	6	—	19
Philadelphia	0	7	0	14	—	21

N.Y. — FG Allegre 25
N.Y. — Banks 22 pass from Hostetler (Allegre kick)
Phi — Cunningham 5 run (Zendejas kick)
N.Y. — FG Allegre 41
N.Y. — FG Allegre 45
Phi — Cunningham 1 run (Zendejas kick)
N.Y. — FG Allegre 24
Phi — Toney 2 run (Zendejas kick)
A: 65,688 T: 3:12

San Francisco 24, New Orleans 20—At the Superdome. For the fourth time in five games, 49er quarterback Joe Montana had to rally his team to victory, this time recovering from a 17-3 third-quarter deficit. He was greatly aided by two questionable touchdowns on which San Francisco players appeared to have fumbled the football before crossing the goal line. Montana had another good day, completing 21 of 29 passes for 291 yards and three TDs, as did his Saints counterpart Bobby Hebert, who hit 31 of 49 for a career-high 308 yards and two TDs. The 49ers' Jerry Rice had seven catches for 149 yards.

San Francisco	0	3	7	14	—	24
New Orleans	0	10	7	3	—	20

S.F. — FG Cofer 41
N.O. — Brenner 2 pass from Hebert (Andersen kick)
N.O. — FG Andersen 49
N.O. — Hilliard 19 pass from Hebert (Andersen kick)
S.F. — Rice 60 pass from Montana (Cofer kick)
S.F. — Taylor 21 pass from Montana (Cofer kick)
N.O. — FG Andersen 39
S.F. — Taylor 32 pass from Montana (Cofer kick)
A: 60,488 T: 3:02

Kansas City 20, Seattle 16—At the Kingdome. After trailing 16-3 at the half, the Chiefs rallied with 17 second-half points. They were led by running back Christian Okoye, who rolled over the Seahawk defense for 156 yards on 30 carries. Seattle's only touchdown came on a 97-yard return of the opening kickoff by James Jefferson.

Kansas City	3	0	7	10	—	20
Seattle	7	9	0	0	—	16

Sea — Jefferson 97 kickoff return (Johnson kick)
K.C. — FG Lowery 39
Sea — FG Johnson 37
Sea — FG Johnson 26
Sea — FG Johnson 37
K.C. — Okoye 13 run (Lowery kick)
K.C. — FG Lowery 25
K.C. — Roberts 2 pass from Jaworski (Lowery kick)
A: 60,715 T: 2:59

L.A. Rams 26, Atlanta 14—At Anaheim Stadium. The Ram defense allowed Falcon quarterback Chris Miller to complete 28 of 39 passes for 340 yards but got tough inside its own 20-yard line, twice stopping Atlanta in fourth-and-short situations to preserve the victory and remain undefeated. Los Angeles quarterback Jim Everett threw for 290 yards and two TDs, connecting eight times with wide receiver Henry Ellard for 165 yards. The Rams' Mike Lansford hit on four of four field goal attempts, including two of more than 40 yards.

Atlanta	7	0	7	0	—	14
Los Angeles	10	10	6	0	—	26

L.A. — Holohan 13 pass from Everett (Lansford kick)
Atl — Collins 9 pass from Miller (McFadden kick)
L.A. — FG Lansford 48
L.A. — Delpino 9 pass from Everett (Lansford kick)
L.A. — FG Lansford 35
L.A. — FG Lansford 27
Atl — Jones 3 run (McFadden kick)
L.A. — FG Lansford 42
A: 52,182 T: 2:59

Denver 16, San Diego 10—At Mile High Stadium. Rookie running back Bobby Humphrey broke open a defensive contest with a 17-yard touchdown run with 1:03 remaining to pull out the game for the Broncos. Humphrey, in his first pro start, ran for 102 yards on 23 carries. Neither quarterback, Jim McMahon for the Chargers nor John Elway for Denver, were particularly effective as the two combined for just 315 passing yards. The Broncos twice had to settle for David Treadwell field goals after facing first-and-goal situations.

San Diego	3	0	7	0	—	10
Denver	0	6	0	10	—	16

S.D. — FG Bahr 39
Den — FG Treadwell 46
Den — FG Treadwell 18
S.D. — Butts 2 run (Bahr kick)
Den — FG Treadwell 27
Den — Humphrey 17 run (Treadwell kick)
A: 75,222 T: 3:09

Cincinnati 26, Pittsburgh 16—At Three Rivers Stadium. Clinging to a three-point lead with less than two minutes left, the Bengals faced a third-and-27 from their own 35-yard line. In an apparent passing situation, Cincinnati chose instead to give the ball to running back James Brooks (127 yards on 17 carries), who busted up the middle for a 65-yard TD run that put the game out of reach. Bengal quarterback Boomer Esiason, hobbled with a sore ankle, led his team on two 80-yard TD drives and threw for 219 yards. With :35 left, Steeler QB Bubby Brister suffered a sprained left knee that would sideline him for two weeks.

Cincinnati	0	13	0	13	—	26
Pittsburgh	7	3	3	3	—	16

Pitt — Carter 22 pass from Brister (Anderson kick)
Cin — FG Breech 24
Cin — FG Breech 27
Pitt — FG Anderson 24
Cinn — Martin 7 pass from Esiason (Breech kick)
Pitt — FG Anderson 40
Cin — Brooks 13 run (kick failed)
Pitt — FG Anderson 34
Cin — Brooks 65 run (Breech kick)
A: 52,785 T: 3:19

Minnesota 24, Detroit 17—At the Metrodome. The Viking defense atoned for the team's sluggish offense, returning two interceptions for touchdowns and holding the Lion offense in check except for rookie sensation Barry Sanders, who gained 99 yards on 23 carries. Defensive tackle Keith Millard had a great day for Minnesota, sacking Detroit QBs three times and making six solo tackles and a 48-yard interception return.

Detroit	7	3	0	7	—	17
Minnesota	0	24	0	0	—	24

Det — Hipple 1 run (Murray kick)
Minn — FG Karlis 22
Minn — Merriweather 15 interception return (Karlis kick)
Minn — Holt 90 interception return (Karlis kick)
Minn — Novoselsky 2 pass from Kramer (Karlis kick)
Det — FG Murray 50
Det — Gagliano 1 run (Murray kick)
A: 55,380 T: 3:23

Green Bay 31, Dallas 13—At Lambeau Field. Packer quarterback Don Majkowski continued to surprise, completing 21 of 32 passes for 313 yards and four touchdowns as Green Bay, with the NFL's No. 1-ranked offense, continued to roll. Complementing Majkowski's air attack was running back Brent Fullwood, who ran for 119 yards on 28 carries. Cowboy QB Steve Walsh, making his first start in place of the injured Troy Aikman, connected on 18 of 29 passes for 193 yards.

Dallas	6	7	0	0	—	13
Green Bay	10	7	7	7	—	31

Dall — Irvin 5 pass from Walsh (kick blocked)
G.B. — FG Jacke 26
G.B. — Fontenot 7 pass from Majkowski (Jacke kick)
Dall — Lockhart 40 fumble return (Ruzek kick)
G.B. — Sharpe 79 pass from Majkowski (Jacke kick)
G.B. — Fontenot 38 pass from Majkowski (Jacke kick)
G.B. — Kemp 4 pass from Majkowski (Jacke kick)
A: 56,656 T: 3:05

Miami 13, Cleveland 10—At Joe Robbie Stadium. Bouncing back from a drubbing by Houston in Week 4, the Dolphins upset the Browns in overtime on a 35-yard field goal by rookie Pete Stoyanovich. Both teams had previous opportunities to win the game, Miami when Stoyanovich missed a 45-yarder with three seconds left in regulation and Cleveland when kicker Matt Bahr missed a 44-yard attempt early in overtime. For the 17th straight week, Miami's offensive line did not allow a sack.

Cleveland	0	3	7	0	—	0	10
Miami	3	7	0	0	—	3	13

Mia — FG Stoyanovich 43
Mia — Duper 35 pass from Marino (Stoyanovich kick)
Cle — FG Bahr 50
Cle — Metcalf 8 run (Bahr kick)
Mia — FG Stoyanovich 35
A: 58,444 T: 3:12

Indianapolis 37, Buffalo 14—At the Hoosier Dome. The Bills rolled up 424 yards in total offense, but that wasn't enough to offset four interceptions, three lost fumbles and four sacks. Even worse for Buffalo was the loss of quarterback Jim Kelly, who sustained a separated left shoulder in the third quarter that would sideline him for three weeks. The Colts were paced on offense by Eric Dickerson, who gained 92 yards on 22 carries.

Buffalo	0	0	7	7	—	14
Indianapolis	14	6	3	14	—	37

Ind — Dickerson 1 run (Biasucci kick)
Ind — Trudeau 1 run (Biasucci kick)
Ind — FG Biasucci 32
Ind — FG Biasucci 46
Ind — FG Biasucci 25
Buff — Reed 16 pass from Kelly (Norwood kick)
Ind — Dickerson 4 run (Biasucci kick)
Buff — Davis 17 pass from Reich (Norwood kick)
Ind — Taylor 80 interception return (Biasucci kick)
A: 58,890 T: 3:09

New England 23, Houston 13—At Sullivan Stadium. The Patriots defense sacked Houston quarterback Warren Moon three times, intercepted him twice and limited him to just 227 passing yards, 113 of them coming after New England had taken a 23-6 lead midway through the fourth quarter. New England got a boost from the return of running back John Stephens (59 yards and a TD on 21 carries), who had missed the last three games with a sprained ankle.

Houston	0	3	0	10	—	13
New England	10	0	10	3	—	23

N.E. — FG Davis 30
N.E. — Allen 1 run (Davis kick)
Hou — FG Zendejas 46
N.E. — FG Davis 34
N.E. — Stephens 11 run (Davis kick)
Hou — FG Zendejas 22
N.E. — FG Davis 43
Hou — Hill 20 pass from Moon (Zendejas kick)
A: 59,828 T: 3:05

MONDAY, OCTOBER 9

L.A. Raiders 14, N.Y. Jets 7—At Giants Stadium. It was a team victory for the Raiders but an individual milestone for Art Shell, who became the first black head coach to win a game in the NFL's modern era. The key play was an interception by Raider safety Eddie Anderson, who grabbed the ball at his own 13-yard line, broke a tackle at the 35 and dashed 87 yards for the game-winning TD. Jet quarterback Ken O'Brien completed 25 of 49 passes for 348 yards but was intercepted twice.

Los Angeles	0	0	7	7	—	14
New York	0	0	7	0	—	7

L.A. — Fernandez 73 pass from Schroeder (Jaeger kick)
N.Y. — Vick 1 run (Leahy kick)
L.A. — Anderson 87 interception return (Jaeger kick)
A: 68,040 T: 3:05

STANDINGS

AFC EAST	W	L	T	Pct	PF	PA
Buffalo	4	2	0	.667	156	160
Indianapolis	3	3	0	.500	111	108
Miami	3	3	0	.500	121	139
New England	2	4	0	.333	88	132
N.Y. Jets	1	5	0	.167	119	158

AFC CENTRAL	W	L	T	Pct	PF	PA
Cincinnati	4	2	0	.667	136	94
Cleveland	3	3	0	.500	136	88
Houston	3	3	0	.500	167	170
Pittsburgh	3	3	0	.500	93	142

AFC WEST	W	L	T	Pct	PF	PA
Denver	5	1	0	.833	136	84
L.A. Raiders	3	3	0	.500	134	114
Seattle	3	3	0	.500	112	124
Kansas City	2	4	0	.333	101	131
San Diego	2	4	0	.333	112	126

NFC EAST	W	L	T	Pct	PF	PA
N.Y. Giants	5	1	0	.833	155	96
Philadelphia	4	2	0	.667	152	133
Washington	3	3	0	.500	154	138
Phoenix	2	4	0	.333	103	143
Dallas	0	6	0	.000	68	177

NFC CENTRAL	W	L	T	Pct	PF	PA
Chicago	4	2	0	.667	192	136
Minnesota	4	2	0	.667	126	106
Green Bay	3	3	0	.500	162	158
Tampa Bay	3	3	0	.500	120	120
Detroit	1	5	0	.167	91	150

NFC WEST	W	L	T	Pct	PF	PA
L.A. Rams	5	1	0	.833	162	125
San Francisco	5	1	0	.833	155	115
Atlanta	2	4	0	.333	108	129
New Orleans	2	4	0	.333	135	109

RESULTS

Minnesota 26, Green Bay 14
Denver 14, Indianapolis 3
Houston 33, Chicago 28
Miami 20, Cincinnati 13
N.Y. Giants 20, Washington 17
Detroit 17, Tampa Bay 16
San Francisco 31, Dallas 14
Pittsburgh 17, Cleveland 7
Seattle 17, San Diego 16
New Orleans 29, N.Y. Jets 14
L.A. Raiders 20, Kansas City 14
Philadelphia 17, Phoenix 5
Atlanta 16, New England 15
Buffalo 23, L.A. Rams 20 (Monday night)

SUNDAY, OCTOBER 15

Minnesota 26, Green Bay 14—At the Metrodome. Herschel Walker made his first appearance in a Viking uniform a sensational one, bursting through and around the Packer defense for 148 yards on 18 carries. Minnesota's defense also had a spectacular day, sacking Green Bay quarterback Don Majkowski eight times and intercepting him twice. Defensive tackle Keith Millard recorded four of the sacks, including one in the third quarter for a safety. Viking quarterback Tommy Kramer completed 14 of 24 passing attempts for 172 yards and two touchdowns.

Green Bay	7	0	0	7	—	14
Minnesota	0	17	9	0	—	26

G.B. — Fontenot 1 run (Jacke kick)
Minn — FG Karlis 28
Minn — Fenney 8 run (Karlis kick)
Minn — Gustafson 6 pass from Kramer (Karlis kick)
Minn — Fenney 8 pass from Kramer (Karlis kick)
Minn — Safety, Majkowski tackled in end zone
G.B. — Bland 46 pass from Majkowski (Jacke kick)
A: 62,075 T: 3:09

Denver 14, Indianapolis 3—At Mile High Stadium. The Broncos limited Eric Dickerson to just 35 yards on 13 carries and held the Colts to just 128 yards overall in a dominant defensive performance. Sammy Winder, playing in place of rookie Bobby Humphrey, who left the game in the third quarter with a bruised rib cage, gained 92 yards on 21 carries.

Indianapolis	3	0	0	0	—	3
Denver	0	7	0	7	—	14

Ind — FG Biasucci 55
Den — Humphrey 2 run (Treadwell kick)
Den — Winder 1 run (Treadwell kick)
A: 74,680 T: 2:34

Houston 33, Chicago 28—At Soldier Field. Just one week after giving up 42 points in a surprising loss to Tampa Bay, the Bears defense again failed in the clutch, allowing the Oilers to score 14 unanswered points in the last 3:38 to win. Quarterback Warren Moon had a big day for Houston, completing 16 of 26 passes for 317 yards and two touchdowns, while Chicago's Mike Tomczak had a strange outing, connecting on 20 of 29 passes but also throwing four interceptions. Allen Pinkett had 70 yards on six carries for the Oilers, including a 60-yard romp with 2:44 left to set up the game-winning TD.

Houston	0	10	9	14	—	33
Chicago	0	14	7	7	—	28

Chi — Anderson 6 pass from Tomczak (Butler kick)
Hou — FG Zendejas 27
Hou — Hill 42 pass from Moon (Zendejas kick)
Chi — Anderson 1 run (Butler kick)
Hou — FG Zendejas 19
Chi — Gentry 79 pass from Tomczak (Butler kick)
Hou — Jeffires 45 pass from Moon (kick failed)
Chi — Thornton 7 pass from Tomczak (Butler kick)
Hou — Moon 1 run (Zendejas kick)
Hou — White 12 run (Zendejas kick)
A: 64,383 T: 3:14

Miami 20, Cincinnati 13—At Riverfront Stadium. After falling behind 13-3 in the first half, the Dolphins bounced back with 17 unanswered points in the second, running up 278 yards in total offense while holding the Bengals to just 83. For the first time during quarterback Dan Marino's seven years with the team, Miami won a game in which he failed to throw a touchdown pass, although Marino did run for a TD on a one-yard bootleg. Dolphin wide receiver Mark Duper had five catches for 129 yards.

Miami	0	3	7	10	—	20
Cincinnati	10	3	0	0	—	13

Cin — FG Breech 20
Cin — Holman 38 pass from Esiason (Breech kick)
Mia — FG Stoyanovich 29
Cin — FG Breech 22
Mia — Marino 1 run (Stoyanovich kick)
Mia — FG Stoyanovich 33
Mia — Davenport 5 run (Stoyanovich kick)
A: 58,184 T: 3:15

N.Y. Giants 20, Washington 17—At Giants Stadium. Running back Ottis Anderson continued to dispel the doubts about his age (31), gaining 101 yards on 25 carries for the Giants, his first 100-yard day since 1985. New York trailed 10-6 entering the fourth quarter, but touchdown passes by Phil Simms to tight end Mark Bavaro and wide receiver Odessa Turner put the Giants in front to stay. The win was New York's ninth in its last 12 games against the Redskins.

Washington	0	3	7	7	—	17
New York	3	0	3	14	—	20

N.Y. — FG Allegre 33
Wash — FG Lohmiller 37
N.Y. — FG Allegre 49
Wash — Sanders 29 pass from Rypien (Lohmiller kick)
N.Y. — Bavaro 12 pass from Simms (Allegre kick)
N.Y. — Turner 25 pass from Simms (Allegre kick)
Wash — Monk 5 pass from Rypien (Lohmiller kick)
A: 76,245 T: 2:56

Detroit 17, Tampa Bay 16—At Tampa Stadium. Parity continued to reign as the previously winless Lions, spurred by the play of rookie quarterback Rodney Peete, defeated the Bucs. Peete, in his second NFL start, completed 17 of 31 passes for 268 yards and ran for 78 yards on 10 carries. With his team trailing by six and less than two minutes to go, Peete engineered a stirring drive, completing four passes for 68 yards and scrambling across from the five-yard line for the winning score on fourth down.

Detroit	3	0	7	7	—	17
Tampa Bay	0	10	3	3	—	16

Det — FG Murray 28
T.B. — Reynolds 68 interception return (Igwebuike kick)
T.B. — FG Igwebuike 27
Det — Clark 33 pass from Peete (Murray kick)
T.B. — FG Igwebuike 34
T.B. — FG Igwebuike 33
Det — Peete 5 run (Murray kick)
A: 46,225 T: 3:24

San Francisco 31, Dallas 14—At Texas Stadium. The 49ers struggled for three quarters but got it all together in the fourth, scoring 17 points to bury the Cowboys, who had their best showing in their thus-far dismal season. Quarterback Steve Young, playing in place of the injured Joe Montana, completed 13 of 18 passes for 174 yards and two touchdowns and was San Francisco's leading rusher as well, gaining 79 yards on 11 carries. Steve Walsh had another good day in defeat, hitting 22 of 36 passes for 285 yards.

San Francisco	0	7	7	17	—	31
Dallas	0	7	7	0	—	14

S.F. — Jones 36 pass from Young (Cofer kick)
Dall — Martin 32 pass from Walsh (Ruzek kick)
S.F. — Jackson 75 blocked field goal return (Cofer kick)
Dall — Clack 1 run (Ruzek kick)
S.F. — Rice 8 pass from Young (Cofer kick)
S.F. — FG Cofer 31
S.F. — Craig 1 run (Cofer kick)
A: 61,077 T: 2:56

Pittsburgh 17, Cleveland 7—At Cleveland Stadium. The Steeler defense, much maligned after giving up 51 points in the season opener against the Browns, hounded Cleveland quarterback Bernie Kosar into one of his worst days as a pro, intercepting him four times, sacking him three times and limiting him to just 162 yards passing on a 15-for-41 day. Rookie Eric Metcalf (57 yards on 13 carries) brought the Browns within three points with a two-yard TD run in the fourth quarter, but Dwight Stone returned the ensuing kickoff 73 yards to the Cleveland 25 to set up the TD that sealed the game.

Pittsburgh	3	0	7	7	—	17
Cleveland	0	0	0	7	—	7

Pitt — FG Anderson 49
Pitt — Carter 14 pass from Blackledge (Anderson kick)
Cle — Metcalf 2 run (Bahr kick)
Pitt — Williams 1 run (Anderson kick)
A: 78,840 T: 3:35

Seattle 17, San Diego 16—At Jack Murphy Stadium. The Chargers dominated the game everywhere but on the scoreboard as the Seahawks made the big plays in the fourth quarter, blocking an extra point that would have tied the game and a field goal that would have won it. San Diego still had a chance to win the game in the final minute, but a key holding penalty pushed the Chargers out of field goal range. San Diego QB Jim McMahon deserved a better fate, completing 25 of 39 passes for 286 yards as San Diego outgained Seattle 362-224.

Seattle	10	0	7	0	—	17
San Diego	7	3	0	6	—	16

S.D. — Cox 3 pass from McMahon (Bahr kick)
Sea — Warner 1 run (Johnson kick)
Sea — FG Johnson 50
S.D. — FG Bahr 29
Sea — Williams 6 pass from Krieg (Johnson kick)
S.D. — Butts 2 run (kick failed)
A: 50,079 T: 3:02

New Orleans 29, N.Y. Jets 14—At the Superdome. The Saints, who entered the game with a 1-4 record in spite of never trailing at halftime, played sixty solid minutes for once as their defense sacked New York quarterbacks five times and recovered three fumbles en route to the win. Dalton Hilliard and Craig Heyward combined for 136 yards on the ground for New Orleans, and quarterback Bobby Hebert completed 18 of 29 passes for 281 yards and three TDs. The Jets, in search of a lift, started Kyle Mackey at quarterback in place of Ken O'Brien, but Mackey was ineffective and was replaced by O'Brien in the fourth quarter.

New York	0	7	0	7	—	14
New Orleans	6	7	7	9	—	29

N.O. — FG Andersen 42
N.O. — FG Andersen 29
N.Y. — Hasty 34 interception return (Leahy kick)
N.O. — Hill 3 pass from Hebert (Andersen kick)
N.O. — Martin 4 pass from Hebert (Andersen kick)
N.O. — Safety, Schreiber holding penalty in end zone
N.O. — Martin 53 pass from Hebert (Andersen kick)
N.Y. — McMillan 74 fumble return (Leahy kick)
A: 59,521 T: 3:27

L.A. Raiders 20, Kansas City 14—At Memorial Coliseum. Bo Jackson, late of baseball's Kansas City Royals, made a lot of his former fans unhappy with a smashing season debut for the Raiders, gaining 85 yards on 11 carries, including a 45-yard gallop in the fourth quarter that set up the game-winning touchdown. The Chiefs contributed mightily to the loss, committing four turnovers on three fumbles and an interception.

Kansas City	7	0	0	7	—	14
Los Angeles	3	7	3	7	—	20

K.C. — Okoye 2 run (Lowery kick)
L.A. — FG Jaeger 24
L.A. — Jackson 2 run (Jaeger kick)
L.A. — FG Jaeger 50
L.A. — Mueller 6 run (Jaeger kick)
K.C. — Thomas 11 pass from DeBerg (Lowery kick)
A: 40,453 T: 3:01

Philadelphia 17, Phoenix 5—At Sun Devil Stadium. Cardinals quarterback Tom Tupa had a horrible afternoon, throwing six interceptions and suffering six sacks, as the Eagles rallied in the second half behind QB Randall Cunningham, who threw two third-quarter touchdown passes to wide receiver Cris Carter to cement the win. Cunningham, who completed only four of 11 passes for 33 yards in the first half, ended the game with 192 yards passing and another 70 yards on the ground.

Philadelphia	0	0	14	3	—	17
Phoenix	0	5	0	0	—	5

Phoe — Safety, Toney tackled by Wilson in end zone
Phoe — FG Del Greco 41
Phi — Carter 2 pass from Cunningham (Zendejas kick)
Phi — Carter 40 pass from Cunningham (Zendejas kick)
Phi — FG Zendejas 42
A: 42,620 T: 3:26

Atlanta 16, New England 15—At Fulton County Stadium. Falcon kicker Paul McFadden, who missed a potential game-winning field goal with 3:21 left, took advantage of his chance for redemption with five seconds remaining and booted a 22-yard field goal to win the game. That was bad news for Patriots kicker Greg Davis, whose missed extra point on a New England TD in the second quarter proved to be the margin of difference. Falcon quarterback Chris Miller completed 19 of 34 passes for 265 yards, and kick returner Deion Sanders had a 60-yard return to set up a touchdown in the second quarter.

New England	6	9	0	0	—	15
Atlanta	3	10	0	3	—	16

N.E. — FG Davis 52
Atl — FG McFadden 30
N.E. — FG Davis 32
N.E. — FG Davis 32
Atl — FG McFadden 30
N.E. — Jones 15 pass from Flutie (kick failed)
Atl — Jones 1 run (McFadden kick)
Atl — FG McFadden 22
A: 39,697 T: 3:23

MONDAY, OCTOBER 16

Buffalo 23, L.A. Rams 20—At Rich Stadium. Twenty-one points were scored in the final 2:23 of a wild game that saw unheralded Bills backup quarterback Frank Reich lead his team on two dramatic fourth-quarter TD drives, the last one culminating in an eight-yard TD strike to wide receiver Andre Reed, with 16 seconds left, to win the game. Reich, who was starting in place of the injured Jim Kelly, connected on 21 of 37 passes for 214 yards, and second-year running back Thurman Thomas had his best day as a pro, rushing for 105 yards on 24 carries.

Los Angeles	7	0	3	10	—	20
Buffalo	0	6	0	17	—	23

L.A. — McGee 3 pass from Everett (Lansford kick)
Buff — FG Norwood 38
Buff — FG Norwood 47
L.A. — FG Lansford 34
Buff — FG Norwood 40
L.A. — FG Lansford 36
Buff — Thomas 1 pass from Reich (Norwood kick)
L.A. — Anderson 78 pass from Everett (Lansford kick)
Buff — Reed 8 pass from Reich (Norwood kick)
A: 76,231 T: 3:39

Week Seven

STANDINGS

AFC EAST	W	L	T	Pct	PF	PA
Buffalo	5	2	0	.714	190	163
Indianapolis	4	3	0	.571	134	120
Miami	4	3	0	.571	144	159
New England	2	5	0	.286	108	169
N.Y. Jets	1	6	0	.143	122	192

AFC CENTRAL	W	L	T	Pct	PF	PA
Cincinnati	4	3	0	.571	148	117
Cleveland	4	3	0	.571	163	95
Houston	4	3	0	.571	194	170
Pittsburgh	3	4	0	.429	93	169

AFC WEST	W	L	T	Pct	PF	PA
Denver	6	1	0	.857	160	105
Kansas City	3	4	0	.429	137	159
L.A. Raiders	3	4	0	.429	141	124
Seattle	3	4	0	.429	133	148
San Diego	2	5	0	.286	125	146

NFC EAST	W	L	T	Pct	PF	PA
N.Y. Giants	6	1	0	.857	175	109
Philadelphia	5	2	0	.714	162	140
Washington	4	3	0	.571	186	166
Phoenix	3	4	0	.429	137	163
Dallas	0	7	0	.000	96	213

NFC CENTRAL	W	L	T	Pct	PF	PA
Minnesota	5	2	0	.714	146	113
Chicago	4	3	0	.571	199	163
Green Bay	3	4	0	.429	182	181
Tampa Bay	3	4	0	.429	148	152
Detroit	1	6	0	.143	98	170

NFC WEST	W	L	T	Pct	PF	PA
San Francisco	6	1	0	.857	192	135
L.A. Rams	5	2	0	.714	183	165
New Orleans	3	4	0	.429	175	130
Atlanta	2	5	0	.286	128	163

RESULTS

Denver 24, Seattle 21, OT
San Francisco 37, New England 20
New Orleans 40, L.A. Rams 21
N.Y. Giants 20, San Diego 13
Philadelphia 10, L.A. Raiders 7
Phoenix 34, Atlanta 20
Houston 27, Pittsburgh 0
Indianapolis 23, Cincinnati 12
Miami 23, Green Bay 20
Minnesota 20, Detroit 7
Washington 32, Tampa Bay 28
Kansas City 36, Dallas 28
Buffalo 34, N.Y. Jets 3
Cleveland 27, Chicago 7 (Monday night)

SUNDAY, OCTOBER 22

Denver 24, Seattle 21—At the Kingdome. The kickers missed four of five field goal attempts, but the one that connected, a 27-yarder by Denver's David Treadwell, won the game in overtime for the Broncos. Treadwell, who had hit 12 of 13 attempts coming into the game, missed three tries in regulation, and Norm Johnson of the Seahawks missed a 40-yarder that would have won the game in overtime. The key play for the Broncos was a 54-yard TD pass from quarterback John Elway to Vance Johnson to tie the game with 2:19 left. Elway, who was sacked four times by the Seahawks, still completed 18 of 35 passes for 344 yards and two TDs.

Denver	0	0	7	14	3	—	24
Seattle	7	7	0	7	0	—	21

Sea — Williams 4 run (Johnson kick)
Sea — Williams 6 pass from Krieg (Johnson kick)
Den — Humphrey 1 run (Treadwell kick)
Den — Kay 2 pass from Elway (Treadwell kick)
Sea — Skansi 24 pass from Krieg (Johnson kick)
Den — Johnson 54 pass from Elway (Treadwell kick)
Den — FG Treadwell 27
A: 62,353 T: 3:42

San Francisco 37, New England 20—At Stanford Stadium. The 49ers struggled against the Patriots before putting the game away in the fourth quarter. The win was costly for San Francisco, which lost QB Joe Montana to a sprained knee—he would miss the following week's game against the Jets—and safety Jeff Fuller to a season-ending and career-threatening neck injury. Steve Young, who replaced Montana with five seconds left in the first half, completed 11 of 12 passes for 188 yards and three TDs, including the key 50-yard TD strike to Jerry Rice that gave the Niners the lead for good.

New England	0	10	7	3	—	20
San Francisco	0	17	7	13	—	37

N.E. — Morgan 55 pass from Grogan (Davis kick)
S.F. — Rice 3 pass from Montana (Cofer kick)
S.F. — FG Cofer 23
N.E. — FG Davis 49
S.F. — Walls 1 pass from Young (Cofer kick)
N.E. — Morgan 19 pass from Grogan (Davis kick)
S.F. — Rice 50 pass from Young (Cofer kick)
N.E. — FG Davis 21
S.F. — Taylor 43 pass from Young (Cofer kick)
S.F. — Craig 3 run (kick failed)
A: 70,000 T: 3:20

New Orleans 40, L.A. Rams 21—At Anaheim Stadium. Saints quarterback Bobby Hebert threw for 276 yards and three touchdowns, the defense sacked Ram QB Jim Everett five times and intercepted him twice and New Orleans cruised to a surprisingly easy upset victory. Running back Dalton Hilliard ran for 87 yards and three TDs.

New Orleans	10	9	14	7	—	40
Los Angeles	7	0	7	7	—	21

N.O. — Hilliard 20 pass from Hebert (Andersen kick)
N.O. — FG Andersen 39
L.A. — Ellard 3 pass from Everett (Lansford kick)
N.O. — Hilliard 2 run (kick failed)
N.O. — FG Andersen 27
N.O. — Turner 54 pass from Hebert (Andersen kick)
N.O. — Martin 37 pass from Hebert (Andersen kick)
L.A. — Johnson 1 pass from Everett (Lansford kick)
N.O. — Hilliard 7 run (Andersen kick)
L.A. — Johnson 3 pass from Everett (Lansford kick)
A: 57,567 T: 3:05

N.Y. Giants 20, San Diego 13—At Jack Murphy Stadium. New York's defense held the Chargers to just 179 yards in total offense, Giants running back Ottis Anderson galloped for 96 yards and two touchdowns and Phil Simms completed 22 of 33 passes for 232 yards in a solid win for New York. San Diego's only TD of the day was scored by the defense on an 81-yard fumble return by safety Vencie Glenn with 2:27 left.

New York	3	3	7	7	—	20
San Diego	0	3	3	7	—	13

N.Y. — FG Allegre 21
S.D. — FG Bahr 26
N.Y. — FG Allegre 40
N.Y. — Anderson 4 run (Allegre kick)
S.D. — FG Bahr 30
N.Y. — Anderson 4 run (Allegre kick)
S.D. — Glenn 81 fumble return (Bahr kick)
A: 48,566 T: 2:52

Philadelphia 10, L.A. Raiders 7—At Veterans Stadium. Two interceptions, one by cornerback Izel Jenkins and the other by linebacker Byron Evans, led to a 10-point third quarter, enough to seal the victory for the Eagles in a tough, defensive game. The Raiders appeared to have staved off Philadelphia after Evans's interception when Luis Zendejas missed a 39-yard field goal attempt, but an offside penalty against cornerback Dan Land gave Zendejas another opportunity, and he hit the 34-yarder that proved to be the game-winner.

Los Angeles	0	0	0	7	—	7
Philadelphia	0	0	10	0	—	10

Phi — Cunningham 1 run (Zendejas kick)
Phi — FG Zendejas 34
L.A. — Gault 24 pass from Beuerlein (Jaeger kick)
A: 64,019 T: 2:53

Phoenix 34, Atlanta 20—At Sun Devil Stadium. The Cardinals broke a four-game losing streak by converting two Falcon fumbles into TDs and getting a three-TD day from running back Earl Ferrell. Phoenix QB Gary Hogeboom completed 17 of 25 passes for 181 yards in spite of taking an uppercut to the jaw in a fight with Atlanta linebacker Marcus Cotton in the second quarter.

Atlanta	0	6	7	7	—	20
Phoenix	14	7	3	10	—	34

Phoe — Ferrell 1 run (Del Greco kick)
Phoe — Ferrell 6 run (Del Greco kick)
Atl — FG McFadden 37
Phoe — Wolfley 5 run (Del Greco kick)
Atl — FG McFadden 37
Phoe — FG Del Greco 50
Atl — Jones 14 run (McFadden kick)
Phoe — Ferrell 3 run (Del Greco kick)
Atl — Settle 16 pass from Miller (McFadden kick)
Phoe — FG Del Greco 22
A: 33,894 T: 3:06

Houston 27, Pittsburgh 0—At the Astrodome. The Oiler offense scored 24 first-half points and the defense held the Steelers to 132 yards (only 42 yards in the first three quarters) as Houston cruised to an easy win. Oiler quarterback Warren Moon threw for 229 yards and three touchdowns, and Mike Rozier and Alonzo Highsmith combined for 93 yards on the ground.

Pittsburgh	0	0	0	0	—	0
Houston	7	17	3	0	—	27

Hou — Highsmith 3 pass from Moon (Zendejas kick)
Hou — FG Zendejas 41
Hou — Duncan 51 pass from Moon (Zendejas kick)
Hou — Highsmith 5 pass from Moon (Zendejas kick)
Hou — FG Zendejas 51
A: 59,091 T: 3:17

Indianapolis 23, Cincinnati 12—At Riverfront Stadium. Eric Dickerson rolled over the Bengals for 152 yards on 31 carries, including a 21-yard burst for the touchdown that put the game out of reach, with 1:22 left. Trailing 12-9 late in the game, the Colts scored two TDs in the last two minutes of the fourth quarter, the first on a three-yard TD pass from QB Jack Trudeau to wide receiver Albert Bentley that followed a fumble by Cincinnati running back James Brooks on his own 16, and the second by Dickerson after defensive back Keith Taylor intercepted a pass from Bengal QB Boomer Esiason.

Indianapolis	0	3	6	14	—	23
Cincinnati	6	3	0	3	—	12

Cin — FG Breech 30
Cin — FG Breech 29
Cin — FG Breech 23
Ind — FG Biasucci 27
Ind — Brooks 2 pass from Trudeau (kick failed)
Cin — FG Breech 21
Ind — Bentley 3 pass from Trudeau (Biasucci kick)
Ind — Dickerson 21 run (Biasucci kick)
A: 57,642 T: 2:58

Miami 23, Green Bay 20—At Joe Robbie Stadium. Pete Stoyanovich kicked a 33-yard field goal with six seconds left to win the game for the Dolphins, but it was a costly victory as running backs Troy Stradford and Marc Logan both went down with knee injuries that put Stradford out for the season and Logan on the sidelines for six games. It appeared that Packer QB Don Majkowski might engineer another fantastic finish when he completed two TD strikes to Sterling Sharpe but Miami QB Dan Marino (24 of 37 passes for 333 yards) quickly marched his team into position for the winning field goal.

Green Bay	3	3	0	14	—	20
Miami	7	3	7	6	—	23

Mia — Jensen 7 pass from Marino (Stoyanovich kick)
G.B. — FG Jacke 44
G.B. — FG Jacke 21
Mia — FG Stoyanovich 36
Mia — Clayton 24 pass from Marino (Stoyanovich kick)
Mia — FG Stoyanovich 21
G.B. — Sharpe 22 pass from Majkowski (Jacke kick)
G.B. — Sharpe 10 pass from Majkowski (Jacke kick)
Mia — FG Stoyanovich 33
A: 56,624 T: 3:12

Minnesota 20, Detroit 7—At the Silverdome. The Viking defense sacked Lion rookie quarterback Rodney Peete eight times, intercepted him twice and forced three Detroit fumbles in a dominant performance. Two of the turnovers led to Viking touchdowns, including a one-yard run by Herschel Walker, who had 89 yards on 20 carries. Minnesota linebacker Mike Merriweather had an outstanding day, with one interception, two sacks, two fumbles caused and one fumble recovered.

Minnesota	3	10	7	0	—	20
Detroit	0	0	0	7	—	7

Minn — FG Karlis 40
Minn — FG Karlis 40
Minn — Walker 1 run (Karlis kick)
Minn — Anderson 4 run (Karlis kick)
Det — Peete 2 run (Murray kick)
A: 51,579 T: 3:05

Washington 32, Tampa Bay 28—At RFK Stadium. The Redskins dominated the Bucs for three quarters, then had to hang on for the win as Tampa Bay quarterback Vinny Testaverde roared back with three fourth-quarter TD passes. When Gerald Riggs (99 yards on 28 carries) gave the Skins a 29-7 lead with a six-yard run late in the third quarter, the game appeared out of reach, but Testaverde struck back with two TDs in the first 50 seconds of the fourth quarter, the second one after the Bucs recovered an onside kick. Testaverde, who completed only four of 14 passes in the first half, finished with 19 completions on 38 attempts for 311 yards.

Tampa Bay	7	0	0	21	—	28
Washington	0	12	17	3	—	32

T.B. — Reynolds 33 blocked punt return (Igwebuike kick)
Wash — FG Lohmiller 33
Wash — Safety, Testaverde tackled by Manley in end zone
Wash — Clark 7 pass from Rypien (Lohmiller kick)
Wash — Clark 10 pass from Rypien (Lohmiller kick)
Wash — FG Lohmiller 42
Wash — Riggs 6 run (Lohmiller kick)
T.B. — Tate 10 pass from Testaverde (Igwebuike kick)
T.B. — Hill 20 pass from Testaverde (Igwebuike kick)
Wash — FG Lohmiller 29
T.B. — Carrier 4 pass from Testaverde (Igwebuike kick)
A: 52,862 T: 3:10

Kansas City 36, Dallas 28—At Arrowhead Stadium. The Chiefs used a balanced offense (221 yards passing, 202 yards rushing) to take the victory and keep the Cowboys winless under new coach Jimmy Johnson. Kansas City running back Christian Okoye, already enjoying a great season, added to his gaudy numbers with a career-high 170 yards on 33 carries, including two touchdowns. Dallas running back Paul Palmer, a Kansas City first-round draft choice in 1987, ran for 85 yards against his old team, including a 63-yard TD romp.

Dallas	7	7	0	14	—	28
Kansas City	14	13	9	0	—	36

K.C. — Okoye 2 run (Lowery kick)
Dall — Palmer 63 run (Ruzek kick)
K.C. — Okoye 13 run (Lowery kick)
K.C. — Saxon 4 run (Lowery kick)
Dall — Dixon 97 kickoff return (Ruzek kick)
K.C. — FG Lowery 43
K.C. — FG Lowery 27
K.C. — Safety, McGovern blocked punt out of end zone
K.C. — Pelluer 5 run (Lowery kick)
Dall — Clack 1 run (Ruzek kick)
Dall — Folsom 4 pass from Walsh (Ruzek kick)
A: 76,841 T: 3:31

Buffalo 34, N.Y. Jets 3—At Rich Stadium. The Bills completely dominated the hapless Jets, controlling the clock with a running game that produced 204 yards and holding New York to just 154 yards in total offense. Running back Larry Kinnebrew had his best day since coming to Buffalo during the off-season, rushing for 77 yards on 17 carries. Bills quarterback Frank Reich had another solid day in relief of the injured Jim Kelly, throwing for 145 yards and three touchdowns.

New York	0	0	3	0	—	3
Buffalo	3	10	7	14	—	34

Buff — FG Norwood 38
Buff — Thomas 3 run (Norwood kick)
Buff — FG Norwood 27
Buff — Reed 20 pass from Reich (Norwood kick)
N.Y. — FG Leahy 41
Buff — Harmon 12 pass from Reich (Norwood kick)
Buff — Davis 7 pass from Reich (Norwood kick)
A: 76,811 T: 3:05

MONDAY, OCTOBER 23

Cleveland 27, Chicago 7—At Cleveland Stadium. The Browns had a surprisingly easy time with the once-powerful Bears, who lost their third game in a row for the first time under coach Mike Ditka and fell out of at least a tie for the lead in the NFC Central for the first time since 1983. Cleveland wide receiver Webster Slaughter had a great day, making eight catches for 186 yards, including a 97-yard TD pass from QB Bernie Kosar in the fourth quarter. Kosar completed 22 of 29 passes for 281 yards and two TDs.

Chicago	0	0	0	7	—	7
Cleveland	7	0	10	10	—	27

Cle — Metcalf 3 pass from Kosar (Bahr kick)
Cle — FG Bahr 31
Cle — Metcalf 7 run (Bahr kick)
Cle — Slaughter 97 pass from Kosar (Bahr kick)
Chi — Davis 5 pass from Harbaugh (Butler kick)
Cle — FG Bahr 35
A: 78,722 T: 3:04

STANDINGS

AFC EAST	W	L	T	Pct	PF	PA
Buffalo	6	2	0	.750	221	180
Indianapolis	4	4	0	.500	154	143
Miami	4	4	0	.500	161	190
New England	3	5	0	.375	131	189
N.Y. Jets	1	7	0	.125	132	215

AFC CENTRAL	W	L	T	Pct	PF	PA
Cincinnati	5	3	0	.625	204	140
Cleveland	5	3	0	.625	191	112
Houston	4	4	0	.500	211	198
Pittsburgh	4	4	0	.500	116	186

AFC WEST	W	L	T	Pct	PF	PA
Denver	6	2	0	.750	184	133
L.A. Raiders	4	4	0	.500	178	148
Seattle	4	4	0	.500	143	155
Kansas City	3	5	0	.375	154	182
San Diego	2	6	0	.250	132	156

NFC EAST	W	L	T	Pct	PF	PA
N.Y. Giants	7	1	0	.875	199	123
Philadelphia	6	2	0	.750	190	164
Phoenix	4	4	0	.500	156	173
Washington	4	4	0	.500	210	203
Dallas	0	8	0	.000	106	232

NFC CENTRAL	W	L	T	Pct	PF	PA
Chicago	5	3	0	.625	219	173
Minnesota	5	3	0	.625	160	137
Green Bay	4	4	0	.500	205	201
Tampa Bay	3	5	0	.375	171	208
Detroit	1	7	0	.125	118	193

NFC WEST	W	L	T	Pct	PF	PA
San Francisco	7	1	0	.875	215	145
L.A. Rams	5	3	0	.625	193	185
New Orleans	4	4	0	.500	195	143
Atlanta	2	6	0	.250	141	183

RESULTS

Chicago 20, L.A. Rams 10
Philadelphia 28, Denver 24
Seattle 10, San Diego 7
New England 23, Indianapolis 20, OT
New Orleans 20, Atlanta 13
Phoenix 19, Dallas 10
Pittsburgh 23, Kansas City 17
Green Bay 23, Detroit 20, OT
Cleveland 28, Houston 17
Cincinnati 56, Tampa Bay 23
Buffalo 31, Miami 17
L.A. Raiders 37, Washington 24
San Francisco 23, N.Y. Jets 10
N.Y. Giants 24, Minnesota 14 (Monday night)

SUNDAY, OCTOBER 29

Chicago 20, L.A. Rams 10—At Soldier Field. The Bears' sluggish offense finally got started behind backup quarterback Jim Harbaugh, who replaced ineffective starter Mike Tomczak in the second quarter. Harbaugh, who completed 10 of 13 passes for 157 yards and scrambled five times for 31 yards and a TD, led Chicago on a 17-point second half to secure the win.

Los Angeles	0	3	0	7	—	10
Chicago	0	3	7	10	—	20

L.A. — FG Lansford 45
Chi — FG Butler 35
Chi — Muster 1 run (Butler kick)
Chi — Harbaugh 1 run (Butler kick)
L.A. — Bell 1 run (Lansford kick)
Chi — FG Butler 46
A: 65,506 T: 3:10

Philadelphia 28, Denver 24—At Mile High Stadium. The Eagle defense sacked Bronco quarterback John Elway seven times and harassed him into three costly interceptions, while the offense unveiled a suddenly potent running game that produced 215 yards, including 93 from running back Keith Byars, who scored the game-winning TD with 5:25 left. Denver hung tough throughout, scoring 17 unanswered points to take a 24-21 lead, with 9:18 remaining, on a four-yard pass from Elway to Melvin Bratton. But a fumbled punt by rookie Darren Carrington after the ensuing series gave Philadelphia the ball on the Denver 24.

Philadelphia	14	0	7	7	—	28
Denver	0	7	10	7	—	24

Phi — Byars 16 run (Zendejas kick)
Phi — Carter 5 pass from Cunningham (Zendejas kick)
Den — Elway 10 run (Treadwell kick)
Phi — Giles 66 pass from Cunningham (Zendejas kick)
Den — Johnson 13 pass from Elway (Treadwell kick)
Den — FG Treadwell 18
Den — Bratton 4 pass from Elway (Treadwell kick)
Phi — Byars 1 run (Zendejas kick)
A: 75,065 T: 3:25

Seattle 10, San Diego 7—At the Kingdome. Charger quarterback Jim McMahon, not starting due to nagging injuries and ineffective play, came off the bench to lead a 55-yard drive that culminated in a 14-yard TD pass to tight end Arthur Cox to give the Chargers a 7-3 lead with 1:53 remaining. But the Seahawks came right back behind QB Dave Krieg, who hit five of seven passes for 83 yards in the final drive, including a 21-yarder to Brian Blades for the game-winning TD with :40 remaining. Krieg threw for 311 yards in spite of being sacked five times.

San Diego	0	0	0	7	—	7
Seattle	3	0	0	7	—	10

Sea — FG Johnson 27
S.D. — Cox 14 pass from McMahon (Bahr kick)
Sea — Blades 21 pass from Krieg (Johnson kick)
A: 59,691 T: 3:15

New England 23, Indianapolis 20—At the Hoosier Dome. Patriots kicker Greg Davis, who had missed an opportunity to win the game with a 46-yard field goal attempt on the last play of regulation, hit a 51-yarder to win the game with 5:03 remaining in overtime. The victory was particularly sweet for New England quarterback Steve Grogan, the third player to start at quarterback for the Pats this season, who hit 28 of 46 passes for 355 yards, including a controversial 28-yard completion to Sammy Martin to keep the game-winning drive going. The Colts claimed that Martin was out of bounds, but the replay official ruled that the videotape was inconclusive.

New England	3	0	7	10	3	—	23
Indianapolis	10	0	0	10	0	—	20

N.E. — FG Davis 47
Ind — Rison 22 pass from Trudeau (Biasucci kick)
Ind — FG Biasucci 32
N.E. — Jones 8 pass from Grogan (Davis kick)
N.E. — FG Davis 48
Ind — Boyer 7 pass from Trudeau (Biasucci kick)
N.E. — Stephens 1 run (Davis kick)
Ind — FG Biasucci 39
N.E. — FG Davis 51
A: 59,356 T: 3:43

New Orleans 20, Atlanta 13—At the Superdome. The Saints outgained the Falcons 392-148 but still needed a one-yard TD plunge by running back Dalton Hilliard with 2:12 left to win the game. Hilliard, who scored the Saints' other touchdown as well, gained 93 yards on 25 carries and 97 yards on seven catches. The New Orleans defense held Atlanta QB Chris Miller to just 135 yards passing and sacked him six times.

Atlanta	0	0	10	3	—	13
New Orleans	7	3	3	7	—	20

N.O. — Hilliard 21 pass from Hebert (Andersen kick)
N.O. — FG Andersen 32
Atl — Collins 18 pass from Miller (McFadden kick)
N.O. — FG Andersen 44
Atl — FG McFadden 41
Atl — FG McFadden 48
N.O. — Hilliard 1 run (Andersen kick)
A: 65,153 T: 3:04

Phoenix 19, Dallas 10—At Texas Stadium. Cowboy miscues led to another loss as the Cards scored 13 points on second-half turnovers for the win. Phoenix safety Michael Zordich intercepted a pass by Dallas QB Steve Walsh late in the third quarter and returned it 16 yards for the TD that gave the Cards a 13-3 lead. Two more mistakes—another Walsh interception and a fumble by Derrick Shepard—led to two Al Del Greco field goals that put the game out of reach in the fourth quarter.

Phoenix	6	0	7	6	—	19
Dallas	0	3	0	7	—	10

Phoe — FG Del Greco 40
Phoe — FG Del Greco 25
Dall — FG Ruzek 37
Phoe — Zordich 16 interception return (Del Greco kick)
Phoe — FG Del Greco 31
Dall — Shepard 37 pass from Walsh (Ruzek kick)
Phoe — FG Del Greco 42
A: 44,431 T: 3:19

Pittsburgh 23, Kansas City 17—At Three Rivers Stadium. The Steelers, up 16-0 in the second quarter, allowed the Chiefs to score 17 points behind QB Steve DeBerg (24 of 36 passes for 338 yards) to take the lead in the third quarter. But Pittsburgh QB Bubby Brister connected on a 64-yard strike with Louis Lipps on the last play of the quarter to put the Steelers in front, and the defense shut Kansas City out the rest of the way. Brister, in his first start since a knee injury three weeks earlier, threw for 253 yards and two TDs.

Kansas City	0	3	14	0	—	17
Pittsburgh	10	6	7	0	—	23

Pitt — FG Anderson 41
Pitt — Lipps 16 pass from Brister (Anderson kick)
Pitt — FG Anderson 47
Pitt — FG Anderson 29
K.C. — FG Lowery 50
K.C. — Mandley 8 pass from DeBerg (Lowery kick)
K.C. — Maas 4 fumble return (Lowery kick)
Pitt — Lipps 64 pass from Brister (Anderson kick)
A: 54,194 T: 3:22

Green Bay 23, Detroit 20—At Milwaukee County Stadium. Rookie running back Barry Sanders had an eye-opening 184 yards on 30 carries for the Lions, but in the end it was another rookie, Packer kicker Chris Jacke, who decided the game with a 38-yard field goal in overtime. Detroit had a chance to win the game in regulation when Sanders burst up the middle for 31 yards to the Green Bay 39, but on the next play, Packer linebacker Tim Harris knocked the ball out of the hands of Lion QB Rodney Peete and recovered it himself to end the threat.

Detroit	7	3	0	10	0	—	20
Green Bay	3	7	10	0	3	—	23

G.B. — FG Jacke 49
Det — Johnson 6 pass from Peete (Murray kick)
Det — FG Murray 42
G.B. — Query 4 pass from Majkowski (Jacke kick)
G.B. — FG Jacke 21
G.B. — Sharpe 2 pass from Majkowski (Jacke kick)
Det — FG Murray 46
Det — Peete 14 run (Murray kick)
G.B. — FG Jacke 38
A: 53,731 T: 3:20

Cleveland 28, Houston 17—At Cleveland Stadium. Browns wide receiver Webster Slaughter made four catches for 184 yards as Cleveland used every trick in their playbook to stage a come-from-behind win. An 18-yard reverse by Reggie Langhorne helped set up the Browns' first TD on a five-yard plunge by quarterback Bernie Kosar; an 80-yard flea-flicker from Kosar to Slaughter accounted for the second score; and a 32-yard option pass from rookie running back Eric Metcalf to Langhorne produced the fourth. The third TD came on another bomb from Kosar to Slaughter, this one good for 77 yards.

Houston	7	3	7	0	—	17
Cleveland	0	0	21	7	—	28

Hou — Jeffires 13 pass from Moon (Zendejas kick)
Hou — FG Zendejas 23
Cle — Kosar 5 run (Bahr kick)
Cle — Slaughter 80 pass from Kosar (Bahr kick)
Hou — Rozier 1 run (Zendejas kick)
Cle — Slaughter 77 pass from Kosar (Bahr kick)
Cle — Langhorne 32 pass from Metcalf (Bahr kick)
A: 78,765 T: 2:58

Cincinnati 56, Tampa Bay 23—At Riverfront Stadium. The Bengals, behind 16-14 in the second quarter, exploded for 42 straight points to bury the Bucs. Running back James Brooks had 131 yards on 17 carries in the Cincinnati onslaught that produced a team-record eight TDs. Bengal quarterback Boomer Esiason threw for 197 yards and five TDs before backup Erik Wilhelm stepped in and threw for 98 yards and another TD.

Tampa Bay	7	9	0	7	—	23
Cincinnati	7	14	21	14	—	56

T.B. — Hill 3 pass from Testaverde (Igwebuike kick)
Cin — Holman 1 pass from Esiason (Breech kick)
Cin — Ball 1 run (Breech kick)
T.B. — Safety, Esiason ran out of end zone
T.B. — Carrier 17 pass from Testaverde (Igwebuike kick)
Cin — Brown 8 pass from Esiason (Breech kick)
Cin — Brooks 4 run (Breech kick)
Cin — McGee 14 pass from Esiason (Breech kick)
Cin — Holman 9 pass from Esiason (Breech kick)
Cin — Brown 18 pass from Esiason (Breech kick)
Cin — McGee 46 pass from Wilhelm (Breech kick)
T.B. — Hill 2 pass from Testaverde (Igwebuike kick)
A: 57,225 T: 3:25

Buffalo 31, Miami 17—At Rich Stadium. The Bills ground down the Dolphins with a crushing running game, highlighted by 100-yard days from both Thurman Thomas (148 yards on 27 carries) and Larry Kinnebrew (121 yards on 21 carries). The Bills defense intercepted Miami QB Dan Marino three times and sacked him twice, the first time Marino had been sacked in 19 games.

Miami	3	0	7	7	—	17
Buffalo	0	21	0	10	—	31

Mia — FG Stoyanovich 45
Buff — Kinnebrew 1 run (Norwood kick)
Buff — Thomas 30 run (Norwood kick)
Buff — Beebe 63 pass from Reich (Norwood kick)
Mia — Clayton 44 pass from Marino (Stoyanovich kick)
Buff — FG Norwood 45
Buff — Jackson 40 interception return (Norwood kick)
Mia — Brown 44 pass from Secules (Stoyanovich kick)
A: 80,208 T: 3:13

L.A. Raiders 37, Washington 24—At Memorial Coliseum. Bo Jackson sparked the Raiders with 144 yards on 19 carries, while the defense victimized the Redskins by sacking their quarterbacks seven times, intercepting them four times and forcing eight fumbles. It was the Raiders' third win in four games under new head coach Art Shell.

Washington	7	3	7	7	—	24
Los Angeles	14	3	20	0	—	37

L.A. — Fernandez 18 pass from Beuerlein (Jaeger kick)
L.A. — Fernandez 8 pass from Beuerlein (Jaeger kick)
Wash — Howard 99 kickoff return (Lohmiller kick)
L.A. — FG Jaeger 26
Wash — FG Lohmiller 43
L.A. — Jackson 73 run (Jaeger kick)
L.A. — FG Jaeger 29
L.A. — FG Jaeger 37
L.A. — Anderson 45 interception return (Jaeger kick)
Wash — Clark 27 pass from Rypien (Lohmiller kick)
Wash — Sanders 14 pass from Humphries (Lohmiller kick)
A: 52,781 T: 3:45

San Francisco 23, N.Y. Jets 10—At Giants Stadium. The 49er defense sacked Jet quarterback Ken O'Brien nine times and held the Jets to just 251 yards overall in a dominating performance made even more remarkable by the loss of Pro Bowl nosetackle Michael Carter to a sprained foot. The 49ers were also playing without starting QB Joe Montana and briefly without backup Steve Young.

San Francisco	7	13	3	0	—	23
New York	0	7	3	0	—	10

S.F. — Jones 10 pass from Young (Cofer kick)
N.Y. — McMillan 45 fumble return (Leahy kick)
S.F. — Rice 45 pass from Bono (Cofer kick)
S.F. — FG Cofer 25
S.F. — FG Cofer 41
N.Y. — FG Leahy 24
S.F. — FG Cofer 40
A: 62,805 T: 2:54

MONDAY, OCTOBER 30

N.Y. Giants 24, Minnesota 14—At Giants Stadium. The Giants defense and special teams were the stars of the game, forcing four turnovers and sacking Viking quarterbacks six times. New York broke the game open in the second half when back-to-back fumbles by Alfred Anderson on kickoff returns set up two Giants TDs within 1:23 of one another. Earlier in the third quarter, linebacker Pepper Johnson had intercepted a pass by Minnesota's Tommy Kramer and run it back 39 yards for New York's first touchdown. Jeff Hostetler, filling in for Phil Simms—who went down early with a sprained ankle—threw only 13 passes for 87 yards, but his four scrambles for 21 yards came at key moments for the Giants.

Minnesota	7	0	0	7	—	14
New York	0	0	17	7	—	24

Minn — Walker 8 pass from Kramer (Karlis kick)
N.Y. — Johnson 39 interception return (Allegre kick)
N.Y. — FG Allegre 39
N.Y. — Manuel 11 pass from Hostetler (Allegre kick)
N.Y. — Anderson 2 run (Allegre kick)
Minn — Fenney 1 run (Karlis kick)
A: 76,014 T: 3:14

Week Nine

STANDINGS

AFC EAST	W	L	T	Pct	PF	PA
Buffalo	6	3	0	.667	249	210
Miami	5	4	0	.556	180	203
Indianapolis	4	5	0	.444	167	162
New England	3	6	0	.333	157	216
N.Y. Jets	2	7	0	.222	159	241

AFC CENTRAL	W	L	T	Pct	PF	PA
Cleveland	6	3	0	.667	233	143
Cincinnati	5	4	0	.556	211	168
Houston	5	4	0	.556	246	229
Pittsburgh	4	5	0	.444	123	220

AFC WEST	W	L	T	Pct	PF	PA
Denver	7	2	0	.778	218	140
L.A. Raiders	5	4	0	.556	206	155
Kansas City	4	5	0	.444	174	192
Seattle	4	5	0	.444	153	175
San Diego	3	6	0	.333	152	173

NFC EAST	W	L	T	Pct	PF	PA
N.Y. Giants	8	1	0	.889	219	136
Philadelphia	6	3	0	.667	207	184
Phoenix	4	5	0	.444	169	193
Washington	4	5	0	.444	213	216
Dallas	1	8	0	.111	119	235

NFC CENTRAL	W	L	T	Pct	PF	PA
Minnesota	6	3	0	.667	183	158
Chicago	5	4	0	.556	232	187
Green Bay	5	4	0	.556	219	214
Tampa Bay	3	6	0	.333	202	250
Detroit	1	8	0	.111	149	228

NFC WEST	W	L	T	Pct	PF	PA
San Francisco	8	1	0	.889	246	158
L.A. Rams	5	4	0	.556	214	208
New Orleans	4	5	0	.444	208	174
Atlanta	3	6	0	.333	171	211

RESULTS

Minnesota 23, L.A. Rams 21, OT
Green Bay 14, Chicago 13
Atlanta 30, Buffalo 28
Houston 35, Detroit 31
Cleveland 42, Tampa Bay 31
Dallas 13, Washington 3
Miami 19, Indianapolis 13
L.A. Raiders 28, Cincinnati 7
San Diego 20, Philadelphia 17
N.Y. Giants 20, Phoenix 13
Denver 34, Pittsburgh 7
N.Y. Jets 27, New England 26
Kansas City 20, Seattle 10
San Francisco 31, New Orleans 13 (Monday night)

SUNDAY, NOVEMBER 5

Minnesota 23, L.A. Rams 21—At the Metrodome. The Vikings failed to score a touchdown, but Rich Karlis kicked an NFL record-tying seven field goals, and linebacker Mike Merriweather blocked a punt in overtime that bounced back through the Rams' end zone to account for the game-winning safety. Los Angeles put up a ferocious fight, scrambling back from an 18-7 deficit by scoring two fourth-quarter touchdowns that put them in the lead, 21-18, with only 28 seconds left. But Viking quarterback Wade Wilson (20 of 39 passing attempts for 281 yards) connected with Hassan Jones on a 43-yard bomb with 12 seconds left to put Minnesota on the Rams' 23-yard line, in position for Karlis's game-tying field goal.

Los Angeles	7	0	0	14	0	—	21
Minnesota	3	9	6	3	2	—	23

Minn — FG Karlis 20
L.A. — Bell 1 run (Lansford kick)
Minn — FG Karlis 24
Minn — FG Karlis 22
Minn — FG Karlis 25
Minn — FG Karlis 29
Minn — FG Karlis 36
L.A. — Ellard 6 pass from Everett (Lansford kick)
L.A. — Bell 1 run (Lansford kick)
Minn — FG Karlis 40
Minn — Safety, Merriweather blocked punt out of end zone
A: 59,600 T: 3:15

Green Bay 14, Chicago 13—At Lambeau Field. Instant replay rode to the rescue for the Packers, who benefited from the replay official's decision that Don Majkowski, contrary to the ruling of the referee on the field, had not thrown the last-minute game-winning touchdown pass to Sterling Sharpe from beyond the line of scrimmage. Chicago had gone ahead 13-7 in the third quarter on a two-yard run by Brad Muster, but Majkowski, who threw for 299 yards and two TDs, mounted a 73-yard drive late in the fourth quarter that culminated in the 14-yard pass to Sharpe with 32 seconds left.

Chicago	3	0	10	0	—	13
Green Bay	7	0	0	7	—	14

G.B. — Didier 24 pass from Majkowski (Jacke kick)
Chi — FG Butler 25
Chi — FG Butler 37
Chi — Muster 2 run (Butler kick)
G.B. — Sharpe 14 pass from Majkowski (Jacke kick)
A: 56,556 T: 3:13

Atlanta 30, Buffalo 28—At Fulton County Stadium. Falcon quarterback Chris Miller threw a 41-yard completion to wide receiver Stacey Bailey to set up a 50-yard game-winning field goal, with two seconds left, by kicker Paul McFadden. Things had looked grim for Atlanta just 27 seconds earlier when Bills fullback Larry Kinnebrew bulled across from the one-yard line to give Buffalo the lead, 28-27. Kinnebrew's TD had been set up by an 85-yard kickoff return by the Bills' Don Beebe.

Buffalo	7	0	14	7	—	28
Atlanta	0	3	17	10	—	30

Buff — Lofton 6 pass from Kelly (Norwood kick)
Atl — FG McFadden 54
Atl — Jones 1 run (McFadden kick)
Buff — McKeller 11 pass from Kelly (Norwood kick)
Atl — Dixon 26 pass from Miller (McFadden kick)
Atl — FG McFadden 26
Buff — Thomas 2 run (Norwood kick)
Atl — Jones 3 run (McFadden kick)
Buff — Kinnebrew 1 run (Norwood kick)
Atl — FG McFadden 50
A: 45,267 T: 3:32

Houston 35, Detroit 31—At the Astrodome. The Oilers, sparked by an outstanding performance by quarterback Warren Moon, scored 21 consecutive points in the second half to defeat the Lions. Moon, who completed 30 of 38 passes for 345 yards and two TDs, scored the eventual game-winner on a two-yard plunge with 3:15 remaining. Detroit still had a chance to win when Terry Taylor returned a fumble by Houston's Curtis Duncan 35 yards to give the Lions the ball at midfield with 1:16 left. But Detroit QB Rodney Peete threw his only interception of the game to end the Lions' hopes.

Detroit	7	10	7	7	—	31
Houston	7	7	14	7	—	35

Det — Sanders 1 run (Murray kick)
Hou — White 1 run (Zendejas kick)
Det — Clark 16 pass from Peete (Murray kick)
Hou — Rozier 1 run (Zendejas kick)
Det — FG Murray 47
Det — White 20 fumble return (Murray kick)
Hou — Givins 6 pass from Moon (Zendejas kick)
Hou — Hill 7 pass from Moon (Zendejas kick)
Hou — Moon 2 run (Zendejas kick)
Det — Sanders 14 run (Murray kick)
A: 48,056 T: 3:24

Cleveland 42, Tampa Bay 31—At Tampa Stadium. Buccaneer QB Vinny Testaverde completed 27 of 50 passes for 370 yards and two TDs, but he also threw four costly interceptions, three of which led directly to touchdowns by the Browns. Early in the second quarter, he was picked off by Cleveland's Frank Minnifield, whose 25-yard return set up a seven-yard TD strike from Browns QB Bernie Kosar to rookie wide receiver Lawyer Tillman. Later in the quarter, Felix Wright picked off another Testaverde pass and ran it 27 yards for a touchdown, to be followed just 19 seconds later by Thane Gash's 15-yard interception return for yet another score. Cleveland rookie Eric Metcalf had 233 all-purpose yards.

Cleveland	7	28	0	7	—	42
Tampa Bay	7	10	7	7	—	31

T.B. — Tate 1 run (Igwebuike kick)
Cle — Metcalf 24 pass from Kosar (Bahr kick)
Cle — Tillman 7 pass from Kosar (Bahr kick)
Cle — Wright 27 interception return (Bahr kick)
Cle — Gash 15 interception return (Bahr kick)
T.B. — Wilder 9 pass from Testaverde (Igwebuike kick)
Cle — Tennell 4 pass from Kosar (Bahr kick)
T.B. — FG Igwebuike 53
T.B. — Wilder 9 pass from Testaverde (Igwebuike kick)
Cle — Metcalf 43 run (Bahr kick)
T.B. — Tate 1 run (Igwebuike kick)
A: 69,162 T: 3:26

Dallas 13, Washington 3—At RFK Stadium. The Cowboys used a conservative ball-control offense paced by running back Paul Palmer to gain their first victory of the season and the first ever in the NFL for coach Jimmy Johnson. Palmer, who gained 110 yards on 18 carries, scored the game's only touchdown on a two-yard plunge in the third quarter.

Dallas	0	3	7	3	—	13
Washington	0	0	3	0	—	3

Dall — FG Ruzek 20
Wash — FG Lohmiller 35
Dall — Palmer 2 run (Ruzek kick)
Dall — FG Ruzek 43
A: 53,187 T: 3:10

Miami 19, Indianapolis 13—At Joe Robbie Stadium. Rookie running back Sammie Smith, a holdout through the entire preseason, finally proved his worth to the Dolphins, running for 123 yards on 25 carries to become the first Miami player since 1987 to rush for 100 yards. It was also the first time since 1985 that the Dolphins' running attack had outgained the passing game, as Miami quarterback Dan Marino completed just 14 of 26 passes for 149 yards.

Indianapolis	3	0	0	10	—	13
Miami	3	9	7	0	—	19

Mia — FG Stoyanovich 18
Ind — FG Biasucci 36
Mia — Clayton 13 pass from Marino (Stoyanovich kick)
Mia — Safety, ball snapped out of end zone
Mia — Brown 10 pass from Marino (Stoyanovich kick)
Ind — FG Biasucci 33
Ind — Rison 7 pass from Trudeau (Biasucci kick)
A: 52,680 T: 3:03

L.A. Raiders 28, Cincinnati 7—At Memorial Coliseum. Los Angeles running back Bo Jackson defeated the Bengals almost single-handedly, rushing for 159 yards on 13 carries, including a seven-yard scamper for the Raiders' first touchdown and a team-record 92-yard run for their second. The Bengals were severely hampered by injuries that put quarterback Boomer Esiason on the sidelines with a bruised lung and left Stanford Jennings as the team's only healthy running back.

Cincinnati	0	0	0	7	—	7
Los Angeles	14	7	7	0	—	28

L.A. — Jackson 7 run (Jaeger kick)
L.A. — Jackson 92 run (Jaeger kick)
L.A. — Mueller 25 pass from Schroeder (Jaeger kick)
L.A. — Gault 84 pass from Schroeder (Jaeger kick)
Cin — McGee 34 pass from Wilhelm (Breech kick)
A: 51,080 T: 3:10

San Diego 20, Philadelphia 17—At Jack Murphy Stadium. The Chargers took advantage of a mistake—their own—to beat the Eagles on a 49-yard field goal by Chris Bahr with four seconds left. Bahr had missed a 44-yard attempt on the previous play, but a false start by San Diego's James FitzPatrick before the snap nullified the miss. Charger quarterback Jim McMahon threw for 264 yards, including two TD tosses to Anthony Miller and a key 49-yard completion to wide receiver Wayne Walker to set up the winning field goal. San Diego linebacker Leslie O'Neal had 3½ sacks.

Philadelphia	0	7	0	10	—	17
San Diego	7	0	10	3	—	20

S.D. — Miller 6 pass from McMahon (Bahr kick)
Phi — Garrity 4 pass from Cunningham (DeLine kick)
S.D. — FG Bahr 23
S.D. — Miller 69 pass from McMahon (Bahr kick)
Phi — FG DeLine 43
Phi — Byars 3 run (DeLine kick)
S.D. — FG Bahr 49
A: 47,019 T: 3:12

N.Y. Giants 20, Phoenix 13—At Sun Devil Stadium. Giants quarterback Jeff Hostetler continued to play well in place of the injured Phil Simms, accounting for all three of New York's touchdowns, throwing for one and rushing for the other two. He finished the day with 177 yards passing and 47 yards rushing. But the Giants still needed an interception by linebacker Pepper Johnson with 1:27 left to seal the victory over the Cards.

New York	7	7	6	0	—	20
Phoenix	3	0	7	3	—	13

N.Y. — Hostetler 19 run (Allegre kick)
Phoe — FG Del Greco 37
N.Y. — Baker 35 pass from Hostetler (Allegre kick)
Phoe — Hogeboom 5 run (Del Greco kick)
N.Y. — Hostetler 3 run (kick failed)
Phoe — FG Del Greco 46
A: 46,588 T: 3:05

Denver 34, Pittsburgh 7—At Mile High Stadium. Bronco QB John Elway threw for 261 yards and a TD and ran for 34 yards and another TD, while rookie running back Bobby Humphrey continued to provide Denver with a solid running game, rushing for 105 yards and two TDs on 25 attempts in a dominant Bronco victory.

Pittsburgh	0	7	0	0	—	7
Denver	10	3	7	14	—	34

Den — Humphrey 22 run (Treadwell kick)
Den — FG Treadwell 26
Pitt — Carter 15 pass from Brister (Anderson kick)
Den — FG Treadwell 26
Den — Johnson 44 pass from Elway (Treadwell kick)
Den — Elway 2 run (Treadwell kick)
Den — Humphrey 12 run (Treadwell kick)
A: 74,739 T: 3:04

N.Y. Jets 27, New England 26—At Sullivan Stadium. Pat Leahy kicked a 23-yard field goal with no time left to give the Jets a much-needed win. After falling behind 24-12 early in the fourth quarter, the Patriots charged back on two TD passes by QB Marc Wilson, who had not played in the NFL since December of 1987. But Jet QB Ken O'Brien, who completed 22 of 29 passes for 386 yards and two TDs on the day, brought his team back with a 36-yard completion to tight end Greg Werner to put the Jets in position for the game-winning field goal. New England kicker Greg Davis had another tough day, missing an extra point and two field goal attempts.

New York	7	7	3	10	—	27
New England	3	0	6	17	—	26

N.Y. — McNeil 19 run (Leahy kick)
N.E. — FG Davis 47
N.Y. — Townsell 35 pass from O'Brien (Leahy kick)
N.E. — Stephens 35 run (kick failed)
N.Y. — FG Leahy 18
N.E. — FG Davis 26
N.Y. — Burkett 29 pass from O'Brien (Leahy kick)
N.E. — Jones 65 pass from Wilson (Davis kick)
N.E. — Dykes 11 pass from Wilson (Davis kick)
N.Y. — FG Leahy 23
A: 53,336 T: 3:17

Kansas City 20, Seattle 10—At Arrowhead Stadium. The Chiefs defense forced eight fumbles—recovering four of them—sacked Seahawk quarterback Dave Krieg five times and held Seattle to just 129 total yards. The stars on offense were running back Christian Okoye, who rushed for 126 yards and a TD on a team-record 37 carries, and quarterback Steve Pelluer, who rushed for 69 yards and a TD. The Seahawks have not won in Kansas City since 1980.

Seattle	7	3	0	0	—	10
Kansas City	7	10	0	3	—	20

Sea — Glasgow 38 fumble return (Johnson kick)
K.C. — Okoye 8 run (Lowery kick)
K.C. — Pelluer 10 run (Lowery kick)
K.C. — FG Lowery 34
Sea — FG Johnson 18
K.C. — FG Lowery 33
A: 54,488 T: 3:04

MONDAY, NOVEMBER 6

San Francisco 31, New Orleans 13—At Candlestick Park. Joe Montana, who had missed the 49ers' previous game due to a sprained knee, returned with a vengeance against the Saints, figuring in all four San Francisco touchdowns. Montana completed 22 of 31 passes for 302 yards and three touchdowns through the air and ran three yards for a TD on the ground. The defense also had a fine day, sacking New Orleans QB Bobby Hebert three times, intercepting him twice and limiting him to 183 yards passing.

New Orleans	7	3	3	0	—	13
San Francisco	7	14	3	7	—	31

S.F. — Rice 32 pass from Montana (Cofer kick)
N.O. — Hilliard 1 run (Andersen kick)
S.F. — Rice 2 pass from Montana (Cofer kick)
N.O. — FG Andersen 39
S.F. — Taylor 46 pass from Montana (Cofer kick)
N.O. — FG Andersen 23
S.F. — FG Cofer 44
S.F. — Montana 3 run (Cofer kick)
A: 60,667 T: 2:55

STANDINGS

AFC EAST	W	L	T	Pct	PF	PA
Buffalo	7	3	0	.700	279	217
Miami	6	4	0	.600	211	226
Indianapolis	4	6	0	.400	174	192
New England	3	7	0	.300	181	244
N.Y. Jets	2	8	0	.200	182	272

AFC CENTRAL	W	L	T	Pct	PF	PA
Cleveland	7	3	0	.700	250	150
Houston	6	4	0	.600	272	253
Cincinnati	5	5	0	.500	235	194
Pittsburgh	4	6	0	.400	123	240

AFC WEST	W	L	T	Pct	PF	PA
Denver	8	2	0	.800	234	153
L.A. Raiders	5	5	0	.500	218	169
Kansas City	4	6	0	.400	187	208
San Diego	4	6	0	.400	166	185
Seattle	4	6	0	.400	160	192

NFC EAST	W	L	T	Pct	PF	PA
N.Y. Giants	8	2	0	.800	229	167
Philadelphia	6	4	0	.600	210	194
Phoenix	5	5	0	.500	193	213
Washington	5	5	0	.500	223	219
Dallas	1	9	0	.100	139	259

NFC CENTRAL	W	L	T	Pct	PF	PA
Minnesota	7	3	0	.700	207	168
Chicago	6	4	0	.600	252	187
Green Bay	5	5	0	.500	241	245
Tampa Bay	3	7	0	.300	212	274
Detroit	2	8	0	.200	180	250

NFC WEST	W	L	T	Pct	PF	PA
San Francisco	9	1	0	.900	291	161
L.A. Rams	6	4	0	.600	245	218
New Orleans	5	5	0	.500	236	198
Atlanta	3	7	0	.300	174	256

RESULTS

L.A. Rams 31, N.Y. Giants 10
Chicago 20, Pittsburgh 0
New Orleans 28, New England 24
San Francisco 45, Atlanta 3
Detroit 31, Green Bay 22
Phoenix 24, Dallas 20
Miami 31, N.Y. Jets 23
Cleveland 17, Seattle 7
Washington 10, Philadelphia 3
Denver 16, Kansas City 13
Minnesota 24, Tampa Bay 10
Buffalo 30, Indianapolis 7
San Diego 14, L.A. Raiders 12
Houston 26, Cincinnati 24 (Monday night)

SUNDAY, NOVEMBER 12

L.A. Rams 31, N.Y. Giants 10—At Anaheim Stadium. Ram quarterback Jim Everett completed 23 of 33 passes—including 18 in a row at one point—for 295 yards and two touchdowns in a game dominated by Los Angeles. The Ram defense sacked Giants QB Phil Simms four times, intercepted him once and limited New York to just 207 total yards, including a measly six rushing yards on the day. A fumbled kickoff by Giants return man Dave Meggett allowed Everett to hit two TD passes within 14 seconds of one another late in the second quarter, the first a 51-yard strike to Aaron Cox and the second a 21-yard toss to Flipper Anderson.

New York	0	3	0	7	—	10
Los Angeles	10	14	7	0	—	31

L.A. — FG Lansford 44
L.A. — Bell 1 run (Lansford kick)
N.Y. — FG Allegre 22
L.A. — Cox 51 pass from Everett (Lansford kick)
L.A. — Anderson 21 pass from Everett (Lansford kick)
L.A. — Bell 2 run (Lansford kick)
N.Y. — Anderson 1 run (Allegre kick)
A: 65,127 T: 3:03

Chicago 20, Pittsburgh 0—At Three Rivers Stadium. The defense carried the day for the Bears, sacking Steeler quarterback Bubby Brister four times, intercepting him three times and recovering three fumbles. Seventeen of Chicago's 20 points came as a result of Pittsburgh turnovers. Bears QB Jim Harbaugh threw for 125 yards and ran for 56 more, while Kevin Butler was 2 for 2 on field goal attempts, giving him 22 consecutive field goals without a miss, one shy of Mark Moseley's NFL record.

Chicago	7	13	0	0	—	20
Pittsburgh	0	0	0	0	—	0

Chi — Anderson 2 run (Butler kick)
Chi — FG Butler 39
Chi — Muster 20 pass from Harbaugh (Butler kick)
Chi — FG Butler 35
A: 56,505 T: 2:51

New Orleans 28, New England 24—At Sullivan Stadium. The Saints took advantage of three Patriots turnovers in the first half to score four touchdowns in a seven-minute span and jump in front 28-0 but then had to hang on to win as New England scored twice in the game's last four minutes. Running back Dalton Hilliard was the workhorse for New Orleans, rushing for 106 yards and two TDs on 28 carries, while New England quarterback Steve Grogan was forced to attempt 59 passes, completing 27 of them for 283 yards and a TD.

New Orleans	7	21	0	0	—	28
New England	0	10	0	14	—	24

N.O. — Hilliard 3 run (Andersen kick)
N.O. — Brenner 1 pass from Hebert (Andersen kick)
N.O. — Maxie 26 interception return (Andersen kick)
N.O. — Hilliard 10 run (Andersen kick)
N.E. — Perryman 1 run (Staurovsky kick)
N.E. — FG Staurovsky 44
N.E. — Dykes 13 pass from Grogan (Staurovsky kick)
N.E. — Perryman 3 run (Staurovsky kick)
A: 47,680 T: 3:15

San Francisco 45, Atlanta 3—At Candlestick Park. The 49ers continued to roll, as San Francisco quarterback Joe Montana ran for one touchdown and completed 16 of 19 passes for 270 yards and three more TDs through the air. Roger Craig ran for 109 yards on 17 carries and Jerry Rice caught three passes for two TDs and 81 yards to give him his fourth consecutive 1,000-yard season. The Falcons' only points were scored on a 25-yard field goal by quarterback Chris Miller, who was forced to make the attempt when regular kicker Paul McFadden strained his right thigh in pregame warmups.

Atlanta	0	3	0	0	—	3
San Francisco	7	21	10	7	—	45

S.F. — Montana 1 run (Cofer kick)
Atl — FG Miller 25
S.F. — Rice 39 pass from Montana (Cofer kick)
S.F. — Haley 3 fumble recovery (Cofer kick)
S.F. — Taylor 2 pass from Montana (Cofer kick)
S.F. — Rice 11 pass from Montana (Cofer kick)
S.F. — FG Cofer 18
S.F. — Henderson 11 run (Cofer kick)
A: 59,914 T: 3:04

Detroit 31, Green Bay 22—At the Silverdome. The Packers outgained the Lions 432-128, but three early turnovers allowed the Lions to take a 24-3 halftime lead that they never relinquished. Green Bay quarterback Don Majkowski completed 34 of 59 passes for 357 yards, but his two interceptions led to Lion TDs, and his first-quarter fumble gave them a field goal as well. Still the Packers had a chance to win, trailing 24-20 in the fourth quarter, but running back Michael Haddix fumbled at midfield and Barry Sanders later dived over from the one-yard line to put the game out of reach.

Green Bay	0	3	14	5	—	22
Detroit	3	21	0	7	—	31

Det — FG Murray 45
Det — Johnson 17 pass from Peete (Murray kick)
Det — Johnson 8 pass from Peete (Murray kick)
G.B. — FG Jacke 34
Det — Holmes 23 interception return (Murray kick)
G.B. — Haddix 6 pass from Majkowski (Jacke kick)
G.B. — Workman 1 run (Jacke kick)
G.B. — FG Jacke 40
Det — Sanders 1 run (Murray kick)
G.B. — Safety, Peete runs out of end zone
A: 44,324 T: 3:41

Phoenix 24, Dallas 20—At Sun Devil Stadium. It was another heartbreaking loss for the Cowboys, who watched as Cardinals backup quarterback Tom Tupa heaved a 72-yard touchdown bomb to Ernie Jones with 58 seconds left to pull out the win for Phoenix. The one bright spot for Dallas was the return of rookie QB Troy Aikman, who had his best day as a pro, completing 21 of 40 passes for 379 yards and two TDs, including a 75-yard pass to James Dixon that had given the Cowboys a 20-17 lead with 1:43 remaining. Tupa, who replaced Gary Hogeboom, completed 14 of 22 passes for 245 yards and two TDs, all in the second half.

Dallas	3	10	0	7	—	20
Phoenix	0	7	0	17	—	24

Dall — FG Zendejas 32
Dall — FG Zendejas 29
Phoe — McDonald 53 interception return (Del Greco kick)
Dall — Martin 5 pass from Aikman (Zendejas kick)
Phoe — FG Del Greco 45
Phoe — Jones 38 pass from Tupa (Del Greco kick)
Dall — Dixon 75 pass from Aikman (Zendejas kick)
Phoe — Jones 72 pass from Tupa (Del Greco kick)
A: 49,657 T: 3:21

Miami 31, N.Y. Jets 23—At Giants Stadium. After an ineffective first half that saw his team fall behind 20-3, Dolphin quarterback Dan Marino came back with a vengeance, throwing for 195 yards and two touchdowns in the third quarter alone. Marino finished the day with 18 completions on 34 attempts for 359 yards and three TDs, while running back Sammie Smith had 61 yards rushing, including a two-yard TD dive in the third quarter that put the game out of reach. Pete Stoyanovich kicked a 59-yard field goal in the second quarter to tie Tony Franklin for the third-longest field goal in NFL history.

Miami	0	10	21	0	—	31
New York	3	17	0	3	—	23

N.Y. — FG Leahy 38
N.Y. — FG Leahy 20
N.Y. — Vick 26 run (Leahy kick)
Mia — FG Stoyanovich 59
N.Y. — McNeil 25 pass from O'Brien (Leahy kick)
Mia — Brown 8 pass from Marino (Stoyanovich kick)
Mia — Clayton 78 pass from Marino (Stoyanovich kick)
Mia — Schwedes 65 pass from Marino (Stoyanovich kick)
Mia — Smith 2 run (Stoyanovich kick)
N.Y. — FG Leahy 22
A: 65,923 T: 3:11

Cleveland 17, Seattle 7—At the Kingdome. Browns quarterback Bernie Kosar threw a 17-yard touchdown pass to rookie wide receiver Lawyer Tillman to break a 7-7 tie in the third quarter and send Cleveland on to the win in a game dominated by the two defenses. The Browns defense intercepted Seahawk QB Dave Krieg three times and held Seattle to just 180 yards in total offense.

Cleveland	0	7	7	3	—	17
Seattle	7	0	0	0	—	7

Sea — Blades 8 pass from Krieg (Johnson kick)
Cle — Manoa 1 run (Bahr kick)
Cle — Tillman 17 pass from Kosar (Bahr kick)
Cle — FG Bahr 29
A: 58,978 T: 2:58

Washington 10, Philadelphia 3—At Veterans Stadium. The Redskins jumped out to a 10-0 lead, then used a ball-control offense to eat up the clock and secure the win. Washington running back Jamie Morris, playing in place of the injured Gerald Riggs, rushed for 88 yards on 38 carries, while the defense held Eagle QB Randall Cunningham to no yards on four carries. Cunningham was victimized by his own receivers, who dropped eight passes, and also by his own errant pass in the third quarter that was intercepted by Redskins linebacker Kurt Gouveia at the Washington 14-yard line.

Washington	3	7	0	0	—	10
Philadelphia	0	3	0	0	—	3

Wash — FG Lohmiller 34
Wash — Byner 1 run (Lohmiller kick)
Phi — FG DeLine 49
A: 65,443 T: 3:04

Denver 16, Kansas City 13—At Arrowhead Stadium. Bronco QB John Elway continued to post mediocre numbers (11 of 22 passing attempts for 133 yards and an interception) but got the job done in the clutch, completing a short shovel pass to Steve Sewell, who scooted 30 yards to set up David Treadwell's 26-yard game-winning field goal with one second left. Rookie Bobby Humphrey had 77 yards on 21 carries for Denver.

Denver	3	7	3	3	—	16
Kansas City	0	6	0	7	—	13

Den — FG Treadwell 18
K.C. — FG Lowery 39
Den — Kragen 17 fumble return (Treadwell kick)
K.C. — FG Lowery 42
Den — FG Treadwell 27
K.C. — Harry 5 pass from Pelluer (Lowery kick)
Den — FG Treadwell 26
A: 76,245 T: 3:02

Minnesota 24, Tampa Bay 10—At Tampa Stadium. The Viking defense performed well all day, sacking Buccaneer quarterback Vinny Testaverde seven times and limiting Tampa Bay to just 201 yards in total offense, while the sputtering offense came through when it had to with a time-consuming 76-yard drive to put the game away in the fourth quarter. The drive culminated in a one-yard TD plunge by Herschel Walker, who was held to 48 yards on 18 carries. Defensive end Chris Doleman had three sacks for the Vikings.

Minnesota	17	0	0	7	—	24
Tampa Bay	0	3	0	7	—	10

Minn — FG Karlis 41
Minn — Rutland 27 fumble return (Karlis kick)
Minn — Jordan 3 pass from Wilson (Karlis kick)
T.B. — FG Igwebuike 22
T.B. — Wilder 5 pass from Testaverde (Igwebuike kick)
Minn — Walker 1 run (Karlis kick)
A: 56,721 T: 3:00

Buffalo 30, Indianapolis 7—At Rich Stadium. Colt kick returner James Pruitt fumbled away the opening kickoff, and running back Eric Dickerson fumbled on Indianapolis's next two possessions to allow the Bills to take a 13-0 lead in the first quarter. When Buffalo quarterback Jim Kelly hit Andre Reed with a pair of second-quarter TD passes to give the Bills a 27-0 lead, the game was all but over. Buffalo running back Thurman Thomas rushed for 127 yards on 29 carries.

Indianapolis	0	0	0	7	—	7
Buffalo	13	14	0	3	—	30

Buff — Thomas 8 pass from Kelly (Norwood kick)
Buff — FG Norwood 42
Buff — FG Norwood 40
Buff — Reed 32 pass from Kelly (Norwood kick)
Buff — Reed 3 pass from Kelly (Norwood kick)
Buff — FG Norwood 32
Ind — Dixon fumble recovery in end zone (Biasucci kick)
A: 79,256 T: 3:05

San Diego 14, L.A. Raiders 12—At Jack Murphy Stadium. The Chargers spotted the Raiders to a 12-0 lead, then charged back and won the game on a 91-yard kickoff return by Anthony Miller in the third quarter and a five-yard scamper by Tim Spencer with 8:48 left. Spencer, who had fumbled on the Los Angeles one-yard line on San Diego's previous possession, ran for 59 yards on 10 carries. Jay Schroeder threw for 173 yards for the Raiders but was intercepted three times, while Bo Jackson had his third straight 100-yard game, gaining 103 yards on 21 carries.

Los Angeles	3	6	3	0	—	12
San Diego	0	0	7	7	—	14

L.A. — FG Jaeger 23
L.A. — FG Jaeger 36
L.A. — FG Jaeger 33
L.A. — FG Jaeger 32
S.D. — Miller 91 kickoff return (Bahr kick)
S.D. — Spencer 5 run (Bahr kick)
A: 59,151 T: 3:11

MONDAY, NOVEMBER 13

Houston 26, Cincinnati 24—At the Astrodome. Oiler QB Warren Moon led his team on a stirring 70-yard drive in the final 4:47 to set up a 28-yard game-winning field goal with no time left by Tony Zendejas. It was a bitter loss for Cincinnati, which grabbed the lead three times only to be overtaken in each case by Houston. Running back James Brooks had 141 yards on 19 carries for Cincinnati, while Moon had 198 yards passing and 23 more on the ground, including a critical 10-yard scramble on the final drive.

Cincinnati	0	14	0	10	—	24
Houston	0	7	6	13	—	26

Cin — Brooks 58 run (Breech kick)
Hou — Seale recovered blocked punt in end zone (Zendejas kick)
Cin — Taylor 1 run (Breech kick)
Hou — FG Zendejas 32
Hou — FG Zendejas 42
Hou — FG Zendejas 47
Cin — Holman 73 pass from Esiason (Breech kick)
Hou — Harris 23 pass from Moon (Zendejas kick)
Cin — FG Breech 38
Hou — FG Zendejas 28
A: 60,694 T: 3:31

Week Eleven

STANDINGS

AFC EAST	W	L	T	Pct	PF	PA
Buffalo	7	4	0	.636	303	250
Miami	7	4	0	.636	228	240
Indianapolis	5	6	0	.455	201	202
New England	4	7	0	.364	214	268
N.Y. Jets	2	9	0	.182	192	299

AFC CENTRAL	W	L	T	Pct	PF	PA
Cleveland	7	3	1	.682	260	160
Houston	7	4	0	.636	295	260
Cincinnati	6	5	0	.545	277	201
Pittsburgh	5	6	0	.455	143	257

AFC WEST	W	L	T	Pct	PF	PA
Denver	9	2	0	.818	248	163
L.A. Raiders	5	6	0	.455	225	192
Kansas City	4	6	1	.409	197	218
San Diego	4	7	0	.364	183	205
Seattle	4	7	0	.364	163	207

NFC EAST	W	L	T	Pct	PF	PA
N.Y. Giants	9	2	0	.818	244	170
Philadelphia	7	4	0	.636	220	203
Phoenix	5	6	0	.455	207	250
Washington	5	6	0	.455	233	233
Dallas	1	10	0	.091	153	276

NFC CENTRAL	W	L	T	Pct	PF	PA
Minnesota	7	4	0	.636	216	178
Chicago	6	5	0	.545	283	219
Green Bay	6	5	0	.545	262	262
Tampa Bay	4	7	0	.364	244	305
Detroit	2	9	0	.182	187	292

NFC WEST	W	L	T	Pct	PF	PA
San Francisco	9	2	0	.818	308	182
L.A. Rams	7	4	0	.636	282	232
New Orleans	6	5	0	.545	262	215
Atlanta	3	8	0	.273	191	282

RESULTS

Philadelphia 10, Minnesota 9
Tampa Bay 32, Chicago 31
Indianapolis 27, N.Y. Jets 10
Cincinnati 42, Detroit 7
Green Bay 21, San Francisco 17
Houston 23, L.A. Raiders 7
L.A. Rams 37, Phoenix 14
N.Y. Giants 15, Seattle 3
New England 33, Buffalo 24
New Orleans 26, Atlanta 17
Miami 17, Dallas 14
Kansas City 10, Cleveland 10, OT
Pittsburgh 20, San Diego 17
Denver 14, Washington 10 (Monday night)

SUNDAY, NOVEMBER 19

Philadelphia 10, Minnesota 9—At Veterans Stadium. Eagle wide receiver Cris Carter made a diving catch of a tipped pass from Randall Cunningham for the game-winning touchdown with 2:32 left. The play was set up when Herschel Walker fumbled near midfield late in the fourth quarter, Eagle linebacker Byron Evans recovered and then lateraled to cornerback Eric Allen, who returned the ball to the Viking 20-yard line before fumbling out of bounds. The Vikings had gone ahead on Herschel Walker's 93-yard kickoff return on the opening play—Rich Karlis missed the extra point—and Karlis's 49-yard field goal in the third quarter.

Minnesota	6	0	3	0	—	9
Philadelphia	3	0	0	7	—	10

Minn — Walker 93 kickoff return (kick failed)
Phi — FG DeLine 34
Minn — FG Karlis 49
Phi — Carter 3 pass from Cunningham (DeLine kick)
A: 65,944 T: 3:12

Tampa Bay 32, Chicago 31—At Soldier Field. The Bucs beat the Bears for the second time this season as Donald Igwebuike kicked a 28-yard field goal with no time left to win the game. It was Igwebuike's fourth field goal of the day, and it thwarted a comeback by the Bears and quarterback Mike Tomczak, who came off the bench to throw three TD passes—two of them to Wendell Davis—in a span of 2:41 and put his team in the lead 31-30. But Tampa Bay QB Vinny Testaverde, who threw for 288 yards on the day, responded by leading the Bucs on an eight-play 56-yard drive in the final two minutes that set up the game-winning kick. Kevin Butler kicked his 23rd consecutive field goal, a 40-yard shot in the second quarter, to tie Mark Moseley for the NFL record.

Tampa Bay	10	0	3	19	—	32
Chicago	0	3	7	21	—	31

T.B. — FG Igwebuike 26
T.B. — Davis 13 interception return (Igwebuike kick)
Chi — FG Butler 40
T.B. — FG Igwebuike 22
Chi — Anderson 59 run (Butler kick)
T.B. — Tate 15 run (Igwebuike kick)
T.B. — FG Igwebuike 29
Chi — Morris 58 pass from Tomczak (Butler kick)
T.B. — Carrier 78 pass from Testaverde (Igwebuike kick)
Chi — Davis 26 pass from Tomczak (Butler kick)
Chi — Davis 52 pass from Tomczak (Butler kick)
T.B. — FG Igwebuike 28
A: 63,826 T: 3:34

Indianapolis 27, N.Y. Jets 10—At the Hoosier Dome. Colt quarterback Jack Trudeau had perhaps his finest afternoon as a pro, completing 17 of 28 passes for 255 yards and a touchdown in leading Indianapolis to an easy win. Eric Dickerson was back in top form for the Colts as well, gaining 131 yards on 31 carries, and rookie wide receiver Andre Rison caught five passes for 108 yards. The Jets were woeful in defeat, scoring their only TD on the last play of the game as the Indianapolis defense sacked New York QB Ken O'Brien five times, intercepted him twice and finally knocked him out of the game with a bruised elbow in the fourth quarter.

New York	0	3	0	7	—	10
Indianapolis	3	17	7	0	—	27

Ind — FG Biasucci 45
Ind — Bentley 1 run (Biasucci kick)
N.Y. — FG Leahy 46
Ind — Beach 1 pass from Trudeau (Biasucci kick)
Ind — FG Biasucci 31
Ind — Dickerson 1 run (Biasucci kick)
N.Y. — Townsell 23 pass from Ryan (Leahy kick)
A: 58,236 T: 3:18

Cincinnati 42, Detroit 7—At Riverfront Stadium. Bengal quarterback Boomer Esiason completed 30 of 39 passes for 399 yards and three TDs as Cincinnati erupted for 42 unanswered points in the final three quarters of the game to bury the Lions. The only bright spot for Detroit was rookie running back Barry Sanders, who rushed for 114 yards and a TD on 18 carries. Bengal wide receiver Tim McGee had 11 catches for 194 yards.

Detroit	7	0	0	0	—	7
Cincinnati	0	28	7	7	—	42

Det — Sanders 2 run (Murray kick)
Cin — McGee 17 pass from Esiason (Breech kick)
Cin — Taylor 3 run (Breech kick)
Cin — Taylor 1 pass from Esiason (Breech kick)
Cin — Bussey blocked punt recovery in end zone (Breech kick)
Cin — Martin 15 pass from Esiason (Breech kick)
Cin — Smith 41 pass from Wilhelm (Breech kick)
A: 55,720 T: 3:40

Green Bay 21, San Francisco 17—At Candlestick Park. The Packer defense sacked 49er quarterback Joe Montana six times, intercepted him once—Montana's first interception in 150 passing attempts—and recovered three fumbles to keep San Francisco in check. The 49ers also contributed to the upset with 10 penalties for 72 yards, committing several of the infractions in critical situations. Green Bay QB Don Majkowski threw for 153 yards and a TD, ran for 15 yards and a second score and Brent Fullwood rushed for 76 yards on 16 carries to pace the Pack. Montana, in spite of the sacks, completed 30 of 42 passes for 325 yards and two TDs, and Jerry Rice had nine catches for 106 yards.

Green Bay	7	7	0	7	—	21
San Francisco	7	7	0	3	—	17

G.B. — Majkowski 2 run (Jacke kick)
S.F. — Craig 4 pass from Montana (Cofer kick)
G.B. — Sharpe 4 pass from Majkowski (Jacke kick)
S.F. — Rice 9 pass from Montana (Cofer kick)
G.B. — Majkowski 8 run (Jacke kick)
S.F. — FG Cofer 44
A: 62,219 T: 3:12

Houston 23, L.A. Raiders 7—At the Astrodome. The Oilers dominated the Raiders to win their third in a row, a first under coach Jerry Glanville. QB Warren Moon completed 20 of 30 passes for 249 yards and two TDs, while Mike Rozier, Allen Pinkett and Alonzo Highsmith combined for 141 yards rushing. The Houston defense was equally dominant, holding Bo Jackson to a season-low 54 yards, intercepting quarterback Steve Beuerlein three times and forcing two fumbles.

Los Angeles	0	7	0	0	—	7
Houston	7	10	3	3	—	23

Hou — Duncan 25 pass from Moon (Zendejas kick)
L.A. — Dyal 22 pass from Beuerlein (Jaeger kick)
Hou — FG Zendejas 20
Hou — Harris 11 pass from Moon (Zendejas kick)
Hou — FG Zendejas 20
Hou — FG Zendejas 46
A: 59,198 T: 3:06

L.A. Rams 37, Phoenix 14—At Anaheim Stadium. The Rams were in command from the opening kickoff, running up a 24-0 half-time lead and cruising to the easy win. L.A. QB Jim Everett completed 15 of 24 passes for 308 yards and two touchdowns, both of them to Henry Ellard, who had five catches for 163 yards. The defense had five sacks and four interceptions on the game, with at least one theft against each of the three quarterbacks used by the Cardinals.

Phoenix	0	0	7	7	—	14
Los Angeles	14	10	3	10	—	37

L.A. — Stewart 41 interception return (Lansford kick)
L.A. — Ellard 49 pass from Everett (Lansford kick)
L.A. — Delpino 32 run (Lansford kick)
L.A. — FG Lansford 27
L.A. — FG Lansford 23
Phoe — Holmes 77 pass from Tupa (Del Greco kick)
L.A. — FG Lansford 40
L.A. — Ellard 42 pass from Everett (Lansford kick)
Phoe — Jordan 1 run (Del Greco kick)
A: 53,176 T: 3:14

N.Y. Giants 15, Seattle 3—At Giants Stadium. The Giants defense dominated the game, holding the Seahawks to just 195 yards, intercepting two passes and sacking Seattle QB Kelly Stouffer for a safety, while their running game dominated the clock, running up 162 yards on 45 carries. In spite of the emphasis on ball control, New York QB Phil Simms completed 17 of 26 passes for 194 yards and the Giants' only TD.

Seattle	0	0	0	3	—	3
New York	7	0	8	0	—	15

N.Y. — Cross 16 pass from Simms (Nittmo kick)
N.Y. — FG Nittmo 32
N.Y. — Safety, Stouffer fumbled ball out of end zone
N.Y. — FG Nittmo 32
Sea — FG Johnson 42
A: 75,014 T: 2:55

New England 33, Buffalo 24—At Sullivan Stadium. The Patriots scored 20 unanswered points in the fourth quarter to come back from a 24-13 deficit and pull away for the win. Bills turnovers figured prominently in the outcome as Buffalo QB Jim Kelly was intercepted by rookie cornerback Maurice Hurst for the go-ahead touchdown, then fumbled the ball away for the game-clinching field goal. Kelly, who threw for 356 yards, was intercepted twice, and the Bills lost four fumbles on the day. John Stephens ran for 126 yards on 23 carries for New England, and Jason Staurovsky kicked four field goals.

Buffalo	7	3	0	14	—	24
New England	0	6	7	20	—	33

Buff — Thomas 3 run (Norwood kick)
N.E. — FG Staurovsky 34
N.E. — FG Staurovsky 24
Buff — FG Norwood 31
N.E. — Egu 15 run (Staurovsky kick)
Buff — Kinnebrew 1 run (Norwood kick)
Buff — Thomas 25 pass from Kelly (Norwood kick)
N.E. — Dykes 14 pass from Grogan (Staurovsky kick)
N.E. — FG Staurovsky 34
N.E. — Hurst 16 interception return (Staurovsky kick)
N.E. — FG Staurovsky 38
A: 49,663 T: 3:22

New Orleans 26, Atlanta 17—At Fulton County Stadium. The Saints used a devastating running game to come back from a 10-3 deficit and overwhelm the Falcons in the second half. New Orleans was led on offense by Dalton Hilliard, who rushed for a career-high 158 yards and a TD on 29 carries, including 106 yards in the second half. The spark plug on defense was linebacker Pat Swilling who sacked Atlanta QB Chris Miller 3½ times for losses of 39 yards.

New Orleans	3	0	9	14	—	26
Atlanta	3	7	7	0	—	17

Atl — FG Davis 45
N.O. — FG Andersen 33
Atl — Settle 27 pass from Miller (Davis kick)
N.O. — Hilliard 22 run (Andersen kick)
N.O. — Safety, Forde blocked punt out of end zone
Atl — Wilkins 19 pass from Miller (Davis kick)
N.O. — Jordan 2 run (Andersen kick)
N.O. — Jordan 1 run (Andersen kick)
A: 53,173 T: 3:06

Miami 17, Dallas 14—At Texas Stadium. The Cowboys outgained the Dolphins 428-303 but scored only twice as Miami came back from a 14-3 deficit to pull out the victory. The Dolphin touchdowns were scored on a Hail Mary pass from QB Dan Marino to Andre Brown at the close of the first half and a one-yard TD run by Sammie Smith in the fourth quarter that came after an interception by safety Liffort Hobley. That errant pass was the only mistake by Dallas quarterback Troy Aikman, who completed 25 of 33 passes for 261 yards and a TD and ran for 71 yards more on eight carries.

Miami	0	10	0	7	—	17
Dallas	7	7	0	0	—	14

Dall — Sargent 1 run (Zendejas kick)
Mia — FG Stoyanovich 23
Dall — Johnston 6 pass from Aikman (Zendejas kick)
Mia — Brown 48 pass from Marino (Stoyanovich kick)
Mia — Smith 1 run (Stoyanovich kick)
A: 56,044 T: 3:14

Kansas City 10, Cleveland 10—At Cleveland Stadium. The Chiefs' Nick Lowery, among the NFL's most accurate kickers over his 10-year career, missed a 45-yard field goal with five seconds left in regulation, missed a second try from 39 yards when a penalty nullified the previous attempt and finally missed a 47-yarder in overtime, all of which allowed the Browns to hold on for the tie. Thirteen of the 20 points scored in the game came after turnovers as Cleveland fumbled the ball away four times, and Kansas City quarterbacks threw three interceptions. The Browns defense had five sacks and held the Chiefs' Christian Okoye to just 40 yards on the day.

Kansas City	0	0	7	3	0	—	10
Cleveland	0	3	7	0	0	—	10

Cle — FG Bahr 40
K.C. — Smith 3 fumble return (Lowery kick)
Cle — Metcalf 1 run (Bahr kick)
K.C. — Lowery 41
A: 77,922 T: 4:14

Pittsburgh 20, San Diego 17—At Three Rivers Stadium. The Steelers gained only 191 offensive yards but were able to win anyway on the strength of their special teams, which recovered two Charger fumbles on punt returns and registered a touchdown on an 84-yard kickoff return by Rod Woodson. It was a tough loss for San Diego QB Jim McMahon, who completed 19 of 36 passes for 226 yards and two TDs, both of them to Anthony Miller, who had seven catches for 104 yards.

San Diego	0	7	10	0	—	17
Pittsburgh	3	3	7	7	—	20

Pitt — FG Anderson 49
S.D. — Miller 20 pass from McMahon (Bahr kick)
Pitt — FG Anderson 28
S.D. — FG Bahr 27
Pitt — Woodson 84 kickoff return (Anderson kick)
S.D. — Miller 19 pass from McMahon (Bahr kick)
Pitt — Hoge 1 run (Anderson kick)
A: 44,203 T: 3:09

MONDAY, NOVEMBER 20

Denver 14, Washington 10—At RFK Stadium. Starting in just his second game in the past five years, backup Bronco QB Gary Kubiak completed only 13 of 27 passes for 123 yards, but he got the job done anyway, tossing a pair of TD passes for the victory in a hard-fought defensive contest. Forced to play without starter John Elway, who was sidelined by a stomach virus, Denver relied heavily on its ground game and rookie Bobby Humphrey, who rushed for 110 yards on 31 carries. The Redskins, who gained just 223 offensive yards, were hurt by a pair of fumbles by running back Jamie Morris.

Denver	7	7	0	0	—	14
Washington	7	0	3	0	—	10

Wash — Morris 8 run (Lohmiller kick)
Den — Bratton 1 pass from Kubiak (Treadwell kick)
Den — Nattiel 5 pass from Kubiak (Treadwell kick)
Wash — FG Lohmiller 32
A: 52,975 T: 2:55

STANDINGS

AFC EAST	W	L	T	Pct	PF	PA
Buffalo	8	4	0	.667	327	257
Miami	7	5	0	.583	242	274
Indianapolis	6	6	0	.500	211	208
New England	4	8	0	.333	235	292
N.Y. Jets	3	9	0	.250	219	306

AFC CENTRAL	W	L	T	Pct	PF	PA
Cleveland	7	4	1	.625	270	173
Houston	7	5	0	.583	295	294
Cincinnati	6	6	0	.500	284	225
Pittsburgh	6	6	0	.500	177	271

AFC WEST	W	L	T	Pct	PF	PA
Denver	10	2	0	.833	289	177
L.A. Raiders	6	6	0	.500	249	213
Kansas City	5	6	1	.458	231	218
San Diego	4	8	0	.333	189	215
Seattle	4	8	0	.333	177	248

NFC EAST	W	L	T	Pct	PF	PA
N.Y. Giants	9	3	0	.750	268	204
Philadelphia	8	4	0	.667	247	203
Washington	6	6	0	.500	271	247
Phoenix	5	7	0	.417	220	264
Dallas	1	11	0	.083	153	303

NFC CENTRAL	W	L	T	Pct	PF	PA
Green Bay	7	5	0	.583	282	281
Minnesota	7	5	0	.583	235	198
Chicago	6	6	0	.500	297	257
Tampa Bay	5	7	0	.417	258	318
Detroit	3	9	0	.250	200	302

NFC WEST	W	L	T	Pct	PF	PA
San Francisco	10	2	0	.833	342	206
L.A. Rams	8	4	0	.667	302	249
New Orleans	6	6	0	.500	279	235
Atlanta	3	9	0	.250	198	309

RESULTS

Detroit 13, Cleveland 10
Philadelphia 27, Dallas 0
Washington 38, Chicago 14
Tampa Bay 14, Phoenix 13
L.A. Raiders 24, New England 21
Indianapolis 10, San Diego 6
N.Y. Jets 27, Atlanta 7
Kansas City 34, Houston 0
Denver 41, Seattle 14
Green Bay 20, Minnesota 19
Buffalo, 24, Cincinnati 7
Pittsburgh 34, Miami 14
L.A. Rams 20, New Orleans 17, OT
San Francisco 34, N.Y. Giants 24 (Monday night)

THURSDAY, NOVEMBER 23

Detroit 13, Cleveland 10—At the Silverdome. Barry Sanders wowed the Thanksgiving Day national television audience with his best performance of the season, running over and around a tough Cleveland defense for 145 yards on 28 carries to give him 1,016 yards overall and make him only the third Lion running back in history to have a 1,000-yard season. The winning points were scored on a third-quarter 35-yard field goal by Eddie Murray that was set up on a 63-yard drive powered almost exclusively by Sanders's runs.

Cleveland	0	10	0	0	—	10
Detroit	0	10	3	0	—	13

Det — FG Murray 39
Cle — FG Bahr 35
Det — Johnson 27 pass from Gagliano (Murray kick)
Cle — Redden 38 run (Bahr kick)
Det — FG Murray 35
A: 65,624 T: 3:09

Philadelphia 27, Dallas 0—At Texas Stadium. The Eagles cruised to an easy win, but the outcome was overshadowed by controversy after the game when Dallas coach Jimmy Johnson accused Philadelphia coach Buddy Ryan of offering illegal bounties: $200 to anyone who could knock Cowboy kicker and ex-Eagle Luis Zendejas out of the game and $500 for a game-ending hit on quarterback Troy Aikman. Zendejas was in fact removed from the game after a blow to the head on the second-half kickoff. Ryan denied the charges, but the NFL later conceded that it was investigating the matter; it eventually ruled that there was no conclusive evidence. The on-field activity was far less interesting as Eagle QB Randall Cunningham threw for 234 yards and two TDs and ran for 46 yards more while the defense intercepted Aikman three times and held the Cowboys to just 191 offensive yards.

Philadelphia	0	10	14	3	—	27
Dallas	0	0	0	0	—	0

Phi — Carter 6 pass from Cunningham (Ruzek kick)
Phi — FG Ruzek 36
Phi — Carter 18 pass from Cunningham (Ruzek kick)
Phi — Byars 1 run (Ruzek kick)
Phi — FG Ruzek 38
A: 54,444 T: 3:07

SUNDAY, NOVEMBER 26

Washington 38, Chicago 14—At RFK Stadium. The Bears went down to their sixth defeat in the last eight games as Redskins QB Mark Rypien had the best game of his career, completing 30 of 47 passes for 401 yards and four TDs with Art Monk on the receiving end for two of the TDs and nine of the passes for 152 yards. Monk's performance moved him into fourth place on the alltime pass receptions list. The Redskins defense held Chicago to just 191 offensive yards.

Chicago	0	14	0	0	—	14
Washington	0	14	10	14	—	38

Wash — Warren 3 pass from Rypien (Lohmiller kick)
Wash — Clark 5 pass from Rypien (Lohmiller kick)
Chi — Sanders 96 kickoff return (Butler kick)
Chi — McKinnon 12 pass from Tomczak (Butler kick)
Wash — FG Lohmiller 28
Wash — Monk 18 pass from Rypien (Lohmiller kick)
Wash — Monk 9 pass from Rypien (Lohmiller kick)
Wash — Byner 4 run (Lohmiller kick)
A: 50,044 T: 3:05

Tampa Bay 14, Phoenix 13—At Sun Devil Stadium. Cardinals kicker Al Del Greco missed a 47-yard field goal with one second left to allow the Bucs to hold on to a hard-fought win. The Bucs had gone ahead just 42 seconds earlier on a five-yard TD pass from Vinny Testaverde to Mark Carrier, capping an 82-yard drive that included two pass completions in fourth-down situations.

Tampa Bay	0	7	0	7	—	14
Phoenix	0	10	3	0	—	13

T.B. — Hill 5 pass from Testaverde (Igwebuike kick)
Phoe — Ferrell 1 run (Del Greco kick)
Phoe — FG Del Greco 21
Phoe — FG Del Greco 28
T.B. — Carrier 5 pass from Testaverde (Igwebuike kick)
A: 33,297 T: 3:31

L.A. Raiders 24, New England 21—At Memorial Coliseum. A 32-yard field goal with 5:57 left by Raider kicker Jeff Jaeger produced the only points in the fourth quarter, but they were enough to win the game for Los Angeles. The Raider defense was dominant throughout, holding New England to just 30 yards rushing and 224 yards in all. Patriots QB Steve Grogan threw three TD passes but was intercepted three times.

New England	0	14	7	0	—	21
Los Angeles	7	7	7	3	—	24

L.A. — Alexander 12 pass from Beuerlein (Jaeger kick)
N.E. — Jones 1 pass from Grogan (Staurovsky kick)
N.E. — Fryar 49 pass from Grogan (Staurovsky kick)
L.A. — Fernandez 13 pass from Beuerlein (Jaeger kick)
L.A. — Smith 11 run (Jaeger kick)
N.E. — Dykes 34 pass from Grogan (Staurovsky kick)
L.A. — FG Jaeger 32
A: 38,747 T: 3:01

Indianapolis 10, San Diego 6—At the Hoosier Dome. With Colt running back Eric Dickerson held to just 30 yards rushing, QB Jack Trudeau picked up the slack for Indianapolis, leading the Colts on an 87-yard drive with less than four minutes left that culminated in a 25-yard TD pass to Bill Brooks to win the game and keep the Colts' hopes of a wild-card berth alive. Trudeau came through in spite of booing from the home fans and a series of cuts and bruises on his throwing hand. The Chargers had 314 yards in total offense but were hurt by their own mistakes, including 13 penalties on the day.

San Diego	0	3	0	3	—	6
Indianapolis	0	3	0	7	—	10

S.D. — FG Bahr 33
Ind — FG Biasucci 22
S.D. — FG Bahr 38
Ind — Brooks 25 pass from Trudeau (Biasucci kick)
A: 58,822 T: 3:19

N.Y. Jets 27, Atlanta 7—At Giants Stadium. The Jets jumped out to a 17-0 halftime lead that they never relinquished, while the defense throttled the Falcons all afternoon, allowing just 213 offensive yards, including a paltry six yards passing in the first half. New York running backs Johnny Hector and Roger Vick combined for 125 yards rushing. Falcon QB Chris Miller had one of his worst days, completing only 13 of 41 passes for 158 yards. There were 36,462 no-shows for the game between the two nonplayoff teams.

Atlanta	0	0	7	0	—	7
New York	3	14	10	0	—	27

N.Y. — FG Leahy 28
N.Y. — Hector 1 run (Leahy kick)
N.Y. — Toon 12 pass from O'Brien (Leahy kick)
N.Y. — FG Leahy 46
Atl — Wilkins 16 pass from Miller (Davis kick)
N.Y. — Hector 1 run (Leahy kick)
A: 40,429 T: 3:14

Kansas City 34, Houston 0—At Arrowhead Stadium. The Chiefs, who had suffered several tough losses this season, broke out in a big way against the Oilers. Kansas City QB Steve DeBerg completed 15 of 25 passes for 224 yards and a TD, while running back Christian Okoye ran for 67 yards to become the first Chief since Joe Delaney in 1981 to rush for 1,000 yards.

Houston	0	0	0	0	—	0
Kansas City	10	10	7	7	—	34

K.C. — FG Lowery 31
K.C. — Saxon 4 run (Lowery kick)
K.C. — FG Lowery 34
K.C. — Pearson 1 blocked punt return (Lowery kick)
K.C. — Hayes 7 pass from DeBerg (Lowery kick)
K.C. — Okoye 17 run (Lowery kick)
A: 51,342 T: 3:15

Denver 41, Seattle 14—At Mile High Stadium. The Broncos easily defeated the Seahawks to clinch the AFC West title, becoming the first NFL team to wrap up its division. Denver jumped all over Seattle early, as John Elway completed 10 of 19 passes for 217 yards and four TDs in the first half alone to power the Broncos to a 38-0 halftime lead. Bronco wide receiver Vance Johnson caught six passes for 154 yards and two TDs, while Bobby Humphrey rushed for 86 yards on 25 carries.

Seattle	0	0	7	7	—	14
Denver	14	24	0	3	—	41

Den — Johnson 4 pass from Elway (Treadwell kick)
Den — Humphrey 4 run (Treadwell kick)
Den — FG Treadwell 30
Den — Johnson 10 pass from Elway (Treadwell kick)
Den — Sewell 32 pass from Elway (Treadwell kick)
Den — Young 9 pass from Elway (Treadwell kick)
Sea — Fenner 5 run (Johnson kick)
Den — FG Treadwell 25
Sea — Largent 31 pass from Krieg (Johnson kick)
A: 75,117 T: 3:11

Green Bay 20, Minnesota 19—At Lambeau Field. Another brilliant performance by Packer QB Don Majkowski, who completed 26 of 35 passes for 276 yards and two TDs, powered Green Bay to the narrow victory and moved the Pack into a first-place tie with the Vikings in the NFC Central. Majkowski became the first quarterback to pass for more than 200 yards against Minnesota this season, while Sterling Sharpe's 157 yards receiving on 10 catches—he had two TDs—was also a high against the Vikings. Minnesota QB Wade Wilson had a fine day, throwing for 309 yards, but his two interceptions proved costly. Minnesota failed to score a TD on four of five possessions inside the Packer 20-yard line.

Minnesota	3	3	10	3	—	19
Green Bay	3	7	3	7	—	20

G.B. — FG Jacke 36
Minn — FG Karlis 19
G.B. — Sharpe 34 pass from Majkowski (Jacke kick)
Minn — FG Karlis 34
Minn — FG Karlis 27
Minn — Walker 6 run (Karlis kick)
G.B. — FG Jacke 42
G.B. — Sharpe 9 pass from Majkowski (Jacke kick)
Minn — FG Karlis 19
A: 55,592 T: 3:20

Buffalo 24, Cincinnati 7—At Rich Stadium. A battle of running games resulted in a solid win for the Bills in spite of the 105 yards gained by Bengal back James Brooks on 20 carries. Thurman Thomas led the way for Buffalo, running for 100 yards on 26 carries. Unlike Cincinnati, the Bills also got substantial rushing yardage from their secondary backs, as Larry Kinnebrew had 66 yards and the team had 228 yards rushing overall. Jim Kelly completed 10 of the only 15 passes he attempted, but they were good for 123 yards and three TDs. The Bengals were hurt by two fumbles and an interception.

Cincinnati	0	0	7	0	—	7
Buffalo	3	7	7	7	—	24

Buff — FG Norwood 24
Buff — Reed 19 pass from Kelly (Norwood kick)
Buff — Harmon 42 pass from Kelly (Norwood kick)
Cin — Jennings 5 run (Breech kick)
Buff — Rolle 1 pass from Kelly (Norwood kick)
A: 80,074 T: 2:59

Pittsburgh 34, Miami 14—At Joe Robbie Stadium. The Dolphins forged a 14-0 lead before the rains came and the Miami offense fell apart, suffering three lost fumbles and two interceptions to let the Steelers back in the game. Miami QB Dan Marino threw for just 128 yards and was forced to miss much of the second half with a bruised shoulder. The game-tying TD came on a fumble recovery by Pittsburgh safety Carnell Lake, who lateraled to Dwayne Woodruff, who ran 21 yards for the score. The offensive stars for the Steelers were rookie running back Tim Worley, who ran for 95 yards on 22 carries, and fullback Merril Hoge, who scored three TDs.

Pittsburgh	0	17	17	0	—	34
Miami	14	0	0	0	—	14

Mia — Smith 1 run (Stoyanovich kick)
Mia — Clayton 66 pass from Marino (Stoyanovich kick)
Pitt — Hoge 1 run (Anderson kick)
Pitt — Woodruff 21 run with lateral after Lake 2 fumble return (Anderson kick)
Pitt — FG Anderson 27
Pitt — Hoge 5 run (Anderson kick)
Pitt — FG Anderson 42
Pitt — Hoge 1 run (Anderson kick)
A: 59,936 T: 3:14

L.A. Rams 20, New Orleans 17—At the Superdome. One of the NFL's deadliest quarterback-receiver combos may have seen its debut in an overtime win for the Rams, as QB Jim Everett and wide receiver Willie Anderson connected on 15 passes for 336 yards to give Anderson the alltime single-game NFL receiving record. Everett, who completed 29 of 51 passes for 454 yards—the most by an NFL QB this season—was particularly hot late in the fourth quarter when L.A. bounced back from a 17-3 deficit with two TDs in the final three minutes, the 15-yard game-tying toss going to Anderson. Anderson was devastating in overtime, catching two passes for 41 yards and drawing a 35-yard interference penalty on the drive that led to Mike Lansford's 31-yard game-winning field goal.

Los Angeles	0	3	0	14	3	—	20
New Orleans	7	3	7	0	0	—	17

N.O. — Martin 19 pass from Hebert (Andersen kick)
N.O. — FG Andersen 36
L.A. — FG Lansford 32
N.O. — Martin 35 pass from Hilliard (Andersen kick)
L.A. — McGee 5 run (Lansford kick)
L.A. — Anderson 15 pass from Everett (Lansford kick)
L.A. — FG Lansford 31
A: 64,274 T: 3:37

MONDAY, NOVEMBER 27

San Francisco 34, N.Y. Giants 24—At Candlestick Park. The Giants charged back from a 24-7 deficit, but a key interception late in the game allowed the 49ers to get the one-yard TD by Tom Rathman that clinched the victory. Both QBs had good days, Joe Montana completing 27 of 33 passes for 292 yards and three TDs for San Francisco and Phil Simms connecting on 25 of 48 tries for 326 yards and two TDs for New York. Simms was also sacked seven times and intercepted three times.

New York	7	3	7	7	—	24
San Francisco	14	10	0	10	—	34

S.F. — Taylor 4 pass from Montana (Cofer kick)
N.Y. — Anderson 2 run (Nittmo kick)
S.F. — Rice 4 pass from Montana (Cofer kick)
S.F. — FG Cofer 44
S.F. — Jones 17 pass from Montana (Cofer kick)
N.Y. — FG Nittmo 39
N.Y. — Meggett 53 pass from Simms (Nittmo kick)
N.Y. — Turner 7 pass from Simms (Nittmo kick)
S.F. — FG Cofer 45
S.F. — Rathman 1 run (Cofer kick)
A: 63,461 T: 3:24

Week Thirteen

STANDINGS

AFC EAST	W	L	T	Pct	PF	PA
Buffalo	8	5	0	.615	343	274
Miami	7	6	0	.538	263	300
Indianapolis	6	7	0	.462	227	230
New England	5	8	0	.385	257	308
N.Y. Jets	4	9	0	.308	239	323

AFC CENTRAL	W	L	T	Pct	PF	PA
Houston	8	5	0	.615	318	310
Cleveland	7	5	1	.577	270	194
Cincinnati	7	6	0	.538	305	225
Pittsburgh	6	7	0	.462	193	294

AFC WEST	W	L	T	Pct	PF	PA
Denver	10	3	0	.769	302	193
L.A. Raiders	7	6	0	.538	265	226
Kansas City	6	6	1	.500	257	239
Seattle	5	8	0	.385	194	264
San Diego	4	9	0	.308	206	235

NFC EAST	W	L	T	Pct	PF	PA
N.Y. Giants	9	4	0	.692	285	228
Philadelphia	9	4	0	.692	271	220
Washington	7	6	0	.538	300	257
Phoenix	5	8	0	.385	230	293
Dallas	1	12	0	.077	184	338

NFC CENTRAL	W	L	T	Pct	PF	PA
Green Bay	8	5	0	.615	299	297
Minnesota	8	5	0	.615	262	214
Chicago	6	7	0	.462	313	284
Tampa Bay	5	8	0	.385	274	335
Detroit	4	9	0	.308	221	316

NFC WEST	W	L	T	Pct	PF	PA
San Francisco	11	2	0	.846	365	216
L.A. Rams	9	4	0	.692	337	280
New Orleans	6	7	0	.462	293	256
Atlanta	3	10	0	.231	208	332

RESULTS

Philadelphia 24, N.Y. Giants 17
Cincinnati 21, Cleveland 0
Green Bay 17, Tampa Bay 16
Houston 23, Pittsburgh 16
San Francisco 23, Atlanta 10
Minnesota 27, Chicago 16
Washington 29, Phoenix 10
N.Y. Jets 20, San Diego 17
L.A. Rams 35, Dallas 31
Detroit 21, New Orleans 14
L.A. Raiders 16, Denver 13, OT
Kansas City 26, Miami 21
New England 22, Indianapolis 16
Seattle 17, Buffalo 16 (Monday night)

SUNDAY, DECEMBER 3

Philadelphia 24, N.Y. Giants 17—At Giants Stadium. The Eagle defense was instrumental in all of Philadelphia's points, as a fumble and an interception, both returned for TDs, gave the Eagles an early 14-0 advantage, a second interception led to a field goal and another fumble set up the game-winning touchdown in the fourth quarter. In spite of the turnovers, New York battled back to a 17-17 tie on a one-yard plunge by Ottis Anderson, but a 91-yard punt from his own two-yard line by Philadelphia QB Randall Cunningham and a subsequent fumble by New York QB Phil Simms led to a two-yard TD run by Keith Byars for the game-winner. Heavy winds gusted through the stadium, as 31 of 41 points were scored by the team with the wind at its back. The victory gave the Eagles a sweep of the season series against the Giants and tied them for the lead in the NFC East.

Philadelphia	14	3	0	7	—	24
New York	7	0	10	0	—	17

Phi — Waters 3 fumble return (Ruzek kick)
Phi — Simmons 60 interception return (Ruzek kick)
N.Y. — Ingram 41 pass from Simms (Nittmo kick)
Phi — FG Ruzek 35
N.Y. — FG Nittmo 38
N.Y. — Anderson 1 run (Nittmo kick)
Phi — Byars 2 run (Ruzek kick)
A: 74,809 T: 3:23

Cincinnati 21, Cleveland 0—At Cleveland Stadium. Bengal wide receiver Tim McGee made a diving catch for a 29-yard gain to set up Cincinnati's first touchdown, then grabbed a 38-yard flea-flicker from QB Boomer Esiason for the second, as the Bengals handed the Browns their first shutout at home since 1977. Cleveland QB Bernie Kosar continued to struggle, completing 15 of 30 passes for only 130 yards.

Cincinnati	0	7	14	0	—	21
Cleveland	0	0	0	0	—	0

Cin — Brooks 1 run (Breech kick)
Cin — McGee 38 pass from Esiason (Breech kick)
Cin — Holman 9 pass from Esiason (Breech kick)
A: 76,236 T: 3:28

Green Bay 17, Tampa Bay 16—At Tampa Stadium. Packer kicker Chris Jacke booted a 47-yard field goal through a swirling wind, as time expired, to pull out the victory for Green Bay. The win added to the legend of Packer quarterback Don Majkowksi, who engineered a 52-yard drive in the last two minutes of the game to get his team into field goal range. Majkowski completed 25 of 53 passes on the day for 331 yards and two TDs, both to Sterling Sharpe, who had eight catches for 169 yards.

Green Bay	7	0	0	10	—	17
Tampa Bay	0	3	3	10	—	16

G.B. — Sharpe 21 pass from Majkowski (Jacke kick)
T.B. — FG Igwebuike 49
T.B. — FG Igwebuike 40
T.B. — Stamps 21 run (Igwebuike kick)
G.B. — Sharpe 55 pass from Majkowski (Jacke kick)
T.B. — FG Igwebuike 36
G.B. — FG Jacke 47
A: 58,120 T: 3:30

Houston 23, Pittsburgh 16—At Three Rivers Stadium. Oiler running back Lorenzo White fought off subzero conditions to rush for 115 yards on 23 carries, including a one-yard dive for the game-winning touchdown with 21 seconds left. Houston QB Warren Moon completed 12 of 20 passes for 171 yards and two TDs, while Tim Worley was the offensive star for the Steelers, running for 103 yards on 18 carries. The Oiler defense scored a safety, held Pittsburgh to just 212 offensive yards and sacked QB Bubby Brister three times.

Houston	0	14	2	7	—	23
Pittsburgh	3	7	3	3	—	16

Pitt — FG Anderson 18
Pitt — Hoge 4 run (Anderson kick)
Hou — Duncan 18 pass from Moon (Zendejas kick)
Hou — Hill 27 pass from Moon (Zendejas kick)
Pitt — FG Anderson 37
Hou — Safety, McDowell tackled Newsome in end zone
Pitt — FG Anderson 18
Hou — White 1 run (Zendejas kick)
A: 40,541 T: 3:27

San Francisco 23, Atlanta 10—At Fulton County Stadium. QB Steve Young came off the bench to lead the 49ers to three second-half scores for the come-from-behind win. Young, who replaced the injured Joe Montana, completed 11 of 12 passes—including his first ten in a row—for 175 yards and a touchdown. Young also ran for a fourth-quarter TD. San Francisco's Roger Craig had 97 yards on 17 carries, wide receiver John Taylor had 162 yards on five catches and the defense held the Falcons to just 101 yards in the second half. The win was the 49ers' 11th in a row on the road.

San Francisco	6	0	7	10	—	23
Atlanta	0	10	0	0	—	10

S.F. — FG Cofer 35
S.F. — FG Cofer 23
Atl — FG Davis 46
Atl — Heller 28 pass from Miller (Davis kick)
S.F. — Taylor 38 pass from Young (Cofer kick)
S.F. — Young 1 run (Cofer kick)
S.F. — FG Cofer 27
A: 43,128 T: 2:52

Minnesota 27, Chicago 16—At the Metrodome. The Vikings jumped out to a 17-3 lead and never looked back en route to a relatively easy win over the Bears. The Chicago defense continued to perform like a shadow of its former self as Minnesota quarterback Wade Wilson connected on 15 of 26 passes for 260 yards, including a 46-yard TD strike to Hassan Jones and a 24-yard TD toss to Anthony Carter. Bears running back Neal Anderson gained 76 yards on 17 carries to give him his second consecutive 1,000-yard rushing season.

Chicago	3	0	7	6	—	16
Minnesota	7	10	7	3	—	27

Chi — FG Butler 33
Minn — Walker 1 run (Karlis kick)
Minn — Jones 46 pass from Wilson (Karlis kick)
Minn — FG Karlis 51
Chi — Boso 3 pass from Tomczak (Butler kick)
Minn — Carter 24 pass from Wilson (Karlis kick)
Chi — Suhey 1 run (kick blocked)
Minn — FG Karlis 45
A: 60,664 T: 3:23

Washington 29, Phoenix 10—At Sun Devil Stadium. Redskins defensive back A.J. Johnson made two key interceptions, one for a touchdown and another to set up a field goal, in sparking Washington to a solid win that eliminated the Cardinals from playoff contention. Earnest Byner had 86 yards rushing and a TD for the Redskins, and the defense held Phoenix to just 29 rushing yards, making it the fifth game in a row that the Cardinals were held to less than 100 yards on the ground.

Washington	3	7	14	5	—	29
Phoenix	0	10	0	0	—	10

Wash — FG Lohmiller 29
Wash — Byner 1 run (Lohmiller kick)
Phoe — FG Del Greco 27
Phoe — Ferrell 1 run (Del Greco kick)
Wash — Riggs 1 run (Lohmiller kick)
Wash — Johnson 59 interception return (Lohmiller kick)
Wash — FG Lohmiller 23
Wash — Safety, Tupa intentional grounding penalty in end zone
A: 38,870 T: 2:54

N.Y. Jets 20, San Diego 17—At Jack Murphy Stadium. Jet safety Erik McMillan picked off a fourth-quarter pass by Charger quarterback Billy Joe Tolliver and ran it back to the San Diego 16 to set up the 14-yard touchdown run by Roger Vick that put New York in command, 20-10, with 7:55 to go. The Chargers came back with a touchdown pass from Tolliver to Anthony Miller and then had a chance to tie with ten second left, but kicker Chris Bahr missed a 37-yard field goal attempt. Johnny Hector led the way for the Jets on the ground, running for 106 yards on 20 carries.

New York	7	0	0	13	—	20
San Diego	0	7	3	7	—	17

N.Y. — Hector 9 pass from O'Brien (Leahy kick)
S.D. — Butts 40 run (Bahr kick)
S.D. — FG Bahr 39
N.Y. — Vick 1 run (Leahy kick)
N.Y. — Vick 14 run (kick failed)
S.D. — Miller 8 pass from Tolliver (Bahr kick)
A: 38,954 T: 3:35

L.A. Rams 35, Dallas 31—At Texas Stadium. The Rams jumped out to a 21-10 lead, watched in dismay as the Cowboys surged in front 31-21, and finally breathed a sigh of relief when L.A. quarterback Jim Everett rallied his team to two touchdowns in the last four minutes to pull out the victory. Four of the Ram touchdowns were scored after Dallas turnovers: three after fumble recoveries and one after an interception. Everett completed 27 of 37 passes for 341 yards and four TDs, including a 23-yarder to Aaron Cox for the game-winner. Dallas QB Troy Aikman had a good game in defeat, connecting on 19 of 34 passes for 179 yards and four TDs. He also ran for 57 yards on four carries.

Los Angeles	14	0	7	14	—	35
Dallas	0	10	7	14	—	31

L.A. — Johnson 1 pass from Everett (Lansford kick)
L.A. — Bell 1 run (Lansford kick)
Dall — Johnston 9 pass from Aikman (Zendejas kick)
Dall — FG Zendejas 47
L.A. — Cox 18 pass from Everett (Lansford kick)
Dall — Dixon 35 pass from Aikman (Zendejas kick)
Dall — Folsom 5 pass from Aikman (Zendejas kick)
Dall — Ford 10 pass from Aikman (Zendejas kick)
L.A. — Brown 39 pass from Everett (Lansford kick)
L.A. — Cox 23 pass from Everett (Lansford kick)
A: 46,100 T: 3:13

Detroit 21, New Orleans 14—At the Silverdome. Lion wide receiver Richard Johnson, out of football for nearly two years, caught eight passes for 248 yards to lead Detroit to its third win in the last four games. The game-winning score was a 75-yard touchdown strike from Lion quarterback Bob Gagliano to Johnson in the third quarter. The resurgent Lions were also effective on defense, holding the Saints to just 169 offensive yards.

New Orleans	0	14	0	0	—	14
Detroit	7	7	7	0	—	21

Det — Peete 6 run (Murray kick)
N.O. — Hilliard 1 run (Andersen kick)
Det — Sanders 3 run (Murray kick)
N.O. — Morris 99 kickoff return (Andersen kick)
Det — Johnson 75 pass from Gagliano (Murray kick)
A: 38,550 T: 3:12

L.A. Raiders 16, Denver 13—At Memorial Coliseum. The Raiders' Jeff Jaeger kicked a 26-yard field goal with 7:58 left in overtime to upset the Broncos. Tight end Mike Dyal was the offensive star for L.A., grabbing a 67-yard TD pass from Steve Beuerlein to tie the game in the fourth quarter as well as passes of 26 and 15 yards in overtime to set up the winning kick. The win spoiled a fine performance by Denver rookie Bobby Humphrey, who ran for a career-high 125 yards on 31 carries.

Denver	0	10	0	3	0	—	13
Los Angeles	3	0	3	7	3	—	16

L.A. — FG Jaeger 37
Den — FG Treadwell 34
Den — Bratton 5 run (Treadwell kick)
L.A. — FG Jaeger 46
Den — FG Treadwell 35
L.A. — Dyal 67 pass from Beuerlein (Jaeger kick)
L.A. — FG Jaeger 26
A: 87,560 T: 3:15

Kansas City 26, Miami 21—At Arrowhead Stadium. Chiefs running back Christian Okoye ran for 148 yards and a TD on 32 carries, and quarterback Steve DeBerg completed 15 of 25 passes for 239 yards and two TDs, including seven passes for 133 yards to wide receiver Stephone Paige, in a ball-control win over the Dolphins. Miami QB Dan Marino, held in check in the first half, came to life in the second with three TD passes, but it was too little, too late; the third TD was scored with only 53 seconds left.

Miami	0	0	7	14	—	21
Kansas City	13	3	3	7	—	26

K.C. — Okoye 3 run (kick failed)
K.C. — Paige 38 pass from DeBerg (Lowery kick)
K.C. — FG Lowery 34
Mia — Jensen 8 pass from Marino (Stoyanovich kick)
K.C. — FG Lowery 28
Mia — Clayton 15 pass from Marino (Stoyanovich kick)
K.C. — Heard 8 pass from DeBerg (Lowery kick)
Mia — Jensen 9 pass from Marino (Stoyanovich kick)
A: 54,610 T: 3:03

New England 22, Indianapolis 16—At Sullivan Stadium. Patriots running back John Stephens, who gained 124 yards on 27 carries, ran 10 yards for the game-winning touchdown with 25 seconds left. The Colts had gone ahead just 1:34 earlier on a pass from Jack Trudeau to Eric Dickerson, but New England QB Marc Wilson engineered a 63-yard drive to pull out the victory. Wilson, making his first start in two years, completed 17 of 31 passes for 255 yards overall. Dickerson gained 80 yards to become the first player to rush for at least 1,000 yards in seven consecutive seasons.

Indianapolis	0	3	7	6	—	16
New England	6	0	3	13	—	22

N.E. — FG Staurovsky 44
N.E. — FG Staurovsky 37
Ind — FG Biasucci 18
N.E. — FG Staurovsky 24
Ind — Benson 9 pass from Trudeau (Biasucci kick)
N.E. — FG Staurovsky 50
N.E. — FG Staurovsky 23
Ind — Dickerson 8 pass from Trudeau (Biasucci kick)
N.E. — Stephens 10 run (Staurovsky kick)
A: 32,234 T: 3:15

MONDAY, DECEMBER 4

Seattle 17, Buffalo 16—At the Kingdome. Things looked grim for the Seahawks when the Bills took advantage of Seattle mistakes to come back from a 10-0 deficit and go in front 16-10 in the third quarter. But Seahawk quarterback Dave Krieg rallied his team in the fourth quarter, heaving a 51-yard touchdown strike to John L. Williams for the game-winning score. Krieg completed 20 of 40 passes overall for 298 yards.

Buffalo	0	10	6	0	—	16
Seattle	10	0	0	7	—	17

Sea — FG Johnson 29
Sea — Warner 1 run (Largent run)
Buff — Reed 61 pass from Kelly (Norwood kick)
Buff — FG Norwood 32
Buff — FG Norwood 40
Buff — FG Norwood 43
Sea — Williams 51 pass from Krieg (Johnson kick)
A: 57,682 T: 3:11

STANDINGS

AFC EAST	W	L	T	Pct	PF	PA
Buffalo	8	6	0	.571	362	296
Miami	8	6	0	.571	294	310
Indianapolis	7	7	0	.500	250	247
New England	5	9	0	.357	267	339
N.Y. Jets	4	10	0	.286	239	336
AFC CENTRAL	**W**	**L**	**T**	**Pct**	**PF**	**PA**
Houston	9	5	0	.643	338	327
Cleveland	7	6	1	.536	287	217
Cincinnati	7	7	0	.500	322	249
Pittsburgh	7	7	0	.500	206	294
AFC WEST	**W**	**L**	**T**	**Pct**	**PF**	**PA**
Denver	10	4	0	.714	309	207
L.A. Raiders	8	6	0	.571	281	240
Kansas City	7	6	1	.536	278	242
Seattle	6	8	0	.429	218	281
San Diego	4	10	0	.286	227	261
NFC EAST	**W**	**L**	**T**	**Pct**	**PF**	**PA**
N.Y. Giants	10	4	0	.714	299	235
Philadelphia	10	4	0	.714	291	230
Washington	8	6	0	.571	326	278
Phoenix	5	9	0	.357	244	309
Dallas	1	13	0	.071	194	358
NFC CENTRAL	**W**	**L**	**T**	**Pct**	**PF**	**PA**
Minnesota	9	5	0	.643	305	231
Green Bay	8	6	0	.571	302	318
Chicago	6	8	0	.429	330	311
Tampa Bay	5	9	0	.357	291	355
Detroit	5	9	0	.357	248	333
NFC WEST	**W**	**L**	**T**	**Pct**	**PF**	**PA**
San Francisco	12	2	0	.857	395	243
L.A. Rams	9	5	0	.643	364	310
New Orleans	7	7	0	.500	315	275
Atlanta	3	11	0	.214	225	375

RESULTS

N.Y. Giants 14, Denver 7
New Orleans 22, Buffalo 19
Kansas City 21, Green Bay 3
Detroit 27, Chicago 17
Washington 26, San Diego 21
Philadelphia 20, Dallas 10
Indianapolis 23, Cleveland 17, OT
L.A. Raiders 16, Phoenix 14
Pittsburgh 13, N.Y. Jets 0
Houston 20, Tampa Bay 17
Seattle 24, Cincinnati 17
Miami 31, New England 10
Minnesota 43, Atlanta 17
San Francisco 30, L.A. Rams 27 (Monday night)

SUNDAY, DECEMBER 10

N.Y. Giants 14, Denver 7—At Mile High Stadium. The Giants drove 85 yards for a touchdown on their first possession, rookie Dave Meggett turned a 10-yard screen pass into a 57-yard TD to put them up 14-0 and the defense held the Broncos in check to secure the win in frigid Mile High Stadium. Linebacker Gary Reasons was the star on defense, making 11 solo tackles and jarring the ball loose from Denver running back Bobby Humphrey on the New York one-yard line to produce a critical turnover late in the third quarter.

New York	0	14	0	0	—	14
Denver	0	0	0	7	—	7

N.Y. — Anderson 3 run (Nittmo kick)
N.Y. — Meggett 57 pass from Simms (Nittmo kick)
Den — Young 32 pass from Elway (Treadwell kick)
A: 63,283 T: 3:01

New Orleans 22, Buffalo 19—At Rich Stadium. Backup quarterback John Fourcade completed 15 of 27 passes for 302 yards and two touchdowns—both after Buffalo turnovers—to lead the Saints to an upset victory over the struggling Bills, who have lost three of their last four games. Buffalo QB Jim Kelly, who would be criticized by his teammates later in the week, completed just 17 of 35 attempts for 211 yards. He also threw three interceptions. Dalton Hilliard had another good game for New Orleans, running for 97 yards on 32 carries. The game-winning points were scored on a 22-yard field goal by Morten Andersen late in the fourth quarter.

New Orleans	13	3	3	3	—	22
Buffalo	0	12	7	0	—	19

N.O. — Tice 12 pass from Fourcade (kick failed)
N.O. — Hilliard 54 pass from Fourcade (Andersen kick)
Buff — Lofton 42 pass from Kelly (kick failed)
N.O. — FG Andersen 31
Buff — FG Norwood 43
Buff — FG Norwood 48
Buff — Metzelaars 2 pass from Kelly (Norwood kick)
N.O. — FG Andersen 26
N.O. — FG Andersen 22
A: 70,037 T: 3:16

Kansas City 21, Green Bay 3—At Lambeau Field. The surging Chiefs won their third consecutive game to keep their hopes of a wild-card playoff spot alive. Their defense held Packer QB Don Majkowski to 123 yards passing and Green Bay to just 208 yards overall. The offensive power was provided by QB Steve DeBerg (15 of 19 passes for 203 yards and two TDs) and running back Christian Okoye (131 yards on 38 carries, his eighth 100-yard game of the season).

Kansas City	0	21	0	0	—	21
Green Bay	0	3	0	0	—	3

K.C. — Hayes 11 pass from DeBerg (Lowery kick)
G.B. — FG Jacke 25
K.C. — Okoye 3 run (Lowery kick)
K.C. — Harry 12 pass from DeBerg (Lowery kick)
A: 56,694 T: 3:12

Detroit 27, Chicago 17—At Soldier Field. Lion running back Barry Sanders put a lock on the rookie of the year award by running all over the Bears, who were eliminated from the playoffs for the first time since 1983. Sanders ran for 120 yards and two TDs on 26 carries, caught three passes for 39 yards and ran two kickoffs back for 59 yards to give him a total of 218 all-purpose yards on the day. The Detroit defense sacked Bears quarterbacks five times to help the improving Lions to their third win in a row.

Detroit	0	17	7	3	—	27
Chicago	3	7	0	7	—	17

Chi — FG Butler 22
Det — Gagliano 14 run (Murray kick)
Det — Sanders 18 run (Murray kick)
Chi — Muster 11 run (Butler kick)
Det — FG Murray 45
Det — Sanders 3 run (Murray kick)
Det — FG Murray 28
Chi — Anderson 1 run (Butler kick)
A: 52,650 T: 3:06

Washington 26, San Diego 21—At RFK Stadium. The Redskins kept their slim playoff hopes alive with a comeback win over the Chargers. After San Diego had taken a 21-16 lead, Washington's Joe Howard answered with a 51-yard kickoff return, and QB Mark Rypien (23 of 39 passes for 302 yards and two TDs) followed that, four plays later, with a 33-yard TD strike to Gary Clark to put the Skins in front for good. The win spoiled a good performance by Charger rookie Billy Joe Tolliver, who completed 24 of 39 passes for 350 yards and two TDs. Washington's Art Monk caught nine passes to move into third place on the NFL's alltime receptions list, with 651, two more than his receivers' coach, Charley Taylor.

San Diego	14	0	0	7	—	21
Washington	0	7	9	10	—	26

S.D. — Miller 25 pass from Tolliver (Bahr kick)
S.D. — Walker 5 pass from Tolliver (Bahr kick)
Wash — Sanders 45 pass from Rypien (Lohmiller kick)
Wash — FG Lohmiller 38
Wash — FG Lohmiller 31
Wash — FG Lohmiller 32
S.D. — Butts 10 run (Bahr kick)
Wash — Clark 33 pass from Rypien (Lohmiller kick)
Wash — FG Lohmiller 28
A: 47,693 T: 3:20

Philadelphia 20, Dallas 10—At Veterans Stadium. Backup QB Matt Cavanaugh threw a 13-yard TD pass to Cris Carter on a fake field goal attempt in the second quarter to stake the Eagles to a 14-0 lead and put the game out of reach. The Philadelphia fans, still incensed over the bounty controversy (see Week 12), pelted the Cowboys with snowballs throughout the game, momentarily dazing back judge Al Jury with an errant throw in the first quarter. It was a good day for rushing quarterbacks, as Dallas's Troy Aikman ran for 60 yards and the Eagles' Randall Cunningham ran for 47.

Dallas	0	3	7	0	—	10
Philadelphia	0	17	3	0	—	20

Phi — Carter 4 pass from Cunningham (Ruzek kick)
Phi — Carter 13 pass from Cavanaugh (Ruzek kick)
Dall — FG Zendejas 47
Phi — FG Ruzek 29
Phi — FG Ruzek 46
Dall — Johnston 18 pass from Aikman (Zendejas kick)
A: 59,842 T: 3:24

Indianapolis 23, Cleveland 17—At the Hoosier Dome. Browns quarterback Bernie Kosar completed 26 of 40 passes for 353 yards, but his two interceptions proved costly, the first leading to the game-tying TD by the Colts' Pat Beach and the second being returned 58 yards by Mike Prior for the game-winning score in overtime. Cleveland had two chances to win the game—once with 28 seconds left in regulation and again in overtime—but kicker Matt Bahr missed both field goal attempts, from 39 and 35 yards, respectively. Eric Dickerson ran for 137 yards on 26 carries to lead Indianapolis.

Cleveland	0	10	7	0	0	—	17
Indianapolis	7	0	3	7	6	—	23

Ind — Rison 51 pass from Trudeau (Biasucci kick)
Cle — Metcalf 12 run (Bahr kick)
Cle — FG Bahr 48
Cle — Tillman recovered blocked punt in end zone (Bahr kick)
Ind — FG Biasucci 35
Ind — Beach 1 pass from Ramsey (Biasucci kick)
Ind — Prior 58 interception return
A: 58,550 T: 3:53

L.A. Raiders 16, Phoenix 14—At Memorial Coliseum. The Raiders missed three field goals, had a touchdown nullified and committed eight penalties, but they still prevailed, fashioning a 46-yard drive in the final two minutes of the game, capped by Marcus Allen's one-yard leap for the game-winning score. Bo Jackson ran for 114 yards on 22 carries for Los Angeles, and quarterback Steve Beuerlein threw for 255 yards.

Phoenix	0	7	0	7	—	14
Los Angeles	0	6	3	7	—	16

L.A. — FG Jaeger 25
Phoe — Jones 35 pass from Hogeboom (Del Greco kick)
L.A. — FG Jaeger 30
L.A. — FG Jaeger 48
Phoe — Novacek 2 pass from Hogeboom (Del Greco kick)
L.A. — Allen 1 run (Jaeger kick)
A: 41,785 T: 3:22

Pittsburgh 13, N.Y. Jets 0—At Giants Stadium. Steeler running backs Tim Worley and Merril Hoge combined for 107 yards and a TD, while the defense shut the Jets out, producing three turnovers in their own territory and limiting New York to just 70 yards on the ground. There were 35,854 no-shows for the hapless Jets, whose record fell to 4-10.

Pittsburgh	7	0	0	6	—	13
New York	0	0	0	0	—	0

Pitt — Worley 35 run (Anderson kick)
Pitt — FG Anderson 42
Pitt — FG Anderson 45
A: 41,037 T: 3:00

Houston 20, Tampa Bay 17—At the Astrodome. The Oilers jumped out to a 20-3 halftime lead, then had to hang on for the victory as the Bucs charged back behind quarterback Vinny Testaverde, who completed 31 of 48 passes for 328 yards and two TDs on the day. Houston was helped by a controversial fumble late in the game, when free safety Jeff Donaldson stripped the ball from James Wilder after a 27-yard pass from Testaverde. The Bucs thought the play should have been ruled an incomplete pass instead of a fumble. Mike Rozier ran for 82 yards for the Oilers, and Tampa Bay's Mark Carrier caught 10 passes for 135 yards to give him a team-record 1,190 yards on the season.

Tampa Bay	3	0	7	7	—	17
Houston	3	17	0	0	—	20

Hou — FG Zendejas 30
T.B. — FG Igwebuike 21
Hou — Hill 12 pass from Moon (Zendejas kick)
Hou — FG Zendejas 37
Hou — Duncan 16 pass from Moon (Zendejas kick)
T.B. — Drewrey 6 pass from Testaverde (Igwebuike kick)
T.B. — Hall 24 pass from Testaverde (Igwebuike kick)
A: 54,532 T: 3:11

Seattle 24, Cincinnati 17—At Riverfront Stadium. Curt Warner scored on a one-yard pass from Dave Krieg with 3:51 remaining to win the game for the Seahawks. The previous play, on which Warner had been thrown for a loss, was nullified by an inadvertent whistle, giving Seattle another shot at the end zone. Wide receiver Steve Largent caught a 10-yard strike from Krieg near the end of the first half for the 100th touchdown reception of his career, a new NFL record.

Seattle	0	7	10	7	—	24
Cincinnati	7	3	0	7	—	17

Cin — McGee 21 pass from Esiason (Breech kick)
Cin — FG Breech 24
Sea — Largent 10 pass from Krieg (Johnson kick)
Sea — FG Johnson 48
Sea — Blades 60 pass from Krieg (Johnson kick)
Cin — Thomas 18 interception return (Breech kick)
Sea — Warner 1 pass from Krieg (Johnson kick)
A: 54,744 T: 3:20

Miami 31, New England 10—At Joe Robbie Stadium. Dolphin quarterback Dan Marino completed 21 of 32 passes for 300 yards, running back Sammie Smith rushed for three touchdowns and the Miami defense sacked Patriots QB Marc Wilson five times in a dominant win that put the Dolphins in a first-place tie with the Buffalo Bills in the AFC East. Marino also scrambled for a touchdown on a broken pass play.

New England	3	0	7	0	—	10
Miami	7	14	0	10	—	31

Mia — Smith 1 run (Stoyanovich kick)
N.E. — FG Staurovsky 36
Mia — Smith 7 run (Stoyanovich kick)
Mia — Marino 1 run (Stoyanovich kick)
N.E. — Stephens 1 run (Staurovsky kick)
Mia — Smith 2 run (Stoyanovich kick)
Mia — FG Stoyanovich 23
A: 62,127 T: 2:59

Minnesota 43, Atlanta 17—At the Metrodome. The Vikings came alive after the Falcons closed to within three points early in the third quarter, scoring 23 unanswered points to turn the game into a rout. The impetus once again was provided by the defense, particularly by defensive end Chris Doleman, who sacked Atlanta QB Chris Miller four times and stripped him of the ball twice. Both fumbles were returned by Minnesota for touchdowns, the first by tackle Keith Millard and the second by tackle Tim Newton. Viking QB Wade Wilson threw for 241 yards and running back Rick Fenney rushed for 89 yards.

Atlanta	3	7	7	0	—	17
Minnesota	7	13	17	6	—	43

Minn — Ingram 2 pass from Wilson (Karlis kick)
Atl — FG Davis 26
Minn — FG Karlis 21
Atl — Wilkins 26 pass from Miller (Davis kick)
Minn — Carter 19 pass from Dozier (Karlis kick)
Minn — FG Karlis 39
Atl — Collins 17 pass from Miller (Davis kick)
Minn — Millard 31 fumble return (Karlis kick)
Minn — FG Karlis 26
Minn — Newton 5 fumble return (Karlis kick)
Minn — FG Karlis 29
Minn — FG Karlis 19
A: 58,116 T: 3:00

MONDAY, DECEMBER 11

San Francisco 30, L.A. Rams 27—At Anaheim Stadium. Joe Montana and the 49ers continued to make the brilliant appear routine, this time coming back from a fourth-quarter 27-10 deficit. The big offensive weapons were Montana, who completed 30 of 42 passes for three TDs and a team-record 458 yards, and wide receiver John Taylor, who grabbed 11 passes for a team-record 286 yards, including TD catches of 92 and 95 yards. San Francisco scored the go-ahead touchdown with 3:42 left on a one-yard plunge by Roger Craig after a fumbled kickoff return by the Rams' Ron Brown.

San Francisco	0	10	0	20	—	30
Los Angeles	17	0	7	3	—	27

L.A. — Bell 3 run (Lansford kick)
L.A. — Johnson 4 pass from Everett (Lansford kick)
L.A. — FG Lansford 25
S.F. — FG Cofer 19
S.F. — Taylor 92 pass from Montana (Cofer kick)
L.A. — McGee 13 pass from Everett (Lansford kick)
L.A. — FG Lansford 22
S.F. — Wilson 7 pass from Montana (Cofer kick)
S.F. — Taylor 95 pass from Montana (kick failed)
S.F. — Craig 1 run (Lansford kick)
A: 68,936 T: 3:18

Week Fifteen

STANDINGS

AFC EAST	W	L	T	Pct	PF	PA
Buffalo	8	7	0	.533	372	317
Indianapolis	8	7	0	.533	292	260
Miami	8	7	0	.533	307	352
New England	5	10	0	.333	277	367
N.Y. Jets	4	11	0	.267	253	374

AFC CENTRAL	W	L	T	Pct	PF	PA
Houston	9	6	0	.600	345	388
Cleveland	8	6	1	.567	310	234
Cincinnati	8	7	0	.553	383	256
Pittsburgh	8	7	0	.553	234	304

AFC WEST	W	L	T	Pct	PF	PA
Denver	11	4	0	.733	346	207
L.A. Raiders	8	7	0	.553	298	263
Kansas City	7	7	1	.500	291	262
Seattle	7	8	0	.467	241	298
San Diego	5	10	0	.333	247	274

NFC EAST	W	L	T	Pct	PF	PA
N.Y. Giants	11	4	0	.733	314	235
Philadelphia	10	5	0	.667	311	260
Washington	9	6	0	.600	357	308
Phoenix	5	10	0	.333	244	346
Dallas	1	14	0	.067	194	373

NFC CENTRAL	W	L	T	Pct	PF	PA
Green Bay	9	6	0	.600	342	346
Minnesota	9	6	0	.600	322	254
Chicago	6	9	0	.400	358	351
Detroit	6	9	0	.400	281	340
Tampa Bay	5	10	0	.333	298	388

NFC WEST	W	L	T	Pct	PF	PA
San Francisco	13	2	0	.867	416	253
L.A. Rams	10	5	0	.667	402	324
New Orleans	8	7	0	.553	345	295
Atlanta	3	12	0	.200	255	406

RESULTS

N.Y. Giants 15, Dallas 0
Denver 37, Phoenix 0
Cincinnati 61, Houston 7
Cleveland 23, Minnesota 17, OT
Indianapolis 42, Miami 13
San Francisco 21, Buffalo 10
Green Bay 40, Chicago 28
L.A. Rams 38, N.Y. Jets 14
Detroit 33, Tampa Bay 7
Washington 31, Atlanta 30
San Diego 20, Kansas City 13
Pittsburgh 28, New England 10
Seattle 23, L.A. Raiders 17
New Orleans 30, Philadelphia 20 (Monday night)

SATURDAY, DECEMBER 16

N.Y. Giants 15, Dallas 0—At Giants Stadium. The Giants clinched at least a wild-card spot in the playoffs with an easy win over the Cowboys. Playing under frigid conditions, New York relied on its running game, which produced 140 yards, and its defense, which held Dallas to a paltry 108 yards in total offense. Ottis Anderson rushed for 91 yards and a TD on 25 carries, while rookie Lewis Tillman chipped in 40 yards on nine.

Dallas	0	0	0	0	—	0
New York	6	3	6	0	—	15

N.Y. — FG Nittmo 33
N.Y. — FG Nittmo 22
N.Y. — FG Nittmo 26
N.Y. — Anderson 1 run (kick blocked)
A: 72,141 T: 2:44

Denver 37, Phoenix 0—At Sun Devil Stadium. The Broncos completely dominated the Cardinals in an easy victory. Rookie Bobby Humphrey ran for 128 yards on 23 carries and threw for his first career TD on a 17-yard halfback option pass to Melvin Bratton, while QB John Elway threw for 247 yards and two TDs. Humphrey became the first Denver rookie to rush for 1,000 yards in a season. The defense held Phoenix to just 101 offensive yards and sacked Cardinal QBs six times on the day. The win ensured the Broncos of home field advantage throughout the playoffs.

Denver	7	13	14	3	—	37
Phoenix	0	0	0	0	—	0

Den — Mecklenburg 23 fumble return (Treadwell kick)
Den — FG Treadwell 38
Den — Sewell 14 pass from Elway (Treadwell kick)
Den — FG Treadwell 33
Den — Bratton 17 pass from Humphrey (Treadwell kick)
Den — Kay 20 pass from Elway (Treadwell kick)
Den — FG Treadwell 35
A: 56,071 T: 3:01

SUNDAY, DECEMBER 17

Cincinnati 61, Houston 7—At Riverfront Stadium. The Bengals jumped out to a 31-0 halftime lead and didn't let up until they had handed the Oilers their worst defeat in franchise history. In a clear attempt to run up the score, Cincinnati tried an onside kick after taking a 45-0 lead and kicked a field goal with 21 seconds left. The stars for the Bengals were QB Boomer Esiason, who completed 20 of 27 passes for 326 yards and four TDs; wide receiver Tim McGee, who had six catches for 147 yards and a TD; and safety David Fulcher, who had three interceptions and a fumble recovery.

Houston	0	0	0	7	—	7
Cincinnati	21	10	21	9	—	61

Cin — Brown 22 pass from Esiason (Breech kick)
Cin — Brooks 14 run (Breech kick)
Cin — Brown 35 pass from Esiason (Breech kick)
Cin — Holman 5 pass from Esiason (Breech kick)
Cin — FG Breech 27
Cin — Taylor 5 run (Breech kick)
Cin — McGee 74 pass from Esiason (Breech kick)
Cin — Ball 5 run (Breech kick)
Hou — White 1 run (Zendejas kick)
Cin — Hillary 10 pass from Wilhelm (kick failed)
Cin — FG Breech 30
A: 47,510 T: 3:35

Cleveland 23, Minnesota 17—At Cleveland Stadium. When the Browns lined up for a field goal with 9:30 gone in overtime, the stage appeared set for kicker Matt Bahr, who had tied the score with 24 seconds left in regulation. But Cleveland stunned the Vikings by faking the field goal instead, winning the game on a 14-yard TD pass from holder Mike Pagel to linebacker Van Waiters. Browns quarterback Bernie Kosar completed 17 of 38 passes for 254 yards and two TDs, including a 19-yard pass to Lawyer Tillman to get into position for the game-tying field goal and a 39-yard strike to Reggie Langhorne to help set up the game-winning score.

Minnesota	0	3	7	7	0	—	17
Cleveland	0	0	14	3	6	—	23

Minn — FG Karlis 44
Cle — Middleton 5 pass from Kosar (Bahr kick)
Minn — Walker 26 run (Karlis kick)
Cle — Langhorne 62 pass from Kosar (Bahr kick)
Minn — Jordan 2 pass from Kramer (Karlis kick)
Cle — FG Bahr 32
Cle — Waiters 14 pass from Pagel
A: 70,777 T: 4:03

Indianapolis 42, Miami 13—At the Hoosier Dome. The Colts executed three touchdown drives of more than 70 yards and converted a blocked punt, an interception and a fumble recovery into three more scores, as Indianapolis romped to an easy win. Colt QB Jack Trudeau connected on 23 of 35 passes for 195 yards and four TDs, while running back Eric Dickerson rushed for 107 yards and two TDs on 21 carries.

Miami	10	3	0	0	—	13
Indianapolis	7	7	14	14	—	42

Mia — FG Stoyanovich 43
Mia — Schwedes 70 punt return (Stoyanovich kick)
Ind — Rison 6 pass from Trudeau (Biasucci kick)
Mia — FG Stoyanovich 47
Ind — Boyer 1 pass from Trudeau (Biasucci kick)
Ind — Dickerson 1 run (Biasucci kick)
Ind — Pruitt 5 pass from Trudeau (Biasucci kick)
Ind — Bentley 6 pass from Trudeau (Biasucci kick)
Ind — Dickerson 2 run (Biasucci kick)
A: 55,665 T: 3:12

San Francisco 21, Buffalo 10—At Candlestick Park. After being held scoreless in the first half, the 49ers came alive in the second half, converting two interceptions thrown by Bills QB Jim Kelly into scores and dominating Buffalo with a ball-control offense. They were led by running back Roger Craig, who ran for a TD and 105 yards to give him his second straight 1,000-yard season.

Buffalo	3	0	0	7	—	10
San Francisco	0	0	7	14	—	21

Buff — FG Norwood 23
S.F. — Craig 1 run (Cofer kick)
S.F. — Young 2 run (Cofer kick)
S.F. — Rice 8 pass from Young (Cofer kick)
Buff — Kelly 1 run (Norwood kick)
A: 60,927 T: 2:58

Green Bay 40, Chicago 28—At Soldier Field. The Packer offense dominated the once powerful Bears defense, amassing 456 yards in a win that completed a Green Bay sweep of the two-game season series between the teams. Little used running back Keith Woodside rushed for 116 yards on 10 carries, while QB Don Majkowski ran for two TDs and 59 yards and threw for a TD and 244 yards.

Green Bay	14	10	6	10	—	40
Chicago	7	7	14	0	—	28

G.B. — Woodside 68 run (Jacke kick)
Chi — Muster 3 pass from Harbaugh (Butler kick)
G.B. — Kemp 27 pass from Majkowski (Jacke kick)
Chi — Anderson 21 pass from Harbaugh (Butler kick)
G.B. — FG Jacke 19
G.B. — Majkowski 17 run (Jacke kick)
G.B. — FG Jacke 44
Chi — Anderson 49 pass from Harbaugh (Butler kick)
G.B. — FG Jacke 23
Chi — Muster 4 run (Butler kick)
G.B. — Majkowski 1 run (Jacke kick)
G.B. — FG Jacke 21
A: 44,781 T: 3:25

L.A. Rams 38, N.Y. Jets 14—At Anaheim Stadium. All the pieces came together for the Rams in a laugher over the Jets. L.A. quarterback Jim Everett threw for 273 yards and two TDs—he now has 4,129 passing yards for the season, a new Ram record—and running back Greg Bell rushed for 52 yards and two TDs on 15 carries. Linebacker Brett Faryniarz made three of his team's seven sacks and recovered two fumbles.

New York	7	0	0	7	—	14
Los Angeles	7	21	0	10	—	38

L.A. — Holohan 25 pass from Everett (Lansford kick)
N.Y. — Townsell 63 pass from Eason (Leahy kick)
L.A. — Bell 1 run (Lansford kick)
L.A. — Anderson 43 pass from Everett (Lansford kick)
L.A. — Bell 5 run (Lansford kick)
L.A. — FG Lansford 37
L.A. — Gary 5 run (Lansford kick)
N.Y. — Neubert 35 pass from O'Brien (Leahy kick)
A: 55,063 T: 2:57

Detroit 33, Tampa Bay 7—At the Silverdome. The Lions continued their second-half resurgence with a dominant victory over the Bucs. As usual, they were led by explosive rookie Barry Sanders, who carried the ball 21 times for 104 yards and a TD, giving him 1,312 yards for the season, the highest total for any rookie in Detroit franchise history. Lion QB Bob Gagliano completed 19 of 33 passes for 192 yards and two TDs, while Eddie Murray, the NFL's most accurate kicker this season, connected on all four of his field goal attempts.

Tampa Bay	0	0	0	7	—	7
Detroit	14	10	3	6	—	33

Det — Johnson 2 pass from Gagliano (Murray kick)
Det — Phillips 55 pass from Gagliano (Murray kick)
Det — FG Murray 33
Det — Sanders 4 run (Murray kick)
Det — FG Murray 43
Det — FG Murray 35
Det — FG Murray 36
T.B. — Carrier 69 pass from Ferguson (Igwebuike kick)
A: 40,362 T: 3:10

Washington 31, Atlanta 30—At Fulton County Stadium. The Redskins exploded for three touchdowns in a 3:38 span of the third quarter to overcome a 27-10 Falcon lead and go on to the victory. Washington quarterbacks Mark Rypien and Doug Williams combined for 24 completions on 39 passing attempts for 390 yards and two TDs, while Ricky Sanders had seven catches for 167 yards. Atlanta's Michael Haynes had six catches for 190 yards and two TDs. The loss guaranteed the 3-12 Falcons the first pick in the 1990 draft.

Washington	3	7	21	0	—	31
Atlanta	3	24	3	0	—	30

Atl — FG Davis 33
Wash — FG Lohmiller 37
Wash — Monk 34 pass from Williams (Lohmiller kick)
Atl — Haynes 72 pass from Miller (Davis kick)
Atl — Haynes 17 pass from Miller (Davis kick)
Atl — FG Davis 24
Atl — Settle 3 run (Davis kick)
Wash — Monk 60 pass from Rypien (Lohmiller kick)
Wash — Byner 1 run (Lohmiller kick)
Wash — Rypien 9 run (Lohmiller kick)
Atl — FG Davis 32
A: 37,501 T: 3:36

San Diego 20, Kansas City 13—At Arrowhead Stadium. The streaking Chiefs were derailed by the Chargers' ball-control offense, led by rookie running back Marion Butts, who ran 39 times for 176 yards to become the first San Diego player to go over 100 yards this season. The Charger defense held Kansas City to just 214 yards while limiting Christian Okoye, the NFL's leading rusher, to just 60 yards on 18 carries.

San Diego	0	7	3	10	—	20
Kansas City	0	13	0	0	—	13

K.C. — FG Lowery 36
K.C. — FG Lowery 30
K.C. — McNair 11 pass from DeBerg (Lowery kick)
S.D. — Parker 1 pass from Tolliver (Bahr kick)
S.D. — FG Bahr 43
S.D. — Miller 5 pass from Tolliver (Bahr kick)
S.D. — FG Bahr 20
A: 40,623 T: 3:31

Pittsburgh 28, New England 10—At Three Rivers Stadium. The Steelers kept their playoff hopes alive with a solid win over the Patriots. With temperatures dipping to 15 below zero with the windchill factor, Pittsburgh chose to stay on the ground, as rookie Tim Worley carried 19 times for 104 yards and a TD, Merril Hoge ran for 63 yards and two TDs and wide receiver Louis Lipps scampered for the fourth touchdown on a 58-yard reverse. The Steelers, who lost their first two games by a total of 92-10, have won four of their last five.

New England	3	0	0	7	—	10
Pittsburgh	7	7	7	7	—	28

Pitt — Worley 8 run (Anderson kick)
N.E. — FG Staurovsky 20
Pitt — Hoge 1 run (Anderson kick)
Pitt — Lipps 58 run (Anderson kick)
Pitt — Hoge 2 run (Anderson kick)
N.E. — Jones 12 pass from Wilson (Staurovsky kick)
A: 26,954 T: 3:25

Seattle 23, L.A. Raiders 17—At the Kingdome. Seahawk QB Dave Krieg completed 25 of 34 passes for 270 yards and two TDs to deal a near fatal blow to the Raiders' playoff chances. Twelve of his passes for 129 yards and a TD went to John L. Williams, who now has caught 70 passes on the season, a new team record for a running back.

Los Angeles	3	0	14	0	—	17
Seattle	7	6	7	3	—	23

Sea — Skansi 5 pass from Krieg (Johnson kick)
L.A. — FG Jaeger 19
Sea — FG Johnson 29
Sea — FG Johnson 25
L.A. — Gault 36 pass from Beuerlein (Jaeger kick)
L.A. — Junkin 1 pass from Beuerlein (Jaeger kick)
Sea — Williams 13 pass from Krieg (Johnson kick)
Sea — FG Johnson 43
A: 61,076 T: 3:01

MONDAY, DECEMBER 18

New Orleans 30, Philadelphia 20—At the Superdome. The Saints, behind the passing of QB John Fourcade, prevented the Eagles from clinching at least a wild-card berth in the playoffs. Fourcade, who completed 18 of 35 passes for 236 yards, threw a 20-yard TD strike to Eric Martin—his third TD pass of the night—in the fourth quarter to put New Orleans in front to stay. Randall Cunningham threw for 306 yards and two TDs, while running for another 92 yards on eight carries. But one of his two interceptions and both of his lost fumbles led to Saints' touchdowns.

Philadelphia	0	10	10	0	—	20
New Orleans	7	9	0	14	—	30

N.O. — Martin 17 pass from Fourcade (Andersen kick)
N.O. — Hilliard 35 pass from Fourcade (Andersen kick)
Phi — Johnson 13 pass from Cunningham (Ruzek kick)
Phi — FG Ruzek 21
N.O. — Safety, Warren tackled Cunningham in end zone
Phi — Little 1 pass from Cunningham (Ruzek kick)
Phi — FG Ruzek 19
N.O. — Martin 20 pass from Fourcade (Andersen kick)
N.O. — Jordan 1 run (Andersen kick)
A: 68,561 T: 3:48

FINAL STANDINGS

AFC EAST	W	L	T	Pct	PF	PA
Buffalo	9	7	0	.563	409	317
Indianapolis	8	8	0	.500	298	301
Miami	8	8	0	.500	331	379
New England	5	11	0	.313	297	391
N.Y. Jets	4	12	0	.250	253	411

AFC CENTRAL	W	L	T	Pct	PF	PA
Cleveland	9	6	1	.594	334	254
Houston	9	7	0	.563	365	412
Pittsburgh	9	7	0	.563	265	326
Cincinnati	8	8	0	.500	404	285

AFC WEST	W	L	T	Pct	PF	PA
Denver	11	5	0	.688	362	226
Kansas City	8	7	1	.531	318	286
L.A. Raiders	8	8	0	.500	315	297
Seattle	7	9	0	.438	241	327
San Diego	6	10	0	.375	266	290

NFC EAST	W	L	T	Pct	PF	PA
N.Y. Giants	12	4	0	.750	348	252
Philadelphia	11	5	0	.688	342	274
Washington	10	6	0	.625	386	308
Phoenix	5	11	0	.313	258	377
Dallas	1	15	0	.063	204	393

NFC CENTRAL	W	L	T	Pct	PF	PA
Minnesota	10	6	0	.625	351	275
Green Bay	10	6	0	.625	362	356
Detroit	7	9	0	.438	312	364
Chicago	6	10	0	.375	358	377
Tampa Bay	5	11	0	.313	320	419

NFC WEST	W	L	T	Pct	PF	PA
San Francisco	14	2	0	.875	442	253
L.A. Rams	11	5	0	.688	426	344
New Orleans	9	7	0	.563	386	301
Atlanta	3	13	0	.188	279	437

WEEK 16 RESULTS

Cleveland 24, Houston 20
Buffalo 37, N.Y. Jets 0
Washington 29, Seattle 0
New Orleans 41, Indianapolis 6
Pittsburgh 31, Tampa Bay 22
N.Y. Giants 34, L.A. Raiders 17
Kansas City 27, Miami 24
Philadelphia 31, Phoenix 14
L.A. Rams 24, New England 20
San Francisco 26, Chicago 0
Detroit 31, Atlanta 24
San Diego 19, Denver 16
Green Bay 20, Dallas 10
Minnesota 29, Cincinnati 21 (Monday night)

SATURDAY, DECEMBER 23

Cleveland 24, Houston 20—At the Astrodome. The Browns, ahead 17-0, allowed the Oilers to charge back into the lead 20-17, then drove 58 yards to set up the game-winning four-yard TD run by Kevin Mack with 39 seconds left. The victory gave the Browns the AFC Central title and left the Oilers as one of two AFC wild-card playoff teams. Mack, who had returned to the Browns three weeks earlier after missing the entire season due to knee surgery and a month in jail on a drug conviction, gained 62 yards on 12 carries. The win spoiled a fine performance by Houston's Warren Moon, who threw for 414 yards and two TDs, and Drew Hill, who had 10 catches for 141 yards and two TDs.

Cleveland	10	7	0	7	—	24
Houston	0	3	7	10	—	20

Cle — FG Bahr 32
Cle — Metcalf 68 pass from Kosar (Bahr kick)
Cle — Slaughter 40 pass from Kosar (Bahr kick)
Hou — FG Zendejas 30
Hou — Hill 9 pass from Moon (Zendejas kick)
Hou — FG Zendejas 37
Hou — Hill 27 pass from Moon (Zendejas kick)
Cle — Mack 4 run (Bahr kick)
A: 58,342 T: 3:41

Buffalo 37, N.Y. Jets 0—At Giants Stadium. The Jets closed out a dismal 4-12 season with a sound drubbing at the hands of the Bills, who ran up 441 yards of offense while allowing just 200. Buffalo's Larry Kinnebrew had 91 yards on 17 carries, Thurman Thomas had 73 yards on 17 carries and Jim Kelly completed 13 of 21 passes for 208 yards and two TDs.

Buffalo	3	7	20	7	—	37
New York	0	0	0	0	—	0

Buff — FG Norwood 26
Buff — Kinnebrew 1 run (Norwood kick)
Buff — Lofton 18 pass from Kelly (kick failed)
Buff — Harmon 25 pass from Kelly (Norwood kick)
Buff — Thomas 3 run (Norwood kick)
Buff — Davis 17 run (Norwood kick)
A: 21,148 T: 2:52

Washington 29, Seattle 0—At the Kingdome. The Redskins finished their season with a resounding win over the Seahawks. Earnest Byner ran for 63 yards and two TDs on 19 carries, and Mark Rypien completed 22 of 31 passes for 290 yards and a TD. The Washington defense sacked Seattle's Dave Krieg four times and held the Seahawks to just 202 offensive yards.

Washington	10	3	16	0	—	29
Seattle	0	0	0	0	—	0

Wash — FG Lohmiller 29
Wash — Byner 2 run (Lohmiller kick)
Wash — FG Lohmiller 27
Wash — Clark 44 pass from Rypien (Lohmiller kick)
Wash — Safety, Krieg tackled by Stokes in end zone
Wash — Byner 8 run (Lohmiller kick)
A: 60,294 T: 2:40

SUNDAY, DECEMBER 24

New Orleans 41, Indianapolis 6—At the Superdome. Saints quarterback John Fourcade connected on 21 of 28 passes for 291 yards and two TDs as New Orleans rolled to an easy win over the Colts. Fourcade also ran for 30 yards and a TD as the Saints outgained Indianapolis 389-230. The loss eliminated the Colts from playoff consideration. New Orleans finished with a 9-7 record but missed the playoffs for the second consecutive season.

Indianapolis	0	6	0	0	—	6
New Orleans	3	7	7	24	—	41

N.O. — FG Andersen 21
Ind — FG Biasucci 41
N.O. — Martin 3 pass from Fourcade (Andersen kick)
Ind — FG Biasucci 24
N.O. — Hilliard 7 run (Andersen kick)
N.O. — Brenner 30 pass from Fourcade (Andersen kick)
N.O. — Fourcade 2 run (Andersen kick)
N.O. — FG Andersen 29
N.O. — Cook 63 interception return (Andersen kick)
A: 49,009 T: 2:50

Pittsburgh 31, Tampa Bay 22—At Tampa Stadium. The Steelers kept their playoff hopes alive with a solid win over the Bucs, who rallied for nine points in the fourth quarter but never led in the game. Pittsburgh continued to run effectively as Tim Worley and Merril Hoge combined for two TDs and 141 yards on 36 carries.

Pittsburgh	7	17	7	0	—	31
Tampa Bay	7	3	3	9	—	22

Pitt — Worley 1 run (Anderson kick)
T.B. — Carrier 7 pass from Ferguson (Igwebuike kick)
Pitt — Lipps 79 pass from Brister (Anderson kick)
T.B. — FG Igwebuike 45
Pitt — Lipps 12 pass from Brister (Anderson kick)
Pitt — FG Anderson 32
T.B. — FG Igwebuike 24
Pitt — Worley 1 run (Anderson kick)
T.B. — Safety, Cocroft blocked punt out of end zone
T.B. — Carrier 39 pass from Ferguson (Igwebuike kick)
A: 29,690 T: 3:06

N.Y. Giants 34, L.A. Raiders 17—At Giants Stadium. The Giants earned the NFC East title and eliminated the Raiders from playoff contention with a dominant victory. After battling to a 17-17 halftime tie, New York exploded for 17 points in the second half while shutting down the Raider offense. The Giants' Ottis Anderson ran for two TDs and 74 yards to give him 1,023 yards for the season, his first 1,000-yard year since 1984. Rookie Dave Meggett continued to be a spark plug for New York, returning a first-quarter punt 76 yards for a TD and grabbing three passes for 25 yards.

Los Angeles	7	10	0	0	—	17
New York	7	10	10	7	—	34

N.Y. — Meggett 76 punt return (Nittmo kick)
L.A. — Horton 1 pass from Beuerlein (Jaeger kick)
L.A. — Fernandez 30 pass from Beuerlein (Jaeger kick)
N.Y. — Anderson 1 run (Nittmo kick)
L.A. — FG Jaeger 42
N.Y. — FG Nittmo 28
N.Y. — Anderson 1 run (Nittmo kick)
N.Y. — FG Nittmo 21
N.Y. — Simms 3 run (Nittmo kick)
A: 70,306 T: 3:13

Kansas City 27, Miami 24—At Joe Robbie Stadium. The Dolphins rallied from a ten-point deficit to tie the game in the fourth quarter, but Nick Lowery's 41-yard field goal with 1:31 left won the game for the Chiefs. Miami QB Dan Marino completed 28 of 47 passes for 339 yards and three TDs, while Kansas City's Steve DeBerg threw for 230 yards and two TDs and drove his team 44 yards in nine plays for the game-winning field goal. The Chiefs' Christian Okoye ran for 98 yards on 26 carries.

Kansas City	0	21	3	3	—	27
Miami	7	7	0	10	—	24

Mia — Jensen 4 pass from Marino (Stoyanovich kick)
K.C. — Paige 20 pass from DeBerg (Lowery kick)
Mia — Edmunds 3 pass from Marino (Stoyanovich kick)
K.C. — Saxon 6 run (Lowery kick)
K.C. — Okoye 1 run (Lowery kick)
K.C. — FG Lowery 19
Mia — FG Stoyanovich 22
Mia — Clayton 7 pass from Marino (Stoyanovich kick)
K.C. — FG Lowery 41
A: 43,612 T: 3:06

Philadelphia 31, Phoenix 14—At Veterans Stadium. The Eagles dominated the Cardinals in a game that featured a 22-yard TD pass from kicker Roger Ruzek to wide receiver Cris Carter after a bad snap on a field goal attempt. Philadelphia QB Randall Cunningham ran for 41 yards and a TD and passed for 162 yards and a second TD, while running backs Heath Sherman and Anthony Toney combined for a TD and 148 yards on 26 carries.

Phoenix	7	7	0	0	—	14
Philadelphia	7	14	3	7	—	31

Phoe — Green 6 pass from Hogeboom (Del Greco kick)
Phi — Cunningham 14 run (Ruzek kick)
Phi — Carter 22 pass from Ruzek (Ruzek kick)
Phi — Drummond 4 pass from Cunningham (Ruzek kick)
Phoe — Green 36 pass from Hogeboom (Del Greco kick)
Phi — FG Ruzek 39
Phi — Sherman 7 run (Ruzek kick)
A: 43,287 T: 3:14

L.A. Rams 24, New England 20—At Sullivan Stadium. The Rams jumped out to a 17-3 lead, fell behind 20-17 and finally pulled the game out on a three-yard plunge by Greg Bell with 1:55 left. The Patriots still had a chance to win, after driving for a first down at the Ram four-yard line with nine seconds left. But QB Steve Grogan threw three incomplete passes into the end zone, and the game was over. Bell was the workhorse for L.A., rushing for 210 yards on 26 carries.

Los Angeles	3	7	7	7	—	24
New England	0	3	7	10	—	20

L.A. — FG Lansford 19
L.A. — Gray 27 interception return (Lansford kick)
N.E. — FG Staurovsky 44
L.A. — McGee 7 pass from Everett (Lansford kick)
N.E. — Fryar 47 pass from Grogan (Staurovsky kick)
N.E. — Stephens 4 run (Staurovsky kick)
N.E. — FG Staurovsky 48
L.A. — Bell 3 run (Lansford kick)
A: 27,940 T: 3:10

San Francisco 26, Chicago 0—At Candlestick Park. A once exciting matchup of old rivals turned into a rout as the dismal Bears season came to a merciful end in a game completely dominated by the 49ers. Joe Montana had a comfortable day, throwing for 106 yards and a TD before giving way to backup Steve Young, who threw for 100 yards more. Kicker Mike Cofer was four for four in field goal attempts.

Chicago	0	0	0	0	—	0
San Francisco	3	13	3	7	—	26

S.F. — FG Cofer 29
S.F. — FG Cofer 24
S.F. — Rice 29 pass from Montana (Cofer kick)
S.F. — FG Cofer 36
S.F. — FG Cofer 47
S.F. — Flagler 29 run (Cofer kick)
A: 65,675 T: 2:57

Detroit 31, Atlanta 24—At Fulton County Stadium. The Lions streaked to their fifth win in a row, thanks to the hapless Falcons, who needed two TDs in the last four minutes of the game to make the score respectable. Barry Sanders carried the load once again for Detroit, rushing for three TDs and 158 yards on 20 carries to give him 1,470 yards for the season, the most ever by a Detroit running back. Only 7,092 fans attended the game, the smallest crowd of the '89 season.

Detroit	7	7	10	7	—	31
Atlanta	0	10	0	14	—	24

Det — Johnson 34 pass from Gagliano (Murray kick)
Atl — FG Davis 25
Det — Sanders 25 run (Murray kick)
Atl — Lang 9 pass from Miller (Davis kick)
Det — FG Murray 39
Det — Sanders 17 run (Murray kick)
Det — Sanders 18 run (Murray kick)
Atl — Jones 1 run (Davis kick)
Atl — Haynes 6 pass from Miller (Davis kick)
A: 7,092 T: 3:24

San Diego 19, Denver 16—At Jack Murphy Stadium. The Broncos continued to stumble toward the playoffs, losing their third game in the past four outings when Chris Bahr kicked a 45-yard field goal as time expired to win for the Chargers. The Broncos had tied the game just 35 seconds earlier, but San Diego rookie quarterback Billy Joe Tolliver drove his team 45 yards in five plays to get in position for the game-winning kick by Bahr, who kicked three other field goals in the game, including a 53-yarder. Tolliver completed 22 of 48 passes for 305 yards, while Denver quarterbacks John Elway and Gary Kubiak were held to 144 yards.

Denver	0	7	3	6	—	16
San Diego	0	6	3	10	—	19

S.D. — FG Bahr 22
Den — Humphrey 12 pass from Elway (Treadwell kick)
S.D. — FG Bahr 41
S.D. — FG Bahr 53
Den — FG Treadwell 24
S.D. — Spencer 1 run (Bahr kick)
Den — Alexander 1 run (kick failed)
S.D. — FG Bahr 45
A: 50,524 T: 3:22

Green Bay 20, Dallas 10—At Texas Stadium. The Cowboys played a solid defensive game, holding the Packers to just 43 yards rushing and 250 yards overall, but in the end it was just another Dallas loss, giving the team 15 for the season to tie the NFL mark set by New Orleans in 1980. Green Bay was led, as usual, by QB Don Majkowski, who completed 21 of 32 passes for 232 yards and both his team's TDs. The win kept the Packers in the hunt for the playoffs, but a victory by the Vikings the following day would eliminate them from contention.

Green Bay	3	7	7	3	—	20
Dallas	3	0	7	0	—	10

G.B. — FG Jacke 28
Dall — FG Zendejas 41
G.B. — Query 14 pass from Majkowski (Jacke kick)
Dall — Del Rio 57 fumble return (Zendejas kick)
G.B. — West 5 pass from Majkowski (Jacke kick)
G.B. — FG Jacke 24
A: 41,265 T: 2:47

MONDAY, DECEMBER 25

Minnesota 29, Cincinnati 21—At the Metrodome. The defense led the way for the Vikings in a win over the Bengals that made Minnesota the NFC Central champion. Defensive end Chris Doleman had 3½ sacks to increase his league-leading season total to 20½, while the Vikings recorded six sacks in all. QB Wade Wilson threw for 303 yards and two TDs, while Rich Karlis contributed five field goals on six attempts. Cincinnati's Boomer Esiason threw for 367 yards and three TDs, but he also threw three costly interceptions. The Minnesota victory eliminated the Packers from playoff contention and enabled the Steelers to qualify as an AFC wild-card team.

Cincinnati	0	7	7	7	—	21
Minnesota	6	16	0	7	—	29

Minn — FG Karlis 31
Minn — FG Karlis 37
Minn — FG Karlis 22
Minn — Fenney 11 pass from Wilson (Karlis kick)
Minn — FG Karlis 42
Cin — Brown 34 pass from Esiason (Breech kick)
Minn — FG Karlis 24
Cin — Holman 65 pass from Esiason (Breech kick)
Cin — Taylor 18 pass from Esiason (Breech kick)
Minn — Novoselsky 1 pass from Wilson (Karlis kick)
A: 58,829 T: 3:41

RESULTS

Wild-card Games
L.A. Rams 21, Philadelphia 7
Pittsburgh 26, Houston 23

Divisional Playoffs
San Francisco 41, Minnesota 13
Cleveland 34, Buffalo 30
L.A. Rams 19, N.Y. Giants 13, OT
Denver 24, Pittsburgh 23

AFC Championship
Denver 37, Cleveland 21

NFC Championship
San Francisco 30, L.A. Rams 3

Super Bowl XXIV
San Francisco 55, Denver 10

WILD-CARD GAMES

SUNDAY, DECEMBER 31

L.A. Rams 21, Philadelphia 7—At Veterans Stadium. The Rams employed a basic zone defense to keep Philadelphia quarterback Randall Cunningham in check and limit the Eagles to a single fourth-quarter touchdown in a surprisingly easy playoff victory. Los Angeles got a pair of scoring strikes from Jim Everett (18 of 33 passes for 281 yards) in the first quarter to jump in front, then ate up the clock with a relentless running game keyed by Greg Bell, who rushed for 124 yards on 27 carries. Bell's seven-yard run with 2:14 remaining put the game out of reach.

Los Angeles	14	0	0	7	—	21
Philadelphia	0	0	0	7	—	7

L.A. — Ellard 39 pass from Everett (Lansford kick)
L.A. — Johnson 4 pass from Everett (Lansford kick)
Phi — Toney 1 run (Ruzek kick)
L.A. — Bell 7 run (Lansford kick)
A: 57,869 T: 3:05

Pittsburgh 26, Houston 23—At the Astrodome. Gary Anderson kept Pittsburgh's Cinderella season alive with a 50-yard field goal in overtime for the win. It was another improbable victory for the Steelers, who looked all but finished in the fourth quarter when Oiler QB Warren Moon connected with wide receiver Ernest Givins for two touchdown passes that put Houston in front 23-16 with 6:02 to play in regulation. But Pittsburgh bounced back with an 82-yard drive, capped by a two-yard touchdown run with 46 seconds left by fullback Merril Hoge, who had 100 yards rushing on 17 carries for the day. Things again looked grim for the Steelers in overtime when a weak punt gave Houston the ball near midfield. But Steeler cornerback Rod Woodson forced and then recovered a fumble by Lorenzo White, and four plays later Anderson was in position for the winning kick. It was a particularly tough loss for Moon and Givins, each of whom had outstanding days, Moon throwing for 315 yards and Givins making 11 catches for 136 yards.

Pittsburgh	7	3	3	10	3	—	26
Houston	0	6	3	14	0	—	23

Pitt — Worley 9 run (Anderson kick)
Hou — FG Zendejas 26
Hou — FG Zendejas 35
Pitt — FG Anderson 25
Hou — FG Zendejas 26
Pitt — FG Anderson 30
Pitt — FG Anderson 48
Hou — Givins 18 pass from Moon (Zendejas kick)
Hou — Givins 9 pass from Moon (Zendejas kick)
Pitt — Hoge 2 run (Anderson kick)
Pitt — FG Anderson 50
A: 58,306 T: 3:55

DIVISIONAL PLAYOFFS

SATURDAY, JANUARY 6, 1990

San Francisco 41, Minnesota 13—At Candlestick Park. The 49ers began their inexorable drive to the Super Bowl with a convincing win over the Vikings. San Francisco dominated every phase of the game, scoring on four of their first six possessions to take a 27-3 halftime lead. Joe Montana had another fine game, completing 17 of 24 passes for 241 yards and four touchdowns, two of them going to Jerry Rice, who had six catches for 114 yards on the day. The 49ers were also devastating on the ground, as Roger Craig ran for 125 yards on 18 carries. San Francisco's supposedly suspect offensive line kept the Vikings, who led the league in sacks, from getting to Montana even once, while the 49er defense produced five turnovers, including a 58-yard interception return for a touchdown by Ronnie Lott.

Minnesota	3	0	3	7	—	13
San Francisco	7	20	0	14	—	41

Minn — FG Karlis 38
S.F. — Rice 72 pass from Montana (Cofer kick)
S.F. — Jones 8 pass from Montana (Cofer kick)
S.F. — Taylor 8 pass from Montana (kick failed)
S.F. — Rice 13 pass from Montana (Cofer kick)
Minn — FG Karlis 44
S.F. — Lott 58 interception return (Cofer kick)
S.F. — Craig 4 run (Cofer kick)
Minn — Fenney 3 run (Karlis kick)
A: 64,585 T: 3:15

Cleveland 34, Buffalo 30—At Cleveland Stadium. The Browns held on for the victory as Cleveland linebacker Clay Matthews intercepted a pass from Jim Kelly on his own goal line with three seconds left to end a Buffalo scoring threat. On the previous play, Kelly (28 of 54 passes for a career-high 405 yards and four TDs) hit Ronnie Harmon in the end zone, but Harmon dropped the ball, allowing the Browns to keep the lead. Cleveland had used two Matt Bahr field goals, precision passing from Bernie Kosar—who completed 20 of 29 passes for 251 yards and three TDs—and a 90-yard kickoff return from Eric Metcalf to forge a 34-24 lead with 6:50 remaining. But Kelly, relying on short dump passes to running back Thurman Thomas, marched his team 77 yards, connecting with Thomas on a three-yard TD pass to bring the Bills within four. Unfortunately for the Bills, Scott Norwood missed the extra point and Buffalo was forced to go for the touchdown on their final possession.

Buffalo	7	7	7	9	—	30
Cleveland	3	14	14	3	—	34

Buff — Reed 72 pass from Kelly (Norwood kick)
Cle — FG Bahr 45
Cle — Slaughter 52 pass from Kosar (Bahr kick)
Buff — Lofton 33 pass from Kelly (Norwood kick)
Cle — Middleton 3 pass from Kosar (Bahr kick)
Cle — Slaughter 44 pass from Kosar (Bahr kick)
Buff — Thomas 6 pass from Kelly (Norwood kick)
Cle — Metcalf 90 kickoff return (Bahr kick)
Buff — FG Norwood 30
Cle — FG Bahr 47
Buff — Thomas 3 pass from Kelly (kick failed)
A: 77,706 T: 3:42

SUNDAY, JANUARY 7

L.A. Rams 19, N.Y. Giants 13—At Giants Stadium. L.A.'s Flipper Anderson streaked past Giants cornerback Mark Collins with a 30-yard touchdown pass from Jim Everett for the overtime win. The touchdown came two plays after a controversial interference call on an attempted pass to Anderson that the Giants felt should have been ruled uncatchable. It was a bitter loss for New York, which dominated the first half but trailed 7-6 because of an interception late in the second quarter that resulted in a 20-yard TD strike from Everett to Anderson. Still, the Giants were able to grab the lead, 13-7, in the third quarter on a two-yard plunge by Ottis Anderson, who had 120 yards on 24 carries for the day. But by the fourth quarter the Ram offense was clicking, and Everett (25 of 44 passes for 315 yards) was able to engineer two field goal-producing drives to tie the game.

Los Angeles	0	7	0	6	6	—	19
New York	6	0	7	0	0	—	13

N.Y. — FG Allegre 35
N.Y. — FG Allegre 41
L.A. — Anderson 20 pass from Everett (Lansford kick)
N.Y. — Anderson 2 run (Allegre kick)
L.A. — FG Lansford 31
L.A. — FG Lansford 22
L.A. — Anderson 30 pass from Everett
A: 76,325 T: 3:10

Denver 24, Pittsburgh 23—At Mile High Stadium. In spite of a gritty effort by the Steelers, it was Denver and John Elway who came out on top after Melvin Bratton dived across from the one for the game-winning score with 2:27 left. Pittsburgh had gone ahead on two Gary Anderson field goals and seemed in command in the second half as running back Merril Hoge (120 yards on 16 carries) banged away at the Bronco defense. But Elway came up with the big plays in the clutch, including a 36-yard completion to Vance Johnson on a flea flicker during the 71-yard winning drive in the fourth quarter. Elway threw for 239 yards and ran for 44 more, while rookie Bobby Humphrey ran for 85 yards on 18 carries.

Pittsburgh	3	14	3	3	—	23
Denver	0	10	7	7	—	24

Pitt — FG Anderson 32
Pitt — Hoge 7 run (Anderson kick)
Den — Bratton 1 run (Treadwell kick)
Pitt — Lipps 9 pass from Brister (Anderson kick)
Den — FG Treadwell 43
Den — Johnson 37 pass from Elway (Treadwell kick)
Pitt — FG Anderson 35
Pitt — FG Anderson 32
Den — Bratton 1 run (Treadwell kick)
A: 75,868 T: 2:57

AFC CHAMPIONSHIP

SUNDAY, JANUARY 14

Denver 37, Cleveland 21—At Mile High Stadium. John Elway answered all his critics with a tremendous performance to lift the Broncos to their third Super Bowl in the past four seasons. Elway was a dominant force, completing 20 of 36 passes for 385 yards and three touchdowns without an interception. He also ran for 39 yards on five carries, several of them in key third-down situations. The Browns made the game close in the third quarter, closing to within three points, at 24-21, on a 10-yard TD pass from Bernie Kosar to Brian Brennan and a two-yard scoring dive by Tim Manoa. But Elway answered with an 80-yard drive, capped by a 39-yard touchdown pass to Sammy Winder. It was the second TD of the day for Winder, who was playing in relief of injured rookie Bobby Humphrey. Another unsung Bronco, fourth wide receiver Michael Young, also played a critical role, catching a 70-yard TD pass in the second quarter and grabbing a 53-yard reception in the third quarter to set up another TD. The Denver defense, which sacked Kosar four times, shut the Browns out in the fourth quarter to secure the win.

Cleveland	0	0	21	0	—	21
Denver	3	7	14	13	—	37

Den — FG Treadwell 29
Den — Young 70 pass from Elway (Treadwell kick)
Cle — Brennan 27 pass from Kosar (Bahr kick)
Den — Mobley 5 pass from Elway (Treadwell kick)
Den — Winder 7 run (Treadwell kick)
Cle — Brennan 10 pass from Kosar (Bahr kick)
Cle — Manoa 2 run (Bahr kick)
Den — Winder 39 pass from Elway (Treadwell kick)
Den — FG Treadwell 34
Den — FG Treadwell 31
A: 76,046 T: 3:28

NFC CHAMPIONSHIP

SUNDAY, JANUARY 14

San Francisco 30, L.A. Rams 3—At Candlestick Park. The Rams scored first, on a 23-yard field goal by Mike Lansford in the first quarter, but from then on it was all 49ers, as Joe Montana & Co. romped to an easy win that sent them to their second straight Super Bowl. Montana was brilliant as usual, completing 26 of 30 passes for 262 yards and two touchdowns, both of them in the first half, when San Francisco jumped out to a 21-3 lead. Roger Craig brought balance to the 49er attack, running for 93 yards and a touchdown on 23 carries. The San Francisco defense, allegedly the weak link of the team, held the high-powered Ram offense to just 156 total yards, while intercepting Los Angeles QB Jim Everett three times. The Rams had a chance to go ahead 10-0 in the early going, but 49er safety Ronnie Lott raced across the field to knock away the potential touchdown pass from wide receiver Willie Anderson. The Rams never threatened again.

Los Angeles	3	0	0	0	—	3
San Francisco	0	21	3	6	—	30

L.A. — FG Lansford 23
S.F. — Jones 20 pass from Montana (Cofer kick)
S.F. — Craig 1 run (Cofer kick)
S.F. — Taylor 18 pass from Montana (Cofer kick)
S.F. — FG Cofer 28
S.F. — FG Cofer 36
S.F. — FG Cofer 25
A: 64,769 T: 2:51

SUPER BOWL

SUNDAY, JANUARY 28

San Francisco 55, Denver 10—At the Superdome. The 49ers looked invincible as they rolled over the Broncos in the most lopsided Super Bowl ever. Once again, it was the efficient Joe Montana who led the way, completing 22 of 29 passes for 297 yards and a Super Bowl-record five touchdown passes, numbers good enough to earn him a record third Super Bowl MVP award. His 13 straight completions was also a Super Bowl record, as are his Super Bowl career totals of 11 touchdown passes, 1,142 passing yards and 122 passes attempted without an interception. Everything clicked for the Niners, as Roger Craig and Tom Rathman combined for 107 rushing yards and Jerry Rice grabbed seven passes for 148 yards and three TDs through the air. The game was never in doubt as the 49ers scored five unanswered touchdowns to go in front 41-3 in the third quarter; San Francisco's eight touchdowns is the most ever scored in Super Bowl history. The 49er defense was also effective, sacking Denver's John Elway six times and limiting him to just 108 yards passing on a 10-for-26 day. The Broncos gained just 167 yards overall, as coach Dan Reeves ran his Super Bowl record to 0-3.

San Francisco	13	14	14	14	—	55
Denver	3	0	7	0	—	10

S.F. — Rice 20 pass from Montana (Cofer kick)
Den — FG Treadwell 42
S.F. — Jones 7 pass from Montana (kick failed)
S.F. — Rathman 1 run (Cofer kick)
S.F. — Rice 38 pass from Montana (Cofer kick)
S.F. — Rice 28 pass from Montana (Cofer kick)
S.F. — Taylor 35 pass from Montana (Cofer kick)
Den — Elway 3 run (Treadwell kick)
S.F. — Rathman 3 run (Cofer kick)
S.F. — Craig 1 run (Cofer kick)
A: 72,919 T: 3:21

Team Statistics

Atlanta

1989 TEAM RECORD

Preseason (1-3)

Date	Result		Opponent
8/12	L	17-23	at Philadelphia
8/19	L	0-27	at Tampa Bay
8/26	L	7-23	New England
9/1	W	38-17	v. Buffalo in Jacksonville

Regular Season (3-13)

Date	Result		Opponent	Att.
9/10	L	21-31	Rams	38,708
9/17	W	27-21	Dallas	55,285
9/24	L	9-13	at Indianapolis	57,816
10/1	L	21-23	vs. Green Bay in Milwaukee	54,647
10/8	L	14-26	at Rams	52,182
10/15	W	16-15	New England	39,697
10/22	L	20-34	at Phoenix	33,894
10/29	L	13-20	at New Orleans	65,153
11/5	W	30-28	Buffalo	45,267
11/12	L	3-45	at San Francisco	59,914
11/19	L	17-26	New Orleans	53,173
11/26	L	7-27	at Jets	40,429
12/3	L	10-23	San Francisco	43,128
12/10	L	17-43	at Minnesota	58,116
12/17	L	30-31	Washington	37,501
12/24	L	24-31	Detroit	7,792

1989 TEAM STATISTICS

	Falcons	Opp.
Total First Downs	261	336
Rushing	75	156
Passing	173	163
Penalty	13	17
Third Down: Made/Att.	67/206	95/211
Fourth Down: Made/Att.	6/17	7/9
Total Net Yard	4669	6025
Avg. Per Game	291.8	376.6
Total Plays	947	1040
Avg. Per Play	4.9	5.8
Net Yards Rushing	1155	2471
Avg. Per Game	72.2	154.4
Total Rushes	318	572
Net Yards Passing	3514	3554
Avg. Per Game	219.6	222.1
Sacked/Yards Lost	51/389	31/183
Gross Yards	3903	3737
Att./Completions	578/312	437/259
Completion Pct.	54.0	59.3
Had Intercepted	12	20
Punts/Avg.	85/40.8	56/41.8
Net Punting Avg.	33.3	34.3
Penalties/Yards Lost	82/671	79/682
Fumbles/Ball Lost	26/11	26/12
Touchdowns	30	49
Rushing	11	26
Passing	17	19
Returns	2	4
Avg. Time of Possession	25:58	34:02

1989 INDIVIDUAL STATISTICS

Scoring	TD R	TD P	TD Rt	PAT	FG	Saf	TP
McFadden	0	0	0	18/18	15/20	0	63
Jones	6	0	0	0/0	0/0	0	36
Davis	0	0	0	12/12	7/11	0	33
Settle	3	2	0	0/0	0/0	0	30
Haynes	0	4	0	0/0	0/0	0	24
Collins	0	3	0	0/0	0/0	0	18
Wilkins	0	3	0	0/0	0/0	0	18
Dixon	0	2	0	0/0	0/0	0	12
Lang	1	1	0	0/0	0/0	0	12
Beckman	0	1	0	0/0	0/0	0	6
Butler	0	0	1	0/0	0/0	0	6
Flowers	1	0	0	0/0	0/0	0	6
Heller	0	1	0	0/0	0/0	0	6
Sanders	0	0	1	0/0	0/0	0	6
Miller	0	0	0	0/0	1/1	0	3
Falcons	11	17	2	30/30	23/32	0	279
Opponents	26	19	4	48/49	31/36	1	437

Passing	Att.	Comp.	Yds.	Pct.	TD	Int.	Tkld.	Rate
Miller	526	280	3459	53.2	16	10	41/318	76.1
Millen	50	31	432	62.0	1	2	10/71	79.8
Fulhage	1	1	12	100.0	0	0	0/0	116.7
Jones	1	0	0	0.0	0	0	0/0	39.6
Falcons	578	312	3903	54.0	17	12	51/389	76.4
Opponents	437	259	3737	59.3	19	20	31/183	82.5

Rushing	Att.	Yds.	Avg.	LG	TD
Settle	179	689	3.8	20	3
Jones	52	202	3.9	19	6
Lang	47	176	3.7	22	1
Haynes	4	35	8.8	21	0
Paterra	9	32	3.6	8	0
Flowers	13	24	1.8	4	1
Miller	10	20	2.0	7	0
Fulhage	1	0	0.0	0	0
Millen	1	0	0.0	0	0
Dixon	2	-23	-11.5	0	0
Falcons	318	1155	3.6	22	11
Opponents	572	2471	4.3	38	26

Receiving	No.	Yds.	Avg.	LG	TD
Collins	58	862	14.9	47	3
Jones	41	396	9.7	46	0
Haynes	40	681	17.0	t72	4
Lang	39	436	11.2	32	1
Settle	39	316	8.1	33	2
Heller	33	324	9.8	30	1
Dixon	25	357	14.3	t53	2
Beckman	11	102	9.3	21	1
Wilkins	8	179	22.4	36	3
Bailey	8	170	21.3	41	0
Paterra	5	42	8.4	20	0
G. Thomas	4	46	11.5	16	0
Sanders	1	-8	-8.0	-8	0
Falcons	312	3903	12.5	t72	17
Opponents	259	3737	14.4	78	19

Interceptions	No.	Yds.	Avg.	LG	TD
Sanders	5	52	10.4	22	0
Gordon	4	60	15.0	34	0
Cooper	4	54	13.5	38	0
Dimry	2	72	36.0	40	0
Case	2	13	6.5	13	0
Shelley	1	31	31.0	31	0
Zackery	1	3	3.0	3	0
Bruce	1	0	0.0	0	0
Falcons	20	285	14.3	40	0
Opponents	12	85	7.1	27	0

Punting	No.	Yds.	Avg.	In 20	LG
Fulhage	84	3472	41.3	24	65
Falcons	85	3472	40.8	24	65
Opponents	56	2342	41.8	15	64

Punt Returns	No.	FC	Yds.	Avg.	LG	TD
Sanders	28	7	307	11.0	t68	1
Jordan	4	0	34	8.5	15	0
Falcons	32	7	341	10.7	t68	1
Opponents	43	20	460	10.7	39	0

Kickoff Returns	No.	Yds.	Avg.	LG	TD
Sanders	35	725	20.7	72	0
Jones	23	440	19.1	29	0
G. Thomas	7	142	20.3	28	0
Paterra	8	129	16.1	31	0
Jordan	3	27	9.0	13	0
Beckman	2	15	7.5	15	0
Primus	1	16	16.0	16	0
Bruce	1	15	15.0	15	0
Falcons	80	1509	18.9	72	0
Opponents	60	1188	19.8	85	0

Sacks	No.
Cotton	9.0
Bruce	6.0
Green	5.0
Casillas	2.0
Gann	2.0
Bryan	1.0
Case	1.0
Dimry	1.0
Reid	1.0
Taylor	1.0
B. Thomas	1.0
Tuggle	1.0
Falcons	31.0
Opponents	51.0

Buffalo

1989 TEAM RECORD

Preseason (1-4)

Date	Result		Opponent
8/5	L	6-31	vs. Washington at Canton
8/13	L	20-24	at Cincinnati
8/19	W	10-7	New Orleans
8/26	L	24-27	vs. Green Bay at Madison
9/1	L	17-38	vs. Atlanta at Jacksonville

Regular Season (9-7)

Date	Result		Opponent	Att.
9/10	W	27-24	at Miami	54,541
9/18	L	14-28	Denver	78,176
9/24	W	47-41(OT)	at Houston	57,278
10/1	W	31-10	New England	78,921
10/8	L	14-37	at Indianapolis	58,890
10/16	W	23-20	Rams	76,231
10/22	W	34-3	Jets	76,811
10/29	W	31-17	Miami	80,208
11/5	L	28-30	at Atlanta	45,267
11/12	W	30-7	Indianapolis	79,256
11/19	L	24-33	at New England	49,663
11/26	W	24-7	Cincinnati	80,074
12/4	L	16-17	at Seattle	57,682
12/10	L	19-22	New Orleans	70,037
12/17	L	10-21	at San Francisco	60,927
12/23	W	37-0	at Jets	21,148

Postseason (0-1)

Date	Result		Opponent	Att.
1/6	L	30-34	at Cleveland	77,706

1989 TEAM STATISTICS

	Bills	Opp.
Total First Downs	334	299
Rushing	136	117
Passing	177	156
Penalty	21	26
Third Down: Made/Att.	86/203	75/213
Fourth Down: Made/Att.	4/8	7/15
Total Net Yards	5853	5046
Avg. Per Game	365.8	315.4
Total Plays	1045	1030
Avg. Per Play	5.6	4.9
Net Yards Rushing	2264	1840
Avg. Per Game	141.5	115.0
Total Rushes	532	484
Net Yards Passing	3589	3206
Avg. Per Game	224.3	200.4
Sacked/Yards Lost	35/242	38/289
Gross Yards	3831	3495
Att./Completions	478/281	508/255
Completion Pct.	58.8	50.2
Had Intercepted	20	23
Punts/Avg.	67/38.3	75/38.3
Net Punting Avg.	32.2	32.1
Penalties/Yards Lost	103/831	87/616
Fumbles/Ball Lost	30/21	31/13
Touchdowns	49	34
Rushing	15	15
Passing	32	14
Returns	2	5
Avg. Time of Possession	30:12	29:48

1989 INDIVIDUAL STATISTICS

Scoring	TD R	TD P	TD Rt	PAT	FG	Saf	TP
Norwood	0	0	0	46/47	23/30	0	115
Thomas	6	6	0	0/0	0/0	0	72
Reed	0	9	0	0/0	0/0	0	54
Kinnebrew	6	0	0	0/0	0/0	0	36
Harmon	0	4	0	0/0	0/0	0	24
Davis	1	2	0	0/0	0/0	0	18
Lofton	0	3	0	0/0	0/0	0	18
Beebe	0	2	0	0/0	0/0	0	12
Kelly	2	0	0	0/0	0/0	0	12
McKeller	0	2	0	0/0	0/0	0	12
Metzelaars	0	2	0	0/0	0/0	0	12
Jackson	0	0	1	0/0	0/0	0	6
Johnson	0	1	0	0/0	0/0	0	6
Kelso	0	0	1	0/0	0/0	0	6
Rolle	0	1	0	0/0	0/0	0	6
Bills	15	32	2	46/48	23/30	0	409
Opponents	15	14	5	33/34	26/37	1	317

Passing	Att.	Comp.	Yds.	Pct.	TD	Int.	Tkld.	Rate
Kelly	391	228	3130	58.3	25	18	30/216	86.2
Reich	87	53	701	60.9	7	2	4/24	103.7
Johnson	0	0	0	—	0	-	1/2	0.0
Bills	478	281	3831	58.8	32	20	35/242	89.3
Opponents	508	255	3495	50.2	14	23	38/289	62.9

Rushing	Att.	Yds.	Avg.	LG	TD
Thomas	298	1244	4.2	38	6
Kinnebrew	131	533	4.1	25	6
Davis	29	149	5.1	21	1
Kelly	29	137	4.7	19	2
Harmon	17	99	5.8	24	0
Mueller	16	44	2.8	9	0
Reed	2	31	15.5	23	0
Reich	9	30	3.3	9	0
Gelbaugh	1	-3	-3.0	-3	0
Bills	532	2264	4.3	38	15
Opponents	484	1840	3.8	33	15

Receiving	No.	Yds.	Avg.	LG	TD
Reed	88	1312	14.9	t78	9
Thomas	60	669	11.2	t74	6
Harmon	29	363	12.5	t42	4
Johnson	25	303	12.1	36	1
McKeller	20	341	17.1	t39	2
Metzelaars	18	179	9.9	23	2
Beebe	17	317	18.6	t63	2
Lofton	8	166	20.8	47	3
Davis	6	92	15.3	29	2
Kinnebrew	5	60	12.0	18	0
Burkett	3	20	6.7	9	0
Mueller	1	8	8.0	8	0
Rolle	1	1	1.0	t1	1
Bills	281	3831	13.6	t78	32
Opponents	255	3495	13.7	t78	14

Interceptions	No.	Yds.	Avg.	LG	TD
Kelso	6	101	16.8	43	0
Odomes	5	20	4.0	13	0
Smith	2	46	23.0	24	0
Jackson	2	43	21.5	t40	1
Bennett	2	5	2.5	6	0
Drane	1	25	25.0	25	0
Bailey	1	16	16.0	16	0
Still	1	10	10.0	10	0
Sutton	1	3	3.0	3	0
Conlan	1	0	0.0	0	0
Wright	1	0	0.0	0	0
Bills	23	269	11.7	43	1
Opponents	20	364	18.2	t80	2

Punting	No.	Yds.	Avg.	In 20	LG
Kidd	65	2564	39.4	15	60
Bills	67	2564	38.3	18	60
Opponents	75	2870	38.3	18	59

Punt Returns	No.	FC	Yds.	Avg.	LG	TD
Sutton, G.B.-Buff.	31	10	273	8.8	26	0
Sutton, Buff.	26	9	231	8.9	26	0
Tucker	6	3	63	10.5	14	0
Johnson	1	0	7	7.0	7	0
Bills	33	12	301	9.1	26	0
Opponents	25	15	227	9.1	25	0

Kickoff Returns	No.	Yds.	Avg.	LG	TD
Harmon	18	409	22.7	49	0
Beebe	16	353	22.1	85	0
Tucker	10	166	16.6	23	0
Davis	3	52	17.3	20	0
Rolle	2	20	10.0	14	0
Tasker	2	39	19.5	20	0
Jackson	1	0	0.0	0	0
Mueller	1	19	19.0	19	0
Bills	53	1058	20.0	85	0
Opponents	75	1187	15.8	40	0

Sacks	No.
Smith	13
Talley	6
Bennett	5.5
Seals	4
Wright	3
Radecic	1.5
Burroughs	1
Cofield	1
Conlan	1
Odomes	1
Smerlas	1
Bills	38.0
Opponents	35.0

Chicago

1989 TEAM RECORD

Preseason (2-2)

Date	Result		Opponent
8/14	W	28-20	at Miami
8/19	L	7-24	San Diego
8/27	L	17-22	Kansas City
9/2	W	41-38	at Raiders

Regular Season (6-10)

Date	Result		Opponent	Att.
9/10	W	17-14	Cincinnati	64,730
9/17	W	38-7	Minnesota	66,475
9/24	W	47-27	at Detroit	71,418
10/2	W	27-13	Philadelphia	66,625
10/8	L	35-42	at Tampa Bay	72,077
10/15	L	28-33	Houston	64,383
10/23	L	7-27	at Cleveland	78,722
10/29	W	20-10	Rams	65,506
11/5	L	13-14	at Green Bay	56,556
11/12	W	20-0	at Pittsburgh	56,505
11/19	L	31-32	Tampa Bay	63,826
11/26	L	14-38	at Washington	50,044
12/3	L	16-27	at Minnesota	60,664
12/10	L	17-27	Detroit	52,650
12/17	L	28-40	Green Bay	44,781
12/24	L	0-26	at San Francisco	60,207

1989 TEAM STATISTICS

	Bears	Opp.
Total First Downs	302	332
Rushing	136	118
Passing	147	191
Penalty	19	23
Third Down: Made/Att.	94/214	84/206
Fourth Down: Made/Att.	10/18	7/15
Total Net Yards	5375	5729
Avg. Per Game	335.9	358.1
Total Plays	1028	1039
Avg. Per Play	5.2	5.5
Net Yards Rushing	2287	1897
Avg. Per Game	142.9	118.6
Total Rushes	516	446
Net Yards Passing	3088	3832
Avg. Per Game	193.0	239.5
Sacked/Yards Lost	28/174	39/247
Gross Yards	3262	4079
Att./Completions	484/267	554/307
Completion Pct.	55.2	55.4
Had Intercepted	25	26
Punts/Avg.	72/39.5	67/39.6
Net Punting Avg.	33.4	34.6
Penalties/Yards Lost	95/846	95/802
Fumbles/Ball Lost	23/17	24/12
Touchdowns	45	43
Rushing	22	21
Passing	21	21
Returns	2	1
Avg. Time of Possession	31:11	28:49

1989 INDIVIDUAL STATISTICS

Scoring	TD R	TD P	TD Rt	PAT	FG	Saf	TP
Anderson	11	4	0	0/0	0/0	0	90
Butler	0	0	0	43/45	15/19	0	88
Muster	5	3	0	0/0	0/0	0	48
Davis	0	3	0	0/0	0/0	0	18
Harbaugh	3	0	0	0/0	0/0	0	18
McKinnon	0	3	0	0/0	0/0	0	18
Thornton	0	3	0	0/0	0/0	0	18
Sanders	0	1	1	0/0	0/0	0	12
Suhey	1	1	0	0/0	0/0	0	12
Boso	0	1	0	0/0	0/0	0	6
Gentry	0	1	0	0/0	0/0	0	6
Green	1	0	0	0/0	0/0	0	6
Morris	0	1	0	0/0	0/0	0	6
Stinson	0	0	1	0/0	0/0	0	6
Tomczak	1	0	0	0/0	0/0	0	6
Bears	22	21	2	43/45	15/19	0	358
Opponents	21	2	1	41/43	26/36	0	377

Passing	Att.	Comp.	Yds.	Pct.	TD	Int.	Tkld.	Rate
Tomczak	306	156	2058	51.0	16	16	10/68	68.2
Harbaugh	178	111	1204	62.4	5	9	18/106	70.5
Bears	484	267	3262	55.2	21	25	28/174	69.1
Opponents	554	307	4079	55.4	21	26	39/247	72.0

Rushing	Att.	Yds.	Avg.	LG	TD
Anderson	274	1275	4.7	73	11
Muster	82	327	4.0	20	5
Harbaugh	45	276	6.1	t26	3
Sanders	41	127	3.1	19	0
Gentry	17	106	6.2	29	0
Tomczak	24	71	3.0	18	1
Suhey	20	51	2.6	8	1
Green	5	46	9.2	t37	1
Taylor	2	7	3.5	7	0
Buford	1	6	6.0	6	0
McKinnon	3	5	1.7	3	0
Thornton	1	4	4.0	4	0
Morris	1	-14	-14.0	-14	0
Bears	516	2287	4.4	73	22
Opponents	446	1897	4.3	t68	21

Receiving	No.	Yds.	Avg.	LG	TD
Anderson	50	434	8.7	t49	4
Gentry	39	463	11.9	t79	1
Muster	32	259	8.1	25	3
Morris	30	486	16.2	t58	1
McKinnon	28	418	14.9	41	3
Davis	26	397	15.3	t52	3
Thornton	24	392	16.3	t36	3
Boso	17	182	10.7	43	1
Suhey	9	73	8.1	22	1
Green	5	48	9.6	21	0
Kozlowski	3	74	24.7	55	0
Sanders	3	28	9.3	t16	1
Waddle	1	8	8.0	8	0
Bears	267	3262	12.2	t79	21
Opponents	307	4079	13.3	t97	21

Interceptions	No.	Yds.	Avg.	LG	TD
Stinson	4	59	14.8	t29	1
Lynch	3	55	18.3	41	0
Gayle	3	39	13.0	20	0
Woolford	3	0	0.0	0	0
Roper	2	46	23.0	43	0
Jackson	2	16	8.0	16	0
Rivera	2	1	0.5	1	0
Morrissey	2	0	0.0	0	0
Dent	1	30	30.0	30	0
Paul	1	20	20.0	20	0
Duerson	1	2	2.0	2	0
Douglass	1	0	0.0	0	0
Tate	1	0	0.0	0	0
Bears	26	268	10.3	43	1
Opponents	25	182	7.3	53	1

Punting	No.	Yds.	Avg.	In 20	LG
Buford	72	2844	39.5	21	60
Bears	72	2844	39.5	21	60
Opponents	67	2655	39.6	15	63

Punt Returns	No.	FC	Yds.	Avg.	LG	TD
Green	16	5	141	8.8	24	0
McKinnon	10	3	67	6.7	17	0
Kozlowski	4	0	-2	-0.5	4	0
Waddle	1	0	2	2.0	2	0
Woolford	1	0	12	12.0	12	0
Bears	32	8	220	6.9	24	0
Opponents	30	5	262	8.7	34	0

Kickoff Returns	No.	Yds.	Avg.	LG	TD
Gentry	28	667	23.8	63	0
Sanders	23	491	21.3	t96	1
Green	11	239	21.7	37	0
Suhey	6	93	15.5	21	0
Pruitt	2	17	8.5	11	0
Chapura	1	8	8.0	8	0
Kozlowski	1	12	12.0	12	0
Tate	1	12	12.0	11	0
Bears	73	1539	21.1	t96	1
Opponents	68	1375	20.2	62	0

Sacks	No.
Dent	9.0
McMichael	7.5
Armstrong	5.0
Roper	4.5
Perry	4.0
Chapura	3.0
Hampton	2.0
Rivera	2.0
Singletary	1.0
Woods	1.0
Bears	39.0
Opponents	28.0

Cincinnati

1989 TEAM RECORD

Preseason (2-2)

Date	Result		Opponent
8/13	W	24-20	Buffalo
8/19	W	35-3	at Detroit
8/28	L	10-27	at New Orleans
9/1	L	10-17	at Minnesota

Regular Season (8-8)

Date	Result		Opponent	Att.
9/10	L	14-17	at Chicago	64,730
9/17	W	41-10	Pittsburgh	53,885
9/25	W	21-14	Cleveland	55,996
10/1	W	21-17	at Kansas City	61,165
10/8	W	26-16	at Pittsburgh	52,785
10/15	L	13-20	Miami	58,184
10/22	L	12-23	Indianapolis	57,642
10/29	W	56-23	Tampa Bay	57,225
11/5	L	7-28	at Raiders	51,080
11/13	L	24-26	at Houston	60,694
11/19	W	42-7	Detroit	55,720
11/26	L	7-24	at Buffalo	80,074
12/3	W	21-0	at Cleveland	76,236
12/10	L	17-24	Seattle	54,744
12/17	W	61-7	Houston	47,510
12/25	L	21-29	at Minnesota	58,829

1989 TEAM STATISTICS

	Bengals	Opp.
Total First Downs	348	280
Rushing	136	114
Passing	183	151
Penalty	29	15
Third Down: Made/Att.	100/220	82/209
Fourth Down: Made/Att.	12/24	6/19
Total Net Yards	6101	5297
Avg. Per Game	381.3	331.1
Total Plays	1083	997
Avg. Per Play	5.6	5.3
Net Yards Rushing	2483	2162
Avg. Per Game	155.2	135.1
Total Rushes	529	482
Net Yards Passing	3618	3135
Avg. Per Game	226.1	195.9
Sacked/Yards Lost	41/332	33/248
Gross Yards	3950	3383
Att./Completions	513/288	482/256
Completion Pct.	56.1	53.1
Had Intercepted	13	21
Punts/Avg.	65/38.5	75/39.1
Net Punting Avg.	29.9	34.7
Penalties/Yards Lost	85/637	121/1045
Fumbles/Ball Lost	29/19	26/16
Touchdowns	52	32
Rushing	17	9
Passing	32	22
Returns	3	1
Avg. Time of Possession	30:51	29:09

1989 INDIVIDUAL STATISTICS

Scoring	TD R	TD P	TD Rt	PAT	FG	Saf	TP
Breech	0	0	0	37/38	12/14	0	73
Brooks	7	2	0	0/0	0/0	0	54
Holman	0	9	0	0/0	0/0	0	54
McGee	0	8	0	0/0	0/0	0	48
Brown	0	6	0	0/0	0/0	0	36
Taylor	3	2	0	0/0	0/0	0	30
Gallery	0	0	0	13/13	2/6	0	19
Ball	3	0	0	0/0	0/0	0	18
Jennings	2	1	0	0/0	0/0	0	18
Martin	0	2	0	0/0	0/0	0	12
Woods	2	0	0	0/0	0/0	0	12
Bussey	0	0	1	0/0	0/0	0	6
Hillary	0	1	0	0/0	0/0	0	6
Smith	0	1	0	0/0	0/0	0	6
Thomas	0	0	1	0/0	0/0	0	6
White	0	0	1	0/0	0/0	0	6
Johnson	0	0	0	0/1	0/0	0	0
Bengals	17	32	3	50/52	14/20	0	404
Opponents	9	22	1	31/32	20/27	1	285

Passing	Att.	Comp.	Yds.	Pct.	TD	Int.	Tkld.	Rate
Esiason	455	258	3525	56.7	28	11	36/288	92.1
Wilhelm	56	30	425	53.6	4	2	3/17	87.3
Schonert	2	0	0	0.0	0	0	2/27	39.6
Bengals	513	288	3950	56.1	32	13	41/332	91.2
Opponents	482	256	3383	53.1	22	21	33/248	72.6

Rushing	Att.	Yds.	Avg.	LG	TD
Brooks	221	1239	5.6	t65	7
Ball	98	391	4.0	27	3
Jennings	83	293	3.5	17	2
Esiason	47	278	5.9	24	0
Taylor	30	111	3.7	16	3
Woods	29	94	3.2	12	2
McGee	2	36	18.0	25	0
Wilhelm	6	30	5.0	14	0
Holifield	11	20	1.8	11	0
Hillary	1	-2	-2.0	-2	0
Johnson	1	-7	-7.0	-7	0
Bengals	529	2483	4.7	t65	17
Opponents	482	2162	4.5	t92	9

Receiving	No.	Yds.	Avg.	LG	TD
McGee	65	1211	18.6	t74	8
Brown	52	814	15.7	46	6
Holman	50	736	14.7	t73	9
Brooks	37	306	8.3	25	2
Hillary	17	162	9.5	17	1
Martin	15	160	10.7	21	2
Kattus	12	93	7.8	16	0
Smith	10	140	14.0	t41	1
Jennings	10	119	11.9	t43	1
Ball	6	44	7.3	15	0
Riggs	5	29	5.8	9	0
Taylor	4	44	11.0	t18	2
Garrett	2	29	14.5	18	0
Holifield	2	18	9.0	14	0
Parker	1	45	45.0	45	0
Bengals	288	3950	13.7	t74	32
Opponents	256	3383	13.2	t84	22

Interceptions	No.	Yds.	Avg.	LG	TD
Fulcher	8	87	10.9	22	0
Thomas	4	18	4.5	t18	1
Dixon	3	47	15.7	28	0
Billups	2	0	0.0	0	0
Kelly	1	25	25.0	25	0
White	1	22	22.0	22	0
Carey	1	5	5.0	5	0
Bussey	1	0	0.0	0	0
Bengals	21	204	9.7	28	1
Opponents	13	42	3.2	19	0

Punting	No.	Yds.	Avg.	In 20	LG
Johnson	61	2446	40.1	14	62
Breech	2	58	29.0	1	32
Bengals	65	2504	38.5	15	62
Opponents	75	2935	39.1	16	57

Punt Returns	No.	FC	Yds.	Avg.	LG	TD
Martin	15	4	107	7.1	17	0
Smith	12	2	54	4.5	15	0
Hillary	6	4	19	3.2	10	0
Carey	3	2	29	9.7	13	0
Bengals	36	12	209	5.8	17	0
Opponents	33	5	323	9.8	45	0

Kickoff Returns	No.	Yds.	Avg.	LG	TD
Jennings	26	525	20.2	33	0
Hillary	14	223	15.9	29	0
Carey	6	104	17.3	23	0
Smith	5	65	13.0	19	0
Ball	1	19	19.0	19	0
Holifield	1	0	0.0	0	0
Taylor	1	5	5.0	5	0
Bengals	54	941	17.4	33	0
Opponents	55	1203	21.9	66	0

Sacks	No.
Buck	6.0
Skow	4.5
Williams	3.5
Krumrie	3.0
Bussey	2.5
Tuatagaloa	2.5
Thomas	2.0
White	2.0
Hammerstein	1.5
McClendon	1.5
Zander	1.5
Kelly	1.0
Wilcots	1.0
Grant	0.5
Bengals	33.0
Opponents	41.0

Cleveland

1989 TEAM RECORD

Preseason (1-4)

Date	Result		Opponent
8/6	L	13-17	vs. Philadelphia at London
8/12	W	25-24	at Detroit
8/19	L	21-24	Pittsburgh
8/26	L	7-21	at Phoenix
9/2	L	10-27	Tampa Bay

Regular Season (9-6-1)

Date	Result		Opponents	Att.
9/10	W	51-0	at Pittsburgh	57,928
9/17	W	38-24	Jets	73,516
9/25	L	14-21	at Cincinnati	55,996
10/1	W	16-13	at Miami	58,444
10/8	L	10-13(OT)	at Miami	58,444
10/15	L	7-17	Pittsburgh	78,840
10/23	W	27-7	Chicago	78,722
10/30	W	28-17	Houston	78,765
11/5	W	42-31	at Tampa Bay	69,162
11/12	W	17-7	at Seattle	58,978
11/19	T	10-10(OT)	Kansas City	77,922
11/23	L	10-13	at Detroit	65,624
12/3	L	0-21	Cincinnati	76,236
12/10	L	17-23	at Indianapolis	58,550
12/17	W	23-17(OT)	Minnesota	70,777
12/23	W	24-20	at Houston	58,852

Postseason (1-1)

Date	Result		Opponent	Att.
1/6	W	34-30	Buffalo	77,706
1/14	L	21-37	at Denver	76,046

1989 TEAM STATISTICS

	Browns	Opp.
Total First Downs	285	276
Rushing	101	93
Passing	161	161
Penalty	23	22
Third Down: Made/Att.	82/213	82/230
Fourth Down: Made/Att.	1/9	10/16
Total Net Yards	5042	4831
Avg. Per Game	315.1	301.9
Total Plays	1011	1031
Avg. Per Play	5.0	4.7
Net Yards Rushing	1609	1670
Avg. Per Game	100.6	104.4
Total Rushes	448	446
Net Yards Passing	3433	3161
Avg. Per Game	214.6	197.6
Sacked/Yards Lost	34/192	45/359
Gross Yards	3625	3520
Att./Completions	529/309	540/269
Completion Pct.	58.4	49.8
Had Intercepted	15	27
Punts/Avg.	97/39.4	94/40.4
Net Punting Avg.	33.8	33.4
Penalties/Yards Lost	128/973	122/985
Fumbles/Ball Lost	23/15	32/11
Touchdowns	41	30
Rushing	14	8
Passing	20	20
Returns	7	2
Avg. Time of Possession	30:27	29:32

1989 INDIVIDUAL STATISTICS

Scoring	TD R	TD P	TD Rt	PAT	FG	Saf	TP
Bahr	0	0	0	40/40	16/24	0	88
Metcalf	6	4	0	0/0	0/0	0	60
Slaughter	0	6	0	0/0	0/0	0	36
Manoa	3	2	0	0/0	0/0	0	30
Tillman	0	2	1	0/0	0/0	0	18
Grayson	0	0	2	0/0	0/0	0	12
Gash	0	0	2	0/0	0/0	0	12
Langhorne	0	2	0	0/0	0/0	0	12
Tennell	0	1	0	0/0	0/0	0	6
Oliphant	1	0	0	0/0	0/0	0	6
Matthews	0	0	1	0/0	0/0	0	6
Jones	1	0	0	0/0	0/0	0	6
Wright	0	0	1	0/0	0/0	0	6
Redden	1	0	0	0/0	0/0	0	6
Waiters	0	1	0	0/0	0/0	0	6
Kosar	1	0	0	0/0	0/0	0	6
Middleton	0	1	0	0/0	0/0	0	6
Mack	1	0	0	0/0	0/0	0	6
Newsome	0	1	0	0/0	0/0	0	6
Browns	14	20	7	40/40	16/24	0	334
Opponents	8	20	2	29/29	15/28	0	254

Passing	Att.	Comp.	Yds.	Pct.	TD	Int.	Tkld.	Rate
Kosar	513	303	3533	59.1	18	14	34/192	80.3
Pagel	14	5	60	35.7	1	1	0/0	43.8
Metcalf	2	1	32	50.0	1	0	0/0	135.4
Browns	529	309	3625	58.4	20	15	34/192	80.1
Opponents	540	269	3520	49.8	20	27	45/359	62.3

Rushing	Att.	Yds.	Avg.	LG	TD
Metcalf	187	633	3.4	t43	6
Manoa	87	289	3.3	22	3
Redden	40	180	4.5	t38	1
Jones	43	160	3.7	15	1
Mack	37	130	3.5	12	1
Oliphant	15	97	6.5	t21	1
Kosar	30	70	2.3	23	1
McNeil	2	32	16.0	18	0
Langhorne	5	19	3.8	18	0
Pagel	2	-1	-0.5	4	0
Browns	448	1609	3.6	t43	14
Opponents	446	1670	3.7	t39	8

Receiving	No.	Yds.	Avg.	LG	TD
Slaughter	65	1236	19.0	t97	6
Langhorne	60	749	12.5	t62	2
Metcalf	54	397	7.4	t68	4
Newsome	29	324	11.2	31	1
Brennan	28	289	10.3	38	0
Manoa	27	241	8.9	32	2
Jones	15	126	8.4	36	0
McNeil	10	114	11.4	32	0
Tillman	6	70	11.7	19	2
Redden	6	34	5.7	8	0
Oliphant	3	22	7.3	9	0
Mack	2	7	3.5	4	0
Waiters	1	14	14.0	t14	1
Middleton	1	5	5.0	t5	1
Tennell	1	4	4.0	t4	1
Kosar	1	-7	-7.0	—	0
Browns	309	3625	11.7	t97	20
Opponents	269	3520	13.1	68	20

Interceptions	No.	Yds.	Avg.	LG	TD
Wright	9	91	10.1	t27	1
Gash	3	65	21.7	t36	2
Johnson	3	43	14.3	23	0
Minnifield	3	29	9.7	25	0
Harper	3	8	2.7	8	0
Grayson	2	25	12.5	t14	1
Matthews	1	25	25.0	25	0
Kramer	1	12	12.0	12	0
Dixon	1	2	2.0	2	0
Lyons	1	0	0.0	0	0
Browns	27	300	11.1	t36	4
Opponents	15	306	20.4	77	1

Punting	No.	Yds.	Avg.	In 20	LG
Wagner	97	3817	39.4	32	60
Browns	97	3817	39.4	32	60
Opponents	94	3797	40.4	20	57

Punt Returns	No.	FC	Yds.	Avg.	LG	TD
McNeil	49	15	496	10.1	49	0
Browns	49	15	496	10.1	49	0
Opponents	49	13	418	8.5	27	0

Kickoff Returns	No.	Yds.	Avg.	LG	TD
Metcalf	31	718	23.2	49	0
Oliphant	5	69	13.8	28	0
McNeil	4	61	15.3	21	0
Jones	4	42	10.5	25	0
Braggs	2	20	10.0	18	0
Redden	2	2	1.0	2	0
Joines	1	12	12.0	12	0
Johnson	1	8	8.0	8	0
Browns	50	932	18.6	49	0
Opponents	58	1175	20.3	73	0

Sacks	No.
Baker	7.5
Perry	7.0
Hairston	6.5
Banks	4.0
Blaylock	4.0
Matthews	4.0
Stewart	3.0
Gash	2.0
Gibson	2.0
Charlton	1.0
Pike	1.0
Grayson	1.0
Johnson	1.0
Harper	1.0
Browns	45.0
Opponents	34.0

Dallas

1989 TEAM RECORD

Preseason (3-1)

Date	Result		Opponents
8/13	W	20-3	at San Diego
8/19	W	27-20	at Raiders
8/26	L	21-24(OT)	at Denver
9/2	W	30-28	Houston

Regular Season (1-15)

Date	Result		Opponent	Att.
9/10	L	0-28	at New Orleans	66,977
9/17	L	21-27	at Atlanta	55,285
9/24	L	7-30	Washington	63,200
10/1	L	13-30	Giants	51,785
10/8	L	13-31	at Green Bay	56,656
10/15	L	14-31	San Francisco	61,077
10/22	L	28-36	at Kansas City	76,841
10/29	L	10-19	Phoenix	44,431
11/5	W	13-3	at Washington	53,187
11/12	L	20-24	at Phoenix	49,657
11/19	L	14-17	Miami	56,044
11/23	L	0-27	Philadelphia	54,444
12/3	L	31-35	Rams	46,100
12/10	L	10-20	at Philadelphia	59,842
12/16	L	0-15	at Giants	72,141
12/24	L	10-20	Green Bay	41,265

1989 TEAM STATISTICS

	Cowboys	Opp.
Total First Downs	246	321
Rushing	78	116
Passing	145	183
Penalty	23	22
Third Down: Made/Att.	62/187	106/229
Fourth Down: Made/Att.	8/19	7/12
Total Net Yards	4294	5556
Avg. Per Game	268.4	347.3
Total Plays	898	1060
Avg. Per Play	4.8	5.2
Net Yards Rushing	1409	1991
Avg. Per Game	88.1	124.4
Total Rushes	355	543
Net Yards Passing	2885	3565
Avg. Per Game	180.3	222.8
Sacked/Yards Lost	30/239	29/183
Gross Yards	3124	3748
Att./Completions	513/266	488/301
Completion Pct.	52.0	61.7
Had Intercepted	27	7
Punts/Avg.	82/39.8	73/39.9
Net Punting Avg.	34.2	35.3
Penalties/Yards Lost	99/766	102/723
Fumbles/Ball Lost	29/15	22/10
Touchdowns	25	44
Rushing	7	17
Passing	14	21
Returns	4	6
Avg. Time of Possession	25:34	34:26

1989 INDIVIDUAL STATISTICS

Scoring	TD R	TD P	TD Rt	PAT	FG	Saf	TP
Ruzek	0	0	0	5/11	14/15	0	29
Zendejas	0	0	0	5/9	10/10	0	25
Dixon	0	2	1	0/0	0/0	0	18
Johnston	0	3	0	0/0	0/0	0	18
Walker	2	1	0	0/0	0/0	0	18
Clack	2	0	0	0/0	0/0	0	12
Folsom	0	2	0	0/0	0/0	0	12
Irvin	0	2	0	0/0	0/0	0	12
Martin	0	2	0	0/0	0/0	0	12
Palmer	2	0	0	0/0	0/0	0	12
Del Rio	0	0	1	0/0	0/0	0	6
Ford	0	1	0	0/0	0/0	0	6
Jeffcoat	0	0	1	0/0	0/0	0	6
Lockhart	0	0	1	0/0	0/0	0	6
Sargent	1	0	0	0/0	0/0	0	6
Shepard	0	1	0	0/0	0/0	0	6
Cowboys	7	14	4	10/20	24/25	0	204
Opponents	17	21	6	28/35	43/44	1	393

Passing	Att.	Comp.	Yds.	Pct.	TD	Int.	Tkld.	Rate
Aikman	293	155	1749	52.9	9	18	19/155	55.7
Walsh	219	110	1371	50.2	5	9	11/84	60.5
Saxon	1	1	4	100.0	0	0	0/0	—
Cowboys	513	266	3124	51.9	14	27	30/239	57.8
Opponents	488	301	3748	61.7	21	7	29/183	93.9

Rushing	Att.	Yds.	Avg.	LG	TD
Palmer	112	446	4.0	t63	2
Aikman	38	302	7.9	25	0
Walker	81	246	3.0	t20	2
Johnston	67	212	3.2	13	0
Sargent	20	87	4.4	43	1
Clack	14	40	2.9	17	2
Dixon	3	30	10.0	13	0
Walsh	6	16	2.7	14	0
Tautalatasi	6	15	2.5	6	0
Shepard	3	12	4.0	12	0
Irvin	1	6	6.0	6	0
Saxon	1	1	1.0	1	0
Bates	1	0	0.0	0	0
Scott	2	-4	-2.0	-1	0
Cowboys	355	1409	4.0	t63	7
Opponents	543	1991	3.7	25	17

Receiving	No.	Yds.	Avg.	LG	TD
Martin	46	644	14.0	46	2
Folsom	28	265	9.5	26	2
Irvin	26	378	14.5	t65	2
Dixon	24	477	19.9	t75	2
Walker	22	261	11.9	52	1
Shepard	18	268	14.9	t37	1
Tautalatasi	17	157	9.2	23	0
Burbage	17	134	7.9	15	0
Palmer	17	93	5.5	13	0
Johnston	16	133	8.3	28	3
Scott	9	63	7.0	12	0
Ford	7	78	11.1	21	1
Sargent	6	50	8.3	21	0
Jennings	6	47	7.8	14	0
Clack	4	69	17.3	44	0
Alexander	1	16	16.0	16	0
Ruzek	1	4	4.0	4	0
Aikman	1	-13	-13.0	-13	0
Cowboys	266	3124	11.7	t75	14
Opponents	301	3748	12.5	t79	21

Interceptions	No.	Yds.	Avg.	LG	TD
Lockhart	2	14	7.0	12	0
Bates	1	18	18.0	18	0
Albritton	1	3	3.0	3	0
Francis	1	2	2.0	2	0
Burton	1	0	0.0	0	0
Horton	1	0	0.0	0	0
Cowboys	7	37	5.3	18	0
Opponents	27	396	14.7	t53	3

Punting	No.	Yds.	Avg.	In 20	LG
Saxon	79	3233	40.9	18	56
Ruzek	1	28	28.0	0	28
Cowboys	82	3261	39.8	28	56
Opponents	73	2911	39.9	28	58

Punt Returns	No.	FC	Yds.	Avg.	LG	TD
Shepard	24	1	160	6.7	17	0
Martin	4	5	32	8.0	12	0
Burbage	3	5	5	1.7	5	0
Cowboys	31	11	197	6.4	17	0
Opponents	38	17	334	8.8	t56	1

Kickoff Returns	No.	Yds.	Avg.	LG	TD
Dixon	47	1181	25.1	t97	1
Shepard	19	394	20.7	32	0
Clack	3	56	18.7	24	0
Burbage	3	55	18.3	22	0
Ankrom	2	6	3.0	5	0
Tautalatasi	1	9	9.0	9	0
Chandler	1	8	8.0	8	0
Sargent	1	0	0.0	0	0
Cowboys	77	1709	22.2	t97	1
Opponents	46	853	18.5	34	0

Sacks	No.
Jeffcoat	11.5
Hamel	3.5
Broughton	3.0
Norton	2.5
Lockhart	2.0
Tolbert	2.0
Horton	1.0
Noonan	1.0
Jones	1.0
Hendrix	0.5
Cowboys	29.0
Opponents	30.0

Denver

1989 TEAM RECORD

Preseason (2-2)

Date	Result		Opponent
8/12	W	17-13	Rams
8/19	L	17-35	at San Francisco
8/26	W	24-21(OT)	Dallas
9/2	L	34-38	at Indianapolis

Regular Season (11-5)

Date	Result		Opponent	Att.
9/10	W	34-20	Kansas City	74,284
9/18	W	28-14	at Buffalo	78,176
9/24	W	31-21	Raiders	75,754
10/1	L	13-16	at Cleveland	78,637
10/8	W	16-10	San Diego	75,222
10/15	W	14-3	Indianapolis	74,680
10/22	W	24-21(OT)	at Seattle	62,353
10/29	L	24-28	Philadelphia	75,065
11/5	W	34-7	Pittsburgh	74,739
11/12	W	16-13	at Kansas City	76,245
11/20	W	14-10	at Washington	52,975
11/26	W	41-14	Seattle	75,117
12/3	L	13-16(OT)	at Raiders	87,560
12/10	L	7-14	Giants	63,283
12/16	W	37-0	at Phoenix	56,071
12/14	L	16-19	at San Diego	50,524

Postseason (2-1)

Date	Result		Opponent	Att.
1/7	W	24-23	Pittsburgh	75,868
1/14	W	37-21	Cleveland	76,046
1/28	L	10-55	vs. San Francisco at New Orleans	72,919

1989 TEAM STATISTICS

	Broncos	Opp.
Total First Downs	308	246
Rushing	125	90
Passing	163	142
Penalty	20	14
Third Down: Made/Att.	111/240	73/216
Fourth Down: Made/Att.	2/9	12/24
Total Net Yards	5093	4407
Avg. Per Game	318.3	275.4
Total Plays	1071	977
Avg. Per Play	4.8	4.5
Net Yards Rushing	2092	1580
Avg. Per Game	130.8	98.8
Total Rushes	554	426
Net Yards Passing	3001	2827
Avg. Per Game	187.6	176.7
Sacked/Yards Lost	43/351	47/374
Gross Yards	3352	3201
Att./Completions	474/351	504/268
Completion Pct.	54.0	53.2
Had Intercepted	20	21
Punts/Avg.	80/39.8	84/41.0
Net Punting Avg.	33.7	35.0
Penalties/Yards Lost	83/594	102/823
Fumbles/Ball Lost	26/12	43/22
Touchdowns	40	25
Rushing	15	10
Passing	21	13
Returns	4	2
Avg. Time of Possession	32:17	27:43

1989 INDIVIDUAL STATISTICS

Scoring	TD R	TD P	TD Rt	PAT	FG	Saf	TP
Treadwell	0	0	0	39/40	27/33	0	120
Humphrey	7	1	0	0/0	0/0	0	48
Johnson	0	7	0	0/0	0/0	0	42
Bratton	1	3	0	0/0	0/0	0	24
Elway	3	0	0	0/0	0/0	0	18
Sewell	0	3	0	0/0	0/0	0	18
Alexander	2	0	0	0/0	0/0	0	12
Jackson	0	2	0	0/0	0/0	0	12
Kay	0	2	0	0/0	0/0	0	12
Winder	2	0	0	0/0	0/0	0	12
Young	0	2	0	0/0	0/0	0	12
Braxton	0	0	1	0/0	0/0	0	6
Kragen	0	0	1	0/0	0/0	0	6
Mecklenburg	0	0	1	0/0	0/0	0	6
Nattiel	0	1	0	0/0	0/0	0	6
Robbins	0	0	1	0/0	0/0	0	6
Brooks	0	0	0	0/0	0/0	1	2
Broncos	15	21	4	39/40	27/33	1	362
Opponents	10	13	2	25/25	17/27	0	226

Passing	Att.	Comp.	Yds.	Pct.	TD	Int.	Tkld.	Rate
Elway	416	223	3051	53.6	18	18	35/298	73.7
Kubiak	55	32	284	58.2	2	2	8/53	69.1
Humphrey	2	1	17	50.0	1	0	0/0	118.8
Johnson	1	0	0	0.0	0	0	0/0	39.6
Broncos	474	256	3352	54.0	21	20	43/351	73.7
Opponents	504	268	3201	53.2	13	21	47/374	64.1

Rushing	Att.	Yds.	Avg.	LG	TD
Humphrey	294	1151	3.9	40	7
Winder	110	351	3.2	16	2
Elway	48	244	5.1	31	3
Alexander	45	146	3.2	11	2
Bratton	30	108	3.6	9	1
Sewell	7	44	6.3	10	0
Kubiak	15	35	2.3	10	0
Jackson	5	13	2.6	8	0
Broncos	554	2092	3.8	40	15
Opponents	426	1580	3.7	24	10

Receiving	No.	Yds.	Avg.	LG	TD
Johnson	76	1095	14.4	69	7
Jackson	28	446	15.9	49	2
Sewell	25	416	16.6	56	3
Young	22	402	18.3	47	2
Humphrey	22	156	7.1	13	1
Kay	21	197	9.4	t20	2
Mobley	17	200	11.8	36	0
Winder	14	91	6.5	19	0
Nattiel	10	183	18.3	43	1
Bratton	10	69	6.9	t17	3
Alexander	8	84	10.5	28	0
Kelly	3	13	4.3	6	0
Broncos	256	3352	13.1	69	21
Opponents	268	3201	11.9	t75	13

Interceptions	No.	Yds.	Avg.	LG	TD
Braxton	6	103	17.2	t34	1
Henderson	3	58	19.3	25	0
Atwater	3	34	11.3	30	0
D. Smith	2	78	39.0	50	0
Robbins	2	18	9.0	t18	1
Munford	2	16	8.0	10	0
Corrington	1	8	8.0	8	0
Carrington	1	2	2.0	2	0
Dennison	1	1	1.0	1	0
Broncos	21	318	15.1	50	2
Opponents	20	194	9.7	t32	1

Punting	No.	Yds.	Avg.	In 20	LG
Horan	77	3111	40.4	24	63
Elway	1	34	34.0	0	34
Kubiak	2	43	21.5	1	29
Broncos	80	3188	39.8	25	63
Opponents	84	3440	41.0	18	64

Punt Returns	No.	FC	Yds.	Avg.	LG	TD
Bell	21	3	143	6.8	24	0
Johnson	12	6	118	9.8	34	0
Nattiel	9	0	77	8.6	38	0
Woods	2	0	6	3.0	11	0
Carrington	1	0	0	0.0	0	0
Broncos	45	9	344	7.6	38	0
Opponents	28	18	370	13.2	52	0

Kickoff Returns	No.	Yds.	Avg.	LG	TD
Bell	30	602	20.1	33	0
Carrington	6	152	25.3	68	0
Humphrey	4	86	21.5	29	0
Bratton	2	19	9.5	10	0
Woods	1	17	17.0	17	0
Broncos	43	876	20.4	68	0
Opponents	72	1256	17.4	36	0

Sacks	No.
Fletcher	12.0
Holmes	9.0
Mecklenburg	7.5
Carreker	5.5
Powers	3.0
Kragen	2.0
Lucas	2.0
Townsend	2.0
Brooks	1.0
Dennison	1.0
Munford	1.0
Broncos	47.0
Opponents	43.0

Detroit

1989 TEAM RECORD

Preseason (0-4)

Date	Result		Opponent
8/12	L	24-25	Cleveland
8/19	L	3-35	Cincinnati
8/25	L	7-13	at Seattle
9/2	L	14-24	at Rams

Regular Season (7-9)

Date	Result		Opponent	Att.
9/10	L	13-16	Phoenix	36,735
9/17	L	14-24	at Giants	76,021
9/24	L	27-47	Chicago	71,418
10/1	L	3-23	Pittsburgh	43,804
10/8	L	17-24	at Minnesota	55,380
10/15	W	17-16	at Tampa Bay	46,225
10/22	L	7-20	Minnesota	51,579
10/29	L	20-23	at Green Bay	53,731
11/5	L	31-35	at Houston	48,056
11/12	W	31-22	Green Bay	44,324
11/19	L	7-42	at Cincinnati	55,720
11/23	W	13-10	Cleveland	65,624
12/3	W	21-14	New Orleans	38,550
12/10	W	27-17	at Chicago	52,650
12/17	W	33-7	Tampa Bay	40,362
12/24	W	31-24	at Atlanta	7,792

1989 TEAM STATISTICS

	Lions	Opp.
Total First Downs	274	314
Rushing	117	98
Passing	139	189
Penalty	18	27
Third Down: Made/Att.	63/189	83/220
Fourth Down: Made/Att.	8/13	10/14
Total Net Yards	4992	5537
Avg. Per Game	312.0	346.1
Total Plays	923	1064
Avg. Per Play	5.4	5.2
Net Yards Rushing	2053	1621
Avg. Per Game	128.3	101.3
Total Rushes	421	454
Net Yards Passing	2939	3916
Avg. Per Game	183.7	244.8
Sacked/Yards Lost	57/343	40/277
Gross Yards	3282	4193
Att./Completions	450/229	570/370
Completion Pct.	50.9	64.9
Had Intercepted	24	16
Punts/Avg.	83/42.6	80/41.2
Net Punting Avg.	36.0	31.8
Penalties/Yards Lost	121/977	107/993
Fumbles/Ball Lost	37/24	28/16
Touchdowns	36	42
Rushing	23	18
Passing	11	19
Returns	2	5
Avg. Time of Possession	26:15	33:50

1989 INDIVIDUAL STATISTICS

Scoring	TD R	TD P	TD Rt	PAT	FG	Saf	TP
Murray	0	0	0	36/36	20/21	0	96
Sanders	14	0	0	0/0	0/0	0	84
Johnson	0	8	0	0/0	0/0	0	48
Gagliano	4	0	0	0/0	0/0	0	24
Peete	4	0	0	0/0	0/0	0	24
Clark	0	2	0	0/0	0/0	0	12
Hipple	1	0	0	0/0	0/0	0	6
White	0	0	1	0/0	0/0	0	6
Holmes	0	0	1	0/0	0/0	0	6
Phillips	0	1	0	0/0	0/0	0	6
Lions	23	11	2	36/36	20/21	0	312
Opponents	18	19	5	41/42	23/32	1	364

Passing	Att.	Comp.	Yds.	Pct.	TD	Int.	Tkld.	Rate
Gagliano	232	117	1671	50.4	6	12	25/145	61.1
Peete	195	103	1479	52.8	5	9	27/172	67.2
Hipple	18	7	90	38.9	0	3	5/26	13.8
Long	5	2	42	40.0	0	0	0/0	70.4
Lions	450	229	3282	50.9	11	24	57/343	60.8
Opponents	570	370	4193	64.9	19	16	40/277	86.2

Rushing	Att.	Yds.	Avg.	LG	TD
Sanders	280	1470	5.3	34	14
Gagliano	41	192	4.7	19	4
Peete	33	148	4.5	14	4
Paige	30	105	3.5	16	0
Painter	15	64	4.3	9	0
Johnson	12	38	3.2	14	0
Gray	3	22	7.3	14	0
Hipple	2	11	5.5	10	1
Brown	1	3	3.0	3	0
Long	3	2	0.7	6	0
McDonald	1	-2	-2.0	-2	0
Lions	421	2053	4.9	34	23
Opponents	454	1621	3.6	t53	18

Receiving	No.	Yds.	Avg.	LG	TD
Johnson	70	1091	15.6	t75	8
Clark	41	748	18.2	69	2
Phillips	30	352	11.7	t55	1
Stanley	24	304	12.7	37	0
Sanders	24	282	11.8	46	0
Mobley	13	158	12.2	30	0
McDonald	12	138	11.5	24	0
Ford	5	56	11.2	37	0
Painter	3	41	13.7	27	0
Gray	2	47	23.5	30	0
Johnson	2	29	14.5	22	0
Paige	2	27	13.5	15	0
Chadwick	1	9	9.0	9	0
Lions	229	3282	14.3	t75	11
Opponents	370	4193	11.3	t69	19

Interceptions	No.	Yds.	Avg.	LG	TD
Holmes	6	77	12.8	36	1
J. Williams	5	15	3.0	9	0
Gibson	1	10	10.0	10	0
Crockett	1	5	5.0	5	0
White	1	0	0.0	0	0
Noga	1	0	0.0	0	0
Taylor	1	0	0.0	0	0
Lions	16	107	6.7	36	1
Opponents	24	447	18.6	t90	3

Punting	No.	Yds.	Avg.	In 20	LG
Arnold	82	3538	43.1	15	64
Team	1	0	0.0	0	0
Lions	83	3538	42.6	15	64
Opponents	80	3293	41.2	22	58

Punt Returns	No.	FC	Yds.	Avg.	LG	TD
Stanley	36	4	496	13.8	74	0
Gray	11	2	76	6.9	15	0
Woods	0	1	0	0.0	0	0
Miller	0	1	0	0.0	0	0
Lions	47	8	572	12.2	74	0
Opponents	46	12	373	8.1	30	0

Kickoff Returns	No.	Yds.	Avg.	LG	TD
Gray	24	640	26.7	57	0
Palmer	11	255	23.2	62	0
Stanley	9	95	10.6	19	0
Sanders	5	118	23.6	43	0
Alexander	5	100	20.0	25	0
Woods	2	28	14.0	15	0
Dallafior	2	13	6.5	13	0
Painter	1	14	14.0	14	0
Crockett	1	8	8.0	8	0
Lions	60	1271	21.2	62	0
Opponents	65	1037	16.0	t99	1

Sacks	No.
Cofer	9.5
Ball	9.0
E. Williams	6.0
Spielman	4.5
J. Williams	3.5
Brooks	2.0
Jamison	2.0
White	1.0
Pete	1.0
McNorton	1.0
Griffin	0.5
Lions	40.0
Opponents	57.0

Green Bay

1989 TEAM RECORD

Preseason (3-1)

Date	Result		Opponent
8/12	W	28-27	vs. Jets in Milwaukee
8/19	L	23-24	Indianapolis
8/26	W	27-24	vs. Buffalo in Madison
9/1	W	16-0	at New England

Regular Season (10-6)

Date	Result		Opponent	Att.
9/10	L	21-23	Tampa Bay	55,650
9/17	W	35-34	New Orleans	55,809
9/24	L	38-41	at Rams	57,701
10/1	W	23-21	vs. Atlanta in Milwaukee	54,647
10/8	W	31-13	Dallas	56,656
10/15	L	14-26	at Minnesota	62,075
10/22	L	20-23	at Miami	56,624
10/29	W	23-20(OT)	vs. Detroit in Milwaukee	53,731
11/5	W	14-13	Chicago	56,556
11/12	L	22-31	at Detroit	44,324
11/19	W	21-17	at San Francisco	62,219
11/26	W	20-19	vs. Minnesota in Milwaukee	55,592
12/3	W	17-16	at Tampa Bay	58,120
12/10	L	3-21	Kansas City	56,694
12/17	W	40-28	at Chicago	44,781
12/24	W	20-10	at Dallas	41,265

1989 TEAM STATISTICS

	Packers	Opp.
Total First Downs	342	307
Rushing	114	116
Passing	207	179
Penalty	21	12
Third Down: Made/Att.	93/204	85/191
Fourth Down: Made/Att.	8/12	5/6
Total Net Yards	5780	5347
Avg. Per Game	361.3	334.2
Total Plays	1045	969
Avg. Per Play	5.5	5.5
Net Yards Rushing	1732	2008
Avg. Per Game	108.3	125.5
Total Rushes	397	460
Net Yards Passing	4048	3339
Avg. Per Game	253.0	208.7
Sacked/Yards Lost	48/277	34/214
Gross Yards	4325	3553
Att./Completions	600/354	475/302
Completion Pct.	59.0	63.6
Had Intercepted	20	25
Punts/Avg.	66/40.6	65/40.7
Net Punting Avg.	31.0	35.9
Penalties/Yards Lost	81/666	104/846
Fumbles/Ball Lost	35/13	28/15
Touchdowns	42	41
Rushing	13	15
Passing	27	22
Returns	2	4
Avg. Time of Possession	30:21	29:39

1989 INDIVIDUAL STATISTICS

Scoring	TD R	TD P	TD Rt	PAT	FG	Saf	TP
Jacke	0	0	0	42/42	22/28	0	108
Sharpe	0	12	1	0/0	0/0	0	78
Fullwood	5	0	0	0/0	0/0	0	30
Majkowski	5	0	0	0/0	0/0	0	30
West	0	5	0	0/0	0/0	0	30
Fontenot	1	3	0	0/0	0/0	0	24
Bland	0	1	1	0/0	0/0	0	12
Kemp	0	2	0	0/0	0/0	0	12
Query	0	2	0	0/0	0/0	0	12
Didier	0	1	0	0/0	0/0	0	6
Haddix	0	1	0	0/0	0/0	0	6
Woodside	1	0	0	0/0	0/0	0	6
Workman	1	0	0	0/0	0/0	0	6
Packers	13	27	2	42/42	22/28	1	362
Opponents	15	22	4	39/41	23/30	1	356

Passing	Att.	Comp.	Yds.	Pct.	TD	Int.	Tkld.	Rate
Majkowski	599	353	4318	58.9	27	20	47/268	82.3
Dilweg	1	1	7	100.0	0	0	0/0	95.8
Fontenot	0	0	0	—	0	0	1/9	0.0
Packers	600	354	4325	59.0	27	20	48/277	82.4
Opponents	475	302	3583	63.6	22	25	34/214	79.7

Rushing	Att.	Yds.	Avg.	LG	TD
Fullwood	204	821	4.0	38	5
Majkowski	75	358	4.8	20	5
Woodside	46	273	5.9	t68	1
Haddix	44	135	3.1	10	0
Fontenot	17	69	4.1	19	1
Kemp	5	43	8.6	14	0
Sharpe	2	25	12.5	26	0
Workman	4	8	2.0	3	1
Packers	397	1732	4.4	t68	13
Opponents	460	2008	4.4	73	15

Receiving	No.	Yds.	Avg.	LG	TD
Sharpe	90	1423	15.8	t79	12
Woodside	59	527	8.9	33	0
Kemp	48	611	12.7	39	2
Fontenot	40	372	9.3	t38	3
Query	23	350	15.2	45	2
West	22	269	12.2	31	5
Fullwood	19	214	11.3	67	0
Matthews	18	200	11.1	25	0
Haddix	15	111	7.4	23	1
Bland	11	164	14.9	t46	1
Didier	7	71	10.1	t24	1
Spagnola	2	13	6.5	14	0
Packers	354	4325	12.2	t79	27
Opponents	302	3553	11.8	61	22

Interceptions	No.	Yds.	Avg.	LG	TD
D. Brown	6	12	2.0	12	0
Murphy	3	31	10.3	20	0
Stills	3	20	6.7	12	0
Stephen	2	16	8.0	8	0
Lee	2	10	5.0	10	0
Noble	2	10	5.0	10	0
Dent	1	53	53.0	53	0
Pitts	1	37	37.0	37	0
Holland	1	26	26.0	26	0
Cecil	1	16	16.0	16	0
Anderson	1	1	1.0	1	0
Greene	1	0	0.0	0	0
Jakes	1	0	0.0	0	0
Packers	25	232	9.3	53	0
Opponents	20	321	16.1	t81	2

Punting	No.	Yds.	Avg.	In 20	LG
Bracken	66	2682	40.6	17	63
Packers	66	2682	40.6	17	63
Opponents	65	2644	40.7	16	55

Punt Returns	No.	FC	Yds.	Avg.	LG	TD
Query	30	7	247	8.2	15	0
Sutton	5	1	42	8.4	17	0
Pitts	0	1	0	—	0	0
Packers	35	9	289	8.3	17	0
Opponents	30	11	416	13.9	74	0

Kickoff Returns	No.	Yds.	Avg.	LG	TD
Workman	33	547	16.6	46	0
Bland	13	256	19.7	37	0
Fullwood	11	243	22.1	35	0
Query	6	125	20.8	28	0
Fontenot	2	30	15.0	20	0
Woodside	2	38	19.0	23	0
Didier	1	0	0.0	0	0
Mandarich	1	0	0.0	0	0
Stephen	0	0	—	0	0
Packers	69	1239	18.0	46	0
Opponents	63	1389	22.0	90	0

Sacks	No.
Harris	19.5
R. Brown	3.0
Greene	2.0
Noble	2.0
Winter	2.0
Hall	1.0
Murphy	1.0
Nelson	1.0
Stephen	1.0
Weddington	1.0
Patterson	0.5
Packers	34.0
Opponents	48.0

Houston

1989 TEAM RECORD

Preseason (2-2)

Date	Result		Opponent
8/12	L	23-41	at Tampa Bay
8/19	W	26-10	vs. Miami at Jacksonville
8/26	W	23-21	vs. Raiders at Oakland
9/2	L	28-30	at Dallas

Regular Season (9-7)

Date	Result		Opponent	Att.
9/10	L	7-38	at Minnesota	54,015
9/17	W	34-27	at San Diego	42,013
9/24	L	41-47(OT)	Buffalo	57,278
10/1	W	39-7	Miami	53,326
10/8	L	13-23	at New England	59,828
10/15	W	33-28	at Chicago	64,383
10/22	W	27-0	Pittsburgh	59,091
10/29	L	17-28	at Cleveland	78,765
11/5	W	35-31	Detroit	48,056
11/13	W	26-24	Cincinnati	60,694
11/19	W	23-7	Raiders	59,198
11/26	L	0-34	at Kansas City	51,342
12/3	W	23-16	at Pittsburgh	40,541
12/10	W	20-17	Tampa Bay	54,532
12/17	L	7-61	at Cincinnati	47,510
12/23	L	20-24	Cleveland	58,852

Postseason (0-1)

Date	Result		Opponent	Att.
12/31	L	23-26	at Houston	58,306

1989 TEAM STATISTICS

	Oilers	Opp.
Total First Downs	327	314
Rushing	112	119
Passing	185	165
Penalty	30	30
Third Down: Made/Att.	83/203	87/191
Fourth Down: Made/Att.	10/14	10/13
Total Net Yards	5427	5211
Avg. Per Game	339.2	325.7
Total Plays	1028	940
Avg. Per Play	5.3	5.5
Net Yards Rushing	1928	1669
Avg. Per Game	120.5	104.3
Total Rushes	495	437
Net Yards Passing	3499	3542
Avg. Per Game	218.7	221.4
Sacked/Yards Lost	37/287	36/277
Gross Yards	3786	3819
Att./Completions	496/295	467/269
Completion Pct.	59.5	57.6
Had Intercepted	16	21
Punts/Avg.	58/41.8	56/37.6
Net Punting Avg.	36.1	34.0
Penalties/Yards Lost	148/1138	109/903
Fumbles/Ball Lost	39/17	25/16
Touchdowns	41	52
Rushing	16	20
Passing	23	28
Returns	2	4
Avg. Time of Possession	31:59	28:01

1989 INDIVIDUAL STATISTICS

Scoring	TD R	TD P	TD Rt	PAT	FG	Saf	TP
Zendejas	0	0	0	40/40	25/37	0	115
Hill	0	8	0	0/0	0/0	0	48
Highsmith	4	2	0	0/0	0/0	0	36
Duncan	0	5	0	0/0	0/0	0	30
White	5	0	0	0/0	0/0	0	30
Moon	4	0	0	0/0	0/0	0	24
Givins	0	3	0	0/0	0/0	0	18
Harris	0	2	0	0/0	0/0	0	12
Jeffires	0	2	0	0/0	0/0	0	12
Pinkett	1	1	0	0/0	0/0	0	12
Rozier	2	0	0	0/0	0/0	0	12
Dishman	0	0	1	0/0	0/0	0	6
Seale	0	0	1	0/0	0/0	0	6
McDowell	0	0	0	0/0	0/0	1	2
Oilers	16	23	2	40/41	25/37	2	365
Opponents	20	28	4	49/51	17/21	0	412

Passing	Att.	Comp.	Yds.	Pct.	TD	Int.	Tkld.	Rate
Moon	464	280	3631	60.3	23	14	35/267	88.9
Carlson	31	15	155	48.4	0	1	2/20	49.8
Zendejas	1	0	0	0.0	0	1	0/0	0.0
Oilers	496	295	3786	59.5	23	16	37/287	85.5
Opponents	467	269	3819	57.6	28	21	36/277	85.4

Rushing	Att.	Yds.	Avg.	LG	TD
Highsmith	128	531	4.1	25	4
Pinkett	94	449	4.8	60	1
White	104	349	3.4	33	5
Rozier	88	301	3.4	17	2
Moon	70	268	3.8	19	4
Montgomery	3	17	5.7	11	0
Johnson	4	16	4.0	8	0
Duncan	1	0	0.0	0	0
Carlson	3	-3	-1.0	0	0
Oilers	495	1928	3.9	60	16
Opponents	437	1669	3.8	t58	20

Receiving	No.	Yds.	Avg.	LG	TD
Hill	66	938	14.2	50	8
Givins	55	794	14.4	48	3
Jeffires	47	619	13.2	t45	2
Duncan	43	613	14.3	55	5
Pinkett	31	239	7.7	23	1
Highsmith	18	201	11.2	32	2
Harris	13	202	15.5	36	2
White	6	37	6.2	11	0
Verhulst	4	48	12.0	21	0
Jackson	4	31	7.8	18	0
Rozier	4	28	7.0	8	0
Mrosko	3	28	9.3	14	0
Johnson	1	8	8.0	8	0
Oilers	295	3786	12.8	55	23
Opponents	269	3819	14.2	t80	28

Interceptions	No.	Yds.	Avg.	LG	TD
Brown	5	54	10.8	41	0
Lyles	4	66	16.5	48	0
McDowell	4	65	16.3	21	0
Dishman	4	31	7.8	31	0
Eaton	3	33	11.0	20	0
Johnson	1	0	0.0	0	0
Donaldson	0	14	—	14	0
Oilers	21	263	12.5	48	0
Opponents	16	171	10.7	43	0

Punting	No.	Yds.	Avg.	In 20	LG
Montgomery	56	2422	43.3	15	63
Oilers	58	2422	41.8	15	63
Opponents	56	2107	37.6	10	55

Punt Returns	No.	FC	Yds.	Avg.	LG	TD
Johnson	19	21	122	6.4	19	0
Oilers	19	21	122	6.4	19	0
Opponents	24	7	191	8.0	28	0

Kickoff Returns	No.	Yds.	Avg.	LG	TD
Johnson	21	372	17.7	39	0
White	17	303	17.8	29	0
Harris	14	331	23.6	63	0
T. Johnson	13	224	17.2	27	0
Mrosko	3	46	15.3	19	0
Williams	2	8	4.0	8	0
Fairs	1	1	1.0	1	0
Lyles	1	0	0.0	0	0
Montgomery	1	0	0.0	0	0
Verhulst	1	0	0.0	0	0
Oilers	74	1285	17.4	63	0
Opponents	59	1024	17.4	t97	1

Sacks	No.
Childress	8.5
Fuller	6.5
Jones	6.0
Meads	4.0
Brown	3.0
Fairs	2.5
Lyles	2.0
Montgomery	1.5
McDowell	1.0
Smith	1.0
Oilers	36.0
Opponents	37.0

Indianapolis

1989 TEAM RECORD

Preseason (4-0)

Date	Result		Opponent
8/12	W	31-7	at New Orleans
8/19	W	24-23	at Green Bay
8/26	W	30-0	Tampa Bay
9/2	W	38-34	Denver

Regular Season (8-8)

Date	Result		Opponent	Att.
9/10	L	24-30	San Francisco	60,111
9/17	L	17-31	at Rams	63,995
9/24	W	13-9	Atlanta	57,816
10/1	W	17-10	at Jets	65,542
10/8	W	37-14	Buffalo	58,890
10/15	L	3-14	at Denver	74,680
10/22	W	23-12	at Cincinnati	57,642
10/29	L	20-23(OT)	New England	59,356
11/5	L	13-19	at Miami	52,680
11/12	L	7-30	at Buffalo	79,256
11/19	W	27-10	Jets	58,236
11/26	W	10-6	San Diego	58,822
12/3	L	16-22	at New England	32,234
12/10	W	23-17(OT)	Cleveland	58,550
12/17	W	42-13	Miami	55,665
12/24	L	6-41	at New Orleans	49,009

1989 TEAM STATISTICS

	Colts	Opp.
Total First Downs	273	336
Rushing	118	126
Passing	140	192
Penalty	15	18
Third Down: Made/Att.	72/211	95/220
Fourth Down: Made/Att.	7/16	4/10
Total Net Yards	4813	5611
Avg. Per Game	300.8	350.7
Total Plays	979	1109
Avg. Per Play	4.9	5.1
Net Yards Rushing	1853	2077
Avg. Per Game	115.8	129.8
Total Rushes	458	507
Net Yards Passing	2960	3534
Avg. Per Game	185.0	220.9
Sacked/Yards Lost	28/174	46/384
Gross Yards	3134	3918
Att./Completions	493/253	556/322
Completion Pct.	51.3	57.9
Had Intercepted	17	21
Punts/Avg.	80/42.4	65/41.6
Net Punting Avg.	32.9	34.5
Penalties/Yards Lost	89/704	103/772
Fumbles/Ball Lost	33/10	34/15
Touchdowns	34	29
Rushing	11	10
Passing	18	15
Returns	5	4
Avg. Time of Possession	27:15	32:45

1989 INDIVIDUAL STATISTICS

Scoring	TD R	TD P	TD Rt	PAT	FG	Saf	TP
Biasucci	0	0	0	31/32	21/27	0	94
Dickerson	7	1	0	0/0	0/0	0	48
Bentley	1	3	1	0/0	0/0	0	30
Brooks	0	4	0	0/0	0/0	0	24
Rison	0	4	0	0/0	0/0	0	24
Beach	0	2	0	0/0	0/0	0	12
Boyer	0	2	0	0/0	0/0	0	12
Trudeau	2	0	0	0/0	0/0	0	12
Verdin	0	1	1	0/0	0/0	0	12
Chandler	1	0	0	0/0	0/0	0	6
R. Dixon	0	0	1	0/0	0/0	0	6
Prior	0	0	1	0/0	0/0	0	6
Pruitt	0	1	0	0/0	0/0	0	6
Taylor	0	0	1	0/0	0/0	0	6
Colts	11	18	5	31/33	21/27	0	298
Opponents	10	15	4	29/29	32/43	1	301

Passing	Att.	Comp.	Yds.	Pct.	TD	Int.	Tkld.	Rate
Trudeau	362	190	2317	52.5	15	13	20/125	71.3
Chandler	80	39	537	48.8	2	3	3/17	63.4
Ramsey	50	24	280	48.0	1	1	4/26	63.8
Bentley	1	0	0	0.0	0	0	0/0	39.6
Dickerson	0	0	0	—	0	0	1/6	0.0
Colts	493	253	3134	51.3	18	17	28/174	69.1
Opponents	556	322	3918	57.9	15	21	46/384	73.0

Rushing	Att.	Yds.	Avg.	LG	TD
Dickerson	314	1311	4.2	t21	7
Bentley	75	299	4.0	22	1
Trudeau	35	91	2.6	17	2
Chandler	7	57	8.1	23	1
Hunter	13	47	3.6	11	0
Verdin	4	39	9.8	26	0
Rison	3	18	6.0	18	0
Ramsey	4	5	1.3	3	0
Brooks	2	-3	-1.5	0	0
Stark	1	-11	-11.0	-11	0
Colts	458	1853	4.0	26	11
Opponents	507	2077	4.1	27	10

Receiving	No.	Yds.	Avg.	LG	TD
Brooks	63	919	14.6	t55	4
Rison	52	820	15.8	61	4
Bentley	52	525	10.1	61	3
Dickerson	30	211	7.0	22	1
Verdin	20	381	19.1	t82	1
Beach	14	87	6.2	17	2
Boyer	11	58	5.3	15	2
Weathers	6	62	10.3	19	0
Pruitt	5	71	14.2	40	1
Colts	253	3134	12.4	t82	18
Opponents	322	3918	12.2	t58	15

Interceptions	No.	Yds.	Avg.	LG	TD
Taylor	7	225	32.1	t80	1
Prior	6	88	14.7	t58	1
Banks	2	13	6.5	11	0
Young	2	2	1.0	6	0
Daniel	1	34	34.0	34	0
Plummer	1	18	18.0	18	0
Bickett	1	6	6.0	6	0
Ball	1	5	5.0	5	0
Colts	21	391	18.6	t80	2
Opponents	17	345	20.3	t92	2

Punting	No.	Yds.	Avg.	In 20	LG
Stark	79	3392	42.9	14	64
Colts	80	3392	42.4	14	64
Opponents	65	2702	41.6	19	58

Punt Returns	No.	FC	Yds.	Avg.	LG	TD
Verdin	23	5	296	12.9	t49	1
Rison	2	2	20	10.0	12	0
C. Washington	1	0	6	6.0	6	0
Prior	0	3	0	—	0	0
Colts	26	10	322	12.4	t49	1
Opponents	51	7	558	10.9	t70	1

Kickoff Returns	No.	Yds.	Avg.	LG	TD
Verdin	19	371	19.5	29	0
Bentley	17	328	19.3	29	0
Pruitt	12	257	21.4	49	0
Rison	8	150	18.8	30	0
Hunter	4	58	14.5	19	0
Colts	60	1164	19.4	49	0
Opponents	63	1208	19.2	48	0

Sacks	No.
Hand	10.0
Johnson	8.5
Bickett	8.0
Thompson	7.0
Herrod	2.0
McDonald	2.0
Young	2.0
Alston	1.0
Armstrong	1.0
Banks	1.0
Larson	1.0
Plummer	1.0
Clancy	0.5
Colts	46.0
Opponents	28.0

Kansas City

1989 TEAM RECORD

Preseason (1-3)

Date	Result		Opponent
8/12	L	13-23	vs. Miami at Memphis
8/20	L	7-45	Giants
8/27	W	22-17	at Chicago
9/1	L	13-15	Jets

Regular Season (8-7-1)

Date	Result		Opponent	Att.
9/10	L	20-34	at Denver	74,284
9/17	W	24-19	Raiders	71,741
9/24	L	6-21	at San Diego	40,128
10/1	L	17-21	Cincinnati	61,165
10/8	W	20-16	at Seattle	60,715
10/15	L	14-20	at Raiders	40,453
10/22	W	36-28	Dallas	76,841
10/29	L	17-23	at Pittsburgh	54,194
11/5	W	20-10	Seattle	54,589
11/12	L	13-16	Denver	76,245
11/19	T	10-10	at Cleveland	77,922
11/26	W	34-0	Houston	51,342
12/3	W	26-21	Miami	54,610
12/10	W	21-3	at Green Bay	56,694
12/17	L	13-20	San Diego	40,623
12/24	W	27-24	at Miami	43,612

1989 TEAM STATISTICS

	Chiefs	Opp.
Total First Downs	304	253
Rushing	120	92
Passing	165	141
Penalty	19	20
Third Down: Made/Att.	88/208	71/211
Fourth Down: Made/Att.	6/9	8/15
Total Net Yards	5265	4293
Avg. Per Game	329.1	268.3
Total Plays	1017	952
Avg. Per Play	5.2	4.5
Net Yards Rushing	2227	1766
Avg. Per Game	139.2	110.4
Total Rushes	559	445
Net Yards Passing	3038	2527
Avg. Per Game	189.9	157.9
Sacked/Yards Lost	23/182	36/294
Gross Yards	3220	2821
Att./Completions	435/259	471/236
Completion Pct.	59.5	50.1
Had Intercepted	23	15
Punts/Avg.	67/40.1	82/39.1
Net Punting Avg.	33.8	32.9
Penalties/Yards Lost	116/878	102/797
Fumbles/Ball Lost	32/18	32/18
Touchdowns	35	32
Rushing	18	9
Passing	14	16
Returns	3	7
Avg. Time of Possession	32:35	27:25

1989 INDIVIDUAL STATISTICS

Scoring	TD R	TD P	TD Rt	PAT	FG	Saf	TP
Lowery	0	0	0	34/35	24/33	0	106
Okoye	12	0	0	0/0	0/0	0	72
Saxon	3	0	0	0/0	0/0	0	18
Harry	0	2	0	0/0	0/0	0	12
Hayes	0	2	0	0/0	0/0	0	12
Paige	0	2	0	0/0	0/0	0	12
Pelluer	2	0	0	0/0	0/0	0	12
Thomas	0	2	0	0/0	0/0	0	12
Carson	0	1	0	0/0	0/0	0	6
Dressel	0	1	0	0/0	0/0	0	6
Gamble	1	0	0	0/0	0/0	0	6
Heard	0	1	0	0/0	0/0	0	6
Maas	0	0	1	0/0	0/0	0	6
Mandley	0	1	0	0/0	0/0	0	6
McNair	0	1	0	0/0	0/0	0	6
Pearson	0	0	1	0/0	0/0	0	6
Roberts	0	1	0	0/0	0/0	0	6
Smith	0	0	1	0/0	0/0	0	6
McGovern	0	0	0	0/0	0/0	1	2
Chiefs	18	14	-3	34/35	24/33	1	318
Opponents	9	16	7	31/32	21/26	0	286

Passing	Att.	Comp.	Yds.	Pct.	TD	Int.	Tkld.	Rate
DeBerg	324	196	2529	60.5	11	16	14/111	75.8
Jaworski	61	36	385	59.0	2	5	1/10	54.3
Pelluer	47	26	301	55.3	1	0	8/61	82.0
Elkins	2	1	5	50.0	0	1	0/0	16.7
Saxon	1	0	0	0.0	0	1	0/0	71.2
Chiefs	435	259	3220	59.5	14	23	23/182	71.2
Opponents	471	236	2821	50.1	16	15	36/294	66.8

Rushing	Att.	Yds.	Avg.	LG	TD
Okoye	370	1480	4.0	59	12
Saxon	58	233	4.0	19	3
Heard	63	216	3.4	28	0
Pelluer	17	143	8.4	27	2
McNair	23	121	5.3	25	0
Gamble	6	24	4.0	20	1
Harry	1	9	9.0	9	0
Jaworski	4	5	1.3	4	0
Agee	1	3	3.0	3	0
Mandley	2	1	0.5	8	0
DeBerg	14	-8	-0.6	15	0
Chiefs	559	2227	4.0	59	18
Opponents	445	1766	4.0	t63	9

Receiving	No.	Yds.	Avg.	LG	TD
Paige	44	759	17.3	50	2
Mandley	35	476	13.6	44	1
McNair	34	372	10.9	24	1
Harry	33	430	13.0	25	2
Heard	25	246	9.8	27	1
Weathers	17	192	11.3	27	0
Hayes	18	229	12.7	23	2
Saxon	11	86	7.8	18	0
Dressel	9	136	15.1	t49	1
Thomas	8	58	7.3	12	2
Roberts	8	55	6.9	25	1
Carson	7	95	13.6	28	1
Worthen	5	69	13.8	21	0
Okoye	2	12	6.0	8	0
Gamble	2	2	1.0	6	0
Carruth	1	3	3.0	3	0
Chiefs	259	3220	12.4	50	14
Opponents	236	2821	12.0	t64	16

Interceptions	No.	Yds.	Avg.	LG	TD
Lewis	4	37	9.3	22	0
Ross	4	29	7.3	23	0
Cherry	2	27	13.5	27	0
Saleaumua	1	21	21.0	21	0
Snipes	1	16	16.0	16	0
Hill	1	3	3.0	3	0
Ashley	1	0	0.0	0	0
Burruss	1	0	0.0	0	0
Chiefs	15	133	8.9	27	0
Opponents	23	269	11.7	t34	2

Punting	No.	Yds.	Avg.	In 20	LG
Goodburn	67	2688	40.1	25	54
Chiefs	67	2688	40.1	25	54
Opponents	82	3205	39.1	14	62

Punt Returns	No.	FC	Yds.	Avg.	LG	TD
Mandley	19	2	151	7.9	19	0
Worthen	19	5	133	7.0	17	0
Barnes	2	0	41	20.5	21	0
Harry	2	0	6	3.0	7	0
Ross	2	0	0	0.0	0	0
Chiefs	44	7	331	7.5	21	0
Opponents	40	10	325	8.1	20	0

Kickoff Returns	No.	Yds.	Avg.	LG	TD
Copeland	26	466	17.9	36	0
McNair	13	257	19.8	37	0
Worthen	5	113	22.6	27	0
Gamble	3	55	18.3	23	0
Saxon	3	16	5.3	14	0
Mandley	1	0	0.0	0	0
Saleaumua	1	8	8.0	8	0
Chiefs	52	915	17.6	37	0
Opponents	55	1156	21.0	t97	2

Sacks	No.
Thomas	10.0
Smith	7.5
Griffin	6.5
Martin	4.0
Saleaumua	2.0
Bell	1.0
Cherry	1.0
Cooper	1.0
Lewis	1.0
Pearson	1.0
Meisner	0.5
Petry	0.5
Chiefs	36.0
Opponents	23.0

Los Angeles Raiders

1989 TEAM RECORD

Preseason (0-4)

Date	Result		Opponent
8/12	L	7-37	San Francisco
8/19	L	20/27	Dallas
8/26	L	21-23	vs. Houston at Oakland
9/2	L	38-41	Chicago

Regular Season (8-8)

Date	Result		Opponent	Att.
9/10	W	40-14	San Diego	43,086
9/17	L	19-24	at Kansas City	77,649
9/24	L	21-31	at Denver	76,055
10/1	L	20-24	Seattle	48,002
10/9	W	14-7	at Jets	76,891
10/15	W	20-14	Kansas City	44,131
10/22	L	7-10	at Philadelphia	66,883
10/29	W	37-24	Washington	56,763
11/5	W	28-7	Cincinnati	54,241
11/12	L	12-14	at San Diego	62,257
11/19	L	7-23	at Houston	61,824
11/26	W	24-21	New England	41,349
12/3	W	16-13(OT)	Denver	90,016
12/10	W	16-14	Phoenix	46,053
12/17	L	17-23	at Seattle	64,632
12/24	L	17-34	at Giants	77,073

1989 TEAM STATISTICS

	Raiders	Opp.
Total First Downs	259	308
Rushing	93	121
Passing	143	160
Penalty	23	27
Third Down: Made/Att.	67/197	110/225
Fourth Down: Made/Att.	9/13	6/13
Total Net Yards	4989	5003
Avg. Per Game	311.8	312.7
Total Plays	912	1045
Avg. Per Play	5.5	4.8
Net Yards Rushing	2038	1940
Avg. Per Game	127.4	121.3
Total Rushes	454	504
Net Yards Passing	2951	3063
Avg. Per Game	184.4	191.4
Sacked Yards/Lost	44/326	35/248
Gross Yards	3277	3311
Att./Completions	414/201	506/277
Completion Pct.	48.6	54.7
Had Intercepted	22	18
Punts/Avg.	67/40.5	72/40.3
Net Punting Avg.	33.9	33.9
Penalties/Yards Lost	132/1105	105/867
Fumbles/Ball Lost	28/12	40/18
Touchdowns	35	36
Rushing	9	15
Passing	21	18
Returns	5	3
Avg. Time of Possession	28:24	31:36

1989 INDIVIDUAL STATISTICS

Scoring	TD R	TD P	TD Rt	PAT	FG	Saf	TP
Jaeger	0	0	0	34/34	23/34	0	103
Fernandez	0	9	0	0/0	0/0	0	54
Gault	0	4	0	0/0	0/0	0	24
Jackson	4	0	0	0/0	0/0	0	24
Mueller	2	2	0	0/0	0/0	0	24
Allen	2	0	0	0/0	0/0	0	12
Anderson	0	0	2	0/0	0/0	0	12
Dyal	0	2	0	0/0	0/0	0	12
Junkin	0	2	0	0/0	0/0	0	12
Washington	0	0	2	0/0	0/0	0	12
Alexander	0	1	0	0/0	0/0	0	6
Horton	0	1	0	0/0	0/0	0	6
King	0	0	1	0/0	0/0	0	6
Smith	1	0	0	0/0	0/0	0	6
Adams	0	0	0	0/0	0/0	1	2
Raiders	9	21	5	34/35	23/34	1	315
Opponents	15	18	3	36/36	15/21	0	297

Passing	Att.	Comp.	Yds.	Pct.	TD	Int.	Tkld.	Rate
Beuerlein	217	108	1677	49.8	13	9	22/175	78.4
Schroeder	194	91	1550	46.9	8	13	20/132	60.3
Evans	2	2	50	100.0	0	0	0/0	118.8
Gossett	1	0	0	.000	0	0	0/0	39.6
Raiders	414	201	3277	48.6	21	22	44/326	70.3
Opponents	506	277	3311	54.7	18	18	35/248	72.0

Rushing	Att.	Yds.	Avg.	LG	TD
Jackson	173	950	5.5	92	4
Smith	117	471	4.0	21	1
Allen	69	293	4.2	15	2
Mueller	48	161	3.4	19	2
Porter	13	54	4.2	23	0
Beuerlein	16	39	2.4	10	0
Schroeder	15	38	2.5	19	0
Evans	1	16	16.0	16	0
Fernandez	2	16	8.0	12	0
Raiders	454	2038	4.5	92	9
Opponents	504	1940	3.8	50	15

Receiving	No.	Yds.	Avg.	LG	TD
Fernandez	57	1069	18.8	75	9
Gault	28	690	24.6	84	4
Dyal	27	499	18.5	67	2
Allen	20	191	9.6	26	0
Smith	19	140	7.4	14	0
Mueller	18	240	13.3	29	2
Alexander	15	295	19.7	61	1
Jackson	9	69	7.7	20	0
Horton	4	44	11.0	20	1
Junkin	3	32	10.7	28	2
Brown	1	8	8.0	8	0
Raiders	201	3277	16.3	84	21
Opponents	277	3311	12.0	51	18

Interceptions	No.	Yds.	Avg.	LG	TD
Anderson	5	233	46.6	87	2
Washington	3	46	15.3	32	1
McDaniel	3	21	7.0	20	0
Benson	2	36	18.0	19	0
Harden	2	1	0.5	1	0
McElroy	2	0	0.0	0	0
Robinson	1	25	25.0	25	0
Raiders	18	362	20.1	87	3
Opponents	22	298	13.5	41	0

Punting	No.	Yds.	Avg.	In 20	LG
Gossett	67	2711	40.5	13	60
Raiders	67	2711	40.5	13	60
Opponents	72	2902	40.3	19	74

Punt Returns	No.	FC	Yds.	Avg.	LG	TD
Adams	19	5	156	8.2	15	0
Edmonds	16	4	168	10.5	20	0
Brown	4	0	43	10.8	29	0
Harden	1	0	11	11.0	11	0
Raiders	40	9	378	9.5	29	0
Opponents	41	9	301	7.3	76	1

Kickoff Returns	No.	Yds.	Avg.	LG	TD
Adams	22	425	19.3	37	0
Edmonds	14	271	19.4	43	0
Mueller	5	120	24.0	49	0
Ware	4	86	21.5	29	0
Brown	3	63	21.0	25	0
Smith	2	19	9.5	15	0
Gault	1	16	16.0	16	0
Turk	1	2	2.0	2	0
Junkin	1	0	0.0	0	0
Lee	1	0	0.0	0	0
Raiders	54	1002	18.6	49	0
Opponents	59	1001	17.0	99	2

Sacks	No.
Townsend	10.5
Davis	6.0
Long	5.0
Wise	4.0
Pickel	3.0
Golic	2.5
Benson	2.0
McDaniel	1.0
Mraz	0.5
Robinson	0.5
Raiders	34.5
Opponents	tk.k

Los Angeles Rams

1989 TEAM RECORD

Preseason (3-1)

Date	Result		Opponent
8/5	W	16-13	vs. San Francisco in Tokyo
8/12	L	13-17	at Denver
8/21	W	23-20	Phoenix
8/26	W	24-14	Minnesota
9/2	W	24-14	Detroit

Regular Season (11-5)

Date	Result		Opponent	Att.
9/10	W	31-21	at Atlanta	38,708
9/17	W	31-17	Indianapolis	63,995
9/24	W	41-38	Green Bay	57,701
10/1	W	13-12	at San Francisco	64,250
10/8	W	26-14	Atlanta	52,182
10/16	L	20-23	at Buffalo	76,231
10/22	L	21-40	New Orleans	57,567
10/29	L	10-20	at Chicago	65,506
11/5	L	21-23(OT)	at Minnesota	59,600
11/12	W	31-10	Giants	65,127
11/19	W	37-14	Phoenix	53,176
11/26	W	20-17(OT)	at New Orleans	64,274
12/3	W	35-31	at Dallas	49,647
12/11	L	27-30	San Francisco	67,959
12/17	W	38-14	Jets	53,063
12/24	W	24-20	at New England	37,940

Postseason (2-1)

Date	Result		Opponent	Att.
12/31	W	21-7	at Philadelphia	57,869
1/7	W	19-13	at Giants	76,325
1/14	L	3-30	at San Francisco	64,769

1989 TEAM STATISTICS

	Rams	Opp.
Total First Downs	321	306
Rushing	107	101
Passing	197	181
Penalty	17	24
Third Down: Made/Att.	87/215	81/215
Fourth Down: Made/Att.	9/15	6/13
Total Net Yards	6042	5567
Avg. Per Game	377.6	347.9
Total Plays	1027	1023
Avg. Per Play	5.9	5.4
Net Yards Rushing	1909	1543
Avg. Per Game	119.3	96.4
Total Rushes	472	404
Net Yards Passing	4133	4024
Avg. Per Game	258.3	251.5
Sacked/Yards Lost	32/236	42/278
Gross Yards	4369	4302
Att./Completions	523/308	577/345
Completion Pct.	58.9	59.8
Had Intercepted	18	21
Punts/Avg.	74/38.3	81/41.5
Net Punting Avg.	32.1	34.7
Penalties/Yards Lost	102/823	93/802
Fumbles/Ball Lost	26/11	38/15
Touchdowns	51	38
Rushing	19	13
Passing	29	24
Returns	3	1
Avg. Time of Possession	30:35	29:25

1989 INDIVIDUAL STATISTICS

Scoring	TD R	TD P	TD Rt	PAT	FG	Saf	TP
Lansford	0	0	0	51/51	23/30	0	120
Bell	15	0	0	0/0	0/0	0	90
Ellard	0	8	0	0/0	0/0	0	48
Anderson	0	5	0	0/0	0/0	0	30
Johnson	0	5	0	0/0	0/0	0	30
McGee	1	4	0	0/0	0/0	0	30
Cox	0	3	0	0/0	0/0	0	18
Delpino	1	1	0	0/0	0/0	0	12
Holohan	0	2	0	0/0	0/0	0	12
Brown	0	1	0	0/0	0/0	0	6
Everett	1	0	0	0/0	0/0	0	6
Gary	1	0	0	0/0	0/0	0	6
Gray	0	0	1	0/0	0/0	0	6
Newsome	0	0	1	0/0	0/0	0	6
Stewart	0	0	1	0/0	0/0	0	6
Rams	19	29	3	51/51	23/30	0	426
Opponents	13	24	1	36/38	26/29	1	344

Passing	Att.	Comp.	Yds.	Pct.	TD	Int.	Tkld.	Rate
Everett	518	304	4310	58.7	29	17	29/214	90.6
Herrmann	5	4	59	80.0	0	1	3/22	76.3
Rams	523	308	4369	58.9	29	18	32/236	90.1
Opponents	577	345	4302	59.8	24	21	42/278	81.7

Rushing	Att.	Yds.	Avg.	LG	TD
Bell	272	1137	4.2	47	15
Delpino	78	368	4.7	t32	1
Gary	37	163	4.4	18	1
McGee	21	99	4.7	15	1
Green	26	73	2.8	9	0
Everett	25	31	1.2	t13	1
Brown	6	27	4.5	12	0
Ellard	2	10	5.0	6	0
Holohan	1	3	3.0	3	0
Hatcher	1	0	0.0	0	0
Anderson	1	-1	-1.0	-1	0
Herrmann	2	-1	-0.5	0	0
Rams	472	1909	4.0	47	19
Opponents	404	1543	3.8	40	13

Receiving	No.	Yds.	Avg.	LG	TD
Ellard	70	1382	19.7	53	8
Holohan	51	510	10.0	31	2
Anderson	44	1146	26.0	t78	5
McGee	37	303	8.2	25	4
Delpino	34	334	9.8	25	1
Johnson	25	148	5.9	22	5
Cox	20	340	17.0	t51	3
Bell	19	85	4.5	14	0
Brown	5	113	22.6	t39	1
Gary	2	13	6.5	8	0
Green	1	-5	-5.0	-5	0
Rams	308	4369	14.2	t78	29
Opponents	345	4302	12.5	t95	24

Interceptions	No.	Yds.	Avg.	LG	TD
Gray	6	48	8.0	t27	1
Irvin	3	43	14.3	18	0
Stewart	2	76	38.0	t41	1
Strickland	2	56	28.0	29	0
Hicks	2	27	13.5	27	0
Newsome	1	81	81.0	t81	1
Stams	1	20	20.0	20	0
Henley	1	10	10.0	10	0
Owens	1	4	4.0	4	0
Wilcher	1	4	4.0	4	0
Miller	1	3	3.0	3	0
Rams	21	372	17.7	t81	3
Opponents	18	207	11.5	42	0

Punting	No.	Yds.	Avg.	In 20	LG
Hatcher	73	2834	38.8	15	54
Rams	74	2834	38.3	15	54
Opponents	81	3364	41.5	13	57

Punt Returns	No.	FC	Yds.	Avg.	LG	TD
Henley	29	19	273	9.4	25	0
Hicks	4	3	39	9.8	15	0
Ellard	2	0	20	10.0	10	0
Irvin	0	2	0	—	0	0
Rams	35	24	332	9.5	25	0
Opponents	34	20	315	9.3	t68	1

Kickoff Returns	No.	Yds.	Avg.	LG	TD
Brown	47	968	20.6	74	0
Delpino	17	334	19.6	30	0
McDonald	2	22	11.0	12	0
Gary	1	4	4.0	4	0
Rams	67	1328	19.8	74	0
Opponents	84	1633	19.4	47	0

Sacks	No.
Greene	16.5
Wilcher	5.0
Piel	4.0
Faryniarz	3.0
Reed	3.0
Wright	3.0
Bethune	2.0
B. Smith	2.0
Strickland	2.0
Miller	1.0
Jerue	0.5
Rams	42.0
Opponents	32.0

Miami

1989 TEAM RECORD

Preseason (0-4)

Date	Result		Opponent
8/14	L	20-28	Chicago
8/19	L	10-26	vs. Houston at Jacksonville
8/25	L	21-35	at Washington
9/2	L	10-20	Philadelphia

Regular Season (8-8)

Date	Result		Opponent	Att.
9/10	L	24-27	Buffalo	54,541
9/17	W	24-10	at New England	57,043
9/24	L	33-40	Jets	65,908
10/1	L	7-39	at Houston	53,326
10/8	W	13-10(OT)	Cleveland	58,444
10/15	W	20-13	at Cincinnati	58,184
10/22	W	23-20	at Green Bay	56,624
10/29	L	17-31	at Buffalo	80,208
11/5	W	19-13	Indianapolis	52,680
11/12	W	31-23	at Jets	65,923
11/19	W	17-14	at Dallas	56,044
11/26	L	14-34	Pittsburgh	59,936
12/3	L	21-26	at Kansas City	54,610
12/10	W	31-10	New England	55,918
12/17	L	13-42	at Indianapolis	55,665
12/24	L	24-27	Kansas City	43,612

1989 TEAM STATISTICS

	Dolphins	Opp.
Total First Downs	311	337
Rushing	88	139
Passing	202	180
Penalty	21	18
Third Down: Made/Att.	101/209	67/194
Fourth Down: Made/Att.	7/14	8/21
Total Net Yards	5546	5696
Avg. Per Game	346.6	356.0
Total Plays	1011	1045
Avg. Per Play	5.5	5.5
Net Yards Rushing	1330	2153
Avg. Per Game	83.1	134.6
Total Rushes	400	493
Net Yards Passing	4216	3543
Avg. Per Game	263.5	221.4
Sacked/Yards Lost	10/86	39/268
Gross Yards	4302	3811
Att./Completions	601/331	513/315
Completion Pct.	55.1	61.4
Had Intercepted	25	15
Punts/Avg.	59/41.7	62/39.0
Net Punting Avg.	35.3	31.6
Penalties/Yards Lost	83/614	106/831
Fumbles/Ball Lost	30/16	19/8
Touchdowns	39	43
Rushing	10	19
Passing	26	21
Returns	3	3
Avg. Time of Possession	28:15	31:45

1989 INDIVIDUAL STATISTICS

Scoring	TD R	TD P	TD Rt	PAT	FG	Saf	TP
Stoyanovich	0	0	0	38/39	19/26	0	95
Clayton	0	9	0	0/0	0/0	0	54
Jensen	0	6	0	0/0	0/0	0	36
Smith	6	0	0	0/0	0/0	0	36
Brown	0	5	0	0/0	0/0	0	30
Edmunds	0	3	0	0/0	0/0	0	18
Logan	0	0	2	0/0	0/0	0	12
Marino	2	0	0	0/0	0/0	0	12
Schwedes	0	1	1	0/0	0/0	0	12
Banks	0	1	0	0/0	0/0	0	6
Davenport	1	0	0	0/0	0/0	0	6
Duper	0	1	0	0/0	0/0	0	6
Stradford	1	0	0	0/0	0/0	0	6
Dolphins	10	26	3	38/39	19/26	1	331
Opponents	19	21	3	42/43	25/33	2	379

Passing	Att.	Comp.	Yds.	Pct.	TD	Int.	Tkld.	Rate
Marino	550	308	3997	56.0	24	22	10/86	76.9
Secules	50	22	286	44.0	1	3	0/0	44.3
Jensen	1	1	19	100.0	1	0	0/0	158.3
Dolphins	601	331	4302	55.1	26	25	10/86	74.9
Opponents	513	315	3811	61.4	21	15	39/268	85.7

Rushing	Att.	Yds.	Avg.	LG	TD
Smith	200	659	3.3	25	6
Stradford	66	240	3.6	13	1
Logan	57	201	3.5	14	0
Davenport	14	56	4.0	9	1
Jensen	8	50	6.3	14	0
Hampton	17	47	2.8	9	0
Secules	4	39	9.8	17	0
Brown	13	26	2.0	6	0
Faaola	2	10	5.0	5	0
Clayton	3	9	3.0	11	0
Roby	2	0	0.0	0	0
Reaves, Wash.-Mia.	1	-1	-1.0	-1	0
Marino	14	-7	-0.5	2	2
Dolphins	400	1330	3.3	25	10
Opponents	493	2153	4.4	33	19

Receiving	No.	Yds.	Avg.	LG	TD
Clayton	64	1011	15.8	t78	9
Jensen	61	557	9.1	20	6
Duper	49	717	14.6	41	1
Edmunds	32	382	11.9	30	3
Banks	30	520	17.3	61	1
Stradford	25	233	9.3	32	0
A. Brown	24	410	17.1	t48	5
T. Brown	13	117	9.0	23	0
Hampton	8	25	3.1	12	0
Schwedes	7	174	24.9	t65	1
Smith	7	81	11.6	34	0
Logan	5	34	6.8	11	0
Davenport	3	19	6.3	9	0
Kinchen	1	12	12.0	12	0
Faaola	1	8	8.0	8	0
Hardy	1	2	2.0	2	0
Dolphins	331	4302	13.0	t78	26
Opponents	315	3811	12.1	t63	21

Interceptions	No.	Yds.	Avg.	LG	TD
Oliver	4	32	8.0	23	0
McNeal	3	-6	-2.0	0	0
Williams	2	43	21.5	24	0
Judson	2	31	15.5	28	0
Thomas	2	4	2.0	4	0
Hobley	1	22	22.0	22	0
Lankford	1	0	0.0	0	0
Dolphins	15	126	8.4	28	0
Opponents	25	335	13.4	48	1

Punting	No.	Yds.	Avg.	In 20	LG
Roby	58	2458	42.4	18	58
Dolphins	59	2458	41.7	18	58
Opponents	62	2416	39.0	17	63

Punt Returns	No.	FC	Yds.	Avg.	LG	TD
Schwedes	18	3	210	11.7	t70	1
Stradford	14	5	129	9.2	19	0
Gibson	1	0	-1	-1.0	-1	0
Williams	0	3	0	—	0	0
Dolphins	33	11	338	10.2	t70	1
Opponents	26	13	256	9.8	18	0

Kickoff Returns	No.	Yds.	Avg.	LG	TD
Logan	24	613	25.5	t97	1
Hampton	17	303	17.8	34	0
Reaves	6	84	14.0	22	0
Schwedes	3	24	8.0	13	0
A. Brown	2	9	4.5	9	0
Faaola	2	30	15.0	17	0
Kinchen	2	26	13.0	17	0
Ahrens	1	10	10.0	10	0
Brudzinski	1	6	6.0	6	0
Davenport	1	19	19.0	19	0
Goode	1	8	8.0	8	0
Williams	1	21	21.0	21	0
Dolphins	61	1153	18.9	t97	1
Opponents	63	1215	19.3	40	0

Sacks	NO.
Cross	10.0
Green	7.5
Sochia	5.0
Bosa	2.0
Kumerow	2.0
Offerdahl	1.5
Ahrens	1.0
Cline	1.0
Frye	1.0
Graf	1.0
Hobley	1.0
Junior	1.0
Krauss	1.0
Lankford	1.0
Thomas	1.0
Williams	1.0
Dolphins	39.0
Opponents	10.0

Minnesota

1989 TEAM RECORD

Preseason (3-1)

Date	Result		Opponent
8/12	W	23-13	vs. Kansas City in Memphis
8/21	W	24-13	Washington
8/26	L	14-21	at Rams
9/1	W	17-10	Cincinnati

Regular Season (10-6)

Date	Result		Opponent	Att.
9/10	W	38-7	Houston	54,015
9/17	L	7-38	at Chicago	66,475
9/24	L	14-27	at Pittsburgh	50,744
10/1	W	17-3	Tampa Bay	54,817
10/8	W	24-17	Detroit	55,380
10/15	W	26-14	Green Bay	62,075
10/22	W	20-7	at Detroit	51,579
10/30	L	14-24	at Giants	76,041
11/5	W	23-21(OT)	Rams	59,600
11/12	W	24-10	at Tampa Bay	56,271
11/19	L	9-10	at Philadelphia	65,944
11/26	L	19-20	at Green Bay	55,592
12/3	W	27-16	Chicago	60,664
12/10	W	43-17	Atlanta	58,116
12/17	L	17-23(OT)	at Cleveland	70,777
12/25	W	29-21	Cincinnati	58,829

Postseason (0-1)

Date	Result		Opponent	Att.
1/6	L	13-41	at San Francisco	64,585

1989 TEAM STATISTICS

	Vikings	Opp.
Total First Downs	326	266
Rushing	126	100
Passing	172	140
Penalty	28	26
Third Down: Made/Att.	73/215	78/233
Fourth Down: Made/Att.	11/16	16/25
Total Net Yards	5255	4184
Avg. Per Game	328.4	261.5
Total Plays	1053	1021
Avg. Per Play	5.0	4.1
Net Yards Rushing	2066	1683
Avg. Per Game	129.1	105.2
Total Rushes	514	462
Net Yards Passing	3189	2501
Avg. Per Game	199.3	156.3
Sacked/Yards Lost	40/279	71/502
Gross Yards	3468	3003
Att./Completions	499/272	488/252
Completion Pct.	54.5	51.6
Had Intercepted	19	18
Punts/Avg.	72/39.8	95/40.6
Net Punting Avg.	33.4	34.6
Penalties/Yards Lost	119/974	116/903
Fumbles/Ball Lost	28/14	29/18
Touchdowns	36	34
Rushing	12	14
Passing	17	18
Returns	7	2
Avg. Time of Possession	30:40	29:20

1989 INDIVIDUAL STATISTICS

Scoring	TD R	TD P	TD Rt	PAT	FG	Saf	TP
Karlis	0	0	0	27/28	31/39	0	120
Walker, Dall.-Minn.	7	2	1	0/0	0/0	0	60
Walker, Minn.	5	1	1	0/0	0/0	0	42
Fenney	4	2	0	0/0	0/0	0	36
Carter	0	4	0	0/0	0/0	0	24
Jordan	0	3	0	0/0	0/0	0	18
Anderson	2	0	0	0/0	0/0	0	12
Gustafson	0	2	0	0/0	0/0	0	12
Novoselsky	0	2	0	0/0	0/0	0	12
Garcia	0	0	0	8/8	1/5	0	11
Merriweather	0	0	1	0/0	0/0	1	8
Holt	0	0	1	0/0	0/0	0	6
Ingram	0	1	0	0/0	0/0	0	6
Jones	0	1	0	0/0	0/0	0	6
Lewis	0	1	0	0/0	0/0	0	6
Millard	0	0	1	0/0	0/0	0	6
Newton	0	0	1	0/0	0/0	0	6
Rutland	0	0	1	0/0	0/0	0	6
Thomas	0	0	1	0/0	0/0	0	6
Wilson	1	0	0	0/0	0/0	0	6
Berry	0	0	0	0/0	0/0	0	2
Vikings	12	17	7	35/36	32/44	2	351
Opponents	14	18	2	32/33	13/21	0	275

Passing	Att.	Comp.	Yds.	Pct.	TD	Int.	Tkld.	Rate
Wilson	362	194	2543	53.6	9	12	27/194	70.5
Kramer	136	77	906	56.6	7	7	12/75	72.7
Dozier	1	1	19	100.0	1	0	0/0	158.3
Rice	0	0	0	—	0	0	1/10	0.0
Vikings	499	272	3468	54.5	17	19	40/279	72.0
Opponents	488	252	3003	51.6	18	18	71/502	67.7

Rushing	Att.	Yds.	Avg.	LG	TD
Walker, Dall.-Minn.	250	915	3.7	47	7
Walker, Minn.	169	669	4.0	47	5
Fenney	151	588	3.9	25	4
Dozier	46	207	4.5	38	0
Anderson	52	189	3.6	14	2
Wilson	32	132	4.1	23	1
Nelson	31	124	4.0	24	0
Clark, Phoe.-Minn.	20	99	5.0	14	0
Clark, Minn.	10	57	5.7	14	0
Jones	1	37	37.0	37	0
Rice	6	25	4.2	10	0
Carter	3	18	6.0	17	0
Lewis	1	11	11.0	11	0
Kramer	12	9	0.8	5	0
Vikings	514	2066	4.0	47	12
Opponents	462	1683	3.6	t37	14

Receiving	No.	Yds.	Avg.	LG	TD
Carter	65	1066	16.4	50	4
Jones	42	694	16.5	50	1
Walker, Dall.-Minn.	40	423	10.6	52	2
Walker, Minn.	18	162	9.0	24	1
Jordan	35	506	14.5	34	3
Fenney	30	254	8.5	26	2
Anderson	20	193	9.7	18	0
Dozier	14	148	10.6	30	0
Gustafson	14	144	10.3	22	2
Lewis	12	148	12.3	t28	1
Nelson	7	52	7.4	11	0
Ingram	5	47	9.4	21	1
Rice	4	29	7.3	14	0
Novoselsky	4	11	2.8	6	2
Clark	2	14	7.0	12	0
Vikings	272	3468	12.8	50	17
Opponents	252	3003	11.9	t65	18

Interceptions	No.	Yds.	Avg.	LG	TD
Browner	5	70	14.0	34	0
Merriweather	3	29	9.7	t15	1
Rutland	2	7	3.5	7	0
Lee	2	0	0.0	0	0
Holt	1	90	90.0	t90	1
Millard	1	48	48.0	48	0
Edwards	1	18	18.0	18	0
Dusbabek	1	2	2.0	2	0
Fullington	1	0	0.0	0	0
Studwell	1	0	0.0	0	0
Vikings	18	264	14.7	t90	2
Opponents	19	138	7.3	t39	2

Punting	No.	Yds.	Avg.	In 20	LG
Scribner	72	2864	39.8	16	55
Vikings	72	2864	39.8	16	55
Opponents	95	3859	40.6	28	61

Punt Returns	No.	FC	Yds.	Avg.	LG	TD
Lewis	44	27	446	10.1	65	0
Carter	1	0	2	2.0	2	0
Vikings	45	27	448	10.0	65	0
Opponents	32	7	300	9.4	26	0

Kickoff Returns	No.	Yds.	Avg.	LG	TD
Nelson	14	317	22.6	32	0
Walker	13	374	28.8	t93	1
Dozier	12	258	21.5	63	0
Anderson	5	75	15.0	36	0
Clark, Phoe.-Minn.	2	6	3.0	6	0
Clark, Minn.	1	6	6.0	6	0
Lewis	2	30	15.0	15	0
Carter	1	19	19.0	19	0
Curtis	1	18	18.0	18	0
Fenney	1	12	12.0	12	0
Rice	1	13	13.0	13	0
Vikings	51	1122	22.0	t93	1
Opponents	68	1287	18.9	44	0

Sacks	No.
Doleman	20.5
Millard	18.0
Noga	11.5
Thomas	9.5
Merriweather	3.5
Berry	3.0
Clarke	2.0
Browner	1.0
Strauthers	1.0
Studwell	1.0
Vikings	71.0
Opponents	40.0

New England

1989 TEAM RECORD

Preseason (2-2)

Date	Result		Opponent
8/12	L	17-20	New York Giants
8/19	W	17-12	vs. Seattle at St. Louis
8/26	W	23-7	at Atlanta
9/1	L	0-16	Green Bay

Regular Season (5-11)

Date	Result		Opponent	Att.
9/10	W	27-24	at Jets	64,541
9/17	L	10-24	Miami	57,043
9/24	L	3-24	Seattle	48,025
10/1	L	10-31	at Buffalo	78,921
10/8	W	23-13	Houston	59,828
10/15	L	15-16	at Atlanta	39,697
10/22	L	20-37	at San Francisco	70,000
10/29	W	23-20(OT)	at Indianapolis	59,356
11/5	L	26-27	Jets	53,366
11/12	L	24-28	New Orleans	47,680
11/19	W	33-24	Buffalo	49,663
11/26	L	21-24	at Raiders	38,747
12/3	W	22-16	Indianapolis	32,234
12/10	L	10-31	at Miami	55,918
12/17	L	10-28	at Pittsburgh	26,594
12/24	L	20-24	Rams	27,940

1989 TEAM STATISTICS

	Patriots	Opp.
Total First Downs	335	297
Rushing	114	110
Passing	187	176
Penalty	34	11
Third Down: Made/Att.	92/240	72/199
Fourth Down: Made/Att.	10/29	5/12
Total Net Yards	5456	5644
Avg. Per Game	341.0	352.8
Total Plays	1129	975
Avg. Per Play	4.8	5.8
Net Yards Rushing	1749	1978
Avg. Per Game	109.3	123.6
Total Rushes	485	495
Net Yards Passing	3707	3666
Avg. Per Game	231.7	229.1
Sacked/Yards Lost	34/265	31/239
Gross Yards	3972	3905
Att./Completions	610/302	449/259
Completion Pct.	49.5	57.7
Had Intercepted	27	16
Punts/Avg.	64/37.4	81/42.1
Net Punting Avg.	31.3	35.2
Penalties/Yards Lost	63/509	111/954
Fumbles/Ball Lost	26/12	22/12
Touchdowns	30	48
Rushing	12	19
Passing	17	27
Returns	1	2
Avg. Time of Possession	30.55	29.05

1989 INDIVIDUAL STATISTICS

Scoring	TD R	TD P	TD Rt	PAT	FG	Saf	TP
Davis	0	0	0	13/16	16/23	0	61
Staurovsky	0	0	0	14/14	14/17	0	56
Stephens	7	0	0	0/0	0/0	0	42
Jones	0	6	0	0/0	0/0	0	36
Dykes	0	5	0	0/0	0/0	0	30
Fryar	0	3	0	0/0	0/0	0	18
Morgan	0	3	0	0/0	0/0	0	18
Perryman	2	0	0	0/0	0/0	0	12
Allen	1	0	0	0/0	0/0	0	6
Dupard	1	0	0	0/0	0/0	0	6
Egu	1	0	0	0/0	0/0	0	6
Hurst	0	0	1	0/0	0/0	0	6
Patriots	12	17	1	27/30	30/40	0	297
Opponents	19	27	2	46/48	19/26	0	391

Passing	Att.	Comp.	Yds.	Pct.	TD	Int.	Tkld.	Rate
Grogan	261	133	1697	51.0	9	14	8/64	60.8
Wilson	150	75	1006	50.0	3	5	10/71	64.5
Eason	105	57	761	54.3	3	4	10/78	71.2
Flutie	91	36	493	39.6	2	4	6/52	46.6
Feagles	2	0	0	0.0	0	0	0/0	39.6
Tatupu	1	1	15	100.0	0	0	0/0	118.8
Patriots	610	302	3972	49.5	17	27	34/265	61.3
Opponents	449	259	3905	57.7	27	16	31/239	91.6

Rushing	Att.	Yds.	Avg.	LG	TD
Stephens	244	833	3.4	t35	7
Perryman	150	562	3.7	18	2
Flutie	16	87	5.4	22	0
Dupard	25	63	2.5	10	1
Allen	11	51	4.6	18	1
Wilson	7	42	6.0	11	0
Tatupu	11	38	3.5	20	0
Egu	3	20	6.7	t15	1
Martin	2	20	10.0	13	0
Grogan	9	19	2.1	7	0
Gryar	2	15	7.5	11	0
Jones	1	3	3.0	3	0
Eason	2	-2	-1.0	0	0
Wonsley	2	-2	-1.0	0	0
Patriots	485	1749	3.6	t35	12
Opponents	495	1978	4.0	t58	19

Receiving	No.	Yds.	Avg.	LG	TD
Sievers	54	615	11.4	46	0
Dykes	49	795	16.2	42	5
Jones	48	670	14.0	t65	6
Fryar	29	537	18.5	52	3
Perryman	29	195	6.7	16	0
Morgan	28	486	17.4	t55	3
Stephens	21	207	9.9	37	0
Martin	13	229	17.6	37	0
Dawson	12	101	8.4	17	0
Tatupu	10	54	5.4	11	0
Dupard	6	70	11.7	45	0
Cook	3	13	4.3	5	0
Patriots	302	3972	13.2	t65	17
Opponents	259	3905	15.1	t74	27

Interceptions	No.	Yds.	Avg.	LG	TD
Hurst	5	31	6.2	t16	1
James	2	50	25.0	28	0
Marion	2	19	9.5	18	0
McSwain	1	18	18.0	18	0
Feggins	1	4	4.0	4	0
Coleman	1	1	1.0	1	0
Clayborn	1	0	0.0	0	0
Rembert	1	0	0.0	0	0
Brown	1	-1	-1.0	-1	0
McGrew	1	-4	-4.0	-4	0
Patriots	16	118	7.4	28	1
Opponents	27	338	12.5	55	2

Punting	No.	Yds.	Avg.	In 20	LG
Feagles	63	2392	38.0	13	64
Patriots	64	2392	37.4	13	64
Opponents	81	3413	42.1	15	76

Punt Returns	No.	FC	Yds.	Avg.	LG	TD
Martin	19	2	164	8.6	28	0
Tucker, Buff.-N.E.	19	4	165	8.7	25	0
Tucker, N.E.	13	1	102	7.8	25	0
Fryar	12	1	107	8.9	20	0
Hurst	1	0	6	6.0	6	0
Taylor	0	2	0	—	0	0
Patriots	45	6	379	8.4	28	0
Opponents	38	6	346	9.1	17	0

Kickoff Returns	No.	Yds.	Avg.	LG	TD
Martin	24	584	24.3	38	0
Tucker, Buff.-N.E.	23	436	19.0	37	0
Tucker, N.E.	13	270	20.8	37	0
Rice	11	242	22.0	46	0
Allen	6	124	20.7	29	0
Taylor	3	52	17.3	22	0
Wonsley	3	69	23.0	40	0
Egu	2	26	13.0	22	0
Hodge	2	19	9.5	11	0
Timpson	2	13	6.5	13	0
Fryar	1	47	47.0	47	0
Rehder	1	14	14.0	14	0
Tatupu	1	2	2.0	2	0
Patriots	69	1462	21.2	47	0
Opponents	61	1199	19.7	60	0

Sacks	No.
Williams	8.0
Jeter	7.0
McGrew	4.5
Brown	4.0
Sims	3.0
Rembert	2.5
Goad	1.0
Patriots	31.0
Opponents	34.0

New Orleans

1989 TEAM RECORD

Preseason (1-3)

Date	Result		Opponent
8/12	L	7-31	Indianapolis
8/19	L	7-10	at Buffalo
8/28	W	27-10	Cincinnati
9/1	L	21-20	Washington

Regular Season (9-7)

Date	Result		Opponent	Att.
9/10	W	28-0	Dallas	66,977
9/17	L	34-35	at Green Bay	55,809
9/24	L	10-20	at Tampa Bay	44,053
10/1	L	14-16	Washington	64,358
10/8	L	20-24	San Francisco	60,488
10/15	W	29-14	Jets	59,521
10/22	W	40-21	at Rams	57,567
10/29	W	20-13	Atlanta	65,153
11/6	L	13-31	at San Francisco	60,667
11/12	W	28-24	at New England	47,680
11/19	W	26-17	at Atlanta	53,173
11/26	L	17-20(OT)	Rams	64,274
12/3	L	14-21	at Detroit	38,550
12/10	W	22-19	at Buffalo	70,037
12/18	W	30-20	Philadelphia	59,218
12/24	W	41-6	Indianapolis	49,009

1989 TEAM STATISTICS

	Saints	Opp.
Total First Downs	304	293
Rushing	108	79
Passing	167	198
Penalty	29	16
Third Down: Made/Att.	89/207	82/216
Fourth Down: Made/Att.	5/10	8/17
Total Net Yards	5328	5186
Avg. Per Game	333.0	324.1
Total Plays	999	997
Avg. Per Play	5.3	5.2
Net Yards Rushing	1948	1326
Avg. Per Game	121.8	82.9
Total Rushes	502	373
Net Yards Passing	3380	3860
Avg. Per Game	211.3	241.3
Sacked/Yards Lost	36/271	47/362
Gross Yards	3651	4222
Att./Completions	461/284	577/320
Completion Pct.	61.6	55.5
Had Intercepted	19	21
Punts/Avg.	71/39.1	75/39.4
Net Punting Avg.	34.2	33.2
Penalties/Yards Lost	90/676	105/850
Fumbles/Ball Lost	28/12	35/18
Touchdowns	46	35
Rushing	19	10
Passing	23	23
Returns	4	2
Avg. Time of Possession	33:43	26:17

1989 INDIVIDUAL STATISTICS

Scoring	TD R	TD P	TD Rt	PAT	FG	Saf	TP
Hilliard	13	5	0	0/0	0/0	0	108
Andersen	0	0	0	44/45	20/29	0	104
E. Martin	0	8	0	0/0	0/0	0	48
Brenner	0	4	0	0/0	0/0	0	24
Hill	0	4	0	0/0	0/0	0	24
Jordan	3	0	0	0/0	0/0	0	18
Cook	0	0	1	0/0	0/0	0	6
Fourcade	1	0	0	0/0	0/0	0	6
Frazier	1	0	0	0/0	0/0	0	6
Heyward	1	0	0	0/0	0/0	0	6
Maxie	0	0	1	0/0	0/0	0	6
Morse	0	0	1	0/0	0/0	0	6
Shepard	0	0	1	0/0	0/0	0	6
Tice	0	1	0	0/0	0/0	0	6
Turner	0	1	0	0/0	0/0	0	6
Forde	0	0	0	0/0	0/0	1	2
Warren	0	0	0	0/0	0/0	1	2
Saints	19	23	4	44/46	20/29	3	386
Opponents	10	23	2	34/35	19/24	0	301

Passing	Att.	Comp.	Yds.	Pct.	TD	Int.	Tkld.	Rate
Hebert	353	222	2686	62.9	15	15	22/171	82.7
Fourcade	107	61	930	57.0	7	4	13/96	92.0
Hilliard	1	1	35	100.0	1	0	0/0	158.3
Hill	0	0	0	—	0	0	1/4	0.0
Saints	461	284	3651	61.6	23	19	36/271	85.9
Opponents	577	320	4222	55.5	23	21	47/362	76.9

Rushing	Att.	Yds.	Avg.	LG	TD
Hilliard	344	1262	3.7	40	13
Heyward	49	183	3.7	15	1
Jordan	38	179	4.7	32	3
Frazier	25	112	4.5	21	1
Fourcade	14	91	6.5	14	1
Hebert	25	87	3.5	11	0
Morse	2	43	21.5	39	0
Turner	2	8	4.0	6	0
Winslow	1	0	0.0	0	0
Hill	1	-7	-7.0	-7	0
Perriman	1	-10	-10.0	-10	0
Saints	502	1948	3.9	40	19
Opponents	373	1326	3.6	38	10

Receiving	No.	Yds.	Avg.	LG	TD
E. Martin	68	1090	16.0	t53	8
Hilliard	52	514	9.9	t54	5
Hill	48	636	13.3	46	4
Brenner	34	398	11.7	t30	4
Turner	22	279	12.7	t54	1
Perriman	20	356	17.8	47	0
Heyward	13	69	5.3	12	0
Tice	9	98	10.9	23	1
Scales	8	89	11.1	26	0
Jordan	4	53	13.3	17	0
Frazier	3	25	8.3	22	0
Shepard	2	36	18.0	23	0
Cook	1	8	8.0	8	0
Saints	284	3651	12.9	t54	23
Opponents	320	4222	13.2	t75	23

Interceptions	No.	Yds.	Avg.	LG	TD
Waymer	6	66	11.0	42	0
Massey	5	26	5.2	22	0
Cook	3	81	27.0	t63	1
Maxie	3	41	13.7	t26	1
Mack	2	0	0.0	0	0
Swilling	1	14	14.0	14	0
Atkins	1	-2	-2.0	-2	0
Saints	21	226	10.8	t63	2
Opponents	19	205	13.9	40	1

Punting	No.	Yds.	Avg.	In 20	LG
Barnhardt	55	2179	39.6	17	56
Winslow	16	595	37.2	4	50
Saints	71	2774	39.1	21	56
Opponents	75	2956	39.4	15	63

Punt Returns	No.	FC	Yds.	Avg.	LG	TD
Harris	27	7	196	7.3	20	0
Morse	10	1	29	2.9	16	0
Hill	7	0	41	5.9	13	0
Shepard	7	1	91	13.0	t56	1
Perriman	1	0	10	10.0	10	0
Turner	1	0	7	7.0	7	0
Massey	0	0	54	—	54	0
Saints	53	9	428	8.1	57	1
Opponents	35	16	244	7.0	28	0

Kickoff Returns	No.	Yds.	Avg.	LG	TD
Harris	19	378	19.9	39	0
Atkins	12	245	20.4	32	0
Morse	10	278	27.8	t99	1
Frazier	8	157	19.6	29	0
Shepard	8	135	16.9	24	0
U. Johnson	2	34	17.0	19	0
Hill	1	13	13.0	13	0
Hilliard	1	20	20.0	20	0
Phillips	1	24	24.0	24	0
Scales	1	0	0.0	0	0
Saints	63	1284	20.4	t99	1
Opponents	55	983	17.9	72	0

Sacks	No.
Swilling	16.5
Warren	9.5
Jackson	7.5
Wilks	4.0
Mills	3.0
W. Martin	2.5
Cook	1.0
Geathers	1.0
V. Johnson	1.0
Mack	1.0
Saints	47.0
Opponents	36.0

New York Giants

1989 TEAM RECORD

Preseason (3-1)

Date	Result		Opponent
8/12	W	20-17	at New England
8/20	W	45-7	at Kansas City
8/26	W	21-17	Jets
9/2	L	10-13	Pittsburgh

Regular Season (12-4)

Date	Result		Opponent	Att.
9/11	W	27-24	at Washington	54,160
9/17	W	24-14	Detroit	76,021
9/24	W	35-7	Phoenix	75,742
10/1	W	30-13	at Dallas	51,785
10/8	L	19-21	at Philadelphia	65,688
10/15	W	20-17	Washington	76,245
10/22	W	20-13	at San Diego	48,566
10/30	W	24-14	Minnesota	76,041
11/5	W	20-13	at Phoenix	46,588
11/12	L	10-31	at Rams	65,127
11/19	W	15-3	Seattle	75,014
11/27	L	24-34	at San Francisco	63,461
12/3	L	17-24	Philadelphia	74,809
12/10	W	14-7	at Denver	63,283
12/16	W	15-0	Dallas	72,141
12/24	W	34-17	Raiders	70,306

Postseason (0-1)

Date	Result		Opponent	Att.
1/7	L	13-19	Rams	76,325

1989 TEAM STATISTICS

	Giants	Opp.
Total First Downs	298	266
Rushing	118	90
Passing	157	159
Penalty	23	17
Third Down: Made/Att.	105/232	79/205
Fourth Down: Made/Att.	17/22	4/17
Total Net Yards	4963	4664
Avg. Per Game	310.2	291.5
Total Plays	1046	946
Avg. Per Play	4.7	4.9
Net Yards Rushing	1889	1539
Avg. Per Game	118.1	96.2
Total Rushes	556	421
Net Yards Passing	3074	3125
Avg. Per Game	192.1	195.3
Sacked/Yards Lost	46/281	39/302
Gross Yards	3355	3427
Att./Completions	444/248	486/273
Completion Pct.	55.9	56.2
Had Intercepted	16	22
Punts/Avg.	70/43.1	74/40.1
Net Punting Avg.	37.8	30.8
Penalties/Yards Lost	83/675	109/800
Fumbles/Ball Lost	30/14	38/15
Touchdowns	37	30
Rushing	17	10
Passing	17	16
Returns	3	4
Avg. Time of Possession	32:23	27:37

1989 INDIVIDUAL STATISTICS

Scoring	TD R	TD P	TD Rt	PAT	FG	Saf	TP
Anderson	14	0	0	0/0	0/0	0	84
Allegre	0	0	0	23/24	20/26	0	83
Nittmo	0	0	0	12/13	9/12	0	39
Meggett	0	4	1	0/0	0/0	0	30
Turner	0	4	0	0/0	0/0	0	24
Bavaro	0	3	0	0/0	0/0	0	18
Baker	0	2	0	0/0	0/0	0	12
Hostetler	2	0	0	0/0	0/0	0	12
Banks	0	1	0	0/0	0/0	0	6
Cross	0	1	0	0/0	0/0	0	6
Ingram	0	1	0	0/0	0/0	0	6
Johnson	0	0	1	0/0	0/0	0	6
Kinard	0	0	1	0/0	0/0	0	6
Manuel	0	1	0	0/0	0/0	0	6
Simms	1	0	0	0/0	0/0	0	6
Marshall	0	0	0	0/0	0/0	1	2
Reasons	0	0	0	0/0	0/0	1	2
Giants	17	17	3	35/37	29/38	2	348
Opponents	10	16	4	30/30	14/21	0	252

Passing	Att.	Comp.	Yds.	Pct.	TD	Int.	Tkld.	Rate
Simms	405	228	3061	56.3	14	14	40/244	77.6
Hostetler	39	20	294	51.3	3	2	6/37	80.5
Giants	444	248	3355	55.9	17	16	46/281	77.9
Opponents	486	273	3427	56.2	16	22	39/302	70.4

Rushing	Att.	Yds.	Avg.	LG	TD
Anderson	325	1023	3.1	t36	14
Tillman	79	290	3.7	19	0
Carthon	57	153	2.7	18	0
Simms	32	141	4.4	15	1
Meggett	28	117	4.2	18	0
Hostetler	11	71	6.5	t19	2
Rouson	11	51	4.6	9	0
Adams	9	29	3.2	8	0
Turner	2	11	5.5	14	0
Reasons	1	2	2.0	2	0
Ingram	1	1	1.0	1	0
Giants	556	1889	3.4	t36	17
Opponents	421	1539	3.7	44	10

Receiving	No.	Yds.	Avg.	LG	TD
Turner	38	467	12.3	44	4
Meggett	34	531	15.6	t62	4
Manuel	33	539	16.3	49	1
Anderson	28	268	9.6	26	0
Mowatt	27	288	10.7	31	0
Bavaro	22	278	12.6	29	3
Ingram	17	290	17.1	t41	1
Carthon	15	132	8.8	18	0
Baker	13	255	19.6	t39	2
Rouson	7	121	17.3	39	0
Cross	6	107	17.8	27	1
Robinson	4	41	10.3	16	0
Adams	2	7	3.5	10	0
Banks	1	22	22.0	t22	1
Tillman	1	9	9.0	9	0
Giants	248	3355	13.5	t62	17
Opponents	273	3427	12.6	t71	16

Interceptions	No.	Yds.	Avg.	LG	TD
Kinard	5	135	27.0	t58	1
Johnson	3	60	20.0	t39	1
Williams	3	14	4.7	14	0
Guyton	2	27	13.5	14	0
S. White	2	18	9.0	18	0
Collins	2	12	6.0	12	0
A. White	2	8	4.0	9	0
Reasons	1	40	40.0	40	0
DeOssie	1	10	10.0	10	0
Banks	1	6	6.0	6	0
Giants	22	330	15.0	t58	2
Opponents	16	240	15.0	t60	2

Punting	No.	Yds.	Avg.	In 20	LG
Landeta	70	3019	43.1	19	71
Giants	70	3019	43.1	19	71
Opponents	74	2964	40.1	15	91

Punt Returns	No.	FC	Yds.	Avg.	LG	TD
Meggett	46	14	582	12.7	t76	1
Giants	46	14	582	12.7	t76	1
Opponents	29	15	236	8.1	23	0

Kickoff Returns	No.	Yds.	Avg.	LG	TD
Meggett	27	577	21.4	43	0
Ingram	22	332	15.1	29	0
Collins	1	0	0.0	0	0
Rouson	1	17	17.0	17	0
Giants	51	926	18.2	43	0
Opponents	73	1306	17.9	63	0

Sacks	No.
Taylor	15.0
Marshall	9.5
Howard	5.5
Banks	4.0
Collins	1.0
Cooks	1.0
Cox	1.0
Johnson	1.0
Reasons	1.0
Giants	39.0
Opponents	46.0

New York Jets

1989 TEAM RECORD

Preseason (2-2)

Date	Result		Opponent
8/12	L	27-28	vs. Green Bay in Milwaukee
8/20	W	19-10	vs. Philadelpiha in Raleigh
8/26	L	17-21	at Giants
9/1	W	15-13(OT)	at Kansas City

Regular Season (4-12)

Date	Result		Opponent	Att.
9/10	L	24-27	New England	64,541
9/17	L	24-38	at Cleveland	73,516
9/24	W	40-33	at Miami	65,908
10/1	L	10-17	Indianapolis	65,542
10/9	L	7-14	Raiders	68,040
10/15	L	14-29	at New Orleans	59,521
10/22	L	3-34	at Buffalo	76,811
10/29	L	10-23	San Francisco	62,805
11/5	W	27-26	at New England	53,366
11/12	L	23-31	Miami	65,923
11/19	L	10-27	at Indianapolis	58,236
11/26	W	27-7	Atlanta	40,429
12/3	W	20-17	at San Diego	38,954
12/10	L	0-13	Pittsburgh	41,037
12/17	L	14-38	at Rams	53,063
12/23	L	0-37	Buffalo	21,148

1989 TEAM STATISTICS

	Jets	Opp.
Total First Downs	292	328
Rushing	91	127
Passing	189	178
Penalty	12	23
Third Down: Made/Att.	68/210	82/213
Fourth Down: Made/Att.	7/15	7/16
Total Net Yards	5011	5994
Avg. Per Game	313.2	374.6
Total Plays	1032	1059
Avg. Per Play	4.9	5.7
Net Yards Rushing	1596	2136
Avg. Per Game	99.8	133.5
Total Rushes	400	517
Net Yards Passing	3415	3858
Avg. Per Game	213.4	241.1
Sacked/Yards Lost	62/477	28/177
Gross Yards	3892	4035
Att./Completions	570/338	314/282
Completion Pct.	59.3	54.9
Had Intercepted	24	15
Punts/Avg.	87/39.4	69/39.8
Net Punting Avg.	35.5	33.7
Penalties/Yards Lost	116/957	90/675
Fumbles/Ball Lost	32/17	32/9
Touchdowns	30	30
Rushing	11	16
Passing	14	31
Returns	5	3
Avg. Time of Possession	29:16	30:44

1989 INDIVIDUAL STATISTICS

Scoring	TD R	TD P	TD Rt	PAT	FG	Saf	TP
Leahy	0	0	0	29/30	14/21	0	71
Vick	5	2	0	0/0	0/0	0	42
Hector	3	2	0	0/0	0/0	0	30
Townsell	0	5	0	0/0	0/0	0	30
McMillan	0	0	3	0/0	0/0	0	18
McNeil	2	1	0	0/0	0/0	0	18
Toon	0	2	0	0/0	0/0	0	12
Burkett	0	1	0	0/0	0/0	0	6
Dressel, K.C.-Jets	0	1	0	0/0	0/0	0	6
Hasty	0	0	1	0/0	0/0	0	6
Neubert	0	1	0	0/0	0/0	0	6
Prokop	1	0	0	0/0	0/0	0	6
Radachowsky	0	0	1	0/0	0/0	0	6
Jets	11	14	5	29/30	14/21	1	253
Opponents	16	31	3	46/50	21/31	1	411

Passing	Att.	Comp.	Yds.	Pct.	TD	Int.	Tkld.	Rate
O'Brien	477	288	3346	60.4	12	18	50/391	74.3
Eason, N.E.-Jets	141	79	1016	56.0	4	6	17/120	70.5
Eason, Jets	36	22	255	61.1	1	2	7/42	68.6
Ryan	30	15	153	50.0	1	3	2/26	36.5
Mackey	25	11	125	44.0	0	1	3/18	42.9
Malone	2	2	13	100.0	0	0	0/0	93.8
Jets	570	338	3892	59.3	14	24	62/477	70.6
Opponents	514	282	4035	54.9	31	15	28/177	88.5

Rushing	Att.	Yds.	Avg.	LG	TD
Hector	177	702	4.0	24	3
Vick	112	434	3.9	t39	5
McNeil	80	352	4.4	t19	2
Brown	12	63	5.3	17	0
O'Brien	9	18	2.0	5	0
Prokop	1	17	17.0	t17	1
Epps	1	14	14.0	14	0
Harper	1	3	3.0	3	0
Mackey	2	3	1.5	5	0
Malone	1	0	0.0	0	0
Ryan	1	-1	-1.0	-1	0
Eason, N.E.-Jets	3	-2	-0.7	0	0
Eason, Jets	1	0	0.0	0	0
Burkett	1	-4	-4.0	-4	0
Lageman	1	-5	-5.0	-5	0
Jets	400	1596	4.0	t39	11
Opponents	517	2136	4.1	t40	16

Receiving	No.	Yds.	Avg.	LG	TD
Toon	63	693	11.0	t37	2
Townsell	45	787	17.5	t63	5
Hector	38	330	8.7	32	2
Vick	34	241	7.1	21	2
McNeil	31	310	10.0	t25	1
Shuler	29	322	11.1	22	0
Neubert	28	302	10.8	t35	1
Burkett, Buff.-Jets	24	298	12.4	30	1
Burkett, Jets	21	278	13.2	30	1
Dressel, K.C.-Jets	12	191	15.9	t49	1
Dressel, Jets	3	55	18.3	43	0
Griggs	9	112	12.4	23	0
Werner	8	115	14.4	36	0
Epps	8	108	13.5	21	0
Walker	8	89	11.1	31	0
Harper	7	127	18.1	48	0
Brown	4	10	2.5	6	0
Dunn	2	13	6.5	8	0
Jets	338	3892	11.5	t63	14
Opponents	282	4035	14.3	t78	31

Interceptions	No.	Yds.	Avg.	LG	TD
McMillan	6	180	30.0	t92	1
Hasty	5	62	12.4	t34	1
Booty	1	13	13.0	13	0
Mersereau	1	4	4.0	4	0
Gordon	1	2	2.0	2	0
Glenn	1	0	0.0	0	0
Jets	15	261	17.4	t92	2
Opponents	24	282	11.8	t87	2

Punting	No.	Yds.	Avg.	In 20	LG
Prokop	87	3426	39.4	29	76
Jets	87	3426	39.4	29	76
Opponents	69	2746	39.8	18	59

Punt Returns	No.	FC	Yds.	Avg.	LG	TD
Townsell	33	12	299	9.1	30	0
Jets	33	12	299	9.1	30	0
Opponents	34	22	257	7.6	t49	1

Kickoff Returns	No.	Yds.	Avg.	LG	TD
Townsell	34	653	19.2	69	0
Humphery	24	414	17.3	52	0
Epps	9	154	17.1	43	0
Dixon	4	67	16.8	21	0
Nichols	2	9	4.5	7	0
Byrd	1	1	1.0	1	0
Washington	1	11	11.0	11	0
Jets	75	1309	17.5	69	0
Opponents	47	1029	21.9	49	0

Sacks	No.
Byrd	7.0
Lageman	4.5
Nichols	4.0
Clifton	2.0
Frase	2.0
McMillan	2.0
Stallworth	2.0
Washington	1.5
Gordon	1.0
Lyons	1.0
Glenn	0.5
Mersereau	0.5
Jets	28.0
Opponents	62.0

Philadelphia

1989 TEAM RECORD

Preseason (4-1)

Date	Result		Opponent
8/6	W	17-13	vs. Cleveland in London
8/12	W	23-17	Atlanta
8/20	L	10-19	vs. Jets in Raleigh
8/26	W	38-14	Pittsburgh
9/2	W	20-10	at Miami

Regular Season (11-5)

Date	Result		Opponent	Att.
9/10	W	31-7	Seattle	64,287
9/17	W	42-37	at Washington	53,493
9/24	L	28-38	San Francisco	66,042
10/2	L	13-27	at Chicago	66,625
10/8	W	21-19	Giants	65,688
10/15	W	17-5	at Phoenix	42,620
10/22	W	10-7	Raiders	64,019
10/29	W	28-24	at Denver	75,065
11/5	L	17-20	at San Diego	47,019
11/12	L	8-10	Washington	65,443
11/19	W	10-9	Minnesota	65,944
11/23	W	27-0	at Dallas	54,444
12/3	W	24-17	at Giants	74,809
12/10	W	20-10	Dallas	59,842
12/18	L	20-30	at New Orleans	59,218
12/24	W	31-14	Phoenix	43,287

Postseason (0-1)

Date	Result		Opponent	Att.
12/31	L	7-21	Rams	57,869

1989 TEAM STATISTICS

	Eagles	Opp.
Total First Downs	321	281
Rushing	120	81
Passing	171	171
Penalty	30	29
Third Down: Made/Att.	97/246	79/217
Fourth Down: Made/Att.	6/13	5/15
Total Net Yards	5320	4894
Avg. Per Game	332.5	305.9
Total Plays	1123	1017
Avg. Per Play	4.7	4.8
Net Yards Rushing	2208	1605
Avg. Per Game	138.0	100.3
Total Rushes	540	426
Net Yards Passing	3112	3289
Avg. Per Game	194.5	205.6
Sacked/Yards Lost	45/343	62/424
Gross Yards	3455	3713
Att./Completions	538/294	529/258
Completion Pct.	54.6	48.8
Had Intercepted	16	30
Punts/Avg.	87/39.0	85/42.0
Net Punting Avg.	35.3	35.5
Penalties/Yards Lost	114/938	118/956
Fumbles/Ball Lost	43/16	44/26
Touchdowns	40	33
Rushing	14	6
Passing	23	26
Returns	3	1
Avg. Time of Possession	30:43	29:17

1989 INDIVIDUAL STATISTICS

Scoring	TD R	TD P	TD Rt	PAT	FG	Saf	TP
Ruzek, Dall.-Phil.	0	0	0	28/29	13/22	0	67
Ruzek, Phil.	0	0	0	14/14	8/11	0	38
Carter	0	11	0	0/0	0/0	0	66
Zendejas	0	0	0	23/23	9/15	0	50
Byars	5	0	0	0/0	0/0	0	30
Cunningham	4	0	0	0/0	0/0	0	24
Jackson	0	3	0	0/0	0/0	0	18
Toney	3	0	0	0/0	0/0	0	18
DeLine	0	0	0	3/3	3/7	0	12
Garrity	0	2	0	0/0	0/0	0	12
Giles	0	2	0	0/0	0/0	0	12
Quick	0	2	0	0/0	0/0	0	12
Sherman	2	0	0	0/0	0/0	0	12
Carson, K.C.-Phil.	0	1	0	0/0	0/0	0	6
Drummond	0	1	0	0/0	0/0	0	6
Everett	0	0	1	0/0	0/0	0	6
Johnson	0	1	0	0/0	0/0	0	6
Little	0	1	0	0/0	0/0	0	6
Simmons	0	0	1	0/0	0/0	0	6
Waters	0	0	1	0/0	0/0	0	6
Harris	0	0	0	0/0	0/0	1	2
Eagles	14	23	3	40/40	20/33	1	342
Opponents	6	26	1	30/33	14/26	2	274

Passing	Att.	Comp.	Yds.	Pct.	TD	Int.	Tkld.	Rate
Cunningham	532	290	3400	54.5	21	15	45/343	75.5
Cavanaugh	5	3	33	60.0	1	1	0/0	79.6
Ruzek	1	1	22	100.0	1	0	0/0	158.3
Eagles	538	294	3455	54.6	23	16	45/343	76.2
Opponents	529	258	3713	48.8	26	30	62/424	64.7

Rushing	Att.	Yds.	Avg.	LG	TD
Cunningham	104	621	6.0	51	4
Toney	172	582	3.4	44	3
Byars	133	452	3.4	t16	5
Higgs	49	184	3.8	13	0
Sherman	40	177	4.4	37	2
Drummond	32	127	4.0	16	0
Reichenbach	1	30	30.0	30	0
Teltschik	1	23	23.0	23	0
Carter	2	16	8.0	11	0
Runager	2	5	2.5	5	0
Johnson	1	3	3.0	3	0
Cavanaugh	2	-3	-1.5	0	0
Carson	1	-9	-9.0	-9	0
Eagles	540	2208	4.1	51	14
Opponents	426	1605	3.8	58	6

Receiving	No.	Yds.	Avg.	LG	TD
Byars	68	721	10.6	60	0
Jackson	63	648	10.3	33	3
Carter	45	605	13.4	42	11
Johnson	20	295	14.8	34	1
Toney	19	124	6.5	15	0
Drummond	17	180	10.6	21	1
Giles	16	225	14.1	t66	2
Quick	13	228	17.5	40	2
Garrity	13	209	16.1	31	2
Carson, K.C.-Phil.	8	107	13.4	28	1
Carson, Phil.	1	12	12.0	12	0
Sherman	8	85	10.6	17	0
Williams	4	32	8.0	11	0
Higgs	3	9	3.0	8	0
Edwards	2	74	37.0	66	0
Little	2	8	4.0	7	1
Ruzek, Dall.-Phil	1	4	4.0	4	0
Eagles	294	3455	11.8	t66	23
Opponents	258	3713	14.4	t80	26

Interceptions	No.	Yds.	Avg.	LG	TD
Allen	8	38	4.8	18	0
Everett	4	64	16.0	t30	1
Frizzell	4	58	14.5	27	0
Jenkins	4	58	14.5	22	0
Evans	3	23	7.7	15	0
Harris	2	18	9.0	11	0
Simmons	1	60	60.0	t60	1
Golic	1	23	23.0	23	0
Waters	1	20	20.0	20	0
Bell	1	13	13.0	13	0
Joyner	1	0	0.0	0	0
Eagles	30	375	12.5	t60	2
Opponents	16	147	9.2	37	0

Punting	No.	Yds.	Avg.	In 20	LG
Teltschik	57	2246	39.4	12	58
Runager	17	568	33.4	5	52
Tuten	7	256	36.6	1	45
Cunningham	6	319	53.2	3	9
Ruzek, Dall.-Phil.	1	28	28.0	0	28
Eagles	87	3389	39.0	21	91
Opponents	85	3571	42.0	19	71

Punt Returns	No.	FC	Yds.	Avg.	LG	TD
Williams	30	7	267	8.9	24	0
Edwards	7	5	64	9.1	28	0
Eagles	37	12	331	8.9	28	0
Opponents	37	21	215	5.8	16	0

Kickoff Returns	No.	Yds.	Avg.	LG	TD
Higgs	16	293	18.3	30	0
Williams	14	249	17.8	28	0
Sherman	13	222	17.1	45	0
Edwards	3	23	7.7	11	0
Little	2	14	7.0	12	0
Byars	1	27	27.0	27	0
Eagles	49	828	16.9	45	0
Opponents	60	1307	21.8	t93	1

Sacks	No.
Simmons	15.5
White	11.0
Brown	10.5
Pitts	7.0
Joyner	4.5
Hopkins	3.5
Golic	3.0
Harris	2.3
Evans	2.0
Frizzell	1.5
Waters	1.0
Eagles	62.0
Opponents	45.0

Phoenix

1989 TEAM RECORD

Preseason (1-3)

Date	Result		Opponent
8/11	L	10-16	Seattle
8/21	L	20-23	at Rams
8/26	W	21-7	Cleveland
9/1	L	20-21	at San Diego

Regular Season (5-11)

Date	Result		Opponent	Att.
9/10	W	16-13	at Detroit	36,735
9/17	W	34-24	at Seattle	60,444
9/24	L	7-35	at Giants	75,742
10/1	L	13-24	San Diego	44,201
10/8	L	28-30	at Washington	53,335
10/15	L	5-17	Philadelphia	42,620
10/22	W	34-20	Atlanta	33,894
10/29	W	19-10	at Dallas	44,431
11/5	L	13-20	Giants	46,588
11/12	W	24-20	Dallas	49,657
11/19	L	14-37	at Rams	53,176
11/26	L	13-14	Tampa Bay	33,297
12/3	L	10-29	Washington	38,870
12/10	L	14-16	at Raiders	41,785
12/16	L	0-37	Denver	56,071
12/24	L	14-31	at Philadelphia	43,287

1989 TEAM STATISTICS

	Cardinals	Opp.
Total First Downs	263	329
Rushing	83	113
Passing	157	185
Penalty	22	31
Third Down: Made/Att.	87/220	104/238
Fourth Down: Made/Att.	4/14	9/11
Total Net Yards	4641	5877
Avg. Per Game	290.1	367.3
Total Plays	986	1100
Avg. Per Play	4.7	5.3
Net Yards Rushing	1361	2302
Avg. Per Game	85.1	143.9
Total Rushes	407	539
Net Yards Passing	3280	3575
Avg. Per Game	205.0	223.4
Sacked/Yards Lost	56/379	30/219
Gross Yards	3659	3794
Att./Completions	523/279	531/286
Completion Pct.	53.3	53.9
Had Intercepted	30	16
Punts/Avg.	82/43.6	76/41.5
Net Punting Avg.	37.6	33.8
Penalties/Yards Lost	113/856	106/916
Fumbles/Ball Lost	24/14	18/11
Touchdowns	29	41
Rushing	10	12
Passing	17	24
Returns	2	5
Avg. Time of Possession	28:27	31:33

1989 INDIVIDUAL STATISTICS

Scoring	TD R	TD P	TD Rt	PAT	FG	Saf	TP
Del Greco	0	0	0	28/29	18/26	0	82
Green	0	7	0	0/0	0/0	0	42
Ferrell	6	0	0	0/0	0/0	0	36
Smith	0	5	0	0/0	0/0	0	30
Jones	0	3	0	0/0	0/0	0	18
Jordan	2	0	0	0/0	0/0	0	12
Hogeboom	1	0	0	0/0	0/0	0	6
Holmes	0	1	0	0/0	0/0	0	6
McDonald	0	0	1	0/0	0/0	0	6
Novacek	0	1	0	0/0	0/0	0	6
Wolfley	1	0	0	0/0	0/0	0	6
Zordich	0	0	1	0/0	0/0	0	6
Wilson	0	0	0	0/0	0/0	0	2
Cardinals	10	17	2	28/29	18/26	1	258
Opponents	12	24	5	40/41	29/40	2	377

Passing	Att.	Comp.	Yds.	Pct.	TD	Int.	Tkld.	Rate
Hogeboom	364	204	2591	56.0	14	19	40/266	69.5
Tupa	134	65	973	48.5	3	9	14/94	52.2
Rosenbach	22	9	95	40.9	0	1	2/19	35.2
Awalt	1	0	0	0.0	0	1	0/0	0.0
Camarillo	1	1	0	100.0	0	0	0/0	79.2
Sikahema	1	0	0	0.0	0	0	0/0	39.6
Cardinals	523	279	3659	53.3	17	30	56/379	62.6
Opponents	531	286	3794	53.9	24	16	30/219	79.2

Rushing	Att.	Yds.	Avg.	LG	TD
Ferrell	149	502	3.4	t44	6
Jordan	83	211	2.5	15	2
Mitchell	43	165	3.8	14	0
Sikahema	38	145	3.8	27	0
Hogeboom	27	89	3.3	15	1
Tupa	15	75	5.0	13	0
Clark	10	42	4.2	9	0
Wolfley	13	36	2.8	t5	1
Baker	20	31	1.6	6	0
Rosenbach	6	26	4.3	8	0
Smith	2	21	10.5	11	0
Jones	1	18	18.0	18	0
Cardinals	407	1361	3.3	t44	10
Opponents	539	2302	4.3	51	12

Receiving	No.	Yds.	Avg.	LG	TD
Smith	62	778	12.5	31	5
Jones	45	838	18.6	t72	3
Green	44	703	16.0	t59	7
Awalt	33	360	10.9	28	0
Sikahema	23	245	10.7	37	0
Novacek	23	225	9.8	30	1
Ferrell	18	122	6.8	25	0
Holmes	13	271	20.8	t77	1
Jordan	6	20	3.3	8	0
Wolfley	5	38	7.6	22	0
Baker	2	18	9.0	9	0
McConkey	2	18	9.0	10	0
Mitchell	1	10	10.0	10	0
Usher	1	8	8.0	8	0
Reeves	1	5	5.0	5	0
Cardinals	279	3659	13.1	t77	17
Opponents	286	3794	13.3	t75	24

Interceptions	No.	Yds.	Avg.	LG	TD
McDonald	7	170	24.3	t53	1
Mack	4	15	3.8	9	0
Downs	1	37	37.0	37	0
Young	1	32	32.0	32	0
Zordich	1	16	16.0	t16	1
Wahler	1	5	5.0	5	0
Burton, Dall.-Phoe.	1	0	0.0	0	0
Carter	1	0	0.0	0	0
Cardinals	16	275	17.2	t53	2
Opponents	30	327	10.9	t59	3

Punting	No.	Yds.	Avg.	In 20	LG
Tupa	6	280	46.7	2	51
Camarillo	76	3298	43.4	21	58
Cardinals	82	3578	43.6	22	58
Opponents	76	3155	41.5	22	64

Punt Returns	No.	FC	Yds.	Avg.	LG	TD
Sikahema	37	13	433	11.7	53	0
Usher, S.D.-Phoe.	4	0	25	6.3	11	0
Usher, Phoe.	1	0	10	10.0	10	0
Jones	1	0	13	13.0	13	0
McConkey	1	0	13	13.0	13	0
5Cardinals	40	13	469	11.7	53	0
Opponents	46	18	371	8.1	20	0

Kickoff Returns	No.	Yds.	Avg.	LG	TD
Sikahema	43	874	20.3	52	0
Usher, S.D.-Phoe.	27	506	18.7	33	0
Usher, Phoe.	17	347	20.4	33	0
Baker	11	245	22.3	33	0
Jones	7	124	17.7	27	0
McConkey	2	40	20.0	21	0
Carr	1	15	15.0	15	0
Clark	1	0	0.0	0	0
Reeves	1	5	5.0	5	0
Cardinals	83	1650	19.9	52	0
Opponents	57	1193	20.9	49	0

Sacks	No.
Harvey	7.0
Galloway	5.5
Nunn	5.0
Saddler	3.5
Bell	2.0
Clasby	2.0
Hill	1.0
Mack	1.0
Wahler	1.0
Wilson	1.0
Zordich	1.0
Cardinals	30.0
Opponents	56.0

Pittsburgh

1989 TEAM RECORD

Preseason (2-2)

Date	Result		Opponent
8/12	L	14-21	Washington
8/19	W	24-21	at Cleveland
8/26	L	14-38	at Philadelphia
9/2	W	13-10	at Giants

Regular Season (9-7)

Date	Result		Opponent	Att.
9/10	L	0-51	Cleveland	57,928
9/17	L	10-41	at Cincinnati	53,885
9/24	W	27-14	Minnesota	50,744
10/1	W	23-3	at Detroit	43,804
10/8	L	16-26	Cincinnati	52,785
10/15	W	17-7	at Cleveland	78,840
10/22	L	0-27	at Houston	59,091
10/29	W	23-17	Kansas City	54,194
11/5	L	7-34	at Denver	74,739
11/12	L	0-20	Chicago	56,505
11/19	W	20-17	San Diego	44,203
11/26	W	34-14	at Miami	59,936
12/3	L	16-23	Houston	40,541
12/10	W	13-0	at Jets	41,037
12/17	W	28-10	New England	26,594
12/24	W	31-22	at Tampa Bay	29,690

Postseason (1-1)

Date	Result		Opponent	Att.
12/31	W	26-23	at Houston	58,306
1/7	L	23-24	at Denver	75,868

1989 TEAM STATISTICS

	Steelers	Opp.
Total First Downs	244	323
Rushing	106	112
Passing	117	177
Penalty	21	34
Third Down: Made/Att.	66/209	106/229
Fourth Down: Made/Att.	6/19	7/20
Total Net Yards	3996	5549
Avg. Per Game	249.8	346.8
Total Plays	955	1077
Avg. Per Play	4.2	5.2
Net Yards Rushing	1818	2008
Avg. Per Game	113.6	125.5
Total Rushes	500	498
Net Yards Passing	2178	3541
Avg. Per Game	136.1	221.3
Sacked/Yards Lost	51/484	31/180
Gross Yards	2662	3721
Att./Completions	404/210	548/290
Completion Pct.	52.0	52.9
Had Intercepted	13	21
Punts/Avg.	83/40.6	69/40.5
Net Punting Avg.	34.1	33.8
Penalties/Yards Lost	116/986	96/785
Fumbles/Ball Lost	32/18	40/21
Touchdowns	29	38
Rushing	17	16
Passing	10	17
Returns	2	5
Avg. Time of Possession	28:50	31:10

1989 INDIVIDUAL STATISTICS

Scoring	TD R	TD P	TD Rt	PAT	FG	Saf	TP
Anderson	0	0	0	28/28	21/30	0	91
Hoge	8	0	0	0/0	0/0	0	48
Lipps	1	5	0	0/0	0/0	0	36
Worley	5	0	0	0/0	0/0	0	30
Carter	1	3	0	0/0	0/0	0	24
Hill	0	1	0	0/0	0/0	0	6
Mularkey	0	1	0	0/0	0/0	0	6
M. Williams	1	0	0	0/0	0/0	0	6
Wallace	1	0	0	0/0	0/0	0	6
Woodruff	0	0	1	0/0	0/0	0	6
Woodson	0	0	1	0/0	0/0	0	6
Steelers	17	10	2	28/29	21/30	0	265
Opponents	16	17	5	37/38	19/27	2	326

Passing	Att.	Comp.	Yds.	Pct.	TD	Int.	Tkld.	Rate
Brister	342	187	2365	54.7	9	10	45/452	73.1
Blackledge	60	22	282	36.7	1	3	4/25	36.9
Carter	1	1	15	100.0	0	0	2/7	118.8
Strom	1	0	0	0.0	0	0	0/0	39.6
Steelers	404	210	2662	52.0	10	13	51/484	67.7
Opponents	584	290	3721	52.9	17	21	31/180	68.8

Rushing	Att.	Yds.	Avg.	LG	TD
Worley	195	770	3.9	38	5
Hoge	186	621	3.3	31	8
Lipps	13	180	13.8	t58	1
M. Williams	37	131	3.5	13	1
Stone	10	53	5.3	32	0
Brister	27	25	0.9	15	0
Blackledge	9	20	2.2	11	0
Carter	11	16	1.5	7	1
Wallace	5	10	2.0	5	1
Tyrrell	1	3	3.0	3	0
Strom	4	-3	-0.8	0	0
Newsome	2	-8	-4.0	0	0
Steelers	500	1818	3.6	t58	17
Opponents	498	2008	4.0	t65	16

Receiving	No.	Yds.	Avg.	LG	TD
Lipps	50	944	18.9	t79	5
Carter	38	267	7.0	t22	3
Hoge	34	271	8.0	22	0
Hill	28	455	16.3	53	1
Mularkey	22	326	14.8	34	1
Worley	15	113	7.5	19	0
Stone	7	92	13.1	16	0
W. Williams	6	48	8.0	16	0
Stock	4	74	18.5	27	0
Thompson	4	74	18.5	28	0
O'Shea	1	8	8.0	8	0
Brister	1	-10	-10.0	-10	0
Steelers	210	2662	12.7	t79	10
Opponents	290	3721	12.8	t66	17

Interceptions	No.	Yds.	Avg.	LG	TD
Woodruff	4	57	14.3	35	0
Everett	3	68	22.7	32	0
Lloyd	3	49	16.3	31	0
Woodson	3	39	13.0	39	0
Little	3	23	7.7	13	0
Griffin	1	15	15.0	15	0
Hall	1	6	6.0	6	0
Hinkle	1	4	4.0	4	0
D. Johnson	1	0	0.0	0	0
Lake	1	0	0.0	0	0
Steelers	21	261	12.4	39	0
Opponents	13	103	7.9	21	1

Punting	No.	Yds.	Avg.	In 20	LG
Newsome	82	3368	41.1	15	57
Steelers	83	3368	40.6	15	57
Opponents	69	2793	40.5	16	62

Punt Returns	No.	FC	Yds.	Avg.	LG	TD
Woodson	29	2	207	7.1	20	0
Hill	5	0	22	4.4	12	0
Lipps	4	0	27	6.8	9	0
J. Johnson	2	0	22	11.0	13	0
Steelers	40	2	278	7.0	20	0
Opponents	45	19	361	8.0	42	0

Kickoff Returns	No.	Yds.	Avg.	LG	TD
Woodson	36	982	27.3	t84	1
Stone	7	173	24.7	73	0
Thompson	4	41	10.3	15	0
J. Williams	4	31	7.8	22	0
J. Johnson	3	43	14.3	19	0
Griffin	1	21	21.0	21	0
Hinnant	1	13	13.0	13	0
Steelers	56	1304	23.3	t84	1
Opponents	53	1096	20.7	42	0

Sacks	No.
Lloyd	7.0
Willis	6.5
Johnson	4.5
G. Williams	3.0
J. Williams	3.0
Jones	2.0
Little	2.0
Lake	1.0
Nickerson	1.0
Olsavsky	1.0
Steelers	31.0
Opponents	51.0

San Diego

1989 TEAM RECORD

Preseason (2-2)

Date	Result		Opponent
8/13	L	3-20	Dallas
8/19	W	24-7	at Chicago
8/23	L	14-17	at San Francisco
9/1	W	21-20	Phoenix

Regular Season (6-10)

Date	Result		Opponent	Att.
9/10	L	14-40	at Raiders	40,237
9/17	L	27-34	Houston	42,013
9/24	W	21-6	Kansas City	40,128
10/1	W	24-13	at Phoenix	44,201
10/8	L	10-16	at Denver	75,222
10/15	L	16-17	Seattle	50,079
10/22	L	13-20	Giants	48,566
10/29	L	7-10	at Seattle	59,691
11/5	W	20-17	Philadelphia	47,019
11/12	W	14-12	Raiders	59,151
11/19	L	17-20	at Pittsburgh	44,203
11/26	L	6-10	at Indianapolis	58,822
12/3	L	17-20	Jets	38,954
12/10	L	21-26	at Washington	47,693
12/17	W	20-13	at Kansas City	40,623
12/24	W	19-16	Denver	50,524

1989 TEAM STATISTICS

	Chargers	Opp.
Total First Downs	267	295
Rushing	95	102
Passing	149	172
Penalty	23	21
Third Down: Made/Att.	81/223	81/227
Fourth Down: Made/Att.	6/18	8/13
Total Net Yards	4910	4764
Avg. Per Game	306.9	297.8
Total Plays	986	1040
Avg. Per Play	5.0	4.6
Net Yards Rushing	1873	1813
Avg. Per Game	117.1	113.3
Total Rushes	432	479
Net Yards Passing	3037	2951
Avg. Per Game	189.8	184.4
Sacked/Yards Lost	39/254	48/360
Gross Yards	3291	3311
Att./Completions	515/270	513/283
Completion Pct.	52.4	55.2
Had Intercepted	19	25
Punts/Avg.	84/39.5	79/38.6
Net Punting Avg	32.4	32.9
Penalties/Yards Lost	122/906	92/726
Fumbles/Ball Lost	24/17	21/13
Touchdowns	31	29
Rushing	13	13
Passing	15	15
Returns	3	1
Avg. Time of Possession	28:55	31:05

1989 INDIVIDUAL STATISTICS

Scoring	TD R	TD P	TD Rt	PAT	FG	Saf	TP
Bahr	0	0	0	29/30	17/25	0	80
A. Miller	0	10	1	0/0	0/0	0	66
Butts	9	0	0	0/0	0/0	0	54
Spencer	3	0	0	0/0	0/0	0	18
Bernstine	1	1	0	0/0	0/0	0	12
Cox	0	2	0	0/0	0/0	0	12
Glenn	0	0	1	0/0	0/0	0	6
Parker	0	1	0	0/0	0/0	0	6
Smith	0	0	1	0/0	0/0	0	6
Walker	0	1	0	0/0	0/0	0	6
Chargers	13	15	3	29/31	17/25	0	266
Opponents	13	15	1	27/29	29/41	1	290

Passing	Att.	Comp.	Yds.	Pct.	TD	Int.	Tkld.	Rate
McMahon	318	176	2132	55.3	10	10	28/167	73.5
Tolliver	185	89	1097	48.1	5	8	9/75	57.9
Archer	12	5	62	41.7	0	1	2/12	23.6
Chargers	515	270	3291	52.4	15	19	39/254	66.7
Opponents	513	283	3311	55.2	15	25	48/360	64.4

Rushing	Att.	Yds.	Avg.	LG	TD
Butts	170	683	4.0	t50	9
Spencer	134	521	3.9	15	3
Nelson, Minn.-S.D.	67	321	4.8	28	0
Nelson, S.D.	36	197	5.5	28	0
McMahon	29	141	4.9	15	0
Bernstine	15	137	9.1	t32	1
Brinson	17	64	3.8	9	0
Holland	6	46	7.7	24	0
A. Miller	4	21	5.3	24	0
Early	1	19	19.0	19	0
Floyd	8	15	1.9	5	0
Archer	2	14	7.0	14	0
Walker	1	9	9.0	9	0
Plummer	1	6	6.0	6	0
Caravello	1	0	0.0	0	0
Tolliver	7	0	0.0	3	0
Chargers	432	1873	4.3	t50	13
Opponents	479	1813	3.8	59	13

Receiving	No.	Yds.	Avg.	LG	TD
A. Miller	75	1252	16.7	t69	10
Nelson, Minn.-S.D.	38	380	10.0	49	0
Nelson, S.D.	31	328	10.6	49	0
Holland	26	336	12.9	37	0
Walker	24	395	16.5	49	1
Cox	22	200	9.1	24	2
Bernstine	21	222	10.6	36	1
Spencer	18	112	6.2	23	0
Brinson	12	71	5.9	11	0
Early	11	126	11.5	21	0
Caravello	10	95	9.5	37	0
McEwen	7	99	14.1	29	0
Butts	7	21	3.0	8	0
Allen	2	19	9.5	11	0
McConkey, Phoe.-S.D.	2	18	9.0	10	0
Parker	2	5	2.5	4	1
Floyd	1	6	6.0	6	0
McMahon	1	4	4.0	4	0
Chargers	270	3291	12.2	t69	15
Opponents	283	3311	11.7	t59	15

Interceptions	No.	Yds.	Avg.	LG	TD
Byrd	7	38	5.4	22	0
Glenn	4	52	13.0	31	0
Bennett	3	4	1.3	4	0
Patterson	2	44	22.0	34	0
Lyles	2	28	14.0	28	0
Smith	1	9	9.0	9	0
Figaro	1	2	2.0	2	0
Bayless	1	0	0.0	0	0
Chargers	25	224	9.0	34	0
Opponents	19	179	9.4	40	0

Punting	No.	Yds.	Avg.	In 20	Lg
Ilesic	76	3049	40.1	11	64
Colbert	8	266	33.3	0	46
Chargers	84	3315	39.5	11	64
Opponents	79	3050	38.6	21	63

Punt Returns	No.	FC	Yds.	Avg.	LG	TD
McConkey, Phoe.-S.D.	15	15	124	8.3	20	0
McConkey, S.D.	14	15	111	7.0	20	0
Brinson	11	0	112	10.2	52	0
Walker	6	4	31	5.2	13	0
Usher	3	0	15	5.0	11	0
Allen	2	0	3	1.5	3	0
Figaro	1	0	0	0.0	0	0
Lyles	1	0	0	0.0	0	0
Byrd	0	1	0	—	0	0
Chargers	38	20	272	7.2	52	0
Opponents	43	10	451	10.5	38	0

Kickoff Returns	No.	Yds.	Avg.	LG	TD
A. Miller	21	533	25.4	t91	1
Holland	29	510	17.6	34	0
Nelson, Minn.-S.D.	14	317	22.6	32	0
Usher	10	159	15.9	26	0
Floyd	3	12	4.0	12	0
McConkey, Phoe.-S.D.	2	40	20.0	21	0
Figaro	1	21	21.0	21	0
Chargers	64	1235	19.3	t91	1
Opponents	57	1249	21.9	t84	1

Sacks	No.
Williams	14.0
O'Neal	12.5
Grossman	10.0
Hinkle	2.5
L. Miller	2.5
Smith	2.5
Bayless	1.0
Glenn	1.0
Lyles	1.0
Phillips	1.0
Chargers	48.0
Opponents	39.0

San Francisco

1989 TEAM RECORD

Preseason (3-2)

Date	Result		Opponent
8/5	L	13-16	vs. Rams in Tokyo
8/12	W	37-7	at Raiders
8/19	W	35-17	Denver
8/23	W	17-14	San Diego
9/1	L	17-28	at Seattle

Regular Season (14-2)

Date	Result		Opponent	Att.
9/10	W	30-24	at Indianapolis	60,111
9/17	W	20-16	at Tampa Bay	64,087
9/24	W	38-28	at Philadelphia	66,042
10/1	L	12-13	Rams	64,250
10/8	W	24-20	at New Orleans	60,488
10/15	W	31-14	at Dallas	61,077
10/22	W	37 20	New England	70,000
10/29	W	23-10	at Jets	62,805
11/6	W	31-13	New Orleans	60,667
11/12	W	45-3	Atlanta	59,914
11/19	L	17-21	Green Bay	62,219
11/27	W	34-24	Giants	63,461
12/3	W	23-10	at Atlanta	43,128
12/11	W	30-27	at Rams	67,959
12/17	W	21-10	Buffalo	60,927
12/24	W	26-0	Chicago	60,207

Postseason (3-0)

Date	Result		Opponent	Att.
1/6	W	41-13	Minnesota	64,585
1/14	W	30-3	Rams	64,769
1/28	W	55-10	Denver	72,919

1989 TEAM STATISTICS

	49ers	Opp.
Total First Downs	350	283
Rushing	124	76
Passing	209	178
Penalty	17	29
Third Down: Made/Att.	80/189	76/210
Fourth Down: Made/Att.	6/9	9/19
Total Net Yards	6268	4618
Avg. Per Game	391.8	288.6
Total Plays	1021	979
Avg. Per Play	6.1	4.7
Net Yards Rushing	1966	1383
Avg. Per Game	122.9	86.4
Total Rushes	493	372
Net Yards Passing	4302	3235
Avg. Per Game	268.9	202.2
Sacked/Yards Lost	45/282	43/333
Gross Yards	4584	3568
Att./Completions	483/339	564/316
Completion Pct.	70.2	56.0
Had Intercepted	11	21
Punts/Avg.	56/39.8	74/38.9
Net Punting Avg.	31.2	32.0
Penalties/Yards Lost	110/922	75/581
Fumbles/Ball Lost	32/14	34/16
Touchdowns	51	26
Rushing	14	9
Passing	35	15
Returns	2	2
Avg. Time of Possession	31:43	28:17

1989 INDIVIDUAL STATISTICS

Scoring	TD R	TD P	TD Rt	PAT	FG	Saf	TP
Cofer	0	0	0	49/51	29/36	0	136
Rice	0	17	0	0/0	0/0	0	102
Taylor	0	10	0	0/0	0/0	0	60
Craig	6	1	0	0/0	0/0	0	42
Jones	0	4	0	0/0	0/0	0	24
Montana	3	0	0	0/0	0/0	0	18
Rathman	1	1	0	0/0	0/0	0	12
Young	2	0	0	0/0	0/0	0	12
Flagler	1	0	0	0/0	0/0	0	6
Haley	0	0	1	0/0	0/0	0	6
Henderson	1	0	0	0/0	0/0	0	6
Jackson	0	0	1	0/0	0/0	0	6
Walls	0	1	0	0/0	0/0	0	6
Wilson	0	1	0	0/0	0/0	0	6
49ers	14	35	2	49/51	29/36	0	442
Opponents	9	15	2	26/26	23/31	1	253

Passing	Att.	Comp.	Yds.	Pct.	TD	Int.	Tkld.	Rate
Montana	386	271	3521	70.2	26	8	33/198	112.4
Young	92	64	1001	69.6	8	3	12/84	120.8
Bono	5	4	62	80.0	1	0	0/0	157.9
49ers	483	339	4584	70.2	35	11	45/282	114.8
Opponents	564	316	3568	56.0	15	21	43/333	68.5

Rushing	Att.	Yds.	Avg.	LG	TD
Craig	271	1054	3.9	27	6
Rathman	79	305	3.9	13	1
Montana	49	227	4.6	19	3
Flagler	33	129	3.9	t29	1
Young	38	126	3.3	22	2
Sydney	9	56	6.2	18	0
Rice	5	33	6.6	17	0
Henderson	7	30	4.3	t11	1
Taylor	1	6	6.0	6	0
Helton	1	0	0.0	0	0
49ers	493	1966	4.0	t29	14
Opponents	372	1383	3.7	23	9

Receiving	No.	Yds.	Avg.	LG	TD
Rice	82	1483	18.1	t68	17
Rathman	73	616	8.4	36	1
Taylor	60	1077	18.0	t95	10
Craig	49	473	9.7	44	1
Jones	40	500	12.5	t36	4
Wilson	9	103	11.4	19	1
Sydney	9	71	7.9	13	0
Flagler	6	51	8.5	30	0
Walls	4	16	4.0	9	1
Henderson	3	130	43.3	78	0
Williams	3	38	12.7	17	0
Greer	1	26	26.0	26	0
49ers	339	4584	13.5	t95	35
Opponents	316	3568	11.3	t65	15

Interceptions	No.	Yds.	Avg.	LG	TD
Lott	5	34	6.8	28	0
Brooks	3	31	10.3	19	0
Wright	2	37	18.5	23	0
Jackson	2	35	17.5	19	0
Griffin	2	6	3.0	3	0
Turner	1	42	42.0	42	0
Holmoe	1	23	23.0	23	0
McKyer	1	18	18.0	18	0
Romanowski	1	13	13.0	13	0
Pollard	1	12	12.0	12	0
Millen	1	10	10.0	10	0
DeLong	1	1	1.0	1	0
49ers	21	262	12.5	42	0
Opponents	11	140	12.7	35	0

Punting	No.	Yds.	Avg.	In 20	LG
Helton	55	2226	40.5	13	56
49ers	56	2226	39.8	13	56
Opponents	74	2875	38.9	18	57

Punt Returns	No.	FC	Yds.	Avg.	LG	TD
Taylor	36	20	417	11.6	37	0
Greer	1	0	3	3.0	3	0
Griffin	1	0	9	9.0	9	0
Romanowski	1	0	0	0.0	0	0
49ers	39	20	429	11.0	37	0
Opponents	35	4	361	10.3	22	0

Kickoff Returns	No.	Yds.	Avg.	LG	TD
Flagler	32	643	20.1	41	0
Tillman	10	206	20.6	60	0
Sydney	3	16	5.3	16	0
Henderson	2	21	10.5	13	0
Taylor	2	51	25.5	27	0
Greer	1	17	17.0	17	0
Jackson	1	0	0.0	0	0
49ers	51	954	18.7	60	0
Opponents	76	1435	18.9	37	0

Sacks	No.
Haley	10.5
Holt	10.5
Fagan	7.0
Stubbs	4.5
Roberts	3.5
Kugler	3.0
Brooks	1.0
Romanowski	1.0
Walter	1.0
49ers	43.0
Opponents	45.0

Seattle

1989 TEAM RECORD

Preseason (3-1)

Date	Result		Opponent
8/11	W	16-10(OT)	at Phoenix
8/19	L	12-17	vs. New England at St. Louis
8/25	W	13-7	Detroit
9/1	W	28-17	San Francisco

Regular Season (7-9)

Date	Result		Opponent	Att.
9/10	L	7-31	at Philadelphia	64,287
9/17	L	24-34	Phoenix	60,444
9/24	W	24-3	at New England	48,025
10/1	W	24-20	at Raiders	44,319
10/8	L	16-20	Kansas City	60,715
10/15	W	17-16	at San Diego	50,079
10/22	L	21-24(OT)	Denver	62,353
10/29	W	10-7	San Diego	59,691
11/5	L	10-20	at Kansas City	54,589
11/12	L	7-17	Cleveland	58,978
11/19	L	3-15	at Giants	75,014
11/26	L	14-41	at Denver	75,117
12/4	W	17-16	Buffalo	57,682
12/10	W	24-17	at Cincinnati	54,744
10/17	W	23-17	Raiders	61,076
10/23	L	0-29	Washington	60,294

1989 TEAM STATISTICS

	Seahawks	Opp.
Total First Downs	290	293
Rushing	86	119
Passing	180	158
Penalty	24	16
Third Down: Made/Att.	85/211	89/213
Fourth Down: Made/Att.	8/17	5/16
Total Net Yards	4596	5215
Avg. Per Game	287.3	325.9
Total Plays	1010	997
Avg. Per Play	4.6	5.2
Net Yards Rushing	1392	2118
Avg. Per Game	87.0	132.4
Total Rushes	405	520
Net Yards Passing	3204	3097
Avg. Per Game	200.3	193.6
Sacked/Yards Lost	46/379	32/235
Gross Yards	3583	3332
Att. Completions	559/316	445/252
Completion Pct.	56.5	56.6
Had Intercepted	23	9
Punts/Avg.	76/39.4	74/39.2
Net Punting Avg.	32.9	33.9
Penalties/Yards Lost	79/738	118/809
Fumbles/Ball Lost	43/14	26/13
Touchdowns	28	37
Rushing	5	11
Passing	21	23
Returns	2	3
Avg. Time of Possession	29:20	30:40

1989 INDIVIDUAL STATISTICS

Scoring	TD R	TD P	TD Rt	PAT	FG	Saf	TP
N. Johnson	0	0	0	27/27	15/25	0	72
Williams	1	6	0	0/0	0/0	0	42
Blades	0	5	0	0/0	0/0	0	30
Skansi	0	5	0	0/0	0/0	0	30
Warner	3	1	0	0/0	0/0	0	24
Largent	0	3	0	1/1	0/0	0	19
Clark	0	1	0	0/0	0/0	0	6
Fenner	1	0	0	0/0	0/0	0	6
Glasgow	0	0	1	0/0	0/0	0	6
Jefferson	0	0	1	0/0	0/0	0	6
Seahawks	5	21	2	28/28	15/25	0	241
Opponents	11	23	3	35/37	22/32	2	327

Passing	Att.	Comp.	Yds.	Pct.	TD	Int.	Tkld.	Rate
Krieg	499	286	3309	57.3	21	20	37/289	74.8
Stouffer	59	29	270	49.2	0	3	9/90	40.9
Rodriguez	1	1	4	100.0	0	0	0/0	83.3
Seahawks	559	316	3583	56.5	21	23	46/379	71.3
Opponents	445	252	3332	56.6	23	9	32/235	89.3

Rushing	Att.	Yds.	Avg.	LG	TD
Warner	194	631	3.3	34	3
Williams	146	499	3.4	21	1
Krieg	40	160	4.0	18	0
Fenner	11	41	3.7	9	1
Harmon	1	24	24.0	24	0
Harris	8	23	2.9	8	0
Stouffer	2	11	5.5	9	0
Blades	1	3	3.0	3	0
Kemp	1	0	0.0	0	0
Rodriguez	1	0	0.0	0	0
Seahawks	405	1392	3.4	34	5
Opponents	520	2118	4.1	38	11

Receiving	No.	Yds.	Avg.	LG	TD
Blades	77	1063	13.8	t60	5
Williams	76	657	8.6	t51	6
Skansi	39	488	12.5	26	5
Largent	28	403	14.4	33	3
Clark	25	260	10.4	28	1
Warner	23	153	6.7	24	1
Tyler	14	148	10.6	27	0
McNeal	9	147	16.3	48	0
Chadwick, Det.-Sea.	9	104	11.6	19	0
Chadwick, Sea.	8	95	11.9	19	0
Kane	7	94	13.4	20	0
Harris	3	26	8.7	11	0
Fenner	3	23	7.7	9	0
Buoyer	1	9	9.0	9	0
Jones	1	8	8.0	8	0
Feasel	1	5	5.0	5	0
Glasgow	1	4	4.0	4	0
Seahawks	316	3583	11.3	t60	21
Opponents	252	3332	13.2	69	23

Interceptions	No.	Yds.	Avg.	LG	TD
Robinson	5	24	4.8	20	0
Harper	2	15	7.5	15	0
J. Johnson	1	18	18.0	18	0
Comeaux	1	0	0.0	0	0
Seahawks	9	57	6.3	20	0
Opponents	23	248	10.8	t30	2

Punting	No.	Yds.	Avg.	In 20	LG
Rodriguez	75	2995	39.9	17	59
Seahawks	76	2995	39.4	17	59
Opponents	74	2902	39.2	21	60

Punt Returns	No.	FC	Yds.	Avg.	LG	TD
Hollis	18	7	164	9.1	21	0
Jefferson	12	10	87	7.3	19	0
Seahawks	30	17	251	8.4	21	0
Opponents	41	12	334	8.1	49	0

Kickoff Returns	No.	Yds.	Avg.	LG	TD
Jefferson	22	511	23.2	t97	1
Harris	18	334	18.6	25	0
Hollis	15	247	16.5	30	0
Harmon	6	84	14.0	19	0
Clark	1	31	31.0	31	0
Comeaux	1	9	9.0	9	0
McNeal	1	17	17.0	17	0
Woods	1	13	13.0	13	0
Seahawks	65	1246	19.2	t97	1
Opponents	44	814	18.5	37	0

Sacks	No.
Porter	10.5
Nash	8.0
Bryant	3.5
Green	3.0
Woods	3.0
Hart	2.0
Hunter	1.0
Mitz	1.0
Seahawks	32.0
Opponents	46.0

Tampa Bay

1989 TEAM RECORD

Preseason (3-1)

Date	Result		Opponent
8/12	W	41-23	Houston
8/19	W	27-0	Atlanta
8/26	L	0-30	at Indianapolis
9/2	W	27-10	at Cleveland

Regular Season (5-11)

Date	Result		Opponent	Att.
9/10	W	23-21	at Green Bay	55,650
9/17	L	16-20	San Francisco	64,087
9/24	W	20-10	New Orleans	44,053
10/1	L	3-17	at Minnesota	54,817
10/8	W	42-35	Chicago	72,077
10/15	L	16-17	Detroit	46,225
10/22	L	28-32	at Washington	53,562
10/29	L	23-56	at Cincinnati	57,225
11/5	L	31-42	Cleveland	69,162
11/12	L	10-24	Minnesota	56,271
11/19	W	32-31	at Chicago	63,826
11/26	W	14-13	at Phoenix	33,297
12/3	L	16-17	Green Bay	58,120
12/10	L	17-20	at Houston	54,532
12/17	L	7-33	at Detroit	40,362
12/24	L	22-31	Pittsburgh	29,690

1989 TEAM STATISTICS

	Buccaneers	Opp.
Total First Downs	288	317
Rushing	84	115
Passing	174	170
Penalty	30	32
Third Down: Made/Att.	95/230	87/208
Fourth Down: Made/Att.	7/13	10/17
Total Net Yards	4842	5460
Avg. Per Game	302.6	341.3
Total Plays	1025	1027
Avg. Per Play	4.7	5.3
Net Yards Rushing	1507	2023
Avg. Per Game	94.2	126.4
Total Rushes	412	479
Net Yards Passing	3335	3437
Avg. Per Game	208.4	214.8
Sacked/Yards Lost	43/331	33/222
Gross Yards	3666	3659
Att./Completions	570/302	515/301
Completion Pct.	53.0	58.4
Had Intercepted	28	21
Punts/Avg.	86/38.5	69/40.3
Net Punting Avg.	32.1	31.4
Penalties/Yards Lost	104/881	109/869
Fumbles/Ball Lost	21/9	30/18
Touchdowns	36	51
Rushing	10	18
Passing	23	29
Returns	3	4
Avg. Time of Possession	29:55	30:05

1989 INDIVIDUAL STATISTICS

Scoring	TD R	TD P	TD Rt	PAT	FG	Saf	TP
Igwebuike	0	0	0	33/35	22/28	0	99
Carrier	0	9	0	0/0	0/0	0	54
Tate	8	1	0	0/0	0/0	0	54
Hill	0	5	0	0/0	0/0	0	30
Wilder	0	3	0	0/0	0/0	0	18
Hall	0	2	0	0/0	0/0	0	12
Howard	1	1	0	0/0	0/0	0	12
Reynolds	0	0	2	0/0	0/0	0	12
Davis	0	0	1	0/0	0/0	0	6
Drewrey	0	1	0	0/0	0/0	0	6
W. Harris	0	1	0	0/0	0/0	0	6
Stamps	1	0	0	0/0	0/0	0	6
Cocroft	0	0	0	0/0	0/0	1	2
S. Smith	0	0	0	0/0	0/0	1	2
Mohr	0	0	0	1(run)	0/0	0	1
Buccaneers	10	23	3	34/36	22/28	1	320
Opponents	18	29	4	51/51	20/24	1	419

Passing	Att.	Comp.	Yds.	Pct.	TD	Int.	Tkld.	Rate
Testaverde	480	258	3133	53.8	20	22	38/294	68.9
Ferguson	90	44	533	48.9	3	6	5/37	50.8
Buccaneers	570	302	3666	53.0	23	28	43/331	66.0
Opponents	515	301	3659	58.4	29	21	33/222	82.2

Rushing	Att.	Yds.	Avg.	LG	TD
Tate	167	589	3.5	48	8
Howard	108	357	3.3	15	1
Wilder	70	244	3.5	14	0
Stamps	29	141	4.9	t21	1
Testaverde	25	139	5.6	16	0
D. Smith	7	37	5.3	17	0
Ferguson	4	6	1.5	7	0
Peebles	2	-6	-3.0	1	0
Buccaneers	412	1507	3.7	48	10
Opponents	479	2023	4.2	t59	18

Receiving	No.	Yds.	Avg.	LG	TD
Carrier	86	1422	16.5	t78	9
Hill	50	673	13.5	53	5
Wilder	36	335	9.3	27	3
Hall	30	331	11.0	32	2
Howard	30	188	6.3	18	1
Stamps	15	82	5.5	21	0
Drewrey	14	157	11.2	18	1
Peebles	11	180	16.4	32	0
W. Harris	11	102	9.3	21	1
Tate	11	75	6.8	19	1
D. Smith	7	110	15.7	44	0
Mitchell	1	11	11.0	11	0
Buccaneers	302	3666	12.1	t78	23
Opponents	301	3659	12.2	t79	29

Interceptions	No.	Yds.	Avg.	LG	TD
Hamilton	6	70	11.7	30	0
Robinson	6	44	7.3	16	0
Reynolds	5	87	17.4	t68	1
O. Harris	1	19	19.0	19	0
Davis	1	13	13.0	t13	1
Futrell	1	1	1.0	1	0
Elder	1	0	0.0	0	0
Buccaneers	21	234	11.1	t68	2
Opponents	28	240	8.6	39	2

Punting	No.	Yds.	Avg.	In 20	LG
Mohr	84	3311	39.4	10	58
Buccaneers	86	3311	38.5	10	58
Opponents	69	2781	40.3	14	60

Punt Returns	No.	FC	Yds.	Avg.	LG	TD
Drewrey	20	2	220	11.0	55	0
Futrell	12	2	76	6.3	15	0
Buccaneers	32	4	296	9.3	55	0
Opponents	54	12	492	9.1	65	0

Kickoff Returns	No.	Yds.	Avg.	LG	TD
Elder	40	685	17.1	30	0
Stamps	9	145	16.1	36	0
Howard	5	82	16.4	19	0
Futrell	4	58	14.5	22	0
Wilder	2	42	21.0	23	0
Drewrey	1	26	26.0	26	0
Pillow	1	17	17.0	17	0
Buccaneers	62	1055	17.0	36	0
Opponents	55	1143	20.8	72	0

Sacks	No.
Murphy	6.0
Moss	5.5
Goff	4.0
Davis	3.0
Jarvis	3.0
Robinson	2.5
Thomas	2.0
Weston	2.0
Cannon	1.0
Lee	1.0
Randle	1.0
S. Smith	1.0
Seals	1.0
Buccaneers	33.0
Opponents	43.0

Washington

1989 TEAM RECORD

Preseason (4-1)

Date	Result		Opponent
8/5	W	31-6	vs. Buffalo in Canton
8/12	W	21-14	at Pittsburgh
8/21	L	13-24	at Minnesota
8/25	W	35-21	Miami
9/1	W	26-21	at New Orleans

Regular Season (10-6)

Date	Result		Opponent	Att.
9/11	L	24-27	Giants	54,160
9/17	L	37-42	Philadelphia	53,493
9/24	W	30-7	at Dallas	63,200
10/1	W	16-14	at New Orleans	53,335
10/8	W	30-28	Phoenix	53,335
10/15	L	17-20	at Giants	76,245
10/22	W	32-28	Tampa Bay	53,862
10/29	L	24-37	at Raiders	52,781
11/5	L	3-13	Dallas	53,187
11/12	W	10-3	at Philadelphia	65,443
11/20	L	10-14	Denver	52,975
11/26	W	38-14	Chicago	50,044
12/3	W	29-10	at Phoenix	38,870
12/10	W	26-21	San Diego	47,693
12/17	W	31-30	at Atlanta	37,501
12/23	W	29-0	at Seattle	60,294

1989 TEAM STATISTICS

	Redskins	Opp.
Total First Downs	338	274
Rushing	101	72
Passing	217	177
Penalty	20	25
Third Down: Made/Att.	105/240	77/202
Fourth Down: Made/Att.	10/19	4/11
Total Net Yards	6253	4915
Avg. Per Game	390.8	307.2
Total Plays	1116	954
Avg. Per Play	5.6	5.2
Net Yards Rushing	1904	1344
Avg. Per Game	119.0	84.0
Total Rushes	514	384
Net Yards Passing	4349	3571
Avg. Per Game	271.8	223.2
Sacked/Yards Lost	21/127	40/304
Gross Yards	4476	3875
Att./Completions	581/337	530/277
Completion Pct.	58.0	52.3
Had Intercepted	17	27
Punts/Avg.	63/42.3	76/40.1
Net Punting Avg.	33.3	34.5
Penalties/Yards Lost	105/881	98/796
Fumbles/Ball Lost	32/20	24/15
Touchdowns	42	38
Rushing	14	9
Passing	24	25
Returns	4	4
Avg. Time of Possession	32:58	27:02

1989 INDIVIDUAL STATISTICS

Scoring	TD R	TD P	TD Rt	PAT	FG	Saf	TP
Lohmiller	0	0	0	41/41	29/40	0	128
Byner	7	2	0	0/0	0/0	0	54
Clark	0	9	0	0/0	0/0	0	54
Monk	0	8	0	0/0	0/0	0	48
Riggs	4	0	0	0/0	0/0	0	24
Sanders	0	4	0	0/0	0/0	0	24
Morris	2	0	0	0/0	0/0	0	12
Coleman	0	0	1	0/0	0/0	0	6
Dupard, N.E.-Wash.	1	0	0	0/0	0/0	0	6
Howard	0	0	1	0/0	0/0	0	6
A. Johnson	0	0	1	0/0	0/0	0	6
Rypien	1	0	0	0/0	0/0	0	6
Walton	0	0	1	0/0	0/0	0	6
Warren	0	1	0	0/0	0/0	0	6
Manley	0	0	0	0/0	0/0	1	2
Stokes	0	0	0	0/0	0/0	1	2
Redskins	14	24	4	41/42	29/40	3	386
Opponents	9	25	4	38/38	14/23	0	308

Passing	Att.	Comp.	Yds.	Pct.	TD	Int.	Tkld.	Rate
Rypien	476	280	3768	58.8	22	13	16/108	88.1
Williams	93	51	585	54.8	1	3	2/10	64.1
Humphries	10	5	91	50.0	1	1	3/9	75.4
Byner	1	0	0	0.0	0	0	0/0	39.6
Sanders	1	1	32	100.0	0	0	0/0	118.8
Redskins	581	337	4476	58.0	24	17	21/127	84.1
Opponents	530	277	3875	52.3	25	27	40/304	70.6

Rushing	Att.	Yds.	Avg.	LG	TD
Riggs	201	834	4.1	58	4
Byner	134	580	4.3	24	7
Morris	124	336	2.7	t12	2
Dupard, N.E.-Wash.	37	111	3.0	19	1
Dupard, Wash.	12	48	4.0	19	0
Rypien	26	56	2.2	15	1
Clark	2	19	9.5	11	0
Sanders	4	19	4.8	13	0
Humphries	5	10	2.0	9	0
Monk	3	8	2.7	14	0
Coleman	1	-1	-1.0	-1	0
Reaves	1	-1	-1.0	-1	0
Williams	1	-4	-4.0	-4	0
Redskins	514	1904	3.7	58	14
Opponents	384	1344	3.5	t73	9

Receiving	No.	Yds.	Avg.	LG	TD
Monk	86	1186	13.8	t60	8
Sanders	80	1138	14.2	68	4
Clark	79	1229	15.6	t80	9
Byner	54	458	8.5	27	2
Warren	15	167	11.1	25	1
Morris	8	65	8.1	17	0
Riggs	7	67	9.6	13	0
Dupard, N.E.-Wash.	6	70	11.7	45	0
J. Johnson	4	84	21.0	39	0
Orr	3	80	26.7	48	0
Tice	1	2	2.0	2	0
Redskins	337	4476	13.3	t80	24
Opponents	277	3875	14.0	t72	25

Interceptions	No.	Yds.	Avg.	LG	TD
A. Johnson	4	94	23.5	t59	1
Walton	4	58	14.5	t29	1
B. Davis	4	40	10.0	15	0
Bowles	3	25	8.3	25	0
Wilburn	3	13	4.3	13	0
Coleman	2	24	12.0	t24	1
Grant	2	0	0.0	0	0
Green	2	0	0.0	0	0
Marshall	1	18	18.0	18	0
W. Davis	1	11	11.0	11	0
Gouveia	1	1	1.0	1	0
Redskins	27	284	10.5	t59	3
Opponents	17	229	13.5	t45	1

Punting	No.	Yds.	Avg.	In 20	LG
Mojsiejenko	62	2663	43.0	21	74
Redskins	63	2663	42.3	21	74
Opponents	76	3047	40.1	22	59

Punt Returns	No.	FC	Yds.	Avg.	LG	TD
Howard	21	18	200	9.5	38	0
Sanders	2	2	12	6.0	7	0
B. Davis	1	0	3	3.0	3	0
Green	1	0	11	11.0	11	0
Mayhew	1	0	0	0.0	0	0
Redskins	26	20	226	8.7	38	0
Opponents	34	5	383	11.3	53	0

Kickoff Returns	No.	Yds.	Avg.	LG	TD
Howard	21	522	24.9	t99	1
A. Johnson	24	504	21.0	38	0
Sanders	9	134	14.9	29	0
Branch	1	6	6.0	6	0
Gouveia	1	0	0.0	0	0
Mandeville	1	10	10.0	10	0
Orr	1	0	0.0	0	0
Redskins	58	1176	20.3	t99	1
Opponents	74	1532	20.7	t96	1

Sacks	No.
Mann	10.0
Manley	9.0
Coleman	4.0
Marshall	4.0
Caldwell	3.5
Grant	3.5
Stokes	3.0
Koch	2.0
Bowles	1.0
Redskins	40.0
Opponents	21.0

Awards

AP:

MVP	Joe Montana, S.F.
Off. Player of the Year	Joe Montana, S.F.
Def. Player of the Year	Keith Millard, Minn.
Off. Rookie of the Year	Barry Sanders, Det.
Def. Rookie of the Year	Derrick Thomas, K.C.
Coach of the Year	Lindy Infante, G.B.

UPI:

AFC Off. Player of the Year	Christian Okoye, K.C.
NFC Off. Player of the Year	Joe Montana, S.F.
AFC Def. Player of the Year	Michael Dean Perry, Cle.
NFC Def. Player of the Year	Keith Millard, Minn.
AFC Coach of the Year	Dan Reeves, Den.
NFC Coach of the Year	Lindy Infante, G.B.

Sporting News:

Player of the Year	Joe Montana, S.F.
Rookie of the Year	Barry Sanders, Det.
Coach of the Year	Lindy Infante, G.B.

Sport Magazine:

Super Bowl XXIV MVP	Joe Montana, S.F.

Maxwell Club:

Player of the Year (Bert Bell Trophy)	Joe Montana, S.F.

AP All-Pro Team

Offense:
WR: Jerry Rice, S.F.; Sterling Sharpe, G.B.
TE: Keith Jackson, Phi.
T: Anthony Munoz, Cin.; Jim Lachey, Wash.
G: Tom Newberry, Rams; Bruce Matthews, Hou.
C: Jay Hilgenberg, Chi.
QB: Joe Montana, S.F.
RB: Christian Okoye, K.C.; Barry Sanders, Det.
Defense:
DE: Chris Doleman, Minn.; Reggie White, Phi.
NT: Michael Dean Perry, Cle.
DT: Keith Millard, Minn.
OLB: Tim Harris, G.B.; Lawrence Taylor, Giants
ILB: Mike Singletary, Chi.; Karl Mecklenburg, Den.
CB: Eric Allen, Phi.; Albert Lewis, K.C.
S: David Fulcher, Cin.; Ronnie Lott, S.F.
Specialists:
P: Sean Landeta, Giants
K: Mike Cofer, S.F.
KR: Rod Woodson, Pitt.

Leaders

TOP TEN LISTS

Scorers/TDs

	TD	Rush	Rec.	Ret.	Pts.
Hilliard, N.O.	18	13	5	0	108
Rice, S.F.	17	0	17	0	102
Anderson, Chi.	15	11	4	0	90
Bell, Rams	15	15	0	0	90
Anderson, Giants	14	14	0	0	84
Sanders, Det.	14	14	0	0	84
Sharpe, G.B.	13	0	12	1	78
Okoye, K.C.	12	12	0	0	72
Thomas, Buff.	12	6	6	0	72
Carter, Phi.	11	0	11	0	66
Miller, S.D.	11	0	10	1	66

Scorers/Kicking

	PAT	FG	Lg.	Pts.
Cofer, S.F.	49/51	29/36	47	136
Lohmiller, Wash.	41/41	29/40	48	128
Karlis, Minn.	27/28	31/39	51	120
Lansford, Rams	51/51	23/30	48	120
Treadwell, Den.	39/40	27/33	46	120
Norwood, Buff.	46/47	23/30	48	115
Zendejas, Hou.	40/40	25/37	52	115
Jacke, G.B.	42/42	22/28	52	108
Lowery, K.C.	34/35	24/33	50	106
Andersen, N.O.	44/45	20/29	49	104

Rushers

	Att.	Yds.	Avg.	Lg.	TD
Okoye, K.C.	370	1480	4.0	59	12
Sanders, Det.	280	1470	5.3	34	14
Dickerson, Ind.	314	1311	4.2	21	7
Anderson, Chi.	274	1275	4.7	73	11
Hilliard, N.O.	344	1262	3.7	40	13
Thomas, Buff.	298	1244	4.2	28	6
Brooks, Cin.	221	1239	5.6	65	7
Humphrey, Den.	294	1151	3.9	40	7
Bell, Rams	272	1137	4.2	47	15
Craig, S.F.	271	1054	3.9	27	6

Receivers/Recs.

	No.	Yds.	Avg.	Lg.	TD
Sharpe, G.B.	90	1423	15.8	79	12
Reed, Buff.	88	1312	14.9	78	9
Carrier, T.B.	86	1422	16.5	78	9
Monk, Wash.	86	1186	13.8	60	8
Rice, S.F.	82	1483	18.1	68	17
Sanders, Wash.	80	1138	14.2	68	4
Clark, Wash.	79	1229	15.6	80	9
Blades, Sea.	77	1063	13.8	60	5
Johnson, Den.	76	1095	14.4	69	7
Williams, Sea.	76	657	8.6	51	6

Receivers/Ydg.

	Yds.	No.	Avg.	Lg.	TD
Rice, S.F.	1483	82	18.1	68	17
Sharpe, G.B.	1423	90	15.8	79	12
Carrier, T.B.	1422	86	16.5	78	9
Ellard, Rams	1382	70	19.7	53	8
Reed, Buff.	1312	88	14.9	78	9
Miller, S.D.	1252	75	16.7	69	10
Slaughter, Cle.	1236	65	19.0	97	6
Clark, Wash.	1229	79	15.6	80	9
McGee, Cin.	1211	65	18.6	74	8
Monk, Wash.	1186	86	13.8	60	8

Punt Returners

	No.	Yds.	Avg.	Lg.	TD
Stanley, Det.	36	496	13.8	74	0
Verdin, Ind.	23	296	12.9	49	1
Meggett, Giants	46	582	12.7	76	1
Sikahema, Phoe.	37	433	11.7	53	0
Taylor, S.F.	36	417	11.6	37	0
Drewrey, T.B.	20	220	11.0	55	0
Sanders, Atl.	28	307	11.0	68	1
McNeil, Cle.	49	496	10.1	49	0
Lewis, Minn.	44	446	10.1	65	0
Howard, Wash.	21	200	9.5	38	0

Interceptions

	No.	Yds.	Lg.	TD
Wright, Cle.	9	91	27	1
Fulcher, Cin.	8	87	22	0
Allen, Phi.	8	38	18	0
Taylor, Ind.	7	225	80	1
McDonald, Phoe.	7	170	53	1
Byrd, S.D.	7	38	22	0

10 players tied with 6 interceptions each

Kickoff Returners

	No.	Yds.	Avg.	Lg.	TD
Woodson, Pitt.	36	982	27.3	84	1
Gray, Det.	24	640	26.7	57	0
Logan, Mia.	24	613	25.5	97	1
Miller, S.D.	21	533	25.4	91	1
Dixon, Dall.	47	1181	25.1	97	1
Howard, Wash.	21	522	24.9	99	1
Martin, N.E.	24	584	24.3	38	0
Gentry, Chi.	28	667	23.8	63	0
Jefferson, Sea.	22	511	23.2	97	1
Metcalf, Cle.	31	718	23.2	49	0

Sacks

	No.
Doleman, Minn.	20.5
Harris, G.B.	19.5
Millard, Minn.	18.0
Greene, Rams	16.5
Swilling, N.O.	16.5
Simmons, Phi.	15.5
Taylor, Giants	15.0
Williams, S.D.	14.0
Smith, Buff.	13.0
O'Neal, S.D.	12.5

Passers

	Att	Comp	Pct.	Yds	Avg. Gain	TD	Pct. TD	Lg	Int	Pct. Int	Rating Pts
Montana, S.F.	386	271	70.2	3521	9.12	26	6.7	95	8	2.1	112.4
Esiason, Cin.	455	258	56.7	3525	7.75	28	6.2	74	11	2.4	92.1
Everett, Rams	518	304	58.7	4310	8.32	29	5.6	78	17	3.3	90.6
Moon, Hou.	464	280	60.3	3631	7.83	23	5.0	55	14	3.0	88.9
Rypien, Wash.	476	280	58.8	3768	7.92	22	4.6	80	13	2.7	88.1
Kelly, Buff.	391	228	58.3	3130	8.01	25	6.4	78	18	4.6	86.2
Hebert, N.O.	353	222	62.9	2686	7.61	15	4.2	54	15	4.2	82.7
Majkowski, G.B.	599	353	58.9	4318	7.21	27	4.5	79	20	3.3	82.3
Kosar, Cle	513	303	59.1	3533	6.89	18	3.5	97	14	2.7	80.3
Simms, Giants	405	228	56.3	3061	7.56	14	3.5	62	14	3.5	77.6

Punters

	No.	Yds.	Lg.	Avg.	TB	Blk	Ret	Ret Yds	In 20	Net Avg
Camarillo, Phoe.	76	3298	58	43.4	6	0	42	330	21	37.5
Montgomery, Hou.	56	2422	63	43.3	7	2	24	191	15	36.1
Arnold, Det.	82	3538	64	43.1	9	1	46	373	14	36.0
Landeta, Giants	70	3019	71	43.1	7	0	29	236	19	37.8
Mojsiejenko, Wash.	62	2663	74	43.0	9	1	34	383	21	33.3
Stark, Ind.	79	3392	64	42.9	10	1	51	558	14	32.9
Roby, Mia.	58	2458	58	42.4	6	1	26	256	18	35.3
Fulhage, Atl.	84	3472	65	41.3	9	1	43	460	24	33.3
Newsome, Pitt.	82	3368	57	41.1	9	1	45	361	15	34.1
Saxon, Dall.	79	3233	56	40.9	6	2	37	334	18	34.3

Team Rankings

	Offense			Defense		
	Total	Rush	Pass	Total	Rush	Pass
Atlanta	24	28	9	28	28	19
Buffalo	5	3	8	11	14	10
Chicago	10	2	19	25	15	24
Cincinnati	3	1	7	15	26	8
Cleveland	16	21	11	7	10	9
Dallas	27	24	27	20	18	20
Denver	15	6	23	3	6	3
Detroit	18	8	26	18	8	27
Green Bay	6	20	5	16	19T	13
Houston	9	12	10	13	9	17
Indianapolis	23	17	24	22	22	15
Kansas City	13	4	21	2	12	2
Raiders	19	9	25	10	16	5
Rams	4	13	4	21	5	28
Miami	7	27	3	24	25	18
Minnesota	14	7	17	1	11	1
New England	8	19	6	23	17	23
New Orleans	11	11	13	12	1	26
Giants	20	15	20	5	4	7
Jets	17	22	12	27	24	25
Philadelphia	12	5	18	8	7	12
Phoenix	25	26	15	26	27	22
Pittsburgh	28	18	28	19	19T	16
San Diego	21	16	22	6	13	4
San Francisco	1	10	2	9	3	11
Seattle	26	25	16	14	23	6
Tampa Bay	22	23	14	17	21	14
Washington	2	14	1	9	2	21

173

Credits

COVER, Richard Mackson/*Sports Illustrated.*

INTRODUCTION

1, Joe Patronite/*Allsport USA*; 2-3, John W. McDonough/*Sports Illustrated*; 7, Walter Iooss, Jr./*Sports Illustrated.*

FIRST QUARTER

8-9, Tony Tomsic/*Sports Illustrated.* 10-11, Bill Smith/*Sports Illustrated*; 12 top, Bill Ballenberg/*Sports Illustrated*; 13 bottom & 14 top, John Biever/*Sports Illustrated*; 14 bottom & 16, Peter Read Miller/*Sports Illustrated*; 17, John Biever/*Sports Illustrated*; 18 & 19, John Iacono/*Sports Illustrated*; 20, © *Duomo*/Bryan Yablonsky; 21 top, © *Duomo*/Al Tielemans; bottom, © *Duomo*/Bryan Yablonsky; 22, © *Duomo*/Dan Helms; 23 top left, Scott Cunningham; bottom left, John Biever/*Sports Illustrated*; top right, John H. Reid III; 24 top, Charles Bernhardt/*Allsport USA*; center & bottom, John Biever/*Sports Illustrated*; 25 left, Manny Rubio; right, Damian Strohmeyer/*Allsport USA*; 26 top, Ronald C. Modra/*Sports Illustrated*; bottom, John Biever/*Sports Illustrated*; 27 top left, Scott Cunningham; bottom left, Fred Vuich/*Allsport USA*; top right, John Biever/*Sports Illustrated*; 28 top, David Walberg/*Sports Illustrated*; bottom, John Biever/*Sports Illustrated*; 29 top, John W. McDonough/*Sports Illustrated*; bottom, Heinz Kluetmeier/*Sports Illustrated*; 30 top, Allen Dean Steele/*Allsport USA*; bottom, Rick Stewart/*Allsport USA*; 31 top left, Scott Cunningham; bottom, John Biever/*Sports Illustrated*; top right, © 1989 *Capital Cities/ABC, Inc.* (Manny Millan); 32, Jonathon Daniels/*Allsport USA*; 33 top left, Peter Read Miller/*Sports Illustrated*; bottom left, David Walberg/*Sports Illustrated*; top right, *Duomo*/Bryan Yablonsky.

SECOND QUARTER

34-35, Walter Iooss Jr./*Sports Illustrated*; 36, Heinz Kluetmeier/*Sports Illustrated*; 37, Cynthia Johnson/*TIME Magazine*; 38-39, Peter Read Miller/*Sports Illustrated*; 40 & 41, John Biever/*Sports Illustrated*; 42 & 43, Joe Ledford/*K.C. Star*; 44, Heinz Kluetmeier/*Sports Illustrated*; 45, John Biever/*Sports Illustrated*; 46, 47 top, Tony Tomsic/*Sports Illustrated*; bottom, Robert Shaver, *NFL Photos*; 48, Tom Reese/Seattle Times; 49 top left, Mike Moore/*NFL Photos*; top right, Herb Weitman/*NFL Photos*; bottom, Brian Masek/*Allsport USA*; 50 top, Andy Hayt/*Sports Illustrated*; bottom, Dave Black/*Sports Illustrated*; 51 top, Scott Cunningham; center, Mary Ann Carter; bottom, © *Duomo*/Al Tielemans; 52 top, Scott Cunningham; bottom, George Long/*NFL Photos*; 53 top left, © *Duomo*/Al Tielemans; center, Scott Cunningham; bottom, Rick Stewart/*Allsport USA*; right, Star Tribune, Brian Peterson; 54, Andy Hayt/*Sports Illustrated*; 55 top, Anthony Neste/*Sports Illustrated*; bottom left, Robert Beck/*Allsport USA*; bottom right, Paul Spinelli/*NFL Photos*; 56 top, Peter Groh/*NFL Photos*; bottom, Phil Huber/*Sports Illustrated*; 57 top, John Biever/*Sports Illustrated*; bottom, Scott Cunningham; 58, John Biever/*Sports Illustrated*; 59 top left, Jerry Wachter/*Sports Illustrated*; bottom, Joe Ledford/*K.C. Star*; top right, *Ft. Worth Star-Telegram*/Jerry W. Hoefer.

THIRD QUARTER

60-61, Michael S. Green/*The Detroit News*; 63 & 64, John Biever/*Sports Illustrated*; 66 & 67, Louis Deluca/*Dallas Times Herald*; 68, Michael S. Green/*The Detroit News*; 69, Al Kamuda/*Detroit Free Press*; 70 & 71, Anthony Neste/*Sports Illustrated*; 72, George Long/*NFL Photos*; 73 top, John Iacono/*Sports Illustrated*; bottom, Bob Breidenbach/*Providence Journal Co.*; 74 top, Mike Fender/*The Indianapolis News*; bottom, Michael Zagaris; 75 right, Kurt Smith/*Seattle Post Intelligencer*; left, Jerry Pinkus/*NFL Photos*; 76 top, Pieter Brouillet/*NFL Photos*; bottom, Otto Greule Jr./*Allsport USA*; 77 top left, Harley Soltes/*The Seattle Times*; bottom left, John Iacono/*Sports Illustrated*; top right, Scott Cunningham; 78, John R. Gentry/*The Indianapolis News*; 79 top, *The San Diego Tribune*/Robert Gauthier; bottom, John Sandhaus/*NFL Photos*.

FOURTH QUARTER

80-81, Walter Iooss, Jr./*Sports Illustrated*; 82, John McDonough/*Sports Illustrated*; 84, Richard Mackson/*Sports Illustrated*; 86, John Biever/*Sports Illustrated*; 87, Andy Hayt/*Sports Illustrated*; 88-89, Richard Mackson/*Sports Illustrated*; 90 top, Tony Tomsic/*Sports Illustrated*; bottom, Lane Stewart/*Sports Illustrated*; 93, Walter Iooss Jr./*Sports Illustrated*; 94, John Iacono/*Sports Illustrated*; 96 & 97, Heinz Kluetmeier/*Sports Illustrated*; 98-99, Heinz Kluetmeier/*Sports Illustrated*; 100, Richard Mackson/*Sports Illustrated*; 101, Peter Read Miller/*Sports Illustrated*; 102, Richard Mackson/*Sports Illustrated*; 103, Walter Iooss Jr./*Sports Illustrated*; 104 top, John Biever/*Sports Illustrated*; bottom, John McDonough/*Sports Illustrated*; 106 top, Walter Iooss Jr./*Sports Illustrated*; bottom, Heinz Kluetmeier/*Sports Illustrated*; 107, John McDonough/*Sports Illustrated*.

HEROES AND FLAKES

109, John Biever/*Sports Illustrated*; 111, Brian Smith/*Sports Illustrated*; 112-113, Jerry Wachter/*Sports Illustrated*; 114, Dave Black/*Sports Illustrated*; 115, Lane Stewart/*Sports Illustrated*; 117, Lee Crum/*Sports Illustrated*; 118, Lane Stewart/*Sports Illustrated*; 120, David Brewster, *Star Tribune*; 122, Andy Hayt/*Sports Illustrated*; 123, David Walberg/*Sports Illustrated*; 125, Joe Ledford, *K.C. Star*; 126-127, Heinz Kluetmeier/*Sports Illustrated*; 128, Andy Hayt/*Sports Illustrated*; 129, © *Duomo*/Dan Helms; 130, Peter Read Miller/*NFL Photos*; 131, Paul Spinelli/*Allsport USA*.

AWARDS

132 left top, © *Duomo*/Al Tielemans; bottom left, Peter Read Miller/*Sports Illustrated*; top right, Richard Mackson/*Sports Illustrated*; center right, Michael S. Green/*Detroit News*; bottom right, Greg Jessen; 133 top left, Andy Hayt/*Sports Illustrated*; center left, Alan Schwartz/*NFL Photos*; bottom left, Don Larson; top right, Craig Molenhouse/*Sports Illustrated*; center right, Ed Webber/*NFL Photos*; bottom right, Walter Iooss Jr./*Sports Illustrated*; 134 top left, Heinz Kluetmeier/*Sports Illustrated*; bottom left, Bill Smith/*Sports Illustrated*; top right, Tony Tomsic/*Sports Illustrated*; center right, Heinz Kluetmeier/*Sports Illustrated*; bottom center, Jerry Wachter/*Sports Illustrated*; bottom right, © *Duomo*/Dan Helms; 135 left & top right, Heinz Kluetmeier; bottom right, John Biever/*Sports Illustrated*.

APPENDIX

140-141, John Iacono/*Sports Illustrated*.

Team Index